AF559571

Social Journalism

Social Journalism

Sanoj Singh

RANDOM PUBLICATIONS
NEW DELHI (INDIA)

Social Journalism

ISBN 978-93-5111-630-1

Published in 2015 in India by
RANDOM PUBLICATIONS
Reprinted 2019
4376-A/4B, Gali Murari Lal, Ansari Road
New Delhi-110 002
Phone : +9111-43580356, 011-23289044, 011-43142548
e-mail: sales@randompublications.com,
info@randompublications.com, randomexports@gmail.com

Reprinted 2024

Type Setting by : Friends Media, Delhi-110089
Digitally Printed at : Replika Press Pvt. Ltd.

Preface

Social journalism is a media model consisting of a hybrid of professional journalism, contributor and reader content. It is similar to open publishing platforms, like Twitter and WordPress.com, except that some or most content is also created and/or screened by professional journalists.

To fully understand the pressures on and performance of the press in any country, one has to consider the economic, political, and socio-cultural contexts of that press, along with the resulting professional orientation of the journalists. Such a holistic approach reflects the complex reality of all human undertakings and has been suggested by a host of theorists and applied to various aspects of communication research. In their seminal volume on media systems, for instance, Siebert, Peterson, and Schramm developed their "four theories of the press"- authoritarian, libertarian, social responsibility, and communist - by analyzing the political, economic, cultural, and philosophical orientations of different groups of countries.

Public relations has become a significant and powerful industry, particularly in recent decades. This industry and its actors mainly work through the media to spread information, persuasion and opinions to the public on behalf of their clients. Publicity is the predominant goal. Networking, relation-building, news production and activities intended to be published in the media are thus part of the everyday work of PR agents such as information officers, PR consultants and spin-doctors. The PR phenomenon needs to be examined and scrutinised as a new party and power in the democratic process. In recent years, some international studies have taken on this mission, but there is scope for more studies on different aspects of the phenomenon, not least in the Nordic countries.

The book is written in a very simple way keeping in view of the general readers.

I would like to thank my team for standing beside me throughout my career and writing this book. My special thanks go to "Random Publications" who have published the book.

– Sanoj Singh

Contents

1

Societal Context of Journalism

INTRODUCTION

To fully understand the pressures on and performance of the press in any country, one has to consider the economic, political, and socio-cultural contexts of that press, along with the resulting professional orientation of the journalists. Such a holistic approach reflects the complex reality of all human undertakings and has been suggested by a host of theorists and applied to various aspects of communication research. In their seminal volume on media systems, for instance, Siebert, Peterson, and Schramm developed their "four theories of the press"- authoritarian, libertarian, social responsibility, and communist - by analyzing the political, economic, cultural, and philosophical orientations of different groups of countries.

Though their thesis has been shown to reflect the cold-war ideology of the time and some specifics of their exposition faulted for undue generalization, the general orientation of their work has endured, with modifications.

Employing similar factors of analysis, Hachten, for instance, modified the Siebert-Peterson-Schramm classification and came up with five categories: authoritarian, Western, communist, revolutionary, and developmental. Even this more realistic classification is flawed, however, as many countries still straddle the categories. An understanding of a given press system requires the analysis of the factors of that press system rather than its slotting into a category.

Downing has suggested the expansion of such factors to include, among other things, insights from anthropology, geography, history, linguistics, and psychology. And Mowlana has referred to aspects of these factors as the ecology of communication, a term he uses "in a broad sense to include all the symbolic environments in which human and technological communication takes place." For purposes of analytical parsimony, three factors - the political, the socio-cultural, and the economic - are specifically discussed here.

However, as should be evident, the three factors are discussed to subsume several others.

Regarding the political factor, the system of government is a determining factor in press practices. Pluralist democracies are inherently more accommodating of press freedom, and dictatorships are less tolerant. However, even among dictatorships, the imperatives of power and legitimation cause governments to negotiate explicitly or implicitly depending on their circumstances.

As several social theorists have noted, power is a relational attribute rather than a boom that is lowered at will. It is at its most effective when exercised without coercion, and each instance of coercion entails some risk of diminution or even loss of power.

As Flathman, among others, has noted, there is a distinction between power and authority: the latter subsumes legitimation and the former does not. Thus, the extent to which power may be exercised non-coercively is partly a function of authority.

Accordingly, even autocratic rulers who have all the instruments of coercion at their disposal often seek legitimation and approval to enhance their authority. Leaders such as Gamal Nassar of Egypt, Kwame Nkrumah of Ghana, and Josip Tito of Yugoslavia, for instance, all relied considerably on populism and charisma to co-opt acquiescence. They employed coercion when their authority and co-opting failed to bring about conformance.

The form of government aside, a country's politics reflects basic facets of the society, including ethnic and religious pluralism and class structures. The distribution of political power varies depending on whether a country is ethnically homogenous or heterogeneous, whether there is a significant middle class, and the extent of the development of civil society.

Countries with diverse ethnic and religious groups - especially those like Nigeria where there is a rough parity in the population of the major groups - require a greater balancing act in matters of governance. Accordingly, they invariably have a built-in opposition, formal or informal, and an inherent capacity for resisting despotism. Similarly, a large middle class and the attendant civil society play a role in shaping the exercise of political power, irrespective of the form of government.

The resulting dynamics of power bears strongly on the function of the press, especially in its relations to the state. Countries such as India and Nigeria that are pluralist in ethnicity and religion also have dynamic press systems that often reflect the fractious nature of their politics. The press in such countries is also more capable of resisting repression.

Even in countries with a monolithic political order there is increasing pressure from global trends towards more open press systems. Such pressures come from new technologies of communication, increasing synchronization in global economic and political values, and diplomatic relations. In some instances, international press attention to a domestic situation has led to reform, as in the case of violence against Brazil's street children, for instance. Regarding the socio-cultural factor, a press system reflects the general character and values of the society in which it is based, as well as the educational background of the people who staff the newsrooms. Studies of the Chinese media system, for instance, note the conforming impact of Confucian values. Similarly, analyses of Nigeria's civic and political culture suggest the impact of the absence of such values in public life.

For instance, in his book We Are All Guilty, Orewa argues that Nigeria's political instability reflects a general indiscipline in institutional and civic culture. Indeed, political culture - a society's values regarding the appropriate form of government - is an important consideration. One has to note, for instance, that the success of dictators often depends on the inclination of people to accept dictatorships. In many developing countries, including Nigeria, where the military have taken over power, the coups have often been preceded by public opinion in their favour. The implicit values bear on the ensuing government's behaviour towards the press.

Studies of the African press have also pointed to the effect of traditional reverence for leaders, polemical tendencies towards opponents, and the dictates of oral communication on mass media content. Doob has written, for instance, that, "In traditional African societies the prestige of established leaders is carefully maintained so that in their normal roles as communicators their communications are likely to evoke approval." Such tendencies have been cited to explain the often adulatory and partisan content of the Nigerian press.

Education also plays a role in the development of a press system. To begin with, literacy is a prerequisite for the use of the print media. Accordingly, newspaper and magazine circulation tends to reflect the literacy rate in the given country. Moreover, the performance of the news media is a reflection of the education and training of the personnel, including their professional socialization.

Regarding the economic factor, the press requires funding and sustenance, and the source of funds has a direct bearing on press content and control. In general, the news media are funded in one of three ways: by governments, by political parties or their supporters, and via the market-place. Of course, these forms of sponsorship are usually not exclusive. Rather a press system may be characterized by its dominant form of sponsorship, which usually determines its orientation.

The press in communist countries, for instance, is funded directly by the government, and its content reflects its role as an agent of the government. Similarly, early in the history of press systems in many non-communist countries, political parties were major owners of newspapers and magazines or were closely aligned with them. Such ownership and alignment typically marry politics and the press, and so determine the content and tenor of the latter. In contrast, the press in contemporary capitalist democracies tends to be funded through the marketplace, making them more independent of the government. In such systems, however, advertisers exercise more clout than the government, and their interests may "have a higher priority than the desires of readers." A critical orientation towards the government is more likely, in part because of the independence from government and in part because such criticism often has popular appeal.

In countries in crisis or those undergoing transition in their political and/or economic system, the inherent tension also manifests in press practices. Such has been the case in Russia, other former Soviet republics, eastern Europe, and African countries. In these countries, stresses in the social system or sudden adjustment to new economic realities cause certain irregularities in press practices, including undisciplined exercise of press freedom and "cash journalism" - the acceptance of money in return for writing favorable stories or covering them up. The practice of cash journalism is also common in China, where there is tension between communist control and officially sanctioned free enterprise. In sum, economic imperatives in any press system produce stresses or pressures that have an impact on journalistic practices.

It should be emphasized that despite the general tendencies just summarized, the relationship between press systems and any given factor described above is not inevitable. Rather, the actual impact of a given factor is a function of other elements of the social system of which the press is a subsystem.

As Vasquez has noted, for instance, government funding of the media in Sweden has much less impact on press freedom there than does similar funding of the press in communist and developing countries. The overall effect of the factors has to be seen in context and in totality.

ORIGINS OF PARTISAN-ADVOCATORIAL ORIENTATION

As already noted, the Nigerian press's partisanship has origins in its history, and that history bears on its fate and performance during the June 12 crisis. The history may be broken up into four periods: the nationalist, regionalist, state-oriented, and independent press eras.

This classification reflects major ownership and editorial orientations dating from the early years of the press to the present day. The Nigerian press became politically aligned quite early in its history. Though the first newspapers, dating back to 1859, were published for educational and entertainment purposes, political advocacy soon became a major thrust.

The first noted case of political journalism in Nigeria was in 1863, when R. Campbell, a West Indian of African descent who has been described as a "brilliant and courageous" writer, "practiced journalism to fight the then existing slave trade." In 1891, John Payne, a Liberian trader in Nigeria, began publishing the

Lagos Weekly Record, in which he attacked the policies of the colonial government. The thrust of the Nigerian press became decidedly political from the 1920s, with the formation of political parties and their establishment of newspapers as organs of agitation. Though most of the papers had obvious regional interests, they aligned in their crusade for independence or some form of self-determination or political rights for Nigerians and other Africans.

The pre-independence press was thus largely nationalist in ideology and orientation. A major exception was the Daily Times, which was established as a commercial enterprise rather than a political instrument and was funded largely by foreign investors. The rest of the Nigerian press began making the transition from nationalism to regionalism as political independence became increasingly a reality and internal political rivalry emerged as a preoccupation.

However, the birth of the regionalist press was not complete until the late 1950s and the years just after independence. This period witnessed the flourishing of newspapers sponsored by the regional and federal governments.

After the Eastern Nigerian government established the Eastern Outlook (later renamed the Nigerian Outlook), other regions and the federal government followed suit. The federal government established the Morning Post in 1961, the Western Regional government established the Daily Sketch in 1964, and the Northern government established the New Nigerian in 1966 (to replace the Nigerian Citizen). The Midwestern Region, which was excised from the West in 1963, established its own newspaper, The Observer, in 1968. The rise of the regionalist press presaged the demise of the nationalist newspapers, most of which were defunct by 1975.

The regionalist newspapers maintained Nigeria's advocatorial press tradition through the early years of independence and democracy. The vibrancy of the press reflected a political structure in which four powerful ethnic-oriented regional governments competed among themselves for resources, while vying for control of or influence at the federal government. As noted earlier, such inherent political pluralism is usually accompanied by a contentious press.

Just before Nigeria's civil war between 1967 and 1970, the country was broken up into 12 states to replace the four regions as political divisions. The state-oriented press emerged during and after the war, as each state sought to establish its own news media. Among the state-owned newspapers established at this time were the Chronicle (South-Eastern State), Daily Sketch (Western), Nigerian Herald (Kwara), Nigerian Standard (Benue Plateau), Renaissance (East Central), and Nigerian Tide (Rivers).

It was during this period, in 1976, that the federal military government bought 100 per cent interest in the New Nigerian, the North's dominant newspaper, and 60 per cent interest in the Daily Times Company, which till then was Nigeria's largest and most successful publishing house. Significantly, the acquisitions were made the same year that the federal government-owned daily Morning Post and Sunday Post ceased publication after years of falling circulation and revenue losses. The acquisitions, coupled with the limited geographic appeal of the state-owned newspapers, created a vacuum for national non-governmental newspapers and so gave rise to the birth of the independent press - the fourth (and current) press era - beginning in the early 1980s.

This era is marked by the rise and dominance of newspapers and magazines established by wealthy entrepreneurs and groups of journalists. The first major publications in this era were the National Concord and The Guardian.

The papers soon became major rivals of the government-owned newspapers, including especially the Daily Times and the New Nigerian, both of which had begun to decline in circulation as well as influence. The Concord, The Guardian and their respective founders - Moshood Abiola and Alex Ibru, respectively - also were to feature prominently in the June 12 crisis.

Though independent, the National Concord became identified with the National Party of Nigeria, the country's ruling party during the four years of what Nigerians call the Second Republic. Dissenting senior staff members subsequently left the Concord group and founded Newswatch in 1984/85, and the magazine gained instant popularity.

This development established a trend that would soon characterize the independent press era, namely the founding of publications by journalists intent on pursuing editorial orientations which though often still partisan were less circumscribed by political affiliation.

Among other publications established this way were the dailies Vanguard and This Day and the weekly magazines Tell and TheNews. The decline of the federal and state government-owned newspapers intensified at this point, and most were reduced to publishing less frequently and in skeletal forms.

Thus, the independent press era is characterized by the dominance of national publications that were not owned by governments or political parties, though their political sympathies or even agendas were transparent in most cases. This era is also marked by the influx into journalism of "a well-educated and politically committed crop of reporters." Olurunyomi writes that "Not only were these young men and women prowling their beats with the confidence of brilliant college graduates, they had also undergone an activist baptism of fire from the anti-apartheid and student movements." This explanation is similar to Flacks's analysis of the ideological ferment within American professions resulting from the influx of graduates radicalized by the campus activism of the 1960s.

The founding of Tell magazine in 1991 and TheNews magazine in 1993 and their subsequent role in the June 12 crisis are particularly illustrative of the ownership trend that characterize the independent press era and the impact of that trend on press performance. The departure of some senior staff members of the Concord group to found Newswatch in 1984 was replicated in 1991 when editors at Newswatch who felt the magazine was becoming too staid and conservative left to found the more radical Tell. Tell's philosophy was to be more advocatorial in the tradition of the nationalist press. Nosa Igiebor, Tell's executive editor and one of the founding publishers, cited the activist journalism of Nnamdi Azikiwe, Obafemi Awolowo, and other nationalists of the colonial era as his inspiration. That philosophy characterized Tell's performance during the June 12 crisis and kept it in the forefront of defiant opposition throughout the crisis.

Like Tell, TheNews was established by a group of senior journalists who left the Guardian group after it was briefly shut down by the military government in 1992. The journalists left the Guardian group rather than agree to an apology for a story as demanded by the government as a condition for ending the shutdown. Like Tell, TheNews was established with an activist journalistic philosophy. The founders believed that "the military had hijacked the [Nigerian] polity," resulting in "a loss of federalism." They saw the magazine then as an "instrument of social engineering" "to catalyze debate and [its] direction," to fight against corruption, and to resist any attempt to muzzle their effort. As will be shown later, the consonant philosophy of the two magazines, along with their relative youth and non-establishment status, informed their reportage and enabled their resilience in the face of concerted effort by the government to muzzle them.

Indeed, it is useful at this point to summarize the factors whose confluence determined the course of the events described below. In politics, there was a legitimation crisis involving military leaders who usurped power at a time the populace was weary of military rule and the economic hardship it helped engender. Along with the ensuing civilian-military divide, there was inter-ethnic tension resulting, in part, from the military's domination by an ethnic/regional segment of the population. Despite the economic difficulties, the press - especially the independent press - also grew at this time, spurred in part by the general resentment of the military government and in part by the growing availability of new technologies that facilitated newspaper and magazine production.

The government also began to license commercial broadcasting at this time. This rapid growth of the news media put a strain on the availability of trained and experienced personnel (despite the influx of graduates noted earlier) and the weak economy strained their viability.

The June 12 crisis therefore featured an illegitimate and insecure government that sought to perpetuate itself through co-opting and coercion, an expanding press that was developing true independence for the first time and was still searching for its professional compass in the midst of an inhospitable economic climate, and a weary populace that included significant numbers of radicalized people. As will become evident below, the tenor of the repression and the press performance reflected all of these factors. In their systems analysis of the mass media and politics, Gurevitch and Blumler propose an approach that emphasizes the "complementarity of roles." They posit that any given political system would tend to produce a corresponding role for journalists and a matching audience expectation. Conversely, any given journalism orientation would tend to produce a certain audience orientation which would put pressure on people in politics to perform in the appropriate direction. As with most structural/functional analyses, Gurevitch and Blumler's tends towards harmony. However, one could envision a situation in which the circumstances and roles in a system become conflictual rather than complementary. That was the situation in the June 12 crisis.

JOURNALISM PROFESSIONALIZATION AND ORIENTATION

As suggested by the review above, journalism professionalization reflects the political, social, and economic system of which a given press system is a part. Indeed, the elements of professionalization, in general, are related to the factors of press systems just summarized. These elements are specialized education, a public service rather than commercial orientation, autonomy, and a high level of related ethical standards in practice.

It has been argued that journalists acquire these attributes through three levels of socialization: the societal, the professional, and the organizational. Societal socialization refers to the overall impact of the social system on individuals and their values, and it accounts for differences among countries even given comparable politics and economies. The professional level refers to processes such as education, training, the development of particular orientations, and the articulation of values and standards through journalism associations. As will be further explained soon, there is an increasing global harmonization in this respect, though differences remain.

The third level of socialization, the organizational, is the process by which individual news media inculcate their particular values and preferences in their journalists. This level of socialization distinguishes, say, one newspaper from another within the same press system in their professional orientation. Beam has suggested that professionalism is best studied at this level. Such an approach does, indeed, have empirical advantages, but it is limited in its representation of professionalization. Analyses that reflect all three levels of socialization better reflect the reality.

Various categories have been developed for classifying journalists' orientations. In a psycho-social taxonomy that reconciled the contradictory claims that journalists are autonomous rebels and that they are motivated by altruistic service to society, Schwartz demonstrated that they fall in either category, what he labeled "inner-directed" or "other-directed." Janowitz identified two orientations as the gatekeeper and the advocate, the gatekeeper being committed to scientific detachment and objectivity and the advocate being oriented towards interpretation and criticism. A similar taxonomy developed by Johnstone, Slawski, and Bowman classifies journalists as neutral and participant.

In a more recent study of American journalists, Weaver and Wilhoit rejected the neutral-participant typology as a misnomer and developed a four-type classification as adversarialist, interpreter, disseminator, and populist mobilizer. They found that the dominant orientation was the interpretive, which entails a blend of investigative reporting and analysis.

This is followed closely by the disseminator orientation, which emphasizes rapid transmission of information to the widest number of people. The adversarialist orientation, with its emphasis on skepticism towards government and business, was found to be a minority orientation. Only a small percentage of journalists were classified as populist mobilizers, those who stressed giving voice to the public and setting public agenda. The various orientations were found to co-exist in various degrees, creating what Lahav has described as "the inherent contradiction between the press as a political organ and the press as an objective medium."

Press systems and the nature of professionalization may be said to be characterized by the dominant orientation at a given time. Historically, press systems have started out in the partisan-advocacy orientation and, to various degrees, moved towards more detached reporting. Janowitz concluded in his analysis that the gatekeeper approach to journalism enhances professionalization and that professionalization, in turn, makes the advocacy orientation more viable.

In the United States, the drive towards professionalization has been traced to the Civil War, when partisanship became so extreme and crude that embarrassed practitioners began to seek reform. The impetus re-emerged after World War I following the resurgence of sensationalistic propaganda. Some early trade publications, undertook the articulation of values and standards and were embraced by journalists. Ultimately, the need to mass-market news accelerated the drive towards objective and non-partisan news.

In the 1920s, Walter Lippmann articulated what became "a central principle in the professionalization of journalism": careful gathering and accurate, balanced, and objective reporting of facts.

Lippmann proposed a scientific orientation to news, which requires "the habits of ascribing no more credibility to a statement than it warrants, a nice sense of the probabilities, and a keen understanding of the quantitative importance of particular facts." Though it cannot be said that Lippmann's high standards have been attained anywhere, journalism professionalization has advanced along the lines of his recommendation. Various professional organizations have long emerged in part for this purpose. Their canons typically reflect the need to maintain credibility with the public, a goal that is broadly defined to encompass the press's independence, social responsibility, and adherence to the standards of facticity, accuracy, objectivity, fairness, and balance. With varying degrees of emphasis, these standards are subscribed to by journalists in various regions of the world. Studies have shown that even in systems where the press is not independent, some journalists aspire to these values or at least subscribe to them in principle.

For instance, while acknowledging that its founding charter imposed "certain political responsibilities," the Pan African News Agency nonetheless stipulates as follows in its stylebook:

A news agency exists to provide news to newspapers, radio and television stations and it lives on credibility. Those who subscribe to its service have the confidence that its news and features will always be factual, objective and balanced and that it can always be relied upon to provide good quality service promptly. Indeed, as Head and Ibelema have noted, professionalization in various press systems has to be judged in terms of journalists' exemplification of these ideals to the extent possible within their systemic constraints.

Studies have shown that professionalization provides some protection from outside interference and attacks. Dimmick's study shows that various media industries moved towards or intensified efforts at professionalization during periods of intense scrutiny or threats from the outside. Some scholars have gone as far as to characterize the practice of objectivity as a mask for journalists' agenda or as a "strategic ritual" and professionalization as an "agent of legitimation."

The rise of journalism professionalization has, however, raised concerns that the watchdog role of the press might be blunted. Merrill contends, for instance, that the American press was becoming so socially responsible that it was "in danger of becoming one vast, gray, bland, monotonous, conformist spokesman for some collectivity of society." Some studies have indicated, however, that professionalization has no such effect. This study provides some insight on this debate.

VISUAL COMMUNICATION IN PUBLIC JOURNALISM

A comparison of the design and photography of public journalism projects with non-public journalism shows there is a difference, but not a radical one. Between 1990 and 1996, more than 400 media outlets had undertaken public journalism projects. Much has been written about the philosophy behind public journalism, its goals, and techniques. Individual public journalism projects have been analysed and compared against these goals and philosophies, and also compared to traditional journalism to see what, if any, difference exists. However, no study has yet focused on the visual communication of public journalism in newspapers. Public journalism practitioners and theoreticians argue that the content of stories generated through public journalism methods is significantly different from the content generated by traditional reporting methods. News designers are taught that the form of their designs must reflect the content of the stories rather than artistic preference or trends.

This prompts the question: If the content of stories generated through public journalism methods is different, and design is driven by content, doesn't it follow that design for public journalism will be different than design for non-public journalism? This is a key question that visual communicators and public journalists must address if the final product is to truly integrate verbal and visual meaning.

The purpose of this research, the first of a two-phase study, is to explore how public journalism projects have been visually communicated in newspapers practicing this approach, and how they differ from the visual communication of non-public journalism.

Through content analysis, textual analysis and telephone interviews, this exploratory study examined the design and photography of projects at six newspapers; four practicing public journalism and two practicing non-public journalism to explore how public journalism projects were visually communicated in newspapers that practiced the genre, and whether the visual communication of public journalism differed from the visual communication of non-public journalism.

Public journalism is a product of the 1990s — its first well-documented experiment was in late 1989 in Columbus, Georgia. Even a decade later, there are as many operational definitions of public journalism as there are media outlets that practice it. For a conceptual definition that speaks to the developing theory of public journalism Jay Rosen has said: "Journalism can and should play a part in strengthening citizenship, improving public debate and reviving public life."

Public or civic journalism is widely understood as an approach designed to address issues that readers say are important, rather than only those issues identified by experts. It seeks to promote a public conversation about those issues that will result in a collective working through of the problem to resolution. Among its goals are strengthening citizenship, improving the quality of public debate, and reviving public life. It proposes a more active role for the press than has traditionally been adopted.

Public journalism derives many of its philosophical foundations from the social responsibility theory of the press and agenda-setting theory. While some scholars of public journalism trace its roots as far back as Thomas Jefferson, John Locke and John Stuart Mill, it seems unarguable that the development of the ideas that infuse public journalism were an outgrowth of the debates between John Dewey and Walter Lippmann over the proper role for the press in a democracy. Dewey and other scholars helped lay the foundation for a gradual shift towards the emerging social responsibility theory of the press, which was akin to Dewey's proposal of the role of the press in helping build a more pluralist and tolerant society. The evolution of the social responsibility theory culminated in the Commission on Freedom of the Press' report in 1947.

The Hutchins Commission's work can be seen as a forerunner of public journalism in that it called for the press to offer "a method of presenting and clarifying the goals and values of the society" and for reporting to project "the opinions and attitudes of the groups in society to one another."

Although social responsibility theory has been challenged as a product of its time, the developing concept of public journalism has drawn heavily from the Hutchins Commission and expanded on the role of the press by incorporating ideas from Dewey, philosophers Jurgen Habermas and Hannah Arendt, and political scientist Michael Sandel. Arendt, Habermas and Sandel all acknowledge the important role media play in society — without communication there is no public sphere. Contemporaries whose thoughts have added fuel to the public journalism fire include Daniel Yankelovich in Coming to Public Judgement, Russell Neuman, Marian Just and Ann Crigler with Common Knowledge, Clifford Christians, John Ferre and Mark Fackler's Good News, James Carey, Jay Rosen, and Davis Merritt.

Public journalism also incorporates aspects of agenda-setting theory, which says that one of the effects of mass communication is to direct the audience's attention to certain problems or issues. By conducting focus groups and taking polls of what the audience considers important before reporting on issues, public journalists make a self-conscious effort to avoid agenda-setting by the media or others, including government and special interests.

While there is no consensus on what public journalism is, or even on what to call it, the premise that all agree on is that it is the duty of the press is to improve the quality of public life by fostering public participation and debate. Some of the methods and techniques public journalists are best known to have used towards these goals include focus groups and citizen advisory boards to discover issues of importance to people; avoiding conflict framing of stories; using ordinary citizens as sources as well as officials and experts; seeking to clarify the core values behind opinions and underlying causes of problems; focusing on solutions and success stories; and taking an active role in promoting discussion among citizens with public forums and town hall meetings.

While public journalists are still focused on inventing their craft, they are understandably concerned with fine-tuning the proper reporting and writing techniques. As is historically typical in journalism, the visual aspects of journalistic storytelling — photography and design — are postponed for attention after the verbal aspects have been worked out. While they may momentarily forget this essential element, journalists have come to realise that visual communication can be just as important, if not more so, as verbal communication.

Inherent in all definitions of design is the idea that it is not simply decoration or dressing up a page, but that form carries a content of its own. The literature laments the use of designs that overemphasize form to the detriment of communication. Originally, design developed in response to the mechanical needs of page make-up. With the advent of photocomposition, mechanical concerns were eliminated as well as the design conventions they necessitated. Today, the story content and needs of the reader drive design.

It is the consensus in design theory that form is inextricably linked to message meaning. The form, or design, of news changes the perception of its content. If newspaper page design is truly to be used to communicate meaning derived from the story's content, and if public journalism has changed that content, then design must change to reflect that. Design must now communicate the public agenda. If public journalism is an attempt to better address the goals laid out by the Hutchins Commission, how can design and photography encourage this? Perhaps public journalism photographs should reflect citizens more often than candidates.

Photojournalists might also refuse to participate in photo opportunities organized by public relations people in the interest of letting the public set the agenda, rather than PR professionals. Public journalism design could also make use of design elements which help communicate its goals, such as summary boxes describing the values in conflict over a certain issue, or graphics telling readers how to get involved, express their opinions, or get more information on an issue. These and other topics must be addressed by public journalism's visual communicators if the final product is to truly integrate verbal and visual meaning.

There is some indication in the public journalism literature that design is beginning to be considered. Most are references made in passing with little follow-up as to how the goals of public journalism might be achieved with visuals. Others offer some specifics. For example, in a speech to the Regional Reporters Association, Jan Schaffer of the Pew Centre for Civic Journalism suggested building in "graphic devices that invite and encourage readers and viewers to contact the news organization and react to an issue, a controversy, a public problem."

Jay Rosen made the connection between public journalism's goals and design when he commented that, "If the pages of the newspaper are thought of as a public space designed by journalists, then what the (Wichita) Eagle did is arrange this space so that the proper concerns of politics (`issues in depth') shone through." He then described how the Eagle accomplished this with visual elements.

For each of the major issues, the Eagle published a list called Places to Start, with the names, addresses and phone numbers of organizations and agencies working on the problem. Repeated invitations were issued to readers to contact the paper with their comments and suggestions. At the Charlotte Observer, the Where They Stand feature was more than a voter's guide. If candidates refused to answer the questions the public posed, then a blank appeared under the candidate's name. This was a powerful use of space, charged with visual meaning. A survey found that one of the most useful features was the Where They Stand box.

The Pew Center's Schaffer also reported that a focus group at one newspaper responded differently to information conveyed graphically than when the same information was reported in a bylined story: "They loved the voter's guide in a grid and asked why we didn't give it to them earlier and repeat it often.... It seemed to them fairer and more factual.

There was no byline and no news peg, just distilled information. Even though it was from bylined stories, the way it was presented seemed to make a difference in how much people believed it."

At the Virginian-Pilot in Norfolk, a new feature was inaugurated on the front page to stimulate more productive dialogue about controversies in the news. The paper also created a new design element that graphically conveyed its new treatment of controversy.

After summarizing the themes of the issue, readers were directed to question themselves. For example: "If you tend to disagree... in what part of (his) argument can you find merit? Even if you tend to agree... what part of (his) argument do you have problems with? Where is the common ground?"

It is much harder to find discussions of photojournalism that promotes the ideals of public journalism. One example that was widely discussed appeared in the Wisconsin State Journal when citizens gathered in the seats of their representatives at the state capitol to question candidates. The result was "a startling visual," according to Rosen, a visual symbol that things had changed.

The value of visual communication to public journalism's goals is even beginning to be addressed tangentially in some scholarly research. Paul Riede concluded that, in the Wichita Eagle's The People Project, the most journalistic depth came in the form of the graphics: "the graphic goes beneath the surface, personality-based coverage of politics typical of traditional journalism." This same study called the "innovative use of the `core values' graphics'... the project's most promising attempt at depth in coverage." In order discover how public journalism projects have been visually communicated and whether they differ from that of non-public journalism, one research question and six hypotheses regarding visual communication were developed based on public journalism characteristics derived from the literature.

They are:

- *H1*: Public journalism will visually convey more mobilizing Information to help citizens participate in their communities than non-public journalism.

- *H2*: Public journalism will visually convey more interactivity, *i.e.*: ways to contact the media.
- *H3*: Public journalism photographs will use fewer managed photo opportunities than non-public journalism.
- *H4*: Public journalism will use more photographs of citizens and "real people" versus candidates or experts than non-public journalism.
- *H5*: Public journalism will use more visual devices to convey views of citizens and "real people" than non-public journalism.
- *H6*: Public journalism will use more visual devices to convey common ground and solutions than non-public journalism.
- *RQ1*: Does the visual communication of public journalism differ with circulation size?

The unit of analysis was all the stories on the public journalism topic in one day's issue of the newspaper. Forty-one newspaper issues were sampled. The 41 issues were drawn from six newspapers in two circulation sizes using one week from each paper. For this study, large newspapers were defined as greater than 200,000 daily circulation. Small newspapers were defined as less than 100,000 daily circulation. Medium newspapers, 100,000 to 200,000 daily circulation, were not included in order to maximize comparisons. It was postulated there would be little difference, for reasons such as resources, between medium and large papers, but the difference would be greater between small and large papers.

One week's issues from two large-circulation non-public journalism newspapers were compared against one week's issues from four public journalism newspapers (both large and small circulation sizes); one week's issues from two small-circulation public journalism newspapers were compared against one week's issues from two large-circulation public journalism newspapers; and one week's issues from two large-circulation public journalism newspapers were compared against one week's issues from two large-circulation non-public journalism newspapers. This allowed comparison of the presentation of public journalism against non-public journalism two ways, and also allowed comparison of the presentation within the genre of public journalism.

Sampling time was limited to one week because one newspaper's series ran for only six days. In addition, the large number of variables examined made a larger sample unwieldy.

All elements associated with the stories in each issue, including stories, headlines, photos, illustrations, sidebars, boxes, logos, refers, graphics, charts, maps, tables, schedules, lists, pullquotes, readouts, and jumps, were coded for size and presence of public journalism criteria.

Since the purpose of this exploratory project was to learn as much as possible about a subject which has not previously been studied, examining all relevant appearance variables was deemed to be more important than a large sample. If even small differences were detected, the results of this exploratory study could help point the way towards future research.

The public journalism stories were sampled using the latest public journalism projects at each newspaper; the non-public journalism stories were sampled using the newspapers' latest series that was on a similar topic as the public journalism series in its comparison paper, or, if that was not feasible, a project that ran as a series of similar magnitude was chosen. This study analysed the content of the appearance variables of all stories dealing with the subject except opinion pieces and letters to the editor. The focus of this study was on differences in photography and design. Editorial pages are highly formatted and generally do not vary in presentation, so they were not deemed suitable for this study. Purposive sampling with newspapers stratified by circulation size and chosen for their experience with the public journalism approach was used because it is better suited the purpose of comparing the visual presentation of public journalism to see how it varies within the genre, and of comparing the visual presentation of public journalism to non-public journalism.

The four public journalism newspapers were initially chosen for a different study by the Pew Centre for Civic Journalism. The basis for this decision included the level of experience each paper had with public journalism philosophies and techniques, and Pew's director's and assistant director's assessment that these particular papers were doing some of the more interesting work within the public journalism genre.

Because of their early entry into the movement, the philosophies and practices of public journalism at these papers are assumed to be more highly developed than those of papers just beginning to practice public journalism. Therefore, the visual communication of public journalism stories should have achieved a deeper level of consideration in these newsrooms. Also, by experimenting with the photographiy and presentation of public journalism for a longer period, their practices should be more finely tuned and may represent the direction that other newspapers will take in public journalism. The two large circulation newspapers not practicing public journalism were chosen by this researcher for their similarities with the public journalism newspapers in circulation size, morning publication, and market demographics, and also to represent specific regions of the country. Their editors have publicly stated their opposition to the public journalism approach. The differences in design styles across the different newspapers were taken into account in the textual analysis.

The characteristics of each newspaper sampled are:

Public journalism - large circulation:

- San Francisco Chronicle: 489,238 daily circulation. Public journalism project on commuter transportation. Published October-December 1996.

- Charlotte Observer: 239,173 daily circulation. Public journalism project on the 1996 election. Published September and October 1996.

Non-public journalism, large circulation:

- Philadelphia Enquirer: 469,398 daily circulation. Corresponds with San Francisco circulation. Series on changes in a suburban neighbourhood in the past 50 years. Published February 1997.
- Omaha World-Herald: 232,360 daily circulation. Corresponds with the Charlotte Observer's circulation. Stories on the 1996 election. Published September and October 1996.

Public journalism - small circulation:

- Wisconsin State Journal, Madison: 86,585 daily circulation. Public journalism project on the 1996 election. Published September-October 1996.
- Binghamton Press and Sun-Bulletin: 68,919 daily circulation. Public journalism project was the community's economic problems. Published September 1996.

Content analysis followed the methods recommended by Klaus Krippendorff and Earl Babbie with two independent coders. Using Scott's Pi, an average reliability estimate was calculated at.98 coder agreement.

Textual analysis followed the methods of Stuart Hall to determine if and how the written content differed from the visual content. Telephone interviews using open-ended questions were conducted with the designers following methods described by Norman Denzin and Y.S. Lincoln, and T.R. Lindlof.

One-way analysis of variance was used on interval data; chi-square was used on categorical data. Since some chi-square cells contained less than five, correlation was also used to determine probability level. Forty-one newspaper issues were analysed. For the purposes of statistical analysis, alpha was set at.05. Because data for this exploratory study were not drawn from a probability sample, the variability of the sample statistics cannot be estimated.

Although the conventional tests of statistical significance have been computed and are reported along with the findings, readers should interpret these with caution. However, in the absence of any research on the visual communication of public journalism, it is hoped these results will add to knowledge and stimulate further study.

When public journalism issues sampled in this study were compared against non-public journalism issues on the six public journalism characteristics, the scores showed a significant difference for two variables, H2: Ways to contact the media, and H6: More visual devices for common ground and solutions. Two other variables, H3: Fewer managed photo ops, and H4: More photos of real people, had means in the direction hypothesized. Two variables showed no significant differences; H1: More mobilizing information, and H5: More visual devices to convey views of real people.

In addition, these same hypotheses were used to compare large public journalism issues against large non-public journalism issues in order to help control for the greater resources of larger circulation newspapers, and to compare the presentation in small public journalism papers to large public journalism papers to see if public journalism is being practiced consistently across circulation sizes. When significant, these results are presented in the discussion section.

THE IMPORTANCE OF UNDERSTANDING

Two final points of interest were revealed in the interviews when designers were asked whether they designed differently for public journalism than for non-public journalism.

Designers at two papers said yes, public journalism design was different from non-public journalism design, and designers at the other two papers replied no, there was no difference.

Interestingly, the no difference responses came from designers whose papers did not have training sessions on the concepts and techniques of public journalism, or who did not include visual journalists in those sessions.

Both affirmative responses came from newspapers whose designers did participate in public journalism education sessions.

Understanding of public journalism principles was one of the explanations offered for some of the findings in this study, and the perception of designers regarding the difference in designing for public journalism reinforces such an explanation.

Visual journalists who did not attend sessions aimed at explaining public journalism's goal and principles may not understand it as well as those who did and, therefore, may not consider ways to visually communicate those goals and principles.

Also, one of the designers interviewed complained that too many journalists at the paper felt like they had been ordered to do public journalism with no opportunity for discussion or input.

This chapter did not offer training sessions in public journalism. "If they're really going to get people on board to do this and do this well, there has to be that discussion," said the designer, who asked to remain anonymous.

"There are numerous ethical challenges in doing this, and they need to at least be explored, as do the possible pitfalls." Both these insights have implications for managing editors contemplating introducing public journalism into their newsrooms.

This study has used the emerging theory of public journalism, which claims a significantly different content than non-public journalism, and the theory of content-driven design, which says that visual meaning must reflect the written content, to examine the question prompted by these theories: If the content of stories generated through public journalism methods is different, and design is driven by content, shouldn't design for public journalism be different than design for non-public journalism?

Table. Large Public Vs. Large Non-Public Journalism: Percentages and Fisher's Exact Test of Public Journalism Characteristics by Size of Paper

Variables (per cent with yes values)	Large PJ stories	Small PJ stories	Exact Probabilities
Common ground and solutions	36%	0%	.025
Interactivity with media	71%	46%	.13
Mobilizing information	25%	63%	.42
Views of real people	50%	39%	.25
N=27			

The results from this study are mixed. Of six hypotheses that speak to the question of whether public journalism is visually different from non-public journalism, two showed significant differences among the newspaper issues sampled. Public journalism stories in this study used more visual devices to convey common ground and solutions, and ways to contact the media than did non-public journalism stories.. Four hypotheses showed no significant differences between public journalism and non-public journalism, but two had means in the direction hypothesized.

The public journalism issues sampled were more likely than non-public journalism to use fewer managed photo opportunities and more photos of real people than candidates or experts, but the differences were not significant These are signs that some of public journalism's goals may be beginning to be translated into practice by visual journalists, but that there are other goals that are not being addressed visually, at least in these newspapers.

The fact that the public journalism issues sampled were not significantly different from the non-public journalism issues in how they visually conveyed views of real people — one of the central tenets of public journalism — should be of concern. That the public journalism issues sampled visually communicated no more mobilizing information than the non-public journalism issues is less cause for worry because mobilizing information is not unique to public journalism the way the other characteristics can be.

This study has also found that, in some cases, public journalism papers that have established new conventions in place of the old have found it easier to adhere consistently to public journalism principles; for instance, the development of standing graphics such as democracy boxes for mobilizing information.

One problem in the consistent communication of public journalism characteristics seems to be with journalists' fundamental understanding of public journalism. Confusion over and even unawareness of public journalism principles seems to be a basic, underlying reason why the practice of public journalism is not significantly different from non-public journalism in terms of visual communication.

In addition, it appears that not all designers are practicing content-driven design. For instance, this research found stories which included views of real people in the text but not in the design.

In conclusion, there appear to be some significant differences in this sample in the way public journalism is visually communicated compared with non-public journalism. However, there is not enough significance to say that it represents a radical departure from non-public journalism, at least in the issues studied here. It appears another researcher's conclusion regarding the content of public journalism may be correct for the visual display as well: "there is no overriding, core philosophy of public journalism at some of the papers practicing it; instead it has become a label used to name a variety of special projects."

The news industry has been undergoing a fundamental paradigm shift since the end of last century. An increasing number of media companies around the United States, such as the Washington Post in Washington, DC, Media General in Virginia, the Tribune Company in Chicago, and New England Cable News, have taken solid steps to merge different media such as newspapers, television stations, radio stations, and online journalism companies to disseminate news content on multiple media platforms.

As a result, in a metropolitan area, one company would own print, TV, and online venues. Media call this industrial trend "media convergence," though the concept means much more than media mergers. Media convergence muddies the lines among broadcast journalism, print journalism, and online journalism, leaving college journalism educators to wonder whether traditional journalism programmes have become dinosaurs.

After surveying 200 newspaper publishers worldwide, the World Association of Newspapers (WAN) found, "Despite a somewhat gloomy outlook for wholesale convergence in media companies worldwide in the near term, convergence is already being implemented with varying degrees of enthusiasm and speed among the world's media companies". The Innovation International Media Consulting Group estimates that at least 100 of the world's multiple media companies are planning and implementing integration strategies. South and Nicholson (2002) drew a sketch of a converged media company:

Daily journalists need to embrace the 24-hour news cycle, with continuous deadlines. And the story needs to be reported and produced for a multi-platform audience. That may mean delivering content first to the Web and cell phones, a streaming video broadcast later in the day, a TV talk-back interview still later, and a "second day" interpretive story for the next morning's newspaper.

Dominic Gates (2002) pointed out, "Convergence with broadcast and online media is the shape of things to come for newspapers." The trend remains controversial. Critics complain that such cross-ownership of both a television station and a newspaper in the same market is a threat to democracy because it limits the number of voices.

Delegates of the Communication Workers of America, a 60,000-member guild, passed a resolution in June of 2002 at the group's annual convention in Las Vegas, pledging to increase public awareness about the risks of ongoing media convergence.

The delegates complained that shrinking media markets are a threat to editorial diversity and job security. In 1975, the Federal Communications Commission (FCC) ruled that no new broadcast licenses would be granted to companies that own a major daily newspaper and a local television station in the same city. Fairness and Accuracy In Reporting (FAIR) calls on the FCC to roll back limits on media consolidation.

The Newspaper Association of America (NAA), on the other hand, has asked the FCC to appeal the rule. On June 2, 2003, the FCC voted 3 to 2 to relax or eliminate some ownership restrictions, such as a rule barring media companies from owning television stations in markets where they publish daily newspapers. Although some lawmakers and advocacy groups are still fighting in the courts and on Capitol Hill to overturn the FCC's new media ownership rules, these rules will be likely to encourage cross-media ownership in the years to come.

The mergers have raised questions about whether they are good for the craft of journalism itself. Critics complain that by requiring journalists to be jacks of both trades, print and broadcast, the journalists will be masters of none. Robert J. Haiman, president emeritus of The Poynter Institute, compared the media convergence trend to an Amphicar, a cross between a boat and a car.

The Amphicar, hawked in Florida during the 1950s, flopped. "It flopped because people quickly discovered that while it really was an ingenious combination of a car and a boat, it was a lousy car (because it also had to be a boat), and it was a lousy boat (because it also had to be a car)".

Willingly or unwillingly, many news practitioners' functions are gradually changing or are expected to change as media convergence rolls on. For a reporter in a converged media environment, knowing how to write is probably no longer enough. S/he could be expected to write the same story for different media in a timely manner. Ideally, s/he can readily talk in front of a video camera. As a photographer, knowing how to tell a story both in video and in still images is more and more in demand.

A designer should know how to prepare still graphics for print, moving graphics for television and dynamic graphics for the Web. At the online version of the Chicago Tribune, for instance, staffers are supposed to cover stories, take pictures, operate video cameras, and create digital pages. The editors, too, need a wider variety of skills than the traditional paper editors. Along with infrastructure changes and the attempt to create synergy among the various media outlets, a new breed of journalists-digital or multimedia journalists-is expected.

As media jobs become more demanding, some news practitioners are beginning to team up to complete projects. At the same time, fear, confusion, and frustration from news practitioners are creeping into newsrooms. Carr (2002c) wrote: "Convergence frightens many people who wonder whether their current skill sets have prepared them for-or will even be needed in-that great undiscovered country, the future.

This is probably the primary reason why I still find such great hostility to convergence among certain journalists." Killebrew (2001), a mass communications professor from the University of South Florida, suggested that "journalists must be prepared to either crosstrain themselves or seek training from other sources while management must be prepared to give them the opportunities and time to do so."

The 1999-2000 president of the Association for Schools of Journalism and Mass Communication (ASJMC), Shirley Staples Carter, questioned whether, in the midst of the "Internet revolution," programmes are prepared to educate journalists of the future. When specifically talking about writing, Keith Hartenberger, manager of news and programming for Tribune Regional Programming, said that journalism schools should make their students aware of the many ways to present the news. "It's a multimedia world out there," he said. "If you're just being prepared to write newspaper stories, you won't be prepared". "At some point, this [cross-media training] is something we're going to expect from everyone".

Media convergence, as a trend that is gradually shaping the landscape of the media industry in the new century, has called into question the conventional journalism school practice of having separate tracks-print, broadcast, etc. Journalism educators around the country also are trying to figure out what they should do, if anything, to better prepare students for the converged media. For instance, should journalism educators consider merging different sequences such as magazine, newspaper, broadcast, and photojournalism, or still teach all such courses as if they were unrelated media?

"Traditionally defined segments of the communications industry are less and less distinguishable for technological and market convergence," observed Moon (2001). Are college journalism educators themselves both theoretically equipped and technologically prepared to teach their students for converged media? What do media companies expect from future news practitioners? What do current news practitioners in converged media feel is lacking? For both news practitioners and professors, the two most urgent questions cry for answers: Should journalism schools train specialists or fit for-all generalists? And how should college journalism education balance the teaching of critical thinking and technical skills? Apart from all these education-related questions, we are also interested in finding out what are the driving forces behind the media mergers, who are regarded as the beneficiaries of this trend, and how people's political beliefs are related to their attitude towards teaching media convergence in colleges? These questions pertain closely to college journalism education, which has been the subject of debate and criticism for two decades.

A national survey was conducted among colleges, daily newspapers, and commercial television stations to explore the issue of how journalism schools should prepare students for the trend of media convergence from the perspectives of news editors, news professionals, and journalism professors. The study measured the level of general support for convergence education and determined if a new model of journalism education was called for.

If so, it examined whether consensus existed among the three groups on the direction educators should take when revisiting programme designs. Where consensus was not apparent, divisions among the sample of educators, editors, and reporters were defined. The goal of the study is to provide evidence that will help journalism educators make informed decisions about how to respond to media convergence in their curricula and courses and lay an empirical foundation for further discussions and conversations about media convergence.

The search results show that media convergence is a comparatively new topic in media research, though articles about it have inundated the Internet, magazines, and newspapers. Most research writings appeared no earlier than 1998. Articles about the relationship between media convergence and higher education are rare and have shown up more recently in trade magazines such as Presstime, Quill, and Journalism Education Today and in Web sites. A few research writings were found in academic conference (*i.e.*, AEJMC) proceedings.

Many writings have addressed one of the toughest questions: What is media convergence? How to define "media convergence" had a direct bearing on how we conducted this study. Out of these writings, we identified four categories of media convergence that directly affect how journalism will be taught in colleges.

CONTENT CONVERGENCE

As Tremayne noted, decades ago, the term media convergence referred to the content convergence between competing newspapers and even among newspapers, magazines, and television.

Today, pure content convergence continues on the Internet. For instance, the St. Petersburg Times has incorporated local Channel 10's TV news into its online newspaper though they are independent business entities. In other words, media convergence may not necessarily be tied to media merger.

Form convergence (or technological convergence). Around the mid-1990s, as Tremayne and Wurtz (2000) noted, computer technology and Internet technology made possible the convergence of all forms of mediated communications including video, audio, data, text, still photo, and graphic art for "on-demand" audiences. Using these different forms to tell news stories on the World Wide Web has been widely regarded as the future of mass communication regardless of the fact that most online news sites have had a hard time making ends meet, let alone making a profit. Form convergence, often called technological convergence, has been a fundamental force to guide and lead convergence in the market, industry, and regulation.

CORPORATE CONVERGENCE

Since the late 1990s, media convergence has been escalated to the level of media mergers. The News Centre located in Tampa, Florida, owned by Media General, and the Tribune Interactive, owned by the Tribune Company, for instance, are the products of media mergers.

In The News Centre, WFLA-TV, The Tampa Tribune, and Tampa Bay Online operate out of the same building. They share daily tips and information, spot news, photography, enterprise reporting, franchises, events, and public service. Each of the three entities in The News Centre has its own independent newsroom, but they issued a joint statement of coverage principles, titled "News Centre Pledge".

The Tribune Interactive has brought together the interactive functions of the company's four newspapers and more than a score of television stations including WGN-TV and CLTV. The individual media outlets have their own newsgathering staff, but their coverage is enhanced by their multimedia desks in the Chicago Tribune newsroom and the Tribune Media Centre in Washington.

"A synergy-team of print editors and TV news veterans at the Chicago Tribune work together to manage resource sharing and the relationship". Media merger has made both content convergence and form convergence handy.

Corporate convergence via vertical and horizontal integration, mergers, alliances, and acquisitions will make traditionally defined segments of the communications industry less and less distinguishable.

ROLE CONVERGENCE

Russial identified several examples of role convergence in newsrooms. For instance, the roles of reporter and librarian, the roles of copyeditor and compositor, the roles of graphic artist and Web designer, and the roles of photo editor, darkroom technician, and photographer are all converging in different media. In more recent years, content convergence, form convergence, and especially corporate convergence have sparked more in-depth role convergence among news practitioners.

For instance, Victoria Lim from The News Centre in Tampa revealed at a February 2002 conference on media convergence at the University of Florida that she primarily works as a television reporter for WFLA-TV, but she also has to write for the company's newspaper, The Tampa Tribune, as a senior consumer investigative reporter and for the Web company TBO.com on a daily basis; at the time of the conference, she was working on 31 stories.

A newspaper reporter may also produce a newspaper in QuarkXPress or serve as a TV news anchor, while a newspaper photographer may shoot video stories or produce interactive online stories in Flash. Role convergence requires that both reporters and editors re-equip themselves both journalistically and technologically.

Of the four types of convergence, role convergence has the most direct effect on future journalism education. Within the media industry, there are serious doubts about whether training cross-media journalists are possible or desirable. When asked whether reporters of the future must be equally skilled in print, TV, and online, Forrest Carr, news director of WFLA-TV at The News Centre in Tampa, said no.

He said he believed that there would always be areas of specialization and students may still choose specialties, but said that it no longer makes any sense to pretend print journalists and electronic journalists are in different professions.

On the other hand, he said that journalists who have skills in TV, print, and online media certainly will be more valuable to their employers; and he emphasized that prospective employees must be willing to work in an environment where reporters cooperate across platforms. In most cases currently, he said, cooperating across platforms simply comes down to the sharing of tips and information.

Charles Kravetz, the vice president for news and station manager of New England Cable News (NECN), the largest regional news network in America, concurs with Forrest Carr. When asked "Do you see a time when all journalists will have to be able to file stories on all platforms (print, TV, radio, online)?" Kravetz said: "I am not sure that is the way it is going to work out.

This notion we had that one-journalist-fits-all-media is perhaps not that realistic.... There are very few people we will talk about in the future that are TV/newspaper/internet reporters". Gates (2002) agreed, "The 'backpack journalist'-a superhack master of multimedia who can do it all and who routinely packs a laptop and a video camera along with the tape recorder and steno notebook-may be the subject of avant-garde j-school courses, but it's not likely to become the norm."

Some other media executives have tried to define the extent to which role convergence is expected. Gil Thelen, executive editor and senior vice president of The Tampa Tribune, for instance, gave suggestions to journalism educators based on his two years of experience in The News Centre.

"The fully formed, all-purpose, multiplatform, gadget-laden journalism grad is NOT what we're looking to hire.... Journalism schools must continue to produce graduates who are competent in one craft area: reporting, design, producing, directing, editing." However, Thelen encouraged journalism schools to train writers to write for print, online, and broadcast and train print photographers to learn how to shoot and produce TV packages. Thelen said that cultural resistance is the biggest hurdle for converging newsrooms, and that employees or current journalism students need to learn to cooperate and collaborate across newsrooms.

What is unclear is whether these media administrators' predictions are limited by the status quo of the current generation of news practitioners who might not be very well prepared for convergence or who might even resist the notion of media convergence. At Brigham Young University, students with multiple skills are more valued and feel more comfortable in the converged media environment.

In addition, sharing tips and information does not entail convergence. Reporters have been doing this for decades. It seems that keeping convergence only on the level of sharing tips and information can hardly justify the high cost of rebuilding infrastructures like The News Centre. We are interested in finding out what expectations media companies have for future journalists. From news professionals' self-evaluations of their preparedness for media convergence, we should also be able to infer what is most desirable in the media industry nowadays.

In the face of increasing demand for technically skilled journalists-conversant with QuarkXPress, Photoshop, Avid, and Dreamweaver and able to crunch statistics using spreadsheets and other statistical methods in order to uncover the hidden story-should longstanding staples such as ethics, law, and theory remain at the heart of journalism curricula?

Or should such materials, commonly grouped together as "critical thinking", share equal hilling with technology or "skills" training? In other words, how should journalism schools balance the teaching of professional skills and that of critical thinking in an era when technology penetrates every facet of news gathering, preparation, editing, production, and delivery?

Convergence further complicates this age-old battle in journalism education. Abraham noticed that the goal of most restructuring in journalism institutions is to provide an integrated skills environment where students would get the chance to practice the skills of multimedia production. Abraham argued: "The role of journalism academy should be very different from that of the industry. Its role should not simply be to inculcate skills that will help students to flag down jobs. They should aim to provide a scholarly background for a deeper intellectual understanding of our lives, media forms and of communication in general".

The dean of the University of Nevada at Reno thinks the ability to use multiple media skills is essential. Brigham Young University, which has built a working converged newsroom into its curriculum, expects students to graduate with multiple skills. University News Director, Dean Paynter, said, "We expect our students to more than anchor, more than report, and more than produce. The best ones can do it all, including write for the newspaper".

Mitchell Stephens, professor of journalism and mass communications at New York University, holds up the other end. "In a world where corporate pressures on 'content providers' seem to be increasing and civic affairs decreasing, the argument for emphasizing the basics does have much to recommend it."

Thomas Kunkel, dean of the Philip Merrill College of Journalism at the University of Maryland, sums it up: "Today's journalists, first and foremost, must be strong critical thinkers who know enough about geography, history and the human condition to understand why events play out as they do. They must be intellectually curious.

They should speak a second language. They should read something other than Jim Romenesko's MediaNews site. They ought to have a world view."

A controversy in late 2002 at Columbia University demonstrates how volatile the argument is currently. The debate arose when the graduate school of journalism at Columbia University halted its search for a dean. The new university president, Lee Bollinger, wanted to re-evaluate the school's mix of craft versus theory, and the move created a flurry of opinion about the journalism school's existing curriculum.

This critical curriculum question is often reflected in the questions of whether and how new technology classes should be included in the existing curriculum and how they should be taught. Some journalism schools are preparing to embrace the wave of media convergence in their new curricula by converging print and electronic media sequences to adapt to the industrial trends and the new technological environment.

Blanchard and Christ warn that universities with limited resources will no longer tolerate duplicating specializations with separate courses such as writing for television, writing for newspapers, writing for public relations, and writing for advertising. Blanchard and Christ add that the communications revolution (the media's convergence and related trends) is making journalism and mass communication's traditional sequences obsolete.

Actually, Blanchard and Christ's opinion is not something new. Early in 1972, the University of Iowa School of Journalism already eliminated its sequences but at the expense of being denied reaccreditation by ACEJMC. About thirty years later, their decision seemed to be finding more sympathy.

Many schools are still exploring where to go. In October 2001, seventeen professors and leaders of new media from thirteen journalism programmes across the country gathered in Berkeley, California, and had a discussion about new media in journalism education. The University of Nevada, Reno, offered several different elective courses in new media, but it did not have a special sequence. It was struggling with how to incorporate them in other classes. The University of Florida had a concentration in online media, which was equivalent to other concentrations such as reporting and editing and photojournalism.

Students who were not in that concentration couldn't always squeeze in the online media courses because they did not have any leftover électives they could take in the school. American University had three divisions, journalism, public communication, and visual media, but they did not work together very well most of the time. The University of South Carolina was restructuring its graduate masters programme in newspaper leadership and was focusing it on convergence. The University of Maryland had an online curriculum, but it was not formally structured as such. Northwestern University had an introductory New Media course at the undergraduate and graduate level, which was offered as an elective.

It was packed with everything from new skills training to wrestling with the business issues of new media to actual production. After three admission cycles, enrollment declined. The University of Minnesota established the Institute for New Media Studies, which merged broadcast journalism and print journalism programmes to make them a concentration with the idea that future journalists would work in a multi-channel environment and should know how to operate within all those channels.

Although editors and academics sometimes agree on the qualifications a journalism student needs, an ideal curriculum doesn't always include convergence preparedness courses. In a 2000 poll, editors and educators agreed "on the same five of 14 types of knowledge considered most necessary for journalism graduates and listed them in the same order of importance". Technical skills were not mentioned in the top five, surpassed instead by "understanding of a journalist's responsibility to the public, understanding of the ethics of journalism, knowledge of current events, broad general knowledge, and knowledge of government".

With so much variance across universities, we are interested in finding out how many journalism schools have revamped their curricula to prepare students for the trend of media convergence, what professors' attitudes are towards teaching critical thinking vs. teaching technical skills and training generalists vs. training specialists, and what editors' and news professionals' attitudes are towards the same issues. In this regard, several scholars and news practitioners have tried to give advice to journalism professors and students in the context of media convergence.

In 2002, David Bulla from the University of Florida presented his "Media convergence: Industry practices and implications for education" to the AEJMC annual conference in Miami. This is the first research writing of its kind. The theme of the paper is the closest to that of this study. Bulla's study looked at the changing nature of contemporary mass communications practices, focusing on multimedia or converged journalism.

It described what scholastic journalism scholars are doing to prepare their students for these changes and provided recommendations to educators about how to update curricula to account for convergence.

The research questions for that study were:

- What are journalism educators currently doing to incorporate convergence into their curricula;
- What abilities, skills, and attitudes do professional journalists expect from their newest employees?

Media convergence in Bulla's study was defined as multimedia journalism, which means reporting, writing, and disseminating content in two or more media platforms.

Because of the controversy about media mergers, Bulla tried to find answers to some hot issues concerning democracy including: Does corporate media merging reduce public discourse and hinder democracy? Will it ultimately mean the need for fewer and fewer reporters, as the development of other technology has meant a decline in the number of employees in other areas of the production process? All these questions pertain to our study.

Bulla obtained a sample of 114 news practitioners working at newspapers, television stations, wire services, magazines, radio stations, and online publications in the United States. The sample was randomly selected from Editor and Publisher and Yahoo lists of media companies in the U.S. Media Web sites. With a response rate of 36 per cent, Bulla interviewed 41 news practitioners. Bulla also interviewed college educators, but he did not state how he sampled them.

What is unclear is the extent to which the Yahoo list and Editor and Publisher list overlap each other and if a sample from two potentially overlapping lists is any longer a random sample. In addition, since Bulla's questions were almost all unstructured, that is, he conducted interviews,10 he did not really need a random sample. Researchers strive for depth rather than breadth and don't mean to claim external validity in the statistical sense by conducting interviews. Finally, if he did need a random sample, a sample of 114 people with a 36 per cent response rate could be statistically defective because of big statistical errors. Bulla needed a better research design to make his study valid and reliable.

Some scholars doubt whether journalism school professors are theoretically and especially technologically prepared to teach media convergence. In an article written for Journalism Education magazine, John Irby, a professor from Washington State University and a veteran newspaper editor and publisher, for instance, was concerned about the disconnection between the newsroom and the classroom. Irby (2000) asked:

Are universities and educators effectively preparing students for the workforce? Do educators understand what newspapers are looking for in future reporters and editors? Does the newspaper industry have a responsibility in the division between educators and professionals? Are journalism educators "discounted" by professionals who believe those who teach couldn't succeed in newspapers?

Irby said older generations of newspaper reporters also appeared on radio and television periodically though they had no training; they never even felt like it was part of their job and thus did not take it very seriously.

But now, he continued, print journalists do need to take it seriously; journalism educators need to re-evaluate, and probably modify, the separatetrack approach in training print and broadcast journalists.

Irby believed that there is still a need for specialization, but he told students to take both broadcast and print courses and told them that computer literacy is as crucial as the old-fashioned kind.

A study about the impact of media convergence on journalism education without consulting Robert J. Haiman's article "Can convergence float?" (2001) should be considered incomplete.

Haiman's fervent talk against media convergence raised some challenging questions that educators must face. Haiman, president emeritus of The Poynter Institute, argued that the converged media world is one from which good journalism, and good journalists, are going to be in great need of defence.

He stuck to his notion of the mission of good journalism he stated 40 years ago: "To inform the public about the public's business, creating a society that is equipped with the knowledge it needs to make the right civic decisions more often than it makes the wrong civic decisions, and thus helping to perpetuate self-government and democracy."

Expressing his deep concern for journalism, Haiman said: "I think that convergence may end up being good, maybe even very good, for media companies. I fear, however, that it is going to be bad, and maybe even very bad, for journalism." He continued to explain:

I think it is going to be bad for journalism because, even if it goes as well as it possibly can, I believe that it is going to distract journalists, journalism teachers, and journalism students away from that single most important imperative of the craft - to create an informed society capable of intelligently governing itself.

And if it does not go well, I fear it is going to subject journalists to time, resource, craft, and ethical pressures, all of which will be bad for journalists, bad for journalism, and bad for the country. In his talk, Haiman mentioned a top education reporter who had done a"superb job" for more than 18 years. Now, he had to do short reports for the TV station with which that newspaper was converged.

However,"he's not exactly ready for prime time." After this reporter retires, Haiman is afraid that that he will be replaced by"someone who may not report like a buzz saw and write like a dream, but who probably will report and write education okay and who will also look good and sound good on television.""When that happens," he continued,"the journalism quality of all of the education reporting coming out of that converged news operation is going to go down."

We believe that few people would disagree with Haiman's point that quality content is the king, to use his own words, but Haiman's above comment could be limited, again, by the performance of the current generation of reporters who are not prepared for media convergence.

Haiman was suggesting that a future reporter who has been trained to work for different media platforms and who has learned more about reporting would produce reporting of less quality.

In our study, we would like to find out to what extent Haiman's concern is shared by editors, news professionals, and professors.

While convergence is still in its infancy, Haiman suggested that journalists, journalism students, and journalism teachers do three"terribly important things":

- For journalists who want to keep good journalism alive in the converged world to take a blood oath to fight, scrap, kick and scream whenever any attempt is made to dilute good journalism values.
- For journalism schools and journalism teachers to offer students the right curriculum to function best in that converged world, and this does not mean offering new courses in convergence.
- For journalism students to emphasize the right areas of study and take the right courses so they will be able to defend themselves against the evils of convergence, prosper in that new world, and contribute to the effort to sustain informed self-government.

Haiman said,"If we decide to teach anything about convergence at Poynter, that is the lesson I hope we'll teach."

To students, Haiman said that the journalists who will be the most successful in the converged world are the same ones who are the most successful today, and they are the ones who are best trained in six areas: reporting, writing, editing, ethics, and media law, research techniques and specialized knowledge such as business, finance, law, science, health, aging, and the environment.

Since the top reporter in education Haiman mentioned can hardly survive the converged media world, our question is whether gaining knowledge in these six areas is sufficient and what else, if any, students need to learn. Do students need to learn any new skills? What new skills do news practitioners need?

Also, we would like to see how the attitudes of the respondents from these three groups towards media merger affect their views of how to train future journalists. As South and Nicholson (2002) commented,"If the industry doesn't agree on what new skills journalists need, it will be hard for journalism schools to know what to teach."

LARGER CONTEXT OF THE STUDY

The questions concerning teaching skills vs. critical thinking and training specialists vs. generalists are not new. They have been contextualized in ongoing conversations across disciplines over decades on many campuses in the United States. But such conversations take on new meanings in journalism schools when many reporting jobs today are becoming high-tech-oriented and many news companies are demanding high-tech skills from new hires upon their graduation.

The impact of such industrial demands on universities brings us back to the core issue-the role of the university in the shaping of the young souls in its charge. In other words, how should a university achieve the desired product-a truly educated human being for newsrooms.

The question of teaching skills vs. critical thinking winds down to a perennial competition between acquiescing pervasive vocationalism with its emphasis on skills training in an attempt to enable college students to survive outside academic institutions and establishing the relevance of the broad spectrum of knowledge to the career goals and lives of individuals. E. D. Hirsch argues: “Narrow vocational education, adjusted to the needs of the moment, is made ever more obsolete by changing technology... What is required is education for change, not for static job competencies”.

Probably no one has better expressed than Joanne G. Kurfiss the importance of imparting critical thinking as skills of analyzing and constructing arguments, as construction of meaning, and as the manifestation of a contextual theory of knowledge. “Critical thinking can result in a new way of approaching significant issues in one’s life or a deeper understanding of the basis for one’s actions. Or it might result in political activity”.

Along the similar line as Kurfiss’s critical thinking theory and unlike Allan Bloom, who condemns the introduction of non-Western materials into the university curricula so as to protect the curriculum from the contamination of ideological conflict, Jerry Herron also highly promotes the teaching of critical thinking by calling on faculty to bring their conflicting ideologies into open engagement so that students can discover what is at stake in different ideas and can see their representational meaning.

The questions are whether universities should totally give up the teaching of skills today and how the needs of the job market and the goal of college education can be in harmony. In other words, can the teaching of common traditional content and the teaching of higher order skills join forces? Patracia Graham, ex-dean of the Harvard Graduate School of Education, argues that we need both commonality and flexibility in American education and there is no reason we cannot have both at once. The question of training specialists vs. generalists is an extension of a larger conversation about reforming the fragmented curricula in higher education. Often classified as "cultural right," Ernest Boyer, Allan Bloom, and E. D. Hirsch share similar views about the problems in higher education. They point out that the university now is anarchistic. There is no vision of what an educated human being is. The curriculum is disjointed and disciplines are fragmented into smaller pieces.

Undergraduates find it hard to see patterns in their courses and relate what they learn to life. Careerism conflicts with the liberal arts. And finally, schools have failed to thoroughly carry out the educational goal of promoting mature literacy for all our citizens. They all agree that an educational reform is needed to teach more common traditional content apart from the higher-order skills that are commonly emphasized.

Boyer calls for a balance between individual interests and shared concerns while the actual priority is given to the latter. To promote a liberal education, Boyer advocates the "integrated core" or "enriched major"-a programme of general education that introduces students not only to essential knowledge, but also to connections across the disciplines, and, in the end, to the application of knowledge to life beyond the campus.

Boyer points out, knowledge becomes important only when we use it and apply it to humane ends; therefore, the undergraduate experience should not only generate new knowledge, but channel that knowledge to the service of the society. It is a matter of invigorating "the claims of community while protecting with full vigour the dignity and origins of each individual," to use Boyer and Kaplan's words.

In a similar vein, Bloom calls on teachers to look towards the goal of human completeness and to provide students a liberal education, in which learning is both synoptic and precise. To Bloom, liberal education feeds the student's love of truth and passion to live a good life. It also requires that a student's whole life be radically changed by it.

Bloom offers an ivory tower vision of the university-"the good old Great Book approach"-undergraduate students spend four years reading certain generally recognized classic texts for answers to philosophical questions of personal and human identity and aspirations. Bloom thinks that man may live more truly and fully in reading Plato and Shakespeare than at any other time because then they are participating in essential being and are forgetting their accidental lives.

In accordance with Boyer's and Bloom's points of view, Hirsch argues that "the greatest human individuality is developed in response to a tradition, not in response to disorderly, uncertain, and fragmented education" and "only by accumulating shared symbols, and the shared information the symbols represent can we learn to communicate effectively with one another in our national community". However, Hirsch places emphasis more on the content of education, ensuring that students acquire all the "right" elements of knowledge that will enable them to get along in the Real World. He believes that neither the content-neutral curriculum of Rousseau and Dewey nor the narrowly specified curriculum of Plato is adequate to the needs of a modern nation. Hirsch calls for a curriculum, including extensive curriculum and intensive curriculum with an emphasis on the former, which is traditional in content and provides students with a common core of cultural information. "The conception of a two-part curriculum avoids the idea that all children should study identical materials" Hirsch says.

Based on our literature review, media convergence in our study is defined as the assimilation of media content for multiple media platforms. Media convergence may involve any combination of the convergences of media contents, media forms, media companies, and roles of news practitioners.

Our general research question is how college professors should prepare students to cope with media convergence. To be specific, should college professors prepare generalists who can competently work in multiple media platforms or prepare specialists who know inside out how to work for one particular medium platform? And how should journalism schools balance the teaching of critical thinking and technical skills?

Corresponding to these two questions, we also would like to find out if college journalism educators themselves are both theoretically equipped and technologically prepared to teach their students about media convergence. The study serves both as an attitude finder and a fact finder.

We believe that professors, editors, and news professionals are the best candidates to answer these questions. Editors represent the media companies to hire news staffers with news reporting abilities desired by the company. News professionals work in the forefront of news reporting and know best about what news reporting abilities they need.

The attitudes of the editors and the current generation of news professionals towards media convergence will have a great implication on future journalism education. Professors run journalism schools, and they have the final say about where their schools are going. Their attitudes towards journalism education in terms of media convergence will have the most direct influence on the kind of education journalism students will receive and how the students will perform in tomorrow's media.

Editors include daily newspaper editors in charge of newsroom operations or online news operations and news directors in charge of newsroom operations in a commercial TV station with news content, both in the United States.

News professionals refer to non-management news staff, such as reporters, anchors, photographers, designers, producers, Web staff, etc., working in American media companies. Journalism professors are defined as full-time instructors with any academic rankings who teach journalism courses in a U.S. journalism school, department, programme, or division, which could be administratively affiliated with an institution with a name like College of Communications or Department of Communications Studies.

To obtain opinions about media convergence, we could have targeted our survey only at those editors and news professionals in a converged media environment. The opinions obtained from those editors and news professionals, however, could be biased. Those media companies that have not gone through convergence must have a reason for not doing so. We also wanted to find out what they are doing about convergence. Balanced views both from the converged and un-converged media companies will better assist colleges in their strategic planning.

We conducted a national survey among editors, news professionals, and journalism professors with three different versions of online survey questionnaires posted on a school Web site. Respondents were asked to fill out the questionnaire online and submit answers online as well. The answers went through a commercial form handler and reached the primary investigator's e-mail address. By doing so, the primary investigator had no way to detect who answered the questionnaire unless the respondent voluntarily revealed his/her e-mail address to request the findings from the study.

There were twenty-two questions in each of these three questionnaires. Almost all questions were close-ended. About half of the questions used a 5-point Likert Scale from "Strongly Agree" to "Strongly Disagree." Some questions across the three questionnaires shared similarity, so that comparisons could be made when analyzing data. A text field was created for respondents to provide feedback to the survey freely.

The textual answers in the text field will be reported along with the statistics to illustrate and explain the quantitative findings. All questionnaires went through pilot tests. The unit of analysis was each participant.

In order to conduct a systematic random sampling of editors and news professionals, we needed a list of newspaper editors and TV news directors in the United States and a list of newspaper and TV news staffers. We found that such lists did not exist, though lists of newspapers and lists of TV stations did exist in multiple places online like Editor and Publisher Yearbook and Broadcasting Sr Cable Yearbook. Therefore, we decided to construct our own.

To do so, we went through two steps. First, we constructed a combined list of daily newspapers and TV stations so that we could sample these news institutions. Second, we visited the Web sites of all sampled news institutions to find the e-mail of the editor/news director and the e-mail of one news professional randomly chosen.

After further research, we decided that newslink.org's daily newspaper list was the most comprehensive and workable list for sampling daily newspapers. In total, 1,190 U.S. daily newspapers with a valid URL were listed alphabetically by state. We sampled one out of every four dailies. Then, we visited each of those Web sites to find the e-mail address of the managing editor, chief editor, online editor, or equivalent in each of those dailies and sent out a survey invitation e-mail to him/her. If an individual e-mail address was not available, we replaced it with a generic e-mail address listed on their Web site and specified that the e-mail was for the editor.

In total, there were 1,093 companies ordered alphabetically by state. From the list, we removed PBS network companies, which mostly did not provide staff information, companies that did not generate news content such as WB network companies and UPN network companies, religious TV stations, and foreign language stations. In total, we extracted 674 TV stations with a valid URL. Since this population is smaller than that of the newspapers, we over-sampled it. Instead of sampling every other four, we sampled every other station.

Then, we visited each of those Web sites to find the e-mail address of the news director or equivalent in each of those TV stations and sent out a survey invitation e-mail to him/her. If an individual e-mail address was not available, we replaced it with a generic e-mail address and specified that the e-mail was for the news director. In total, we successfully sent out invitation e-mails to 523 newspaper editors and TV news directors as our sample.

We also sampled one news professional out of each of the sampled U.S. dailies and TV stations for the survey. Since there was always more than one professional in a company, we simply randomly clicked on one name and picked him/her and made sure that s/he was on the news staff.

Then, we sent him/her a survey invitation e-mail. If an individual e-mail address was not available, we replaced it with a generic e-mail address and specified whom the e-mail was for. S/he was asked to fill out a questionnaire that was worded in a slightly different manner. In total, we successfully sent out invitation e-mails to 398 news professionals.

We also needed to conduct a systematic random sampling of college journalism professors, but we were disappointed that all lists we found had many J-schools, even major ones, missing. Therefore, a new list was built upon the existing lists and upon the findings from a more careful search in the Yahoo U.S. Colleges and Universities site. In total, the new list contains 205 alphabetically ordered U.S. J-schools that contain 2,194 journalism professors.

We sampled one out of every four professors from the virtually running list of all journalism professors across the schools. For instance, if a school had six journalism professors, we picked the fourth one; then, the second journalism professor from next school was picked. We sent an invitation e-mail to every professor in the sample. In total, we successfully sent out 500 e-mails.

The three samples of editors, news professionals, and professors included 1,421 cases.

We understood that non-response had been a serious problem with online surveys in recent years. In order to counter possible low response rates in our survey, we created three samples for editors, news professionals, and professors containing roughly 500 people for each group, which were much larger than the sample sizes for populations recommended by Mildred Patten (2000) in her book Understanding Research Methods: An Overview of the Essentials so that, if low response rates occurred, we could base our confidence limits on the actual number of responses themselves. We also sent out one reminder e-mail to the samples, which drastically boosted the response rates, especially for professors and news professionals.

After two weeks of online data collecting in November 2002, we received 223 responses from professors (a 44 per cent response rate), 151 responses from editors (a 29 per cent response rate), and 142 responses from news professionals (a 35 per cent response rate).

The overall response rate is 36 per cent. As Singletary notes, returns of 30 per cent to 40 per cent are common in mail surveys. The response rates of this online survey seem typical. However, the response rates are still comparatively low. A response bias is potentially present. Many respondents (41 per cent) left textual answers to explain and illustrate their answers to the close-ended questions and/or made comments on the topic.

- What is the status quo of media convergence in the industry?

By the end of 2002, 19 per cent of the newspapers and commercial television stations with news content in the United States had gone through media mergers. Being merged or not has to do with the size of a company. Larger companies tend to have been merged while smaller ones have not.

Roughly half of the news professionals surveyed (48 per cent) reported that they produced news content for multiple media platforms on a routine basis; that was true both in merged media (50 per cent) and non-merged media (48 per cent). In other words, media merger is not the precondition for practicing news for multiple media platforms. The pressure on news professionals to learn to produce multimedia content is also felt in many non-merged media companies. This finding confirms that media convergence is not necessarily related to media merger.

A typical editor or news director was a man (71 per cent) between 36-45 years old (42 per cent) with a bachelor's degree (76 per cent) who had worked for at least two media (57 per cent) for more than 20 years (53 per cent). A typical news professional was either a man (52 per cent) or woman (48 per cent) between 26-35 years old (43 per cent) with a bachelor's degree (84 per cent) who had worked for at least two media (60 per cent) less than ten years (62 per cent).

Editors had generally worked for more years than news professionals, but they did not have more multiplatform experience than news professionals. As more news companies are practicing cross-media reporting with or without their companies being merged, it is important that editors with multiplatforrn experiences are chosen to direct newsroom businesses. Many editors need cross-media training more urgently than news professionals do if the news company they work for produces news contents for multiple media platforms on a daily basis.

- Should J-schools train specialists or generalists?

Gil Thelen (2002) said that writers should learn how to write for multimedia and still photographers should learn how to shoot videos, but he was not interested in hiring people with multiple sets of skills. We designed four questions to test how popular Thelen's opinion was.

The majority of the respondents (84 per cent) agreed or strongly agreed with Thelen that journalism students should learn how to write for multiple media platforms. One-way ANOVA shows significant difference among the means for professors (4.35), professionals (4.05), and editors. Tukey HSD post hoc tests show that professors were more positive on this statement than editors and professionals, while no significant difference existed between editors and professionals.

A similar number of respondents (85 per cent) agreed or strongly agreed with Thelen that journalism students with a visual emphasis should learn how to produce and edit photos, videos, and online interactive images. One-way ANOVA shows significant difference among the means for professors (4.55), professionals (4.22), and editors. Tukey HSD post hoc tests show that professors were more positive on this statement than professionals, while professionals were more positive than editors.

Most respondents (78 per cent) agreed or strongly agreed that all journalism majors should learn multiple sets of skills, such as writing, editing, TV production, digital photography, newspaper design, and Web publishing.

Oneway ANOVA shows significant differences among the means for professionals (4.28), editors (3.99), and professors (3.86).

Tukey HSD post hoc tests show that news professionals who worked in the forefront of news production felt this need more deeply than other respondents. Editors also had such an expectation for them.

There is no significant difference between editors and professors. These findings support the growing evidence that news professionals are being asked to wear multiple hats. The findings also indicate that Thelen's view has its market at this moment when news professionals with multiple sets of skills are highly desirable but not easy to find. Such a view may change as more journalism graduates equipped with multiple sets of skills enter the job market.

The professors' textual answers show that some of the difficulties J-schools have come across include the lack of a friendly curriculum, lack of credit hours to include the components of convergence content, lack of willing cooperation among faculty from different sequences, and lack of expertise, interest, or even time for some professors to develop new courses on convergence. When asked whether journalism students should still have a specialization, such as writing, photojournalism, broadcasting, and new media, over half (63 per cent) of the respondents agreed or strongly agreed. Over a quarter of the respondents (28 per cent) were negative and 9 per cent were not sure. One-way ANOVA mean comparisons show no significant difference of attitude among professionals (3.42), editors (3.51), and professors (3.72).

Comparing the support rate for this question to those for the first three questions, it is fair to argue that editors, news professionals, and professors emphasized the importance of cross-media training more than that of specialization, though they believed that specialization should not be neglected either. Currently, students in many J-schools specialize in one area by subscribing to a sequence such as news-editorial, magazine, photojournalism, and broadcast. When asked whether sequences should be reorganized considering the trend of media-platforms merging in the industry, 56 per cent of the professors agreed or strongly agreed, 22 per cent were not sure, and another 22 per cent disagreed or strongly disagreed.

The concept of sequences is being shaken among professors though it is still being accepted as a legitimate means of training students in various specialization areas in some J-schools. Speaking on behalf of herself and her colleagues, Professor #93 offered some special insight on this issue: We can't teach for the"now." We have to prepare students for when they graduate...which in most instances is now five years out. And, we feel a commitment to expose them to all types of writing in all platforms so they can be flexible about their career choice at the front end of their academics. Then, they can apply the skills to a specialty area where they are totally proficient.

"Flexible" is a key term repeatedly seen in editors' and news professionals' textual answers as a suggestion for future journalists. Editor's statement is typical:

Our job descriptions are open ended and new hires understand that they are being hired for their skills. They may be hired today to cover the city beat. In six months or in two weeks, if necessary, a person with Quark skills may be asked to fill in or shift duties to include pagination of a particular section. It is important that hires stay flexible.

The new hires, wrote Editor, "need to understand that the information they gather and process can have many different uses, audiences and shelf lives. They need to understand the complexities of the audience mix and be able to respond." "Those unwilling to be flexible may find themselves in a difficult scenario later in their careers".

From a different perspective, Professional concurred: "Students must be flexible, have a vigorous skill set and be prepared to get laid off and move around in the changing media arena." In short, "young journalists must be prepared to fill a variety of roles if they hope to succeed". "The most successful journalists are those that take on assignments willingly, can learn and want to learn".

Specialization in journalistic jobs is still honored, but is losing its favour to cross-media capability in converged media. Today, professionals with different specializations team together to work on multiple media projects. Tomorrow, it is likely that one-man bands will be more and more desired in newsrooms.

- How should J-schools balance the teaching of critical thinking and that of technical skills?

Most respondents (93 per cent), especially professors, agreed or strongly agreed that journalism students should both learn technical skills, such as online information search and Web design, while learning critical thinking skills in media law, ethics, etc.

One-way ANOVA shows significant difference among the means for professionals (4.35), editors (4.38), and professors (4.76). Tukey HSD post hoc tests show that professors were more positive on this point than editors and professionals, while no significant difference existed between editors and professionals.

But, should journalism students spend more time on learning critical thinking skills than on technical skills? Opinions were divided.

More than half of the respondents (62 per cent) believed that should be the case, but 19 per cent of the respondents were not sure and another 19 per cent of them did not agree. Oneway ANOVA shows significant difference among the means for professors (3.21), professionals (3.87), and editors (4.3). Tukey HSD post hoc tests show that editors were more positive on this point than professionals, and professionals were more positive than professors.

Throughout all the answers from the three groups of respondents, critical thinking was highly regarded as being more important than technical skills. Editors, news professionals, and professors all liked to see good stories, and good stories come from good thinking ability. An editor said: "Journalism graduates need to have a broad, well-rounded education; be critical thinkers; have the ability to write clearly; have a serious work ethic; and know computer basics - in that order".

"You can teach a monkey to type," echoes a writer. Therefore, he strongly suggested that J-schools "get more critical thinking skills pounded into the skulls of the students". While highly emphasizing the importance of critical thinking ability, editors did not mean to neglect the importance of teaching technical skills in schools.

We will develop this point when we discuss the next question. Comparing the professors' highest mean for the first question and their lowest mean for the second question, it is clear that professors saw critical thinking as highly important, but preferred a comparatively balanced approach for the teaching of the two sets of knowledge. One professor's comment illustrated this observation:

Knowing technical skill alone will not make you a "good" journalist. Critical thinking is vital not just to a career but to life itself. Without developing your ability to discern and evaluate, you will become "the prey" of society. Next, a technical skill is critical to a career in journalism today.

Even print Journalism is very high tech these days and all electronic media require extensive computer knowledge as well as other technical skills. I would place critical thinking skills first on your list of things to do because a developed mind will make it that much easier to develop a creative and technically sound understanding of the technical side of the business.

From a holistic view, there was no substantial disagreement between classrooms and newsrooms when we examine the issue of teaching critical thinking vs. teaching technical skills.

Compared to Terry's 2000 poll, this study shows that professors gave a higher status to technical skills in journalism curricula in 2002 than they did in 2000.

This is a period during which media convergence garnered its momentum. In short, all respondents generally agreed that J-schools should place emphasis on teaching critical thinking, but at the same time, should not neglect teaching technical skills.

- Should technical skills be learned at work or in school?

News professionals were asked, "If you wish to possess the technical skills you don't have now, do you prefer to learn them at work or wish you had learned in school?" Editors were given the same question with a slightly different wording.

Chi-Square test shows that the difference between editors and news professionals is significant. This finding well supplements the findings from the preceding questions. It suggests that editors not only looked at future journalists' critical thinking ability, but also hoped that future journalists would already possess the skills needed in a converged newsroom when they are hired.

On the other hand, most professionals preferred that they spend most of their school time on gaining critical thinking ability and learn skills largely at work. The professionals' general preference, to some extent, also reflected their need for technological update at their current positions, so that they can better qualify for multimedia productions.

Many editors and reporters said that school is the best place for journalism students to explore every facet of the media and acquire basic technical skills, though some advanced skills can only be learned on the job.

Learning skills while in school, they said, can build confidence and an expansive and broad understanding of the entire field and help with damage control and communication in newsrooms. "If editing and the technical skills were more prevalent in college courses," wrote a multi-tasking editor, "I think I could stave off a lot of headaches when the students become professionals."

An internship was the news professionals' and editors' most recommended venue for enhancing and learning more technical skills and gaining other practical experience. Reporter said: "While I value my college education, my internship and first job provided me with the most valuable skills today."

Another reporter said: "While education is great, students who work in media while in school fare much better in the real world." Some editors had complaints about graduates with a 3.5 GPA but no practical experience and no published news work. An anchor/reporter said that it is important even "for a freshman or sophomore in college to visit a newsroom and shadow someone. So many students wait until they are juniors and seniors to do this and then they realise they made a mistake in selecting their major. You will learn more by watching and doing". One reporter said, "To remain competitive, education must continue throughout a career". The implication of the discrepancy from this finding suggests that Jschools should place emphasis on teaching critical thinking, expose students to new technology, and design a comprehensive internship programme for students to gain real-world knowledge and further develop their crossmedia technical skills.

- What skills do news professionals need to learn most at their current positions?

Both editors and news professionals were given this unstructured question with slightly different wordings. We read through all the answers, and categorized them into the following nine facets in random order:

Multimedia production: producing and editing news stories on video, for the Web, and for print; re-purposing the same story for different media.

New technology: knowledge of software for producing video, Web sites, graphics, newspapers, and magazines; knowledge of how to operate a computer and use the Internet.

Good writing: knowing how to write to make people remember and/or take action, write about the beats with an expert's view.

Good editing is also expected:

Critical thinking: Having good news judgement, understanding what is legal and ethical, knowing how to report with insight, knowing how to crunch statistics.

Computer-assisted reporting: Expert's knowledge of conducting online information search, database knowledge.

On-camera exposure: How to report like a TV news anchor before a camera for a newspaper reporter.

Visual production: A newspaper writer must know how to take photos, or a TV reporter must know how to shoot video.

Second language: Knowing how to fluently speak and read a foreign language.

Time management: Well organizing time to work for multiple media platforms; the ability and willingness to work as a team to produce multimedia news stories.

Then we ranked these facets according to the percentage scores each facet got separately from the editors and the news professionals:

This ranking shows more agreement than disagreement between editors and news professionals. No matter how technology changes and whether media are converged, editors and news professionals believed that learning how to write good stories is still the top priority and writing is the very basic skill all news professionals should learn.

One editor pushed the importance of good writing to the extreme:"I've worked in markets 170 to 20, and having training in multiple media will not help you get a job, but being a good writer will".

Most editors and news professionals, however, did believe that learning multimedia production, new technology, and computer-assisted reporting are also among the top priorities."I would strongly urge students to prepare themselves to the best of their ability to be able to report/edit the news in a variety of platforms and to learn how to truly engage readers/listeners/viewers in what they are writing about," said Editor.

Editors and news professionals both believed that it is not very important for a newspaper reporter to learn how to talk like an anchor in front of a video camera.

This skill was even regarded as being less important than knowing how to speak a second language. Some editors and news professionals also mentioned learning how to manage time for producing multimedia news stories. Editor hoped that journalists in a converged environment would learn to avoid"extra" work by working"smarter" and with greater awareness of the requirements of the different publishing media. This finding, again, shows that editors valued critical thinking ability more than news professionals did. Editors wanted news professionals to be good thinkers first, and the latter wanted most to learn how to express their thinking in different media.

- If news professionals have to re-purpose their work for multiple media platforms, will the quality of their work suffer?

Since some authors such as Haiman expressed the concern about the possible decline of work quality if news professionals have to "re-purpose" stories for multiple media platforms, we tried to find out to what extent this concern was shared by editors and news professionals. Opinions split.

Thirty-eight per cent of the editors and professionals agreed or strongly agreed that the quality would deteriorate, 40 per cent disagreed or strongly disagreed, and the other 22 per cent were not sure. Editors and professionals showed no significant difference on this attitude T-test. Such a concern was not prevalent in the news industry. In response to such concerns, the news director from a converged media company wrote: “When reporters do cross platforms we give them the time to finish the project for all three platforms. Quality does not suffer. If we were to try to force reporters to cross platforms while operating under daily deadlines then quality could suffer depending on the nature of the story and the extra time consumed”.

Another editor summed up this issue: “Some employees can capably handle multiple media and tell stories effectively. Others cannot. Certainly strong technical skills and training can help, but it’s not just dependent on that; it depends more on the attitude and aptitude of the journalist”.

Quality multimedia work also involves a solid understanding of different cultures in different media. Editors both for and against media convergence noted the difficulty of merging different media with different cultures, and editors in those merged media called for flexibility in aptitude and willingness to cooperate across platforms. For instance, Editor wrote: Clarity of what convergence means to the news organization is vital and often lacking. This causes unneeded anxiety. Managers have to realise that each medium has its own culture, language, skill set and timetable and is naturally skeptical of anything unfamiliar. It is also true that these same journalists’ stock in trade is learning a new culture, language, skill set and timetable-on a daily basis. Therein lies the hope for an efficient news operation running on all cylinders and an effective -maybe even happy-staff.

If most editors and news professionals are not concerned about the quality of the work prepared for multiple media platforms and if news professionals are given enough time to complete their cross-media work, there is little reason to worry that future journalists, if well trained both theoretically and technologically for multiple media platforms, will produce work of poorer quality.

Training students to practice news in multiple media platforms will help bridge newsroom cultures from different media and eventually erase such differences.

We have noticed that no significant statistical differences existed between the editors and news professionals from the converged media companies and their counterparts from the not-yet-converged media companies when they answered the questions reported above.

- How are J-schools coping with media convergence?

From 1998 to 2002, about 60 per cent of the J-schools in the United States redesigned their curricula or developed new courses to prepare students for practicing news in multiple media platforms.

A typical journalism professor was a man (71 per cent) between 46-55 years old (42 per cent) with a doctoral degree (63 per cent) who worked in news media for one to ten years (48 per cent), may still be practicing news (45 per cent) in one way or another, and conducted academic research (66 per cent). More professors claimed that they were theoretically equipped (81 per cent) than technologically prepared (53 per cent) to teach students how to report news in multiple media platforms.

More than half of the professors (57 per cent) had not taught any journalism courses in the last five years where skill sets were beyond their own expertise; 25 per cent of the professors taught one such course and 11 per cent taught two.

Nevertheless, the majority of the professors (84 per cent) added content about media convergence either to their existing courses or to new courses or participated in cross-media team-teaching in the last five years.

Worries, concerns, and, sometimes, misconceptions about media convergence appeared in professors' textual answers. For instance, a professor from Montana said: "convergence is not happening". A professor who no longer practiced news said, "In my judgement, the writing portion of preparing news for print and for the Web is exactly the same".

Another professor maintained that it was not necessary to teach cross-media news practicing because "few 'want ads' for newspaper reporter and editor positions specifically listed multimedia platform skills as required or preferred experience for new hires". Many professors worried that media mergers would restrict the number of voices in a community. They regarded media mergers as a grand experiment in the profession and waited for the FCC's ruling on the cross-ownership of different media in the same market.

Wait-and-see-that was the strategy some universities took for teaching media convergence. One professor said that he needed to see the substantive contribution media convergence could make before he would be more serious about this phenomenon. He said that J-schools should be cautious about embracing convergence. Some other universities didn't have the time and resources to teach convergence courses or make major curriculum changes.

Most professors, however, did believe that media convergence was a reality; and "anybody serious about practicing media needs at minimal an acquaintance with various media and at best multiple competencies," as Professor said. Many professors (and editors and news professionals as well) had a clear opinion as to which comes first, teaching critical thinking or teaching technical skills.

While acknowledging the need for incorporating media convergence content in curricula, especially the technological components, professors cautioned against sacrificing conceptual and theoretical courses such as law, ethics, history, cultural studies, critical perspectives, etc. Professor analogized critical thinking as meat and potatoes and technical skills as dessert and side dishes and argued that "the meat and potatoes need to come before one begins to worry about the dessert and side dishes (or side shows)." This viewpoint was popular. Professor wrote:

It's the message, not the medium, that is of paramount importance. If students cannot understand and appreciate the underlying concepts, principles and ethics of journalism, then they cannot produce the type of content that will be of value to a free society. A thorough grounding in journalism must come before any training in tools. The tools are means to an end, not the end in and of themselves.

Incidentally, a reporter had similar thoughts: The medium isn't the message, the message is the message. In short, the fundamental analytic and synthetic skills of the news writer are paramount to the message.

The medium does not alter the reporter's craft of interpreting news events in the context of the society in a way that will make sense for the receiver of the information.... Additional skills may be desirable, but for the most part they can be learned on the job.

Obviously, the more skills one can offer, the better the employment opportunity. Those ancillary skills should not come at the expense of thorough proficiency as a news writer.

We fully understand why these respondents emphasize the teaching of critical thinking and the fundamentals of good reporting over the teaching of technical skills, and we strongly agree with their opinions. But, we also see the danger of over-stretching the point by treating the two sets of knowledge as two opposing poles.

Those arguments are based on the presumptions that message and medium can be easily separated, content and form can be detached, and readers for different media are from the same population. But, is that right? It is true that content is the king. It is true that "the medium does not alter the reporter's craft of interpreting news events."

News practice, however, is not only about news-gathering and writing. It also includes production, editing, and delivery. Without a solid grasp of grammar and style, how can a writer effectively express his/her good analytical thinking? Without knowing the available features and limitations of online news delivery, how can messages be constructed to their fullest potential?

Without understanding the technical difference between video news and print news, how can messages be constructed appropriately? In the digital era when almost all steps of news transmission involves technology, if professors don't teach students technical skills, will the computer majors, who know little about news practices, be expected to produce newspapers, TV news, and online news?

Writers, for instance, do not necessarily have to be conversant in constructing news reporting with Flash for online presentation or know how to operate a video camera to shoot video stories.

But knowing the principles and rules of news video-taping and what Flash or other software can offer will surely help writers more effectively convey their messages and better cooperate with visual reporters. Creativity distinguishes artists and artisans. Critical thinking ability distinguishes master journalists and technical writers. But artists must first know what artisans know and a master journalist must possess all that a technical writer knows for a living. Skills are intrinsic instead of extrinsic to ideas.

Teaching critical thinking and teaching technical skills are not mutually exclusive. Teaching journalism students how to express their critical thinking with conversant technical skills in different media seems to be a big challenge for J-school professors in the years to come.

From the professors' textual answers, we have observed different philosophical approaches to teaching convergence. Unlike some professors who took the wait-and-see approach, a professor from the University of Texas at Austin claimed that "convergence is already happening, and journalism schools should be leading the parade and not following it".

A popular viewpoint was that "skills across platforms must be taught, but more importantly storytelling, ethics, and critical thinking skills should be even more important in the journalism school curriculum".

One professor from Texas Christian University said that it maintained the existing sequences but required broadcast students to take print courses and vice versa.

Team-teaching was an often-used approach in some J-schools such as Indiana University for courses involving multiple sets of skills while professors learned from each other. Another professor, from the University of Colorado at Boulder, said convergence meant that "students work together to produce multimedia content for the Web-not that each individual should attempt to become proficient in all media".

To overcome the hurdle of the ratio limited by the ACEJMC accreditation standards between journalism courses and liberal arts courses, a professor from Bowling Green State University suggested that journalism undergraduate students stay for five years and devote the fifth year entirely to practice.

Some professors said that journalism students only need to know a little about the practices in media other than their own while some other professors firmly maintained that students should "be the master of many arts and the explorer of all".

- Who benefits from media convergence?

All respondents were asked, "Do you think that merging media companies such as television station, newspaper, radio station, and online news from a local area will benefit any of the parties listed on the left? Check all entries that apply." The entries included "The general public," "News professionals," "Media companies," "Nobody," and "Not sure." We designed this question about the legitimacy of media merger as a barometer for testing the respondents' political view on media convergence. We presumed that a respondent's answer to this question could be related to his/her way of answering other questions regarding teaching media convergence or requirement for new hires.

Most respondents (66 per cent) from all three groups pointed to media companies as the beneficiary of media mergers. In comparison, only 37 per cent of the respondents said that media mergers also benefit the general public, and even fewer (27 per cent) said that media mergers benefit the news professionals.

By reading the percentage numbers horizontally, we can find that consistently fewer respondents believed that media mergers benefit the general public or news professionals; also consistently more respondents believed that media mergers benefit media companies. It is also noticeable that 47 per cent of editors believed that media mergers benefit the general public while the other 53 per cent didn't. Editors' opinions on this point were roughly equally split. This finding indicates that media merger is a grand experiment in the media industry. Its benefits to the general public, which can better legitimize media mergers, are to be explored in the years to come.

By reading the percentage numbers both vertically and horizontally, we also find that editors were the most positive about the benefits media mergers could bring to all three parties while professors were least sure of such benefits. It is logical to reason that management personnel, such as editors and news directors and the companies they represent, are the primary forces behind today's media merger movement.

The question is that, since most professors, editors, and even news professionals believed that media mergers do not benefit news professionals and hardly benefit the general public, why do most news professionals still want to be trained to be cross-media practitioners and why are so many Jschool professors enthusiastic about training such graduates?

Considering the editors' most positive attitude towards media convergence, we wonder if news professionals are under the pressure to do so, and J-school professors are under the pressure to follow the industrial trend. Our surmise is partially corroborated by some textual answers. A news anchor from a merged media company agreed that new hires should have received cross-media training in writing and visuals and should possess multiple sets of skills. She showed her understanding for media mergers:

The merging of media companies is almost a daily occurrence. The pool of entities providing news services is shrinking. I think there is a danger that the public will lose in this race for media giants to accumulate wealth. At the same time, with the amount of competition in the industry from cable networks, the Internet, DVD's etc., I see the financial need for companies to merge to survive.

A newspaper reporter also from a merged media company expressed a similar feeling: "I am not all for the media convergence... At the same time I find it quite beneficial to be savvy in all branches of the industry. It helps the journalist become more knowledgeable about her or his job". News professionals were not alone in having such feelings. Here are two excerpts from two professors who have expressed similar feelings:

It's a harsh reality that I checked the box saying that news companies are the ones that are sure to benefit from media convergence. It may not be great for the public or even for news professionals who are going to be asked to bring more and more skills to the table and to have more and more responsibility on the job. Even so, convergence in one way or another is gonna happen and we need to prepare our students. Finally, my answer on merging media companies... reflects my disdain for the corporatization and concentration of control in the media. I think we ought to train mass communicators for a converged world, but as professors we ought to fight like hell against media mergers.

Very few respondents (19 per cent) believed that media mergers benefit all three parties, the general public, news professionals, and media companies, but about one third of the respondents (35 per cent) believed that media companies are the only beneficiaries to such a practice. These 35 per cent respondents, who were almost equally proportionally found in editors, news professionals, and professors groups, could be regarded as the most critical towards media mergers.

We compared these 35 per cent respondents with the rest of the sample and found no significant difference in their answers concerning the necessity of teaching journalism students cross-media writing and visuals and teaching multiple sets of skills. Always, more respondents believed that professors should teach all those things. In short, the respondents' political view was not directly tied to their views of teaching students cross-media practices.

2

The Public Journalism

INTRODUCTION

A review of forty-seven public journalism studies conducted from 1995 through 2001 revealed that public journalism has primarily been studied in three areas: content, journalists, and effects of public journalism on the audience. Content and Public Journalism. Studies have found that public journalism content has distinct characteristics. For example, McGregor, Comrie, and Fontaine studied coverage of a New Zealand election campaign, comparing papers that endorsed public journalism and papers that did not, and found the public journalism papers covered the race more constructively.

By comparing the Seattle Times Front Porch Forum Project coverage with the coverage by the Times in earlier years as well as content in the Seattle Post-Intelligencer, Blazier and Lemert found that among eleven public journalism traits, providing mobilizing information was the most distinguishing factor between the public journalism project and earlier coverage by the paper and coverage by the competition.

Moscowitz also found mobilizing information in a study comparing coverage of homelessness in the Knight-Ridder-owned, civic journalism-oriented Charlotte Observer with the Gannett-owned, traditional journalism-oriented Indianapolis Star. The Charlotte Observer was also less likely to use official sources and more likely to include solutions to problems in its coverage seeking out citizen sources rather than relying solely on official sources has been identified as a characteristic of public journalism.

By comparing two papers, one civic, the other not, Kennamer and South found the civic-affiliated paper had a much greater number of unaffiliated sources than the other. Kurpius also studied sources and found that local television news stories, employing public journalism techniques, used a larger percentage of African American sources than represented in the general population. Furthermore African American, Latino, and female journalists were more likely to use minority and female sources in their stories. Rather than focus on the text of a story, Coleman compared the visual elements in public journalism and traditional journalism content. Although for the most part, visual elements did not distinguish public journalism and traditional journalism, Coleman did find that public journalism stories were significantly more likely than traditional journalism stories to include visual elements that facilitated contact of the media by the public.

Because interactivity lends itself to citizen involvement and public journalism principles, Choi compared public journalism and traditional journalism newspapers in an online environment, expecting that online public journalism newspapers would exhibit more public journalism characteristics.

Content analyses of online stories from the Rochester Democrat, Charlotte Observer, Orlando Sentinel, online versions of public journalism-oriented newspapers, and the Buffalo News, Winston-Salem Journal, Florida Times Union, online versions of traditional journalism-oriented newspapers, found little difference in the content of online newspapers that represented public journalism and traditional journalism newspapers.

PRACTICE PUBLIC JOURNALISM

JOURNALISTS AND PUBLIC JOURNALISM

Because a decision to practice public journalism usually rests with a senior editor or producer, Kurpius examined the relationship between management and content. In two separate examinations of local television news, Kurpius found that visionary managers were the key for the civic-model of successful issues coverage at local television stations, but he also discovered that market forces may hinder civic reporting efforts in local media in the long run.

Factors that may influence journalists' attitudes towards public journalism were studied by scholars in New Mexico. After journalists at the Albuquerque Journal and Albuquerque Tribune and journalism students at the University of New Mexico completed self-administered questionnaires as part of a convenience sample, the results showed "a progression of socialization that begins with students supporting civic journalism."

Journalism students without newsroom experience appeared to be more supportive of civic journalism than practicing journalists and journalism students with newsroom experience. The authors suggested that civic journalism appeared to be inconsistent with autonomy, an attribute greatly valued by practicing journalists and journalism students with newsroom experience.

Indiana University scholars asked journalists directly about civic journalism in their most recent national survey. Although their previous national surveys of journalists, which were conducted in 1982 and 1992, had documented the backgrounds, attitudes, and values of journalists, the latest national study represented the first time that specific questions about public or civic journalism practices were asked.

According to "The American Journalist in the 21st Century," 72 per cent of journalists approved of giving ordinary people a chance to express their views on public affairs and 58 per cent endorsed providing possible solutions to society's problems. Only 32 per cent approved of convening meetings to discuss public issues.

EFFECTS OF PUBLIC JOURNALISM ON THE AUDIENCE

The sixteen audience-centreed studies identified in the Massey and Haas review examined the effects of civic journalism on the public rather than the public's expectations of journalism." For example, one study reviewed by Massey and Haas found evidence that public journalism produced positive results.

In a study of broadcast and print media that included Wisconsin Public Television and Radio, WISC-TV, the Wisconsin State Journal, and the Wood Communications Group and their collaborative effort to provide a more civic-oriented approach towards election coverage, Denton and Thorson found respondents in Madison said the project made them more knowledgeable about the election, encouraged them to vote, and gave them useful tools to assess campaign information.

Although the literature found civic journalism practices improved public attitudes and increased knowledge of election issues, overall, the Massey and Haas review of public journalism studies found mixed audience effects. Public journalism was found to both increase and suppress voter turnout, to both increase participation in civic projects and have no impact on civic participation, and to produce both strong and weak agenda-setting effects.

After reviewing forty-seven empirical studies, Massey and Haas criticized the public journalism literature for its lack of methodological rigour and for narrowly focusing on "jewel box" civic journalism projects that were conducted at the Wichita Eagle, Charlotte Observer, and Wisconsin State Journal.

Only one of the authors' six recommendations for future research involved the public and that was to conduct laboratory experiments that "could prove more useful for more convincingly identifying whatever causal factors may be behind any public-journalism influence on news audiences."

Surprisingly, none of the recommendations that resulted from this comprehensive review of public journalism studies focused on the public as an independent, active, and integral component of the communication process with opinions and expectations about a new type of journalism that ventures to re-engage the audience in the civic arena.

RESEARCH QUESTIONS

Although civic journalism has been discussed, practiced, debated, and studied for over a decade and a half, the public's perspective on civic journalism has not been studied empirically. Understanding the public's view of local news and civic journalism is important for the practice and business of journalism as well as society as a whole.

Without an assessment of what the public expects of local news, it will be virtually impossible to identify journalism practices that may help reverse declining attention to news, restore dwindling public trust in news as a whole and journalists in particular, and bring back the vanishing participant in civic affairs.

Unlike much of the research on public journalism, which has focused on the effects of specific public journalism projects on voting rates and other measures of civic participation, this study explores the public's views about journalism as well as the public's expectations of local news and the underlying dimensions of those expectations.

Specifically, the following research questions will be answered:

- *RQ1:* What do survey respondents regard as the important attributes and roles of journalism and how does that compare with the norms of traditional and public journalism?
- *RQ2:* How do survey respondents compare with journalists on the importance of practices and norms associated with traditional and civic journalism?
- *RQ3:* What segments of survey respondents as defined by race or ethnicity, age, income, education, and gender are more likely to endorse civic journalism and traditional journalism norms?
- *RQ4:* What are the underlying dimensions of survey respondents' expectations of local news?

As part of a research project for a local newspaper and local NPR affiliated public radio station that was starting up a local news division to complement the national news broadcast from NPR, the authors worked with the radio station managers to design a research study that would ascertain public opinion about local news. A Pew Centre for Civic Journalism grant provided funding for the audience study. The radio station manager believed that understanding the public's expectations of local news was a prerequisite to building a radio news division that would report local news of importance and meet the public's needs.

The spring 2001 survey, conducted in a southwestern metropolitan area by a professional telephone survey unit, used random digit dialing to select the sample. Interviews were completed with 600 adults, representing a response rate of 62.2 per cent. Calculation of the response rate was based upon the number of completed interviews (n=600) relative to the number of completed interviews plus refusals (n=286), incomplete interviews (n=37), and persons contacted but not interviewed due to illness, language barriers, or other impairments (n=36).

Answers to the four research questions were based on survey respondents' ratings of roles of local news media and characteristics of news coverage. Respondents were asked: What do you think is the most important role of local news media? Rate each on whether you think it's "extremely important," "somewhat important," or "not very important."

The roles were (1) report the widest range of news; (2) concentrate on certain topics; (3) provide a forum for community views; (4) be a watchdog of powerful people and the government; (5) highlight interesting people and groups in the community; and (6) offer solutions to community problems.

Respondents were also asked the following: What is the most important characteristic of news coverage you want? Rate each on whether you think it's "extremely important," "somewhat important," or "not very important." The characteristics were (1) accuracy; (2) rapid reporting; (3) understand the local community; (4) unbiased reporting; (5) care about your community; (6) be inclusive of different points of view; and (7) provide explanation of issues and trends.

To determine how survey respondents compare with journalists, the survey respondents' opinions about practices and norms associated with traditional and civic journalism were matched with journalists' opinions from "The American Journalist in the 21st Century" national survey.

Specifically, the opinions of survey respondents and journalists were compared in four areas: offering solutions, providing a community forum, being a watchdog, and rapid reporting. Although both studies used random sampling and "extremely" on the measurement scale, there were several methodological differences.

The question wording in the national survey of journalists differed on the four opinions that were compared. For offering solutions, the national survey asked journalists how important it was "to point people towards possible solutions to society's problems."

For providing a community forum, the national survey asked journalists how important it was "to convene meetings of citizens and community leaders to discuss public issues." For being a watchdog, the national survey asked how important it was to "investigate claims and statements made by the government."

For rapid reporting, the national survey asked journalists how important it was to "get information to the public quickly." In addition to the difference in wording, the present study relied on a three-point scale to measure opinions about journalistic norms while the national survey of journalists relied on a four-point scale of "extremely," "quite," "somewhat," and "not really important." The difference in question wording and the number of points on the measurement may have affected the number of respondents that chose "extremely" as an option. The final methodological difference was that the present study was conducted in spring 2001 in one southwestern metropolitan area while the national survey of 1,149 journalists was conducted summer and fall of 2002. The survey questionnaire also included questions about socio-economic backgrounds and media use. Standard survey questions were asked to ascertain number of years lived in the area, marital status, level of education, income, age, and race or ethnicity. Respondents were also asked if they had children living at home and their gender was recorded.

To establish media use, respondents were asked if they read the primary daily newspaper 4-6 times a week, 1-3 times a week, less frequently, or never. Similarly, respondents were asked if they read the primary Sunday newspaper 3-4 times a month, 1-2 times a month, less frequently, or never. Respondents were also asked how often they heard news on the radio, which TV stations they watched for local news, and how often they obtained local news from the Internet.

Bivariate analyses with appropriate statistics were used to determine if opinions about public and traditional journalism practices and norms differed by race or ethnicity, age, income, education, or gender. A factor analysis was used to identify underlying dimensions of survey respondents' attitudes about the roles and characteristics of public and traditional journalism.

SOCIO-ECONOMIC BACKGROUND AND MEDIA USE

Survey participants had established roots in this southwestern metropolitan area. The median number of years lived in the area was twelve; 55 per cent were married and 42 per cent had children at home. Although education was high, different educational levels were represented: 21 per cent had a high school degree or less, 27 per cent had some college, 28 per cent were college graduates, and 24 per cent completed at least some graduate school. Different income groups were also represented: 34 per cent had a household income of less than $40,000; 31 per cent had incomes between $40,000 and $69,000, and 35 per cent had incomes of $70,000 or higher. Slightly more than one-third of the respondents were ages 18 to 39; 31 per cent were ages 40 to 69; 35 per cent were 70 years or older. Respondents were fairly diverse: 68 per cent were white, 19 per cent; were Latino, 7 per cent were African American, and 5 per cent were Asian American or other. The remaining 1 per cent did not specify race or ethnicity. When asked how many times a week they read the primary local newspaper, 30 per cent said never or less frequently than 1-3 times a week, 25 per cent said 1-3 times a week, and 44 per cent said 4-6 times a week.

Survey participants were more devoted to the Sunday newspaper with 64 per cent reporting they read it 3-4 times a month. In addition to the newspaper, survey participants relied on other local news sources: 80 per cent watched one of the five local TV news outlets, 59 per cent often heard news on the radio, and 18 per cent often turned to the Internet.

THE PUBLIC'S VIEWS ON JOURNALISTIC NORMS

The overwhelming majorities said that accuracy (94 per cent) and unbiased reporting (84 per cent) are extremely important, but two major tenets of traditional journalism did not receive strong endorsements.

The traditional journalistic norm of being a watchdog of powerful people and the government was supported by only 49 per cent of survey respondents and rapid reporting was endorsed by only 35 per cent.

THE PUBLIC'S VIEWS ON THE ROLE OF LOCAL NEWS

Slightly more than half (51 per cent) said offering solutions to community problems was extremely important, and 49 per cent said providing a forum for community views was extremely important.

To answer RQ2, these views were compared with journalists' views about civic journalism practices.

COMPARING THE PUBLIC AND JOURNALISTS

Although the survey of the public was conducted in a southwestern metropolitan area and the survey of journalists was conducted nationally, results from the two surveys were compared because both studies used random sampling techniques, included similar questions about characteristics of traditional and public journalism, and incorporated "extremely important" on the measurement scale.

A difference in proportions test on independent random samples was used to determine if survey respondents were significantly different from journalists in their endorsement of two civic journalism norms and two traditional journalistic norms. Even though the majority of survey respondents strongly endorsed the fundamental characteristics of journalism, accuracy and unbiased reporting, there was a statistically significant gap between survey respondents and journalists on two roles that are an integral part of traditional journalism: watchdog and rapid reporting.

Only 49 per cent of survey respondents said being a watchdog of powerful people and the government is extremely important, but 70 per cent of journalists said that traditional journalism role is extremely important. Survey respondents were also significantly less likely than journalists to say that rapid reporting was extremely important (35 per cent vs. 59 per cent).

The roles and characteristics of traditional and civic journalism displayed were analysed by five socio-economic characteristics (race or ethnicity, age, income, education, and gender) to better understand survey respondents' opinions about traditional and civic journalism roles and characteristics.

Although there was no statistically significant difference between survey respondents and journalists in their endorsement of the civic journalism role of providing solutions to problems, there were significant differences when this civic journalism role was analysed by sub-segments of survey respondents.

SOLUTIONS

African Americans and Hispanics were significantly more likely than whites and Asian Americans to say that the civic journalism role of offering solutions to community problems was extremely important.

Almost three quarters (72 per cent) of African Americans and 64 per cent of Hispanics said offering solutions was extremely important, but only 45 per cent of whites and 47 per cent of Asian Americans said this civic journalism role was extremely important.

Segments of survey respondents that made less money and had less education were more likely than wealthier and more educated segments to say offering solutions to community problems was extremely important. Almost three-fifths (59 per cent) of adults who had incomes of less than $50,000 compared to 44 per cent of adults with incomes of $50,000 or more said offering solutions was extremely important.

This inverse relationship was also apparent when offering solutions to community problems was analysed by education. Adults with a high school education or less (68 per cent) were more likely than adults with some college (54 per cent) and adults with a college degree or higher (42 per cent) to say offering solutions was extremely important. Females were also more likely than males to attach greater value to the public journalism role of offering solutions with 56 per cent of females compared to 44 per cent of males saying it was extremely important for local news to offer solutions to community problems.

WATCHDOG AND RAPID REPORTING

The traditional journalism characteristics of watchdog and rapid reporting were also analysed by the five socio-economic variables and three were significantly related.

The oldest age group (55+) was more likely than the youngest age groups to value the watchdog role of traditional journalism, with 62 per cent of adults 55 or older compared to 47 per cent of adults 35 to 54 and 45 per cent of adults 18 to 34 saying being a watchdog of powerful people and the government was extremely important. An inverse relationship emerged when the traditional journalistic characteristic of rapid reporting was analysed by education. Among adults with a high school degree or less, 47 per cent said rapid reporting was extremely important; 30 per cent of adults with a college degree or higher said rapid reporting was extremely important. Females attached greater value to rapid reporting than males. Among females, 40 per cent said rapid reporting was extremely important but only 30 per cent of males said this traditional journalistic practice was extremely important.

The Underlying Dimensions of the Public's Expectations of Local News

To better understand the underlying dimensions of survey respondents' expectations of local news reporting, researchers factor analysed the six roles of local news and seven characteristics of journalism. The good neighbour dimension that emerged included attributes of public journalism: caring about your community, highlighting interesting people and groups in the community, understanding the local community, and offering solutions to community problems.

The watchdog dimension was represented by four roles of local news including being a watchdog of powerful people and the government, concentrating on certain topics, providing a forum for community views, and providing explanations of issues and trends.

The unbiased and accurate reporting dimension was defined by those two traditional characteristics of news; the fast dimension was represented by the traditional news characteristic, rapid reporting. Providing a wide range of news and being inclusive of different points of view did not load high on any one dimension. In fact, the inclusive factor loading was similar for the good neighbour, watchdog, and unbiased and accurate dimensions.

DISCUSSION

Although more than fifty empirical studies have been conducted on public or civic journalism, none of the studies has tried to gauge public opinion about this new approach to journalism practice.

This study provided insight into a journalistic practice that developed over the past decade and a half in response to the vanishing newspaper reader and disappearing participant in civic affairs. Furthermore, this study provided insight into the public's views on traditional journalistic characteristics.

At a time when newspaper readership, participation in civic life, and the credibility of journalism are at all-time lows, this study helped answer broader questions about journalism: Is traditional journalism meeting the public's expectations? Is the civic journalism movement on the right track?

The results of this survey suggest that, in many cases, the public and the press, including traditional journalism and the civic journalism movement, are on separate tracks headed in different directions and unless something is done to better meet the public's expectations, civic participation, newspaper readership, and the credibility of the press may continue to decline.

While it is reassuring to know that the survey respondents overwhelmingly endorse accuracy and unbiased reporting, it is important to recognize that these same expectations can cause the public to turn away from the news.

When Jayson Blair fabricates the news at the New York Times or star foreign correspondent Jack Kelley is accused of inventing parts of stories reported by USA Today, the public's trust in the news media is shaken and the reasons for reading the news are threatened. It is also important to note that long-held norms of traditional journalism, being a watchdog and rapid reporting, are not strongly valued by a majority of the survey respondents. Only 49 per cent said being a watchdog of powerful people and the government was extremely important, and 35 per cent said rapid reporting was extremely important.

But when the survey respondents were analysed by age, the press as watchdog was popular in the oldest age group. Over three-fifths of adults 55 years or older said the news media's traditional role of being a watchdog was extremely important.

Offering solutions to community problems, a characteristic of civic journalism, was strongly endorsed by only half of the survey participants as a whole, but when different segments were analysed, this public journalism practice was found to be more popular than first thought. The popularity of offering solutions is most evident among those who have traditionally been disenfranchised from the power sources of government and business: African Americans, Hispanics, adults with less income and education, and women.

Perhaps these groups are looking to news media as a source for help. Do the public's expectations of local news fit the traditional journalism model, the civic journalism movement, or some other ideal? The factor analysis of thirteen roles and characteristics of journalism revealed four dimensions with being a good neighbour-not watchdog, unbiased and accurate, or fast-representing the dominant expectation.

Being a good neighbour included caring about your community, highlighting interesting people and groups in the community, understanding the local community, and offering solutions to community problems. The expectation that the press should be a good neighbour may be related to declining trust in the news media and declining attention to news.

If the public expects the press to be a good neighbour but the press fails in that role because it sees its professional responsibility as a watchdog, there is clearly a disconnect between the public's expectations and the press' expectations which civic journalism practices may not be able to fix.

Buzz Merritt and Maxwell McCombs argue for an expanded watchdog role of the press that is consonant with the good neighbour perspective: News media need to be creative watchdogs and agenda setters scanning the horizon for the gaps in current public life.

Part of this larger watchdog role is functioning as social radar, not just a chronicler of what government and other institutions are doing right now, whether good or bad. This means discovering the concerns of citizens and defining what the public needs to know in very expansive terms.

But for this expanded watchdog role to resonate with the public, the news media must educate the public and even persuade the public that in the role of watchdog, they are looking out for the public in the same way that a good neighbour would. According to Andrew Kohut, director of the Pew Research Centre for the People and the Press, a decade and a half ago, which was about the time of the first civic journalism projects?

The public thought the press was "too sensational, too pushy, too rude, too uncaring about people and the public." But most people saw journalists as moral, professional and caring about the interests of the country. Today, the public considers the news media even less professional, less accurate, less moral, less helpful to democracy, more sensational, more likely to cover up mistakes and more biased.

These are not exactly attributes of a good neighbour. Because this study represents only one metropolitan area in the Southwest, additional studies should be conducted in other parts of the country.

Because different communities have different characteristics and needs, it is possible that they have different expectations of their local news. It is also possible that even with different community characteristics and needs, the public's expectations of local news are similar, regardless of community size or geographic location.

Only by replicating this study in other communities can the public's expectations of local news be determined. According to a 3 May 2005 New York Times article, the 1.9 per cent drop in daily circulation and 2.5 per cent decline in Sunday circulation reported by the Audit Bureau of Circulations represented the "largest circulation losses for the industry in more than a decade, and indicate an acceleration of the decline."

The magnitude of the circulation decline for 814 daily newspapers suggests that it is imperative that future studies determine how the public's expectations of local news relate to readership of newspapers and use of other news media. Future studies should also determine how participation in civic life is related to the public's expectations of local news. Finally, it is important for future studies to focus on the public's expectations of news with special attention paid to the concept of the press as a good neighbour.

By gaining greater insight into the public's expectations of local news, it may be possible to initiate a dialogue between the public and the press. This dialogue may lead to a closing of the gap between the expectations of the public and the press that could, in the long run, reverse declining attention to news and waning participation in civic life.

Perhaps more than any other profession, journalism grapples with an apparent contradiction between autonomy and public service. Sociologists define professional autonomy as wide latitude of judgement in executing occupational duties.' Autonomy provides discretion in the application of techniques and separation from influences that threaten a professional's ability to apply expertise in service to the public.

Thus, practitioners adhere to norms of public service even as the lay public itself is excluded from formal decision making. This conception of autonomy becomes problematic when applied to the press, according to advocates of civic (or public) journalism. This reform movement is based on the premise that news media should go beyond the mere reporting of information to act as a catalyst and as a forum for the revitalization of democracy.

But according to civic journalism opponents, these goals threaten the institutional independence of the press and thereby jeopardize journalistic autonomy. Under the traditional view of journalism, autonomy allows the press to cover public affairs with some protection against partisan bias and other corrupting influences.

If civic journalism is to succeed in the long run as a reform movement, it must meet head on the tension between the profession's autonomous identity and its role in democracy.

Civic journalism has focused on the implementation and consequences of professional values, but it has been less concerned about understanding the origins of these values as a function of professional socialization. The purpose of this study is to model the process by which professional socialization predisposes college students to reject or embrace civic journalism.

We will first assess the extent of support for various dimensions of civic journalism within two groups: journalism students and professional journalists living in the same community. Our general expectation is that students will be relatively supportive of civic journalism while professionals will express reservations in light of their commitment to autonomy.

We will then consider college experiences that might help to explain when and why this gap emerges.' Our intent is not to argue for the merits of civic journalism, but to provide insight into why support for it might erode as a consequence of professional socialization. For those who do support civic journalism, this line of enquiry could suggest implications for curriculum reform geared towards enhancing-or preventing the erosion of-civic journalism support.

This approach will also allow us to make an empirical contribution to the ongoing debate as to whether civic and traditional journalism principles coexist in harmony, or whether the two perspectives necessarily conflict as values take shape during professional socialization.

Why Autonomy Is Important to Journalists. While autonomy for all professions is ostensibly a mechanism of public service, it also accommodates the psychological needs of the practitioners. Autonomy contributes to group identification-the perception of belonging to a particular human group. Cheney and Tompkins observed that identification helps to sustain "an individual's or a group's 'sameness' or 'substance' against a backdrop of change and 'out side' elements." Prior research shows autonomy strongly correlated with both professional identification of journalists and job satisfaction. Management trends in news media have increased the need for autonomy in recent decades. Comparison of the findings of Johnstone, Slawski, and Bowman in 1976 with those of Weaver and Wilhoit for 1986 and 1996 reveals that perceived autonomy declined.

As Johnstone, Slawski, and Bowman surmised, the bureaucratization of media organizations diminishes the sense of autonomy among rank-and-file reporters. In the first two surveys, 60 per cent of respondents reported they were almost entirely free to select the material on which they worked; this dropped to 51 per cent in the third study.

Potential threats to autonomy include increased corporate chain ownership, the crumbling of the metaphorical wall between business and editorial, competition from Internet sources of news and entertainment, and the blurring of editorial and business functions in news organizations. With an erosion of perceived autonomy, and without the organizational protection and academic credentials of other professions, journalists are likely to feel vulnerable in the face of structural changes.

This probably accounts for some of the defensiveness, if not outright hostility, many prominent journalists express towards civic journalism, a reform movement that is itself an explicit challenge to traditional notions of autonomy.

DEMOCRACY AND PUBLIC PARTICIPATION

Dewey's concept of public opinion is rooted in an intellectual tradition that can be traced back to Montesquieu. In this tradition of thought, public opinion is understood as a body of shared beliefs and attitudes that emerged within the public sphere. With the decline of absolutism in the Renaissance, there emerged an independent social sphere, dominated by neither church nor monarch, in which an educated class was able to meet, to exchange ideas, and to formulate improved, shared concepts to benefit society as a whole.

The venues for this discourse were neither churches nor the royal courts, but salons, coffee houses, and the pages of the early newspapers, which offered both a forum for ideas and a stimulus for face-to face discussion. The public itself can thus be seen as in some sense a product of the media. It was the early newspapers that provided a common body of knowledge and ideas among urban residents who were not connected by face-to-face relationships.

The participants in this discourse saw themselves as citizens, not merely giving expression to private interests, but rather participating as representatives of the larger society. Public opinion, as understood in this tradition, was the social consensus that emerged as the result of dialogue. Juergen Habermas traces the decline of the public sphere to the middle of the last century, prompted by, among other factors, the transformation of newspapers from political journals into commercial enterprises, and the development of a broader, more heterogeneous audience.

A great deal has been written about the decline of the public and the decline of community. Both issues are complex, but they are distinct. What is meant by community seems generally to be small groups "bound together by history, faith, and fellowship." The notion of a public, by contrast, is that of private individuals, who do not necessarily share a common history, faith, or fellowship, but who come together to participate in critical rational discourse about common concerns on the basis of common knowledge—a common knowledge provided by shared sources of information.

The concern with revitalizing the public sphere goes back at least to the 1920s, when John Dewey worried, in *The Public and Its Problems*, about the eclipse of the public. Recently, there has been a major upsurge of interest in revitalizing the public sphere, evidenced by such works as *The Good Society* by Robert Bellah, Richard Madsen, William Sullivan, Ann Swidler, and Steven Tipton; Benjamin Barber's *Strong Democracy*; and such civic enterprises as Harry Boyte's *Project Public Life* and Frances Moore Lappe's *Centre for Living Democracy*, as well as the writings of Jay Rosen, James Carey, Noam Chomsky, and Douglas Kellner.

Any defender of participatory democracy must address the objection that, as Benjamin Barber phrases it, "popular government carries within it the seeds of a totalitarian despotism." John Dewey's answer is, in part, that if the people cannot be trusted to take an active role in governing themselves, then it is not plausible to imagine that they can play a meaningful role as watchdogs over their leaders either. The real alternative, in this view, is not elite democracy, but oligarchy.

And, argues Dewey, "the world has suffered more from leaders and authorities than from the masses." Dewey was prepared to acknowledge that the average citizen, considered as an individual, does lack the knowledge necessary to play an effective role in governing. But for Dewey, it was not the individual in isolation who was to play an active role in self-governance; it was the individual as the member of a community and as a participant in the processes of debate and discussion who had the ability to draw on the knowledge of others and participate in the formation of a public will.

Nonetheless, our collective memory is haunted by images of masses out of control: lynchings and pogroms and the mass terrorism of a Kristallnacht. But are these really examples of publics that have become overly active, as social conservatives and political realists would argue, or masses of individuals who have become overly passive, as advocates of participatory democracy maintain? Barber argues that "thin democracy has itself nourished some of the pathologies that it has attributed to direct democracy and... strong democracy may offer remedies for the very diseases it has been thought to occasion."

The frenzied masses feared by democratic realists are most frequently seen in totalitarian or oligarchic societies, and their participants typically have little access to effective mechanisms of democratic participation. By contrast, the very culture of democratic participation fosters a climate of rationality, deliberation, and respect for persons. In participatory democracies, by definition, power and decision-making authority is decentralized and diffused throughout the society. The capacity for collective willformation at the smallest levels of organization is enhanced, but the capacity for the formation of a mass will is diminished.

In the past few years, the theoretical debate between democratic realists and advocates of strong or participatory democracy has been overtaken by events. There has been a devolution of power from the federal to the state and local levels, and a scaling back of our national commitment to provide, through the mechanisms of government, basic social guarantees in the areas of education, housing, welfare, and other social services.

The responsibility for addressing these needs is being shifted to communities and individuals. With a change in the political reality of who must govern and solve problems comes a change in the institutional definitions of who and what is newsworthy.

The Lippmann model of the citizen as interested spectator must be abandoned as citizens become the key players in the social drama.

Some social critics, such as British sociologist John Thompson, question the viability of participatory democracy in a mass media age. The arguments raised by Thompson against the ideal of public participation have less to do with a distrust of the public than with considerations related to technology and scale. Thompson argues that "the idea of the public sphere is largely inapplicable to the circumstances of the late twentieth century," and he offers two arguments for this claim:

- The development of technical media has dramatically altered the nature of mass communications and the conditions under which it takes place, so much so that the original idea of the public sphere could not simply be reactivated on a new footing. The media of print have increasingly given way to electronically mediated forms of mass communication, and especially television, and these new media have transformed the very conditions of interaction, communication and information diffusion in modern societies.
- The second reason why the idea of the public sphere is of limited relevance today is that the idea is linked fundamentally to a notion of participatory opinion formation. The idea of the public sphere assumes that the personal opinions of individuals will become *public opinion* through, and only through participation in a free and equal debate which is open in principle to all. But this assumption, whatever relevance it may have had to eighteenth-century political life (and this may have been considerably less than Habermas suggests) is far

> removed from the political realities and possibilities of the twentieth century.... We live in a world today in which the sheer scale and complexity of decision-making processes limits the extent to which they can be organized in a participatory way. Hence the original idea of the public sphere, in so far as it is linked to the idea of participatory opinion formation, is of limited relevance today.

Neither of these objections seems fatal. If we understand the public sphere as an ideal, realized only in a very partial way even in the Enlightenment, then the prospect of even a partial realization of this ideal in our own era may seem like a partial victory worth striving for, rather than a dream impossible to achieve.

The emergence of new media makes participation more, rather than less possible. It is not face-to-face participation that matters, but rather participation in dialogue, and new technologies have broadened the possibilities for public participation.

However imperfectly realized, such new forms of media as talk radio and electronic bulletin boards offer new forums for public dialogue.

Their potential to serve the common good can only increase if civility is acknowledged as a core value for public communicators. Public access channels on cable television are as yet little used, but they too represent a space in which public dialogue can take place. Although it is true that some decision-making takes place on a scale that makes public participation difficult or impossible, that would seem to constitute an argument for, rather than against, political decentralization.

Even though some decisionmaking must take place on a regional, national, or even international scale, there is also a great deal of decision-making that takes place on a local scale and can be opened up to much greater participation.

OUTCOMES OF PUBLIC JOURNALISM

Initially, six outcomes of public journalism projects were identified: improved citizenship skills, enhanced public deliberative processes, increased private funding and donations, expanded volunteer efforts, and greater public policy and civic organization responsiveness.

These items were dummy coded with "present" coded as 1, "absent" as O. The six items were then examined through exploratory factor analysis and three factors emerged.

First, improved civic competence is an additive index consisting of two measures of public journalism outcomes: improved citizenship skills and improved public deliberative processes second, improved political process was constructed by adding two items: changes in public policy and the formation of new civic organizations. Finally, heightened volunteerism is a two-item additive index consisting of measures of raised private funds and donations, and increased level of volunteer efforts.

FEATURES OF THE NEWS ORGANIZATION

For news organizations' publication schedule, daily publication was coded as 1 and all other scheduling formats as zero. Level of circulation was measured using a six-point scale with 1 representing circulations under 50,000 and 6 representing circulations over 5 million.

Type of population served was measured on a four-point scale with 1 for smaller populations and 4 a national audience. Level of involvement in public journalism represents the length of time in years the news organization experimented with these practices. Partnerships was coded for evidence of other media or civic organizations involved in the project with "none" coded as 0 "either media or civic" as 1, and "both civic and media" as 2.35

FEATURES OF THE PROJECT

Eleven specific categories were identified to code each project according to the primary topic covered, including community, crime, diversity, economy, education, environment, health, poverty, youth, election, and government.

These items were dummy coded with "present" coded as 1, "absent" as 0 Project branding was constructed with three items, each used to develop a unique project identification, including evidence of a formal presentation format, clearly stated aim of the projects, and guide for reader comprehensiveness. Each item was dummy-coded with 1 being "present," O being "absent."

Mobilizing information consisted of two items: empowerment information (to help citizens engage in civic activities) and civic linkages (contact information for public officials and civic leaders). Each item was dummy-coded with "present" coded as 1, "absent" as 0.

STORY FRAMES

Each project was coded according to six frames used in journalistic reporting: investigative frame, conflict frame, issue-oriented frame, problem-solving frame, human-interest frame, and historical frame. These items were dummy-coded with 1 representing a frame being "present," 0 for "absent."

CITIZEN INVOLVEMENT

To measure a project's effort to include citizens' input, each case was coded for evidence of (a) inviting citizens to provide feedback, and (b) giving them a voice in the publication of their community's conversation. These two variables were dummy-coded with 1 for "present," 0 for "absent."

Each project was also coded for evidence of the news organization's effort to assess the climate of opinion on the project and/or issue including (a) survey and (b) focus group research. Surveys could be the organization's own scientific or informal surveys, or surveys provided by other sources. Each was dummy-coded with 1 for "present," 0 for "absent."

OUTLINES OF AN ETHICAL THEORY

An ethical theory grounded in the philosophical tradition of pragmatism offers the news media a much more promising means of fulfilling the social role envisioned for them by democratic theory, that is, enabling citizens to play an active role in self-governance. Ultimately, these principles and practices may also provide a way for journalists to find in daily practice a fulfillment of the ideals of public service that attracted many of them to journalism.

It may be helpful to summarize the key elements of the realist/objectivist view embodied in traditional journalism ethics and then contrast them with the pragmatist view.

ONTOLOGY

In the traditional realist view, the world exists independently of our knowledge of it, and there are facts about the world that are true, independent of any human knowledge of them. In the pragmatist view, reality is socially constructed, emerging out of the human activity of creating words and concepts as tools to meet human needs.

The concepts and categories through which we try to understand and manipulate our environment emerge historically as the products of human interaction with each other and with our environment. As we transform our social reality through our productive activity, we continuously transform our language and the concepts and categories through which we see the world.

EPISTEMOLOGY

In the realist view, truth consists in a correspondence between a statement and an external reality. By the use of scientific methods—or the scientifically based methods of journalistic objectivity—trained observers can come to have knowledge of the world that is objectively true. Expressions of fact must be clearly distinguished from expressions of opinion, which convey beliefs about facts for which we lack sufficient evidence, and from expressions of value, which state attitudes towards the facts.

The current role of the news media is to disseminate the vocabulary and the point of view of those segments of society that are recognized as authorized knowers. Insofar as the ethic of objectivity explicitly defined the news media as a medium for the transmission of an expert discourse, the structure of journalistic communication is designed to guarantee that the flow of vocabulary is overwhelmingly one-way. Journalists interview experts and then transmit their views to the public, but journalists generally do not disseminate "uninformed" public opinion.

In the pragmatist view, by contrast, a statement is true when its truth conditions are satisfied, but what these truth conditions may be is established through human activity. This conception of truth was expressed by William

James when he defined truth as "what it is good for us to believe." What it is good for us to believe is established experientially: the criteria for what it is good for us to believe about how to bake bread bear no direct logical relation to what it is good for us to believe about the existence of an afterlife.

The procedures known as "scientific method" or "journalistic objectivity" are just particular ways of interpreting the world; any special claim that they confer to epistemic authority must rest on their usefulness to particular human ends. Standards of truth and falsity are always internal to a domain of activity.

Some have suggested that this notion of truth invites relativism or even nihilism. Christopher Norris, for example, bitterly attacks the neo-pragmatism of Richard Rorty, Stanley Fish, and others as leading to a moral bankruptcy that easily rationalizes accommodation to power.

This consequence would indeed seem to follow from a notion that holds that multiple domains of activity (or communities of interpretation) entail multiple truths. But within the pragmatist conception, truth is always provisional, subject to revision in the light of new experience, changing values, or the encounter with other communities of interpretation.

If we wish to imagine a kind of truth that is not provisional, it could reside only in the kind of knowledge that would emerge at the end of all such experiments and encounters. Thus, C. S. Peirce describes truth as "the opinion which is fated to be ultimately agreed to by all who investigate."

This notion of ultimate truth seems problematic; why suppose that all who investigate will ever reach agreement? Even if one remains agnostic about whether such ultimate consensus is possible, Peirce's description points to several features of a pragmatist conception of truth that are more widely shared: understanding truth as a product of human activity, and specifically, as the product of a social, rather than individual process of enquiry.

This pragmatist notion of truth seems to be compatible with Habermas' notion that universal consensus under ideal conditions is the criterion of defensible truth claims. The ideal conditions that Habermas envisions are characterized by uncoerced and equal participation in public discourse.

What are the practical implications of the rejection of journalistic objectivity? The rejection of objectivity consists not merely in the assertion that the news media fail to provide an objective picture of reality, or even that objectivity is impossible in practice, but rather that it is impossible even in theory.

There is no neutral standpoint from which we can give an account of reality that is a-perspectival. Denying that there is such a thing as objective truth is not denying that there is such a thing as truth; nor is it saying that all truth claims are of equivalent value. Rather, it is to say that propositions are always true or false relative to some standard that is internal to a theory, language game, or system of beliefs.

One implication of this conceptualization is that journalists should continuously try to explore and to disclose the frame of reference and the conscious and hidden assumptions from within which they and their sources operate. This is a responsibility for journalists to a far greater degree than for practitioners of other disciplines or professions precisely because journalism is not a discipline in which standards of truth and fundamental premises are established by convention and are relatively stable.

Journalism operates in a public sphere in which multiple standards and interpretations come into conflict. Another implication is that the provisional and contestable character of truth claims should be emphasized; where there is significant disagreement, the media should be made accessible to and should disseminate the widest possible range of viewpoints.

SOCIAL ROLE

In the realist view, the primary social function of the news media is the collecting, organizing, and disseminating of information. In order to perform these functions effectively (as observer, gatekeeper, and messenger), the news media must maintain a stance of neutrality and avoid becoming instigators or participants in the events that they cover.

In the pragmatist view, the media of mass communications are one of the most important institutions through which we come to know ourselves as individuals and as members of society. Our common language and values are circulated by the mass media; within the mass media, the news media play a particular role in defining the set of common understandings and values that sustain the social order. The challenge is to perform that role fairly, in a way that addresses not merely individual interests, but also the common interest that defines us as a public.

ETHICS

In the realist view, the primary duty of the news media is to give a true picture of the world that can serve as the basis for political participation. Within this view, theorists disagree about the degree of public participation that is possible or desirable. Whereas social responsibility theorists, such as the authors of the Hutchins Commission report, envision active participation in self-governance, democratic realists like Lippmann favour a more limited role for the public—namely the ratification of expert decisions.

From this ontology, epistemology, and conception of the social roles of the news media is derived the set of values previously discussed: accuracy, fairness, objectivity, truth-telling, avoidance of conflict of interest, and so on. We have seen, though, that this derivation is powerfully influenced by the relations of power within the news media. In the pragmatist view—or at least in this version of pragmatism-there can be no such thing as the one true picture of the world. Rather, we are all continuously in the process of constructing and modifying our pictures in light of new experiences and changing objectives. As individuals, we have the capacity to make use of the experiences of others in modifying our pictures of reality and redefining our objectives. As members of communities, we operate most successfully when a broad range of perceptions and values enters into our deliberations.

From this pragmatist perspective, the proper role of the news media is to facilitate the operation of communities as contexts for democratic decision-making. This means that journalism must serve as a medium for the public exchange of ideas and for the exchange of competing views of reality and the public good; in addition, it should facilitate the formation of public consensus.

The arguments that follow rest upon a view of the ideal social order as one in which all citizens participate, to the limits of their abilities, in determining the course of their common life. Towards that end, the key values of the news media must include accessibility, respect for persons, fairness, interpretation, and skepticism.

EXAMINE THE RELATIONSHIPS BETWEEN PUBLIC JOURNALISM

In order to examine the relationships between public journalism efforts and their purported impact on civic competence, the political process, and volunteerism, we performed hierarchical multiple regression analyses in which organizational factors, project features, story frames, and efforts to involve community members and assess public opinion served as independent variables predicting the three criterion variables.

Tables are organized in a manner that highlights the order in which the different blocks of independent variables were entered into the regression and indicates the incremental variance in the criterion variable explained by each successive block. We consider how each additional block affects the standardized betas of the variables being considered simultaneously, and focus on the final standardized coefficients for the full model.

IMPROVED CIVIC COMPETENCE

The regression model predicting improved civic competence performed quite well, as it accounted for a total of 52.9 per cent of variance. The features of the news organization were substantial predictors (20.4 per cent of variance), with news organizations that served small or medium communities and that partnered either with civic organizations or other media the most successful.

Improved citizenship was also anchored in the actual features of the public journalism project (16.4 per cent of incremental variance). The focus on certain social problems such as poverty seems well suited for the purpose of improving citizenship. On the other hand a focus on negative or individualized concerns such as crime and health counter this objective. The news frames utilized in public journalism stories accounted for 10.3 per cent of the variance in the model. Among the frames, it seems clear that the problem-solving frame was most closely linked with reported improvement in citizenship. Conversely, the human-interest frame appeared to produce the opposite effects, reducing the perception of an increase in civic skills among the audience exposed to public journalism efforts.

Above and beyond characteristics of the news organization, features of the project, and selection of story frames, enhanced citizenship seemed to be contingent on involving citizens in the process of public journalism. In our model this block accounted for 4.6 per cent of the final variance, with inviting audience/reader feedback and giving citizens an actual voice serving as key contributors.

In addition, administering surveys in the community was also positively related to improving citizenship in the community. In the final model, public journalism's reported ability to improve citizenship was linked

- To news organizations that serve smaller communities and partner with other community organizations,
- To projects that focus on topics such as poverty as opposed to crime or health,
- To reporting that adopted problem-solving story frames over human interest story frames, and
- To project elements that involved citizens through feedback, sourcing, and surveys.

These findings support many of the conclusions drawn from case study analysis, while clarifying how these different factors intersect to shape citizenship.

IMPROVED POLITICAL PROCESS

The regression model used to gauge political process improvements— accounted for 22.6 per cent of the variance. In this model, the features of the news organization were not as critical as in the previous model, accounting for only 4.2 per cent of the total variance explained. In the final model, only a single organizational factor-partnerships with other community or media organizations-was a significant predictor of improvements in the political process.

The features of the project were substantial predictors of an improved political process, with 10.8 per cent of the variance explained by this block. Among this group, community and education topics are positively related with the dependent variable, while concentrating on the poverty topic is negatively related.

This suggests limited responsiveness in terms of process responsiveness when projects address the needs of the underprivileged. The framing of news also explained variation in improving the political process, with the investigative frame as the strongest predictor, followed by a problem-solving frame. Conflict, explanatory, and human-interest frames appear to be irrelevant for this purpose, while the use of a historical frame is negatively related.

This seems to indicate that attention to long-standing community issues is less effective at spurring political responsiveness than focused attention on current problems or scandals. Engaging citizens with the project or seeking their opinion does not seem to be particularly consequential for improvements to the political process.

These two blocks only account for.5 per cent of the incremental variance and yield no significant predictors. In the final model, then, partnerships, reporting on community and education (as opposed to poverty), and investigative and problem-solving (but not historical) story frames appear to spur responsiveness in terms of improvements to the political process.

IMPROVED VOLUNTEERISM

The model predicting levels of volunteerism in the community explained 22.7 per cent of the variance. As was the case for improving the political process, organizational features do not play as large a role as they do in improving citizenship, explaining only 3.1 per cent of the variance in reports of improved volunteerism, whereas project features explained a sizable amount (13.5 per cent) of incremental variance.

Again, establishing a partnership with another news or civic organization is positively related to increased volunteerism, making this a consistent predictor across all three models. Project topics such as community, crime, and education are linked with reports of increased volunteerism.

In terms of news framing, concentrating on human-interest seems to increase civic volunteerism, whereas historical frames have the opposite effect, consistent with the negative association in the model explaining political process improvement. This block explains 5.0 per cent of the incremental variance.

Finally it seems that citizens' engagement with the project and seeking citizens' opinions are not necessary to improve volunteerism. The model shows a small incremental contribution of these two blocks (incremental variance explained 1.1 per cent) with only the use of surveys actually being negatively related to volunteerism.

In sum, partnerships; reporting on community, crime, and education; and human-interest (but not historical) story frames appear to spur reported increases in volunteerism. This study is the first to explore a broad range of public journalism projects, incorporating a near census of the field of efforts between 1994 and 2002 and tracing the reported effects on civil society.

Further, it incorporates multiple levels of specificity, examining the effects of organizational features, particular projects, story frames, and citizen involvement in civic and public life. Our findings, thus, provide the first holistic assessment of the impact of public journalism on U.S. civil society and critical insights for future research and practice. Before we discuss these implications, we first offer an interpretation of these findings and discuss some of their limitations.

Although we find organizational features such as publication schedule, circulation level, and population type are associated with certain civil society goals of public journalism, most of these effects appear to be mediated through the structure of public journalism projects and journalistic framing.

One organizational feature is consistently found to shape the general success of these efforts: partnerships with other organizations. In our final models, partnerships predicted improved citizenship, political processes, and volunteerism, indicating me centrality of organizations' connections for efforts to renew civil society.

This seems most true of efforts to improve citizenship, where institutional connections may provide the basis for civic recruitment and broader project scope. Additionally, a project's focus also appears to be linked to certain civil society outcomes.

A focus on education, community, crime, and poverty were found to relate to the achievement (or failure) of civil society goals. The potency of a particular issue varied across these goals. For example, focusing on community and education was related to positive effects on the political process and civic volunteerism, with projects focusing on crime also linked to volunteerism.

The positive association of the these topics on political process and volunteerism outcomes suggests that projects directed at issues affecting larger cross-sections of the population are particularly effective at improving processes and spurring action.

Notably, a negative relationship was detected between a focus on crime and health topics-individualized issues typically directed at those with higher socio-economic status-and the improvement of civic skills, whereas a focus on poverty was found to have a positive effect on the development of civic competencies, as might be expected.

However, a focus on poverty was negatively related to improvements in the political process, suggesting a lack of elite responsiveness to issues affecting the underprivileged. Future research must work to disentangle these effects and identify the types of issues that produce desirable community outcomes.

Particularly notable are the results regarding the emphasis on certain story frames. Our findings suggest that problem-solving frames have the most pronounced effects on efforts to improve citizenship and the political process, and investigative news frames were also positively correlated with improvements in the political process.

In sharp contrast, however, human-interest and historical news frames appeared to generally reduce the success of public journalism efforts at achieving civil society goals, particularly in relation to citizenship. Our results for human-interest frames show a reduction in the development of civic skills, yet an increase in civic volunteerism, which is surprising given past research on episodic framing and the reduction of a sense of shared responsibility.

46 For historical news frames, we observed negative effects on both political process and volunteerism outcomes, suggesting that projects revolving around long-standing issues are less effective at spurring political or public responses. This pattern of results points to the importance of journalistic choices in framing news stories around certain themes and organizing devices.

Investigative and problem-solving frames would appear to spur involvement and action, whereas historical frames, and to a lesser extent human interest frames, appear to reduce responsiveness to community problems. While not invalidating frames that spur long-term reflection on deep-seated problems, these results do question how stories are organized and presented.

Further, it may be that the cross-sectional nature of these case assessments does not allow an observation of the effects of certain story frames over time. Finally, efforts to involve citizens in public journalism-*i.e.*, inviting feedback from citizens, giving them a voice in coverage and their communities, and surveying their attitudes and behaviours-were linked to the improvement of civic competencies.

In total, these results suggest that journalists who understand the perspectives of citizens are more able to construct projects that improve citizens' civic and deliberative skills. It may also be that asking citizens for their perspective and giving them public forums is fundamentally mobilizing, something we might call a type of "civic Hawthorne effect."

This study, while comprehensive, is not without limitations. Most notably, the cases that function as our units of analysis rely on some self assessment of effects by the editors and journalists involved in the projects. This may create some biases. However, these would seem to be equivalent across all news organizations in the study, thereby rendering differences observed meaningful.

Moreover, every effort was made to validate the outcome variables, which were often self-assessed against real world indicators of change. The reliability of these self-assessments was found to be well above the threshold for acceptability, further suggesting the validity of the data. The implications of this study, even with these limitations, are broad-reaching. They can be used to inform the next generation of public journalism efforts and structure research efforts. Future research should consider the longitudinal effects of public journalism projects on civil society. Using small-N comparative historical methods, researchers might more closely explore the precise configurations of organization, project, and story frame that lead to the most effect on civic and public outcomes. Finally, there are broad theoretical implications of our study. If historical frames are demobilizing, for example, what alternative frames could address long-term, deep-seated community problems addressed by journalists interested in democracy? If problem-solving and investigative frames are mobilizing, what are the specific features of these types of projects that encourage changes in civil society? If certain topics seem to lend themselves to successful public journalism outcomes, how might coverage of other issues be constructed to spur responsiveness on the part of the public and policymakers? Clearly, there is much that remains to be learned about the effects of public journalism projects on civil society. Nonetheless, if the findings presented here are any indication, the effects of the projects are considerable and broad reaching, and certainly provide empirical support for the normative project of public journalism.

CIVIC JOURNALISM AS A MULTI-DIMENSIONAL CONCEPT

In efforts to document the amount of support among reporters and editors, researchers have sought to isolate specific values associated with civic journalism. Bare developed a "personal public journalism" scale that formed a continuum from general goals to specific practices.

Support decreased along the scale in the movement from abstract goals to practices that violate professional detachment. One purpose of this study is to identify where students and professionals might depart in their evaluations of specific goals and practices. We will consider first the possible reactions to a questionnaire item that explicitly mentions "civic journalism" as a reform movement.

"CIVIC JOURNALISM" AS A POLITICIZED TERM

Several proponents of civic journalism have lamented that the term itself has become politicized in that it evokes disdain in professional circles instead of contemplation. Consequently, we expect that the professional respondents, and perhaps some students, will react negatively to a question that merely mentions "civic journalism."

Analysis of responses to this item could help us to evaluate responses to the other questionnaire items: if respondents express support for specific goals and practices, yet object to "civic journalism" itself, this would suggest that they are responding to something not captured by the other attitudinal items.

Given the lack of prior research on differences between professionals and students in support for civic journalism, we propose a research question rather than a formal hypothesis: RQ1: In comparison with professionals, will students express stronger support for "civic journalism" as a general description of the reform movement?

CIVIC JOURNALISM GOALS

The press traditionally understands its role as a disseminator of accurate information that allows individuals to participate as competent citizens. This requires neutrality in the coverage of political actors, institutions, and issues. By contrast, civic journalists argue that news media should not be neutral about the quality of civic participation in their communities.

We asked respondents to assess their support for two goals associated with civic journalism: going beyond the mere transmission of information to increase political participation, and focusing on news that helps a community to solve problems. While these goals are potentially problematic in light of the norm of detachment, they are described at a fairly abstract level, with the threat to autonomy more implicit than explicit.

Thus, we again propose a research question instead of a hypothesis: RQ2: In comparison with professionals, will students express stronger support for civic journalism goals? Civic journalism Practices. We do anticipate differences between professionals and students in the evaluation of practices that might jeopardize autonomy.

For example, we asked respondents to assess their support for news media sponsoring meetings to address local problems. According to professional critics, such events cripple the ability of journalists to remain critical of the favored policies. We also asked respondents to evaluate the use of polls to help journalists decide what should be covered.

Critics have dismissed this technique as another manifestation of how marketing has intruded into the newsroom. Handing news judgement over to the public directly violates the profession's traditional understanding of autonomy. H1: In comparison with professionals, students will express stronger support for practices associated with civic journalism.

ANTECEDENTS OF SUPPORT FOR CIVIC JOURNALISM

A review of prior literature suggests that college experiences and attitudes adopted during professional socialization will influence students' acceptance of civic journalism.

Potential predictors of civic journalism support include the amount of college instruction, anticipatory socialization as a psychological construct, working for a campus paper, and support for traditional roles of the press.

FORMAL INSTRUCTION

Participation in a college journalism curriculum should influence the likelihood of students adopting values similar to those of professionals. Weaver and Wilhoit reported that alumni of journalism programmes expressed a connection between their formal education and their current news values. Students are likely to adopt a commitment to professional autonomy-and consequently a reticence about civic journalism-to the extent that instruction emphasizes the conventional understanding of professional detachment and neutrality. Prior participation in a civic journalism project should also predict support, but we did not include this variable because of the minimal presence of civic journalism in the journalism programme where we recruited respondents. The programme had provided only one civic journalism class (in 1998), with an enrollment of eleven students.

ANTICIPATORY SOCIALIZATION

Individuals typically view themselves as members of a profession long before they join a specific organization. "Anticipatory professional socialization" represents the extent to which an individual has thought seriously about a particular career. An important dimension of this process is "identification," or the perception of belonging to a particular group.

This need for professional membership and acceptance might predispose students to reject civic journalism. A central argument of civic journalism is that news media should display their inner workings, thereby becoming more accountable to the public.

But if students begin to value an insider's perspective on newsroom culture, this group identification could evoke an aversion to the civic journalism critique.

WORKING FOR A COLLEGE NEWSPAPER

While these two factors should facilitate the adoption of traditional values, neither duplicates the degree of autonomy experienced by professionals. Working for an independent college newspaper, however, might represent an indelible socializing experience that produces a resistance to civic journalism.

Campus newspapers vary in their degree of independence from journalism departments and university administrations, but a tradition of American universities is that student newspapers should maintain substantial institutional independence.

The experience of working for a campus newspaper-including the sense of empowerment gained from reporting and editing with little or no instructor supervision— should instill an appreciation for autonomy that cannot be duplicated in the classroom.

Theorists of human development have observed that a young person's identification with an occupation or profession facilitates a realization of self identity, and thus many students might become attracted to journalism precisely because it allows them to express independence and personal identity through their writing and news judgement.

H2: Students with campus newspaper experience will be less supportive of civic journalism compared to other students.

SUPPORT FOR TRADITIONAL ROLES

Civic journalism opponents argue that its goals and practices are not compatible with the traditional mission of the press as an institution that relies on autonomy to provide accurate and balanced information. In the case of journalism training, the question is whether the formation of a professional identity will allow for not only multiple role conceptions among students, but for acceptance of roles that are potentially incompatible.

Prior surveys of professionals provide evidence that journalists do identify with more than one role. Weaver and Wilhoit identified three highly correlated but distinct attitudes about professional purpose: interpretation, dissemination, and adversary orientations."

The interpretive function resonates with a recommendation of the Commission on Freedom of the Press-that journalists should investigate the truth about facts while providing a context that gives them meaning. The disseminator function highlights the need for the press to transmit information that is useful to a large audience, while the adversary function reflects the importance of acting as a "watchdog" of government.

In a survey of newspaper staff members, Arant and Meyer concluded that the majority of journalists do not support practices that violate professional autonomy, but those who did also supported traditional roles of news media. In the context of this study, we anticipate that students would support the traditional roles.

But with relatively little concern about journalistic autonomy, measures of traditional values might correlate strongly with civic journalism support among the students, given that the overarching commitment to public service is reflected in all of these role conceptions. We propose the following research question: RQ3: Will support for the dissemination, interpretive, and adversary roles predict students' support for civic journalism? The student respondents attended the University of New Mexico (Albuquerque), and the professional journalists were recruited from two daily newspapers published in the same city. While the restriction of respondents to one community in the Southwest limits the external validity of findings, the design eliminates regional factors as alternative explanations for possible differences between students and professionals.

SAMPLING

We used a purposive sample of students in courses taught within the university's Communication and Journalism Department. The intent was to include a large percentage of students who identified to some degree with journalism as a profession.

During April of 1999, we administered questionnaires to classes that contained students in four undergraduate major tracks: print journalism, broadcast journalism, public relations, and advertising. We would expect that some students would be sharply focused on journalism, with some fully involved in internships and writing for the campus paper. Other students, however, would have little or no interest in journalism as a career, but they would have at least some knowledge of news media as an academic topic. This diversity of student background creates the possibility for variance within the variables used to predict civic journalism support.

The sampling frame for the professional journalists was defined as all reporters and editors on the staffs of the Albuquerque Journal and the Albuquerque Tribune. The family-owned Journal represents the largest newspaper in New Mexico with a circulation of approximately 121,000. The Tribune is delivered in the afternoon to about 16,000 subscribers, the vast majority of whom live in Albuquerque. It is owned by Scripps Howard.

We were given permission to distribute questionnaires during the same time period in which we sought responses from the students. The staff list for the Journal included 144 reporters and editors while the list for the Tribune totaled.

INTERVIEWING

Questionnaire items for students and professional journalists were identical in every respect practical. We used paper-and pencil, self-administered questionnaires for both groups. The availability of students in classroom settings allowed us to directly distribute and administer their questionnaires (N=317 respondents), but this degree of supervision was not practical for the professionals' questionnaires.

In both newsrooms, we requested that an administrative assistant place a questionnaire, cover letter, and return envelope in the mail slots of all reporters and editors. Two weeks after the questionnaires were distributed, we distributed a reminder letter to coax potential respondents who had failed to complete a questionnaire.

This procedure produced a response rate of 59 per cent for the Journal and 57 per cent for the Tribune. These can be considered relatively high response rates given that the interviews were voluntary and unsupervised. The final sample consists of N=117 professional journalists.

DESCRIPTION OF SAMPLES

Descriptive statistics reveal a range of interest within the student sample regarding journalism as a career goal. When asked if they plan to pursue a career in journalism, 55 per cent disagreed or strongly disagreed, 16 per cent indicated they were not sure, and 29 per cent agreed or strongly agreed.

For the sample of professional journalists, we sought to gather data reflecting variance in newsroom status among reporters and editors. When asked how many years they had worked in journalism, 42 per cent indicated 1 to 10 years, 26 per cent indicated 11-20 years, and 32 per cent reported more than 20 years.

CIVIC JOURNALISM MEASURES

One question asked explicitly about civic journalism: "Several newspapers in recent years have initiated projects known as 'civic journalism.'

Indicate the extent to which you agree with the goals of civic journalism." Respondents were asked to answer using a 1-5 scale for each question, with 1 meaning "strongly disagree" and 5 indicating "strongly agree." No answer (NA) was coded as 3.

Two items described goals: "Local media should focus on news that directly helps a community solve its problems." "Local media should go beyond simply reporting news in efforts to increase public participation."

Two items described practices: "Local media should sponsor community meetings to help citizens solve problems." "Reader or viewer interest polls should be used to help journalists decide what should be covered."

Predictors of Support for Civic Journalism. Variables used to predict students' support for civic journalism include journalism experiences in college and support for traditional media roles.

College Journalism Instruction. A summed two-item scale (r=.40) assessed the extent of formal instruction:

- "Are you a major in the UNM Department of Communication and Journalism?"
- "How many news writing courses have you taken at the college level? Include any courses taken this semester." Career Anticipation. A summed 6-item scale (alpha=.85) measured the extent to which students had anticipated a career in journalism. Responses to the first two questions were coded as yes=2; no, NA=1.
- "Do you plan to write news for the Daily Lobo?"
- "Do you plan to undertake a news writing or editing internship?"
- For the remaining questions, respondents used a 1-5 scale with 1 meaning "strongly disagree" and 5 "strongly agree."
- "I plan to pursue a career in journalism."
- "I hope to work in a newsroom."
- "My interest in a news-related career is growing stronger.
- "I have always wanted to be a journalist."
- College Newsroom Experience. A summed two-item scale (r=.38) assessed the extent of involvement with the university newspaper.
- "Have you been a news writer for the Daily Lobo?"
- "Have you worked as an editor for the Daily Lobo?"
- Dissemination Role. A single item measured support for the role of news media in disseminating information. Respondents used a 1-5 scale, with 1 meaning "not important" and 5 indicating "extremely important."
- "How important is it for the media to concentrate on news that is of

interest to the widest possible public?" Interpretive Role. A single item scale measured support for the interpretive role of news media in covering public affairs.

- "How important is it for the media to provide analysis and interpretation of complex problems?"
- *Adversary Role:* A summed two-item scale (r=.18) measured support for the role of the media in acting as an adversary of government.
- "How important is it for the media to be an adversary of public officials by being constantly skeptical of their decisions?"
- "How important is it for the media to investigate claims and statements made by government?"

The five civic journalism measures were first entered together in a one-way repeated-measures multivariate analysis of variance (MANOVA), with journalism experience (student without newsroom experience, student with newsroom experience, professional) as the independent variable. Using all four algorithms, the analysis showed a significant effect for the dependent variables considered together.

When the civic journalism measures were subjected to separate one-way ANOVAs, significant effects were obtained for the following items: local media should go beyond reporting news to increase participation, local media should sponsor meetings, and polls should be used to help journalists decide on news coverage.

With respect to the premise that news media should attempt to increase participation, there was not a significant difference between students with newsroom experience and professionals-both expressed significantly less support for this goal compared to the students without newsroom experience. The same pattern occurred with the practice of local media sponsoring meetings.

These results suggest that students with newsroom experience were becoming more like professionals and less like their fellow students in their evaluations of civic journalism. Finally, the professionals expressed significantly less support, in comparison to both groups of students, for the use of polls to help journalists decide on coverage. Collectively, the three cases show a clear pattern of decreasing support for civic journalism as the respondents gain experience via newsroom participation.

The first research question asks whether college students, in comparison to professionals, express stronger support for the attitudinal item that explicitly mentions "civic journalism" as a reform movement.

No significant difference was found. RQ2 addresses whether college students express stronger support for civic journalism goals. The means for students and professionals are nearly identical with respect to the premise that local media should focus on news that helps a community to solve problems. But in the comparison between students without newsroom experience and professionals, a statistically significant difference exists for the item that concerns media going beyond reporting to increase public participation. While the first goal describes an agenda-setting function that facilitates a community response to a problem, it apparently does not evoke suspicion among the professionals to the extent of the second goal.

To "go beyond" the reporting of news might have suggested a kind of advocacy journalism to the professional respondents. Hi states that the students will express stronger support for practices associated with civic journalism. Both measures generated significant differences between the student and professional respondents, in support of Hl.

The second practice in particular (use of polls) would challenge autonomy if respondents interpreted it as diminishing the importance of professional expertise. In the interpretation of these results, it is useful to consider that civic journalism has existed for only about ten years, and consequently the older professional respondents would not have been exposed to it while in college.

Meanwhile, neither of the Albuquerque papers had conducted projects identified as civic journalism. As for the students' exposure, their journalism programme had not adopted civic journalism as a regular component of the curriculum.

Thus, we urge caution in making inferences that would generalize these results. For example, Arant and Meyer found that the amount of civic journalism support was related to whether a newspaper had previously conducted a project.

H2 proposes that students with campus newspaper experience will be less supportive of civic journalism compared to other students. Lending support to H2, students with newsroom experience were less supportive of the goal in which media go beyond reporting to increase participation. This is also the case for the practice of news media sponsoring meetings.

We consider next the importance of campus newspaper experience in relation to other experiences that might explain the erosion of civic journalism support. We decided to examine this deterioration of support with respect to a civic journalism practice in light of our theoretical argument that specific techniques, rather than abstract goals, would more likely generate opposition as professional socialization proceeds.

The largest variance in student responses occurred with the item that advocates media sponsorship of meetings. This variable was used as the dependent variable in a multiple regression model in which the three indicators of educational experiences are entered as an initial block of independent variables. The second block includes the measures of support for traditional media roles.

In the first equation, only newspaper experience accounted for a significant amount of variance. The beta is negative, demonstrating that writing and editing for a campus newspaper diminish potential support for civic journalism.

The second equation addresses RQ3: Will support for traditional media roles predict support for civic journalism? The attitudinal measure for the interpretive role did account for significant incremental variance, but support for the dissemination and adversary roles did not.

All of the betas were positive, however. While these results do not provide overwhelming support in favour of RQ3, they certainly do not suggest a scenario in which the adoption of civic journalism values is accompanied by a rejection of the traditional roles for news media. This study represents the first empirical effort to model the origins of civic journalism values as a function of professional socialization during the college years.

The results confirmed that students tended to be more supportive of civic journalism in comparison to professionals who work in the same community. Gaps between the student and professional respondents emerged when questionnaire items described specific practices that violate the norm of detachment, such as news media promotion of town hall meetings. A subsequent analysis of factors that might explain these results suggests a scenario of professional socialization that begins with students predisposed to support civic journalism. Acquisition of these values during the college years, meanwhile, is not associated with an erosion of commitment to traditional roles.

However, in leaving the classroom for the newsroom, the unmaking of civic journalists might occur as reporters and editors develop a stronger sense of autonomy. One experience in particular— working for the campus paper-appears to instill a sense of autonomy that diminishes acceptance of civic journalism.

A BROADER VIEW OF AUTONOMY

College instruction would ideally promote an open-minded orientation to journalistic roles and an appreciation for both the limitations of routine reporting and the potential for innovation. But those who would reform the curriculum to promote civic journalism must acknowledge the inherent need for increased autonomy during the beginning stages of professional socialization.

The desire for autonomy is an inevitable outcome of the process by which students identify with the profession. Journalistic autonomy, consequently, should be appreciated not as a fixed disposition but as a developmental process.

From the perspective of civic journalism advocates, the results of this study highlight the need for college instruction to encourage a broader conception of journalistic autonomy. However, would-be reformers should acknowledge the importance of autonomy for students and for professionals rather than issuing a wholesale attack on editorial detachment.

The irony of professional autonomy is that it is the best hope for implementing reform even as editorial detachment appears to preclude civic journalism. Civic journalism can challenge students and professionals to reconceptualize autonomy as the independence to transcend conventional practices that would otherwise limit the contribution of the press to democratic life.

MEDIA ORGANIZATIONS AND NEWS VALUES

There are two broad types of newsroom studies: (1) of news organizations; and (2) of journalists' beliefs and attitudes. While there are no inherent methodological contradictions between them, each tends to have its own understandings of how public journalism is established in newsrooms.

Organizational studies see the adoption of public journalism from the top down, with publisher and editor orientations as the important predictors of public journalism practice. An investment by news organizations in public journalism shapes reporting routines and story content, and accounts for the adoption of the practice over longer periods of time.

This approach posits institutionalization as a property of the organization, with organizational decisions molding the actions and routines, if not beliefs, of individuals within them. Evidence suggests that newsrooms institutionalizing public journalism (*i.e.*, commitments to partnerships with other community organizations and lengthy projects) produce stronger public effects.

A second approach looks at the effect of values of journalists on attitudes and behaviour. Here, the adoption of public journalism values is a prerequisite for genuine individual transformation that leads to newsroom change. Proponents of this approach hold that positive attitudes towards public journalism should precede behavioural change."

This values approach, then, sees change in beliefs and attitudes as generating new public reporting behaviour that underlies the transformation of news organizations. From their review of public journalism studies, Massey and Haas found that journalists are most comfortable with the more "traditional" shadings of public journalism, though some support for more "activist" roles exists. These mixed results indicate traditional and public journalism beliefs seem to coexist in many newsrooms and within individual journalists, suggesting an "occupational pragmatism." Not surprisingly, "mixed-change" characterizes virtually every case of public journalism, positing a kind of "tipping point" within newsrooms and individuals.

If newsrooms have not tipped, public journalism practice should be weak. As this suggests, both the organizational approach and the news values approach ultimately focus on the degree to which newsrooms have adopted and integrated public journalism practices into the newsroom culture, regardless of whether the spur of this transformation is from the top down or the bottom up.

NEWS COVERAGE AND CONTENT

Research on changes in reporting spurred by public journalism is sparse, with little attention to whether certain topics or frames of reporting are particularly suited to public journalism. Although public journalism often implicitly focuses on community, efforts have addressed a plethora of issues confronting localities, including crime, diversity, education, environment, health, poverty, and, of course, elections and government.

Public journalists have utilized a range of issue frames to structure their reporting, from established conflict and human-interest frames to more novel problem-solving and historical frames. However, little is known about the potency of these framing devices for civil society outcomes or whether certain topics lend themselves to successful public journalism as defined by increases in civic competence and volunteerism.

Instead, most coverage studies focus on the type of content and sources used in public journalism stories, with inconsistent evidence. Some indicate little difference in content, while others have found that public journalism efforts have a greater focus on local concerns and help citizens engage in civic activities.

There is also inconsistent evidence on sourcing. Thus, it remains unclear whether certain public journalism tools, such as encouraging citizen involvement or giving citizen voices greater prominence, improves civil society outcomes.

EFFECTS OF PUBLIC JOURNALISM

The evidence for public journalism effects on civic and public life is partial and incomplete. Studies divide broadly into those investigating the effect of public journalism on electoral outcomes and those addressing civic and public problem solving.

First, there is evidence supporting a positive relationship between citizenfocused journalism and knowledge, trust, and civic participation in elections. There is, however, some evidence to the contrary. Thus, on the whole, studies support a moderate effect of civic electoral coverage in the areas of voter awareness of issues and traditional forms of political participation.

Although untangling political cause and effect is difficult, there is a case for public journalism efforts and broader public engagement. Studies have found an increase in political participation. There is also some evidence that public journalism increases public deliberation and civic problem solving. Moreover, Friedland's study of the "We the People" project in Madison, Wisconsin, found project longevity to have substantial cumulative impact on opinion leaders, media cooperation, and institutional effectiveness, with mixed effects on citizen engagement. If there is episodic coverage with little follow-up, however, a project's cumulative problem-solving effects were attenuated.

In sum, the case-based evidence shows effects of increased civic and public problem solving in limited areas. Past theorizing and case studies concerning the practices and effects of public journalism do not present a clear picture of the consequences of this shift in coverage for civil society. Scholars have focused on different levels of analysis-organization, newsroom, story, and citizens-and attended to a wide range of outcome variables.

Results have not been consistent, though this inconsistency may be a function of community and organizational factors that are not the focus of a particular case study. After a decade of broad practice, it is unclear which organizational factors beyond length of adoption and integration of public journalism contribute to the success of public journalism efforts.

Likewise, beyond attention to certain patterns of sourcing and shifts in content, it is not known whether the success of public journalism efforts is connected with attention to certain topics-such as poverty or crime-and particular frames of reference - such as human interest or problem-solving.

On a more basic level, evidence is lacking on whether particular ways of giving voice to the perspectives of citizens improve civil society in the ways that theorists of public journalism attest. Accordingly, we examine here the effects of a wide range of potentially explanatory variables on assessments of the outcomes of a wide cross-section of public journalism efforts between 1994 and 2002. This study attempts to answer how the influence of organizational factors, project features, story frames, and efforts to involve community members and assess public opinion uniquely contribute to three broad goals of public journalism: (1) improving civic skills among citizens; (2) influencing the policymaking process; and (3) increasing levels of civic volunteerism.

Accordingly, we offer the following research questions to guide our analysis:

- RQ1: What features of news organizations involved in public journalism projects appear to influence whether sponsored efforts increase civic skills of citizens, public input on policymaking, and levels of civic volunteerism?
- RQ2: What features of public journalism projects appear to influence whether sponsored efforts increase civic skills of citizens, public input on policymaking, and levels of civic volunteerism?
- RQ3: What types of story frames used by journalists involved in public journalism projects appear to influence whether sponsored efforts increase civic skills of citizens, public input on policymaking, and levels of civic volunteerism?
- RQ4: What types of efforts to involve community members and assess public opinion appear to influence whether sponsored efforts increase civic skills of citizens, public input on policymaking, and levels of civic volunteerism?

METHODS

Data

This study is based on data collected at the University of Wisconsin-

Madison from the archives of the Pew Centre for Civic Journalism. During its ten years of operation as the principle incubator for the movement, between 1993 and 2003, the Pew Centre collected examples of public journalism projects submitted by U.S. newsrooms seeking funding, competing for awards, and/or seeking informal recognition and advice.

Between January 2000 and May 2001, this archive was systematically examined for all evidence of public journalism experiments, with the archive structured into a set of cases organized by discrete projects and publication dates.

A qualitative coding scheme was developed to capture a descriptive account of project attributes, including, but not limited to: the news organization (circulation, population served, partnerships); the project (topic, publication dates, presentation format); the news frames, sources, and civic linkages used in news construction; and the civic practices, polls, and public deliberative events used to give citizens a voice.

In addition, outcomes such as improved civic and deliberative skills, increased public funding and volunteerism, and improved public policy processes were gauged from these reports.

A quantitative coding guide was developed so that statistical tools could be used to more systematically analyse these data. The final inventory of the archive contained a total of 651 cases of public journalism completed between 1994 and 2002. Although the study sample is limited to public journalism projects in the Pew Centre's archive and undercounts the full range of public journalism work conducted by U.S. newsrooms during this period, it captures public journalism as practiced by the most dedicated of self-identified public journalism practitioners. Thus, the sample, while biased in favour of best practices, provides a solid foundation upon which to assess a broad range of public journalism practices and evaluate the movement's reach and impact on community life.

Measures

Items coded from the public journalism projects were used to operationalize six general clusters of variables: (1) outcomes of the public journalism project, (2) features of the news organization, (3) features of the project, (4) features of the stories, particularly story frames, (5) citizen involvement, and (6) public assessment. In the analyses reported in this chapter, the outcomes of public journalism were used as dependent variables predicted by the other five sets of variables.

ACCEPTANCE OF PUBLIC JOURNALISM VALUES

Not surprisingly, considering the public statements by editors of several large papers in the Northeast, public journalism is stronger among small and medium papers and in other regions.

Readers served by small- and medium-circulation newspapers were more likely to be exposed to public journalism projects than those served by large newspapers. Four questions asked about the importance of values associated with public journalism practice. These items constitute a scale of Personal Public Journalism, representing staff members' attitudes towards personal involvement in solving community problems.

Bare found that journalists at the *Wichita Eagle*, which had been involved in public journalism efforts for several years, scored significantly higher on these factors than did journalists at *Raleigh News and Observer* and *Omaha World-Herald*.

For journalists in Raleigh and Omaha the dominant belief system was the traditional investigative and interpretive values. The items attempted to tap into journalists' views of their personal responsibilities not the duties of the newspapers in general. The question presented was as follows:

To you personally, how important are each of the following items in your daily work? (1 = not really important, 2 = somewhat important, 3 = quite important, 4 = extremely important):

- Helping people in my community.
- Helping the community solve problems.
- Improving community morale.
- Working with civic groups on community improvement projects.

These four items represent a continuum of the journalist's involvement in or attachment to the community. These variables represent a shift from "the traditional ideal of maintaining distance between themselves and the communities they serve".

Table: Personal Public Journalism Scale

	1 (Not Important) %	2 (Somewhat Important) %	3 (Quite Important) %	4 (Extremely Important) %	Mean Response
Help community	3	24	38	35	3.07
Solve problems	8	29	39	24	2.80
Improve morale	35	42	16	7	1.96
Work with groups	43	37	16	4	1.80
Four-item scale: α = .7534					

Table above shows the majority of respondents said the first two items were quite or extremely important (74 per cent for helping people in the community and 64 per cent for helping the community solve problems).

Twenty-three per cent believed that improving community morale was quite or extremely important, and fewer, 20 per cent, indicated that working with civic groups was quite or extremely important. Although a range of response showed less support as the items moved from describing general values (helping people) to specific actions (working with civic groups), the four items constitute a scale of personal public journalism. The reliability function in Statistical Package for the Social Sciences (SPSS) was used for evaluating and creating the scale. Spector suggested that a scale must produce an alpha of at least.70 for the scale's items to be considered internally consistent and representative of a belief system. The alpha for these items was.7534.

The typical national answers on the personal public journalism variables fell in the middle of the range found by Bare survey of three distinctive newspapers. The nationwide sample fell closer to the journalists at the two newspapers with more traditional journalism practice, the *Omaha World-Herald* and the *Raleigh News and Observer*.

On the two general public journalism values, helping people in my community and helping the community solve problems, the differences among average responses for the three newspapers and the national sample were small. However, on the non-traditional journalism values, the differences among papers were large, with the greatest importance being attached to improving community morale and working with community groups by journalists at the *Wichita Eagle*, a practitioner of public journalism for 4 years prior to the survey.

Some of the earliest public journalism initiatives began with top management; for example Knight-Ridder's 1989 symposium on editorial pages called by CEO James K. Batten. Newsroom supervisors were more supportive of public journalism values than were those in lower staff positions.

Twenty-four per cent of the supervisors said improving community morale was not important versus 43 per cent of the other staff.

Although 33 per cent of the supervisors said working with civic groups on community improvement projects was not important, 50 per cent of the reporters and other staff members said so.

Table. Comparison of Personal Public Journalism Mean Responses

	World Herald	News and Observer	Wichita Eagle	National Sample
Help community	2.75	3.00	3.00	3.07
Solve problems	2.49	2.84	2.74	2.80
Improve morale	2.12	2.18	2.69	1.96
Work with groups	1.70	1.79	2.35	1.80
Sum	9.07	9.81	10.77[a]	9.63

[a]Sum is significantly different at the.05 level.

Table. Difference Between Newsroom Supervisors and Staff Members Who Said ThesePublic Journalism Values Were Extremely or Quite Important

	Supervisors%	Staff Members%	X	df	p
Help community	81	69	11.38	1	.001
Solve problems	70	58	9.17	1	.01
Improve morale	28	19	6.24	1	.05
Work with groups	25	16	7.11	1	.01

Whether or not journalists worked at newspapers that had done public journalism projects was a significant predictor of the importance of these public journalism values. Twenty-seven per cent of the journalists working at papers that had done public journalism said improving community morale was not important versus 48 per cent of those whose papers had not done public journalism projects.

Although 36 per cent of the journalists at papers with public journalism said working with civic groups was not important, 54 per cent of the others said it was so. Circulation was a consistent predictor of support for public journalism values, ranging from most support by journalists at small papers, less support by those at medium-size papers, and least support by those at large papers.

The findings support the observation that public journalism is a small- and medium-circulation newspaper phenomenon.

Journalists from different regions of the country showed significant differences in their regard for the importance of helping the community solve problems: 16 per cent of Northeasterners said it was not important versus 7 per cent of the Westerners, 6 per cent of the Midwesterners, and 5 per cent of the Southerners, x $(9, N = 61) = 18.31, p < .05$.

Region was a significant predictor of the importance of improving community morale: 43 per cent of Northeasterners and Westerners said it was not important versus 35 per cent of the Southerners and 21 per cent of the Midwesterners x $(9, N = 61) = 22.93, p < .01$.

Journalists active in church were more likely to support public journalism values.

More of the journalists who attend church (25 per cent) said improving community morale was quite or extremely important than those who do not attend (14 per cent), x $(3, N = 61) = 15.15, p < .01$.

Likewise more of those who attend church (22 per cent) thought working with civic groups on community projects was quite or extremely important than did those who do not (10 per cent), x $(3, N = 61) = 12.88, p < .01$.

Table. Relation of Working at Newspapers That Had Done Public Journalism Projects and Whether Respondents Said Public Journalism Values Were Extremely or Quite Important.

	Work at Public Journalism Papers %	Not at Public Journalism Papers %	χ	df	p
Help community	78	66	10.54	1	.001
Solve problems	68	55	1.02	1	.001
Improve morale	28	15	2.96	1	.001
Work with groups	24	13	9.42	1	.01

Table. Relation of Size of Newspapers Where Respondents Worked and Whether They Said Public Journalism Values Were Extremely or Quite Important

Circulation	Small %	Medium %	Large %	χ	df	p
Help community	82	75	68	10.33	2	.01
Solve problems	72	67	54	14.18	2	.001
Improve morale	39	24	13	36.53	2	.0001
Work with groups	36	21	9	40.85	2	.0001

When asked whether their newspaper should engage in practices associated with public journalism, fewer than 30 per cent of the respondents agreed that their newspapers should do so:

For each of the following statements, please tell me whether you agree or disagree:

- My newspaper has an obligation not just to point out community problems and explain alternative solutions but also to set up meetings and organize programmes to solve the problems.
- Those of us in the newspaper business have an obligation to go beyond merely reporting the news to join with civic groups to push specific ideas for improving the quality of life in our community.

Twenty-eight per cent agreed with the first statement, whereas 29 per cent agreed with the second statement. The percentages of support for these two items are similar to the percentages of support for the second two items in the Personal Public Journalism scale and reinforce the finding that, although journalists are supportive of general public journalism values, they are less likely to support specific public journalism practices that deviate from traditional journalism practice.

LIMITATIONS AND FUTURE RESEARCH

The results of this chapter are based on a single study in one community, thus restricting any inferential claims based on an assumption of external validity. But the findings reflect a certain degree of construct validity given our emphasis on autonomy as a professional value that should dampen support for civic journalism.

Students who work for a campus newspaper should be moving closer to professionals and away from fellow students; the data consistently fit this pattern across various measures of civic journalism support.

Future research would ideally incorporate a panel design of at least two years' duration, with a larger and broader sample of respondents, to track the development of journalistic values as students enter the initial stage of their professional careers. Studies should also incorporate direct attitudinal measures of autonomy as a professional value to supplement the attitudinal and experiential measures used in this study. We suggest a framework for field research based on the development of operational measures that represent the twentieth-century ethos of professional journalism (*e.g.*, detachment, free press, watchdog role, people's right to know, criticizing institutions) alongside the civic journalism approach (*e.g.*, social responsibility, community building, self-criticizing press institutions, problem-solving).

This approach might generate insight that can be used for the reform of journalism instruction as educators promote autonomy in service to democracy. Public journalism began as a series of experiments in the late 1980s and early 1990s, and soon developed into what Schudson has called "the most impressive critique of journalistic practice inside journalism in a generation" and "the best organized social movement inside journalism in the history of the American press."

Also known as civic journalism, the movement arose in response to a perceived crisis in the role of the press in constituting a public sphere in which citizens could understand and engage productively with the issues of the day. During the first decade, the movement generated an array of innovative practices in newsrooms and communities, as well as an extensive network of journalism practitioners and educators committed to reshaping professional and institutional norms.

The primary philosophical emphasis of public journalism, as manifest in the writings of its leading theorists and practitioners, is on the relationship between the practice of journalism and the democratic work of citizens in a self-governing republic, and suggests journalists are ideally suited to help constitute vital "publics" to deliberate complex issues and engage in collective problem-solving activities.

Public journalism, thus, has set out to help members of the public come to see themselves as citizens, and hold them accountable for grappling with the full complexity of issues and become participants in civil society rather than mere spectators of it.

Still, after more than a decade of practice of public journalism, empirical knowledge of whether and how public journalism has met these goals remains largely based on in-depth case studies. Early literature focused on cases generally acknowledged as the seed-beds of the public journalism movement.

Subsequent comparative research examined other best cases, focusing on changes in newsroom reporting and editing practices, community recognition of public journalism efforts, and shifts in community problem-solving and public deliberation. While researchers found positive evidence in each area, elements were not disaggregated and case studies were often idiosyncratic, making it difficult to measure impact or establish clear relationships among elements.

In their critical review of forty-seven evaluative studies of public journalism, Massey and Haas found that public journalism practices have had limited effects on the attitudes, beliefs, and behaviours of news audiences. They criticize existing research for focusing on "a handful of showcase public-journalism news organizations and projects." In doing so, they highlight the methodological shortcomings of many of the efforts to assess public journalism, and recommend that future research capture a wider array of experiments and trace the effects of these efforts on community life. With prior research lacking a broad, systematic assessment of public journalism efforts, we set out to provide a holistic analysis of the movement, shedding light on participating organizations, practices, and effects.

An inventory of the archives of the Pew Centre for Civic Journalism found 651 public journalism projects conducted from 1994 to 20027 Our research analyses the inventory using hierarchical regression analysis to trace the effects of organizational factors, project features, story frames, and efforts to involve community members and assess public opinion on three civil society goals:

- Improving citizens' civic competencies,
- Influencing policymaking processes, and
- Increasing civic volunteerism.

The literature on public journalism is extensive, but extracting clear empirical propositions is challenging. First, much of the best literature is normative, advocating a role of the press in improving public life, and tends to draw case-based observations about changes public journalism creates in news organizations.

Second, the large body of case literature is very uneven, ranging from anecdotal and polemic to qualitative and comparative case observation. While it is difficult to untangle the effects of public journalism on civil society given these inconsistencies, there are important insights to be gained from the extant research.

Public journalism research has primarily concentrated on several flagship public journalism newsrooms and projects. Additionally, there are numerous case studies of other cities and regions. These cases, however, have not been analysed using a systematic empirical-quantitative framework.

Here, we consider the scholarship in three domains of public journalism:

- Organization of newsrooms and their effects on individual journalists' values, norms, and behaviour;
- Links between public journalism efforts and changes in news content, framing, and sourcing; and
- Public journalism's impact on electoral knowledge and behaviour, and on citizen participation in public life.

3

The Importance of Media for the Social Construction of Leadership

INTRODUCTION

Many social analysts have recognized the importance of mass media in shaping views of ourselves and the world around us. Research in mass communication has shown that the media influence people's cognition in a variety of ways. The media may determine what issues are important and set agenda for what the public thinks about, transmit knowledge and information, reinforce or crystalize existing beliefs, change existing beliefs, and cultivate perceptions of the nature of social reality. The last decade has witnessed an unprecedented growth in the level and type of media coverage devoted to matters of organization and management. Interested publics are now routinely served by various business media outlets, perhaps most conspicuously by a business press with mass appeal.

According to the Standard Rate and Data Service, the six-month average circulation in 1989 of the Wall Street Journal was 1.93 million, that of Fortune, Business Week, and Inc. were.707.870, and.754 million, respectively. In addition to such dedicated business publications, popular newspapers and magazines, such as the New York Times and Time, with their own huge circulations (1.17 and 1.68 million), regularly feature business and management reports. Such mammoth figures are complemented by the extensive reach and appeal of television and other mass media outlets. While an ostensible mission of the business media is to provide facts and information about business organizations, it is clear theat business journalism extends into areas well beyond simple reporting, transmitting to us a variety of deeper messages regarding organizations and their functioning. Media analysts have recognized its ideological and constructive aspects.

The media achieves its impact through its consideration of and interaction with the audience. News organizations are directly dependent on market forces and appeal directly to popular opinions. To maintain the allegiance of the audience, news selection and treatment has to take into account its viewing and reading behaviour and be responsive to its needs and gratifications. Furthermore, the interpretation of meanings by readers is not passive reception or discovery of what is inherent in the news but active interaction with the text involving pre-existing cognition and attitudes, previous and current expectations, and the nature of the perceived social and physical environment. The relationships between the press and the audience are therefore indicative of a confluence of societal interests in supplying and consuming certain kinds of information.

In this regard, constructions of leadership are regularly and widely produced for our consumption, with transmissions often taking the form of portraits and images of great leadership figures, both in the public and private sectors. These images feed and expand our appetites for leadership products, appealing not only to our collective commitments to the concept but fixating us in particular on the personas and characteristics of leaders themsevels. In this research we were interested in understanding how the business press, in conjunction with their reading publics, construct a leaders's image over time in light of radical changes in the fortunes of a firm. When we say "the business press" or "the media" we refer to a field of news organizations in general, not to individual news writers and reporters.

We keep in mind the fact that authors who are credited with having written some news article are only one part of the hierrarchy in typical news organizations, whose ranks include policymakers, top editors, section heads, writers, reporters, and researchers as well as support, dissemination, and business staffs.

Furthermore, news making is a process entailing news selection, editing, writing, information gathering, and information checking. Thus it is appropriate to treat news reports and articles as products of organizations rather than products of individual journalist. Admittedly, newsworkers are not just organizational members but also professionals with professional norms and values. But, as Tuchman found, news professionalism has developed in conjunction with modem news organizations, and professional practices serve organziational needs.

Consequently, the dichotomy between organizational commitment and professional allegiance the characterized traditional professionals is very much obsolete in this domain. Previous research has studied the media in terms of political ideologies of different news organizations. For the purpose of the present study, however, we adopted a cultural perspective, examining how the news industry as a whole influences and shapes news consumers' cultural conceptions and beliefs. We therefore treated news organizations in aggregate as an organizational field that constitutes "a recognized area of institutional life" by sharing a rather homogeneous structure and values.

The basic question we sought to address was, Given the initial success of a firm, what image of the CEO will be constructed? And how will the image be reconstructed (if at all) with new, negative performance information that is also associated with the tenure of the same leader? We intended both to explicate the content of the leader image associated with given performance outcomes and to examine the degree of continuity and change of the image as the performance drama of a firm unfolds over time.

Organizational researchers have studied leadership attributions as a function of "performance cues," but they have not typically considered that, realistically, leaders can and often are associated with variable performance outcomes over time and that attributions made at any given time are often made within the historical context of previous attributions.

Although questions of the kind raised above typically have been studied at the individual level, we contend that they can also be explored at the collective level of news organizations, on the assumption that there is much communality in knowledge, assumptions, and routine practices. As we will argue, organizational credibility is the primary concern across news organizations, which makes both performance information and attribution history essential in the process of image construction.

ANALYSIS OF READERS' DESCRIPTIONS

In this first analysis we focused on the images formed by readers in response to the news articles selected as stimulus data by the following procedure.

IMAGE DATA

Before the stimulus data were presented to respondents, they filled out a questionnaire about whether they had read or heard about People Express nd Burr and, if yes, whether they thought People Express and Burr had been successful. Most of the respondents (86 per cent) reported having read or heard about People Express. Twenty per cent thought the airline was a success, 33 per cent thought it was not a success, and 47 per cent were not sure.

There were no differences among the three groups of respondents regarding their familiarity with the company and their perceived success of the company. Although the majority of the respondents showed some familiarity with the airline, very few reported knowledge of Donald Burr: 91.4 per cent of the respondents had not read or heard about Burr, and 90 per cent did not know whether he was successful or not. Of the 10 per cent who reported they did, 5.7 per cent considered Burr a success, and 4.3 per cent considered him not a success. The stimulus data of three historical periods were randomly presented to 74 undergraduate business students, with 25 respondents for each period. Respondents were asked to write a description of Donald Burr both as a person and as a CEO, based on the materials they had just read. To ensure that each and every article in the package was read, a question was placed after each article: "Have you read the whole article? Did you understand the article? If No, please read it again. If Yes, go on the the next chapter." Three of the descriptions were discarded because the respondent failed to write about Burr. Seventy-two portrayals served as the image data on which our analysis was performed.

CONTENT ANALYSIS

The image descriptions were first read for their generl structure of presentation. They were then screened for descriptions of Burr, which could be a word, a phrase, or a sentence. The descriptive units were similar to what some content analysts call "propositions". These propositional descriptions were then grouped into more superordinate theme categories.

For example, "a man of drive" and "he worked very hard" would be grouped under the theme of Motivation. Other examples of the Motivation theme included "ambitious," "a need for achievement," "desire to be the best," "high spirited," "energetic," "enthusiastic," "aggressive," "commitment," "determined," etc. When questions arose concerning the meaning of a linguistic unit, we consulted respondents again for clarification.

Across three periods, 14 different themes were abstracted. The propositions and themes provided qualitative data for examining the structure of the leader image within and across the performance periods. In this procedure, twenty original descriptive units from each category were randomly selected and each was recorded on a card. A total of 120 cards were given to each of the five judges, in random order, to be classified into six categories. Agreement of individual categories by the judges with those by the researcher ranged from 80 per cent to 100 per cent, with the average being 91 per cent.

In addition, coeffient Kappa, which takes into account the level of chance agreement, was calculated for each judge's overall categorization agreement with the researcher. The average of the Kappa coefficients was.89. Frequencies. Two types of theme frequencies were counted. One was the percentage frequency of propositions in a given theme for a given performance period.

This frequency by propositions provided statistics for examining the relative salience and importance of individual themes within the performance periods and for analyzing the trend of the themes across the periods. The second theme frequency was the percentage of respondents in a period that made reference to a given theme. This frequency by individuals served as an index of consensus, indicating the convergence of the leader image among the readers. We will refer to this frequency as the consensus rate.

RESULTS

The presentational structure of the articles of period 1 followed a pattern of attributes, achievements, and means. Burr's attributes were introduced as causes of the success of People Express, followed by details about how the success had been achieved. Eight image themes for period 1 were extracted.

Those themes that had an above-average frequency of references (12.5 per cent) were People, Motivation, Ability, and Innovation, constituting altogether 86 per cent of the total propositions. People, which denoted Burr's humanistic management philosophy and practice and his charismatic appeal, was the most salient theme.

All image themes were positive and complemented each other. The descriptions were permeated with exuberant praise and admiration, such as "very versatile," "extremely intelligent," "with people's interest at heart," "created a family in his organization," "a dreamer who realized his dreams," "noted for his unorthodox style of management ideas and innovations," "a man with a mission," and "oozes enthusiasm and optimism," etc.

The image themes formed a pattern, with substantive themes denoting the leadership traits of Burr and methathemes commenting on the substantive themes. The metatheme in the first period was Balance. It pointed out that Burr not only possessed positive characteristics, but these fitted his mission as well as each other perfectly to make him an ideal business leader. The balance theme consisted of propositions that were typically presented in pairs of couplets.

For example, Burr was seen as not only ambitious but also capable and willing to work hard; not only willing to take chances but also possessing a fundamental understanding of the business; not only wanted to do well for himself but also for others, employees and customers alike; not only a perfectionist but also a businessman who wanted to make a profit, etc.

The high consensus rate (the first three themes were all above 90 per cent) indicates that there was high consensus among the respondents that Burr was an all-around ideal leader: charismatic, innovative, dedicated, and competent. In the second period, the general presentational structure followed a sequential pattern of positive attributes, achievements, problems, and causes.

While illustration of the positive personal characteristics and great achievements continued, problems began to emerge and were traced by some to Burr's weaknesses. There were ten themes, six of which were positive and four negative. Yet none of the negative reached the average frequency of 10 per cent or the consensus rate of 50 per cent, whereas the major themes remained positive, with equal or above-average frequency and higher than 50 per cent consensus rate.

The most salient theme was still People. There were two metathemes. One was Overdone, which consisted of propositions that Burr had too much of some otherwise positive characteristics, such as desire to succeed and idealism. The other was Change, which suggested that as the company expanded, Burr had altered some of his previously good leadership ideas and styles or developed some undesirable attitudes. However, as pointed out above, they were of quite low salience.

Compared with the image constructed in period 1, the metatheme of Balance was replaced by Overdone, and all four of the added themes were negative. These negative themes, although with low frequency and consensus rates, introduced some minor contradictions to the exclusively positive themes generated in the first period. Overdone confliected with Balance, Unethical with Ethical, and Autocratic with People.

Change did not represent a rejection of any of the previous attributions but claimed that the leader himself had changed. Nevetheless, the four most prominent themes were all positive ones and enjoyed the highest four consensus rates; the total number of positive propositions constituted 80 per cent, whereas the total number of negative propositions accounted for only 20 per cent.

All in all, the leader images had gone through considerable reconstruction; however, despite the questions and doubts about the previously constructed image of an ideal leader, the image of the second period was still overwhelmingly positive. When it came to the failure period, period 3, the general structure of presentation in the articles consisted of an ordering of positive attributes, negative attributes, and failure.

That the positive descriptions preceded the negative ones seemed to indicate an obligation not to forget Burr's strengths while pointing out his weaknesses. There were nine images themes, four of which were positive and five negative. The four themes that had an above-average frequency rate (11 per cent) were People, Overdone, Motivation, and Innovation.

They constituted 76 per cent of the propositions of the third period. The major themes were no longer all positive. The negative theme, Overdone, which emeged from the second period, was prominent second only to the People theme. There seemed to be a greater deal of reconstruction resulting in a rather negative image. However, semantic analysis revealed some significant qualifications on the negativeness.

First, the most prominent theme was still People, and within the major themes, only 28 per cent of the propositions were negative. Second, two of the five negative themes were metathemes, which constituted 67 per cent of all the negative propositions. Overdone, as mentioned above, referred to an excessive amount of otherwise good personal qualities.

Some of the Overdone propositions were negative in view of the changed situation. The "too much of a good thing" was conceived by respondents as a state not solely caused by an absolute oversupply of the leader's endowment, but by its interaction with a changed external situation.

This was articulated by the second metatheme, III-adaptation, which emphasized the insufficiency of attributes and skills relative to the changed demands of the environment. So, although the previous all-positive image in terms of major themes was now broken, the negative themes of Overdone and Ill-adaptation did not directly conflict with the positive substantive themes.

The consensus rate of period 3 showed high agreement on all the major themes, with Vision and Overdone scoring highest, followed by People and Motivation. Ill-adaptation also showed a marginal majority rate. The overall image of the leader was of an admirable leader with otherwise basically good qualities that unfortunately ill-fitted a changed environment. The message conveyed through the image was that the cause of the failure by and large lay not in the inherent quality of the leader but in the changed situation.

Looking across the performance periods, images were reconstructed as performance varied. As problems arose and performance suffered, the total number of positive propositions decreased, whereas the total number of negative propositions increased.

Yet throughout the periods, positive propositions outnumbered negative ones. Furthermore, the aggregate percentage frequency of positive propositions in major themes did not show a significant over-time difference.

The percentage frequency of the negative propositions in the major theme Overdone differed significantly over time. These statistics and the semantic features of the major negative attributions presented above revealed a serious effort by the press to account for the performance failure without rejecting previous positive leader attributes.

STIMULUS DATA

The search for information about People Express and its CEO, Donald Burr, started with all the sources available to the authors, including Business Periodical Index, Business Index, Infotrac Academic Index, National Newspaper Index, and Magazine Index. In addition, computer searches were done on Business Data Base and Popular Magazine Review Online. A huge volume of information about the airline company was identified.

Business Index alone recorded 295 People Express entries by about forty business journals over six years. To make this information manageable, we decided to search only entries under Donald Burr. This trimmed the articles down to about 100, split almost evenly between journals and newspapers.

A quick look at the articles, however, showed that the indexing was far from stringent: many of the articles under the entry of Donald Burr in fact provided little information about him. It was therefore decided that we collect only articles that made references to Burr in their titles.

In addition, we retained those articles that had been contributed by news organizations that reported on Burr over all three periods. The rationale for this criterion was that journals or newspapers that carried reports about Burr over the total life of the company were appropriate for testing the self-consistency expectation. Finally, we dropped those articles that had fewer than ten descriptive clauses on Burr. A descriptive clause on Burr was one that had as its topic Burr, his characteristics, his activities, or any other reference to him. The resultant stimulus data comprised 22 articles representing five journals and two newspapers. These included the New York Times, Wall Street Journal, Business Week, Fortune, Inc., Newsweek, and Time. This material was divided into three groups according to the historical periods in which they were published. The entire procedure netted a total of about 10,000 words of text per period. The material for each period was subdivided into two groups so that the reading load for any individual was not more than 5,000 words of text.

A CONSTRUCTION-CONSTRAINT MODEL OF LEADERSHIP IMAGES

A traditional perspective on journalism is that news "mirrors" or "reflects" the actual nature of the world; journalists are thus objective reporters of actual events. A constructionist approach to social reality rejects the notion of an objectivity that is independently of social actors. In practice, business leaders are rarely observed and described as individuals per se but are seen as representatives or personifications of the organizations in their charge.

Thus, seeking "unbiased" knowledge of the actual activities and endowments of a leader and whatever consistencies exist therein is made less important. In any case, such knowledge cannot tell us much about the nature of the constructions that will emerge. More important is what information will be used or ignored and how such information will be interpreted and given meaning in the constructed image. In theory, then, many alternative constructions are possible, and it would be difficult to predict a priori the contents of an image and the rules by which it is reconstructed over time. In reality, however, the alternative reconstructions that are likely to emerge from the popular press and be tolerated by its reading publics will be constrained to a much smaller set of alternatives, so that the particular construction and reconstruction of leadership images is likely to be the joint product of forces that bear on the popular press and its readership.

We identified the following forces at work in the popular press:

- Antideterminism– a belief that individuals determine the fate of organizations;
- The effects of performance cues and antribution history;
- The professional values and ideology of news organizations; and
- Organizational routinization. These forces are explained in detail below.

ANTIDETERMINISM

One can find evidence of more and less antideterministic perspectives being represented in the writings of organizational scientists, particularly around issues concerning the relative magnitude to the size of the leadership effect versus environmental factors on organizational performances. The antideterministic perspective is reflected in theories that suggest that the fates and fortunes of a firm can be understood in terms of the personal endowments of the leaders in charge. A more deterministic perspective is presented by the so-called external-control models of management, by which a firm's performance is understood more in terms of the environmental and inertial constraints facing managements. A key differences in these two perspectives has been in the assumptions made regarding the extent to which managements are capable of exercising, through their unique endowments, control over an unruly environment in the service of organizational performance.

For the antideterminist, the principal significance of leaders lies in their substantive actions and activities, which effectively isolate their firms from the vagaries of environment or use environment to the advantages of their firms, or both, in direct proportion to their abilities and skills. For the determinist, leadership's role is largely symbolic, aimed at preserving among important constituencies the illusion of a more antideterministic world and continued support for the leaders' stewardships. We argue that the business press is particularly prone to interpret organizational outcomes in terms of leadership. It is widely recognized by both practitioners and researchers that news focuses on individuals in general and leaders in particular: "In the mass mediated reality, organizations, bureaucracies and movements—in fact all larger and more enduring social formations—are reduced to personifications".

While there are practical reasons for the news to emphasize leaders (such as perceived importance of the news), there is an implicit theory of society that the social process, above all others, is shaped by leaders.

Western journalism has sometimes been portrayed as a sort of cult of personality that largely discounts anonymous social, economic, and political forces: journalism shuns these forces, proposing instead that great men and women still alive among us and that it is they who make history.... the media's celebration of personality stems more deeply from a belief in voluntarism—of will—that attributes social change to the deliberate actions of individuals. Journalism, in other words, is strongly antideterministic.

This antideterministic view of organizational performance will orient the business press to attribute organizational outcomes to personal qualities and activities of the leader, leading to a very positive image as the organization performs well. The image will be constructed in a way that accounts for that performance while reflecting the professional values of the news press.

PERFORMANCE CUES AND ATTRIBUTION HISTORIES

Studies of performance-cue effects suggest that the construction of leader images is mainly a process of matching leader characteristics with performance outcomes. The direction of performance outcomes (positive versus negative) therefore determines that of leader images. We call this view of attribution the outcome-primacy approach.

According to this perspective, the CEO of a successful firm will be depicted with positive personal qualities, but if the firm subsequently experiences performance failure, the same leader will now be stigmatized with an image of failure and be depicted with negative image characteristics. The new leader image, constructed to match the performance failure, would depart radically from the original one, which was well-fitted to the performance success.

The obvious omission in this argument is the prestructuring effect of attribution history. If, as we argue, attribution making in real life is often a continuous rather than a one-shot process, past attributions should influence new attributions.

First, past attributions may serve as schema through which performance cues would be selectively processed. Second, as Salanick's theory of commitment would suggest, the very act of attribution has a binding effect on future attributions to the extent that the action is explicit, irrevocable, volitional, and public. Attribution makers are therefore pulled in two different directions. One is to update and revise the leader image to fit the drastically different performance information, the other is to affirm the initial leaders image to maintain consistency with past attribution. Some kind of compromise will have to be reached.

Although the above discussion on attribution thory is typically applied to individuals, news organizations frequently face a similar dilemma. The dilemma arises from the prevalent organizational concern for credibility. As a Bristish newscaster put it, "Credibility in the minds of the audience is the sine qua non of news".

Apart from any professional concern for ethics, news institutions' dependence on market forces makes it essential for them to cultivate a credible image in order to compete for readers and advertisers. How, then, is credibility gained and maintained? Research on journalism mostly points to rules and procedures aimed at the objectivity or factivity of news.

In addition, Gans observed that journalists were very reluctant to change opinions because inconsistency undermines credibility. Accordingly, we argue that consistency is another means by which news organizations maintain credibility. Credibility through objectivity and consistency seems to reflect newsworkers' strategy towards "hard" and "soft" news, respectively. Objectivity implies tending to hard news, such as buying, merging, selling of business, and changes in stock price and profit.

Consistency requires coherent continuity in interpreting those hard events. Interpretation and construction occur more fully in soft news, such as feature stories of successful business leaders.The ideal of objectivity coupled with the antideterministic perspective of journalism predicts the construction of a very positive leader image in the soft feature stories that account for the hard events of business successes.

Once this positive image is formulated and publicized, consistency for the sake of credibility predicts continuation of the positive leader image. However, as time goes on and the company experiences performance failure, the radical development calls for radical revision of the original leader image. The question is whether the positive leader image should be supplanted by a negative one to fit the new performance outcome or whether the highly publicized positive image should be kept intact to maintain consistency.

This is no easy dilemma, because achieving one goal will cost the other. This may be resolved by reducing leadership attributions or by making more external attributions for performance. In veiw of our discussion of antideterminism, this alternative is less than satisfactory, since it would paint the leader as a rather passive actor in the process.

The more preferable alternative is to modify the image to the extent that the initially positive image is still preserved and yet the recent performance failure is also accounted for.

PROFESSIONAL VALUES AND IDEOLOGY

News selection and treatment are not free from values and ideology. From the ideological hegemony perspective, the media is seen as part of the poltiical system, specialized in formulating and distributing the ideology of the dominant social power. Scholars from a cultural perspective, however, seek to identify in the media values of the culture at large, in which journalism is imbedded. The aggregate of the values may be called ideology, which, however, does not necessarily imply hegemony of the dominant ruling coalitions with a system of deliberate and integrated values.

Gans summarized the journalistic values he identified in the national new as the journalistic para-ideology, which both reflects the existing values and shapes future values of the national culture. If news contains values and ideology, the will certainly find expressions in leader images constructed in the news. And since values and ideology are stable and enduring, news organizations will attempt to preserve the image of the leader who is regarded as the embodiment of their cultural values and ideology.

ORGANIZATIONAL ROUTINIZATION

News organizations are professional bureaucracies and journalists are organizational members. News selection and treatment are a function of oganizational structures and requirements. Topics are assigned downward to reporters, stories are reviewed and selected hierarchically, essential facts are verified by special checkers, and records are kept for future assignments. The process routinization produces consistency and predictability. Furthermore, the formal and informal control mechanisms of the organization reinforce uniformity and consistency. Viewed from this inertial perspective of news organizations, a positive leader image, once constructed, is likely to be preserved, even in face of organizational performance change.

Considering the above forces, we formulated a tentative model from which we could derive expectations about the continuity and revision of leadership images in the popular press. Such forces operate as a set of constraints that define the characteristics of the reconstructions that will take place. Initially, performance cues will carry great weight in determining early constructions of the leader's image.

Information about the leader is likely to be used in a way that accounts for or otherwise explains the performance outcomes of the firm. The constructed image will tend to focus on the special endowments of the leader, particularly those consistent with cultural values.

As time passes and as new information on the changing fortunes of the firm are received, an interaction of performance information and elements of the originally constructed image will determine the characteristics of the reconstruction.

This suggests that the reconstructive process yields products that are continuous with the past. It describes a conservative process that does not contradict but, rather, preserves the original image, limiting revisions to the introduction of amendments that render the new performance information interpretable from a leadership point of view. To explore this model, we did a case study of the reports by the popular press on a business leader whose company experienced dramatic changes of performance: Donald Burr, the founder and chairman of People Express Airlines Inc.

Business leaders associated with dramatically performing organizations are often covered extensively by the popular press. Burr and his airline enjoyed very prominent and extensive coverage in popular journals and newspapers during the 1980s. Business Index alone recorded about 50 entries under Burr over a period of six years.

Burr was featured as Man of the Year by Time in 1985 and was further honored in cover stories by Inc., Business Week, Time, and others. In the initial success period, Inc. devoted eight full pages to reporting on Burr and his company. When the company was in trouble, the New York Times organized a case study of Peope Express attended by professionals and academics. Not only was Burr a celebrity in the popular press, he became a model of humanistic management for business school academics.

The long-time prominence of Burr in the popular press ensured a well-portrayed image for analysis. In addition, Burr had been in charge of People

Express throughout its six years of operation, thereby making possible a direct and strong association between leader image and organizational performance.

Finally, the ups and downs of the company's performance were very dramatic, presenting us with an ideal context for examining the dynamic development of leader image. Following is a brief introduction to the state of the airline industry at the time and to Donald Burr and People Express, as depicted in two prominent sources: the U.S. Industrial Outlook and Current Biography 1986.

DEREGULATION AND THE AIRLINE INDUSTRY

Prior to 1978, airlines were subject to the economic regulatory jurisdiction of the Civil Aeronautic Board (CAB). Competition was restricted and rates and fares were tightly controlled. After 1978, when the Airline Deregulation Act was passed, many new airlines were certified, and 1983 greeted all airlines with complete freedom of pricing. As a result of the deregulation, the airline industry entered into a period of fierce competition, characterized by a rapid increase in the number of air carriers and rapid reduction of fares.

The new entrants, taking advantage of low operating costs, quickly expanded their markets by offering low prices. The major pre-deregulation carriers, in an effort to retain their traditional markets, offered discount fares that were even below their cost of providing services. Fare wars thus ensued. The industry as a whole operated at a loss between 1979 and 1982.

The fare wars, on the one hand, stimulated air travelling by luring passengers who might otherwise travel by rail or bus, but, on the other hand, forced the major airlines to streamline their operating costs. The industry started to recover financially in 1983 and continued into 1984 and 1985. Other factors that contributed to the recovery and continued economic growth of the airline industry included the general national economic growth, the decreasing and stabilizing of jet fuel prices, and labour concessions.

As the fare wars continued, the sustained price discounts seemed ultimately to hurt more the newer and smaller air carriers. Merger activities started in 1985 and became widespread in 1986. As a result, the industry was becoming highly concentrated, and by 1987 nine major passenger carriers accounted for 90 per cent of all revenue passenger miles. At the time, U.S. Industrial Outlook predicted that the airline industry would evolve into a few mega-carriers, with numerous smaller carriers controlling secondary markets and providing supplementary service in selected major metropolitan centres.

DONALD BURR AND PEOPLE EXPRESS

Taking advantage of industry deregulation, Donald Burr resigned from his executive position in Texas International Airlines Inc. to found People Express Airline Inc. Although credited with saving Texas International from going under,

Burr publicized that he was not at all happy with the way it was run. Through People Express he wanted to demonstrate "a better way of doing things," "a better way for people to work together within the American system of democracy".

At People Express, every employee was required to buy 100 shares of the company. There was no corporate hierarchy and no rigid job specialization. Everyone was an owner-manager: a pilot was a "flight manager," and a flight attendant a "customer-service manager." Everyone was "cross-utilized": The flight manager might do inventory control and the customer-service manager might work at the ticket counter.

Burr himself had no secretary, and he often pitched in to fill whatever happened to be a vacancy. The company also did away with traditionally standard services such as free meals, free baggage handling, and comfortable lounges. Consequently, the high employee motivation, low labour cost, and elimination of the "frills" made it possible for People to offer very cheap fares that made flight a popular product for the people.

In April 1981, the company made its first flights. After an initial loss of $9.2 million in the first year, People began to earn a profit somewhere between $500,000 and $1 million in 1982. By 1983, the company was servicing 19 cities in the U.S. and, in May, started its foreign service to London.

Owing to its skyrocketing sales volume, People's shares hit an all-time high of nearly $50 in July 1983. And the company appeared in the 100 Best Companies to Work for in America. People's participative management became case-study models for business schools. Burr summarized his "six precepts" of People Express:

The first, of course, is service, growth and development of people. The second is to be the best provider of transportation for people. The third is to develop the best leadership. The fourth is to be a role model. The fifth is simplicity. And the sixth is to maximize profits.

Although sales continued to grow, 1984 witnesses a loss of profit, and stock prices tumbled to as low as $8 a share. There were also increasing passenger complaints about delayed flights, lost luggage, and overbooking. People Express was known as "People Distress." Internally there was growing disenchantment with Burr, which culminated in the departure of the company's chairman, Pareti, who was quickly joined by adozen other key employees.

People managed to come back from this nosedive by curbing expansion and cutting expenses. Profit for the second quarter of 1985 jumped to $13 million and $16.5 million in the third. To meet the challenges from major airlines that reduced fares as a way to cut into People's market, the company decided to expand its geographic base by buying a number of smaller airlines.

The major acquisition of Frontier Airlines made People Express the fifth largest airline in the U.S. The explosive growth of People coupled with its ensuing debt load and increasing competition from the full-service carriers sent the company into another tailspin in 1986. During the first quarter, the company suffered a crushing loss of $458 million. The management tried to save the airline by selling some of the larger planes and by upgrading service to attract a wider range of customers.

When this failed to work, People agreed to sell Frontier to United Airlines. But the sale was canceled because of United's wage dispute with the pilots' union. People had to file for bankruptcy for Frontier. Finally, in September 1986, People Express was sold to Texas Air, whose predecessor was Texas International. Burr therefore went full circle, back to his original company to be the executive vice president.

A few months later he resigned to "pursue independent business interests," thus bringing the story to an end. Based on People's performance and on major organizational events, the history of People Express can be divided into three periods. The first period covered 1981 to 1983, which, despite the initial loss, was one of great success.

The second period, from 1984 to 1985, witnessed great expansion, great loss, and great gains. This period can be seen as a period of mixed performance. The last period started in 1986 and ended with the merger of the company to Texas Air in September of the year. This is clearly a period of failure. It is against this backdrop that our analysis takes place.

METHOD

Two analyses were conducted on magazine and newspaper articles about Burr. The first followed traditional content-analytic methods, identifying leader-characteristic themes, recording frequency, and analyzing trends of these themes. The second analysis focused on metaphors about Burr, using the theory and method proposed by Lakoff and Johnson. By design, much of the analysis is interpretive.

Although the mechanics of conducting the content analysis, described below, are quite conventional, the first analysis was performed on image descriptions by 72 readers of the published nmews articles. Involving respondents was primarily aimed at educing possible research bias and improving the reliability and validity of the findings. This assumed a reasonable linkage between the original stimuli of the news articles and the responses of the readers.

Our assumption was supported by previous mass-media research findings that news media have the power to hape news consumers' opinions, especially on topics about which they are ignorant. Furthermore, it was our belief that for the interpretation of image contents in the popular press, the reading public has an equal if not greater claim to reliability and validity than two academic researchers.

Some ethnographic researchers have argued that, since culture is a collective phenomenon, culture as discerned by researchers alone is inevitably more biased than if the researchers work as facilitators with a group of the cultural members. Following this argument, we had reason to expect that the collective judgement of the 72 respondents would help us interpret image meanings in the news articles more objectively.

But objectivity itself may be an illusion. Leader images in the press are more than explicit statements readily collected from the original writings. More often they have to be inferred from writings about the leader. To the extent that an image is impressionistic and holistic, its inference would depend on who makes the inference. As research on uses and gratifications has found, people with different motives (needs, beliefs, and values) may experience different media effects.

If news publishers, editors, and writers have audience considerations for story selection and production, business students would be more typical of their readership than researchers. Hence the readers' image formations may be closer than the researcher's to that of the news producers.

Lastly, the portrayed reality in the press is both an influence on and a reflection of the reading public. Given this collusive relationship, an analysis of the construction of Burr's image can proceed by focusing either on the writer or the reader. Analyzing both may serve as a cross-check of the finding.

TRENDS OF THE MAJOR THEMES ACROSS PERIODS

As performance fluctuated, the percentage frequency of the positive major themes of People, Innovation, and Motivation did not change significantly. The most noticeable theme change, in addition to the negative theme Overdone, was in Ability, the frequency of which decreased sharply. What's more, its very opposite, Inability, was developed in the third period. The consensus rate of Ability also decreased significantly over time.

On the basis of performance-cue studies, one might have expected Inability to emerge as a probable leader characteristic in the mixed period and a major dimension in the failure period. Yet there were no Inability propositions for the second period and only 6 per cent for the theme in the third period. This suggests that instead of overt negative attributions, there was a playing-down of the issue of competence by avoiding the topic (lowering the frequency of the positive propositions of Ability).

Furthermore, a semantic examination revealed that 80 per cent of the Ability propositions in the first period made reference to global propositions, such as "a genius," extremely intelligent," and "very versatile," while only 20 per cent confined Ability to specific areas of knowledge, skill, or expertise.

By contrast, in the failure period, the Inability propositions were mostly restricted to more specific areas, such as "not an organization genius" or "lacked the knowledge to change." Interestingly, only one reader used the globally negative term "a poor businessman" to describe Burr. Furthermore, many Inability statements were presented together with acknowledgments of Burr's past successes and strengths in motivating people.

Although chi-square analysis of both proposition frequencies and consensus rates showed no significant difference over time with People, Innovation, and Motivation, analysis of the content of the themes revealed subtle differences in People and Motivation. Throughout the three periods, the theme People was perceived as positive; but in the first period, it was presented as a personal quality with strong ethical tones: trusting and trustworthy, fair and caring for people.

In the second period, as the company was growing larger and more depersonalized, people orientation become more instrumental, a motivation skill. In the failure period. Burr's people orientation was admired but viewed as ill-fitting to the changed internal and external situations. Motivation in the success period was conceptualized in terms of ambition, need for achievement, enjoyment of the work, mostly intrinsically derived. But in the failure period, Motivation meant more determination, endurance, and courage, a quality demonstrated when confronting externally adverse conditions.

These changes told us again how past attributions interacted with current performance cues to determine the reconstruction of the leader's image. Instead of being rejected, the themes were modified by the injection of new meaning. The resultant new images were subtly different yet consistent with and traceable to the old ones.

ANALYSIS OF METAPHORICAL EXPRESSIONS

We sought to look directly into the original news articles to find independent evidence of the dynamics of leader-image construction. In order to do so, we analysed the metaphors used in the same news stories on which the respondents had based their own descriptions of Burr. We considered the study of metaphors appropriate because of the role of imagery associated with them. As Pondy highlighted, metaphors provide compelling, symbolic images that can link past and present. Journalists' metaphorical descriptions of Burr could help them reconcilek the great initial success with the subsequent decline of People Express.

Finally, according to Lakoff and Johnson, linguistic metaphors are not mere poetical or rhetorical embellishments but reflect the way the world is systematically conceptualized. Metaphors about Burr, besides adding vividness to the story, represent a crystallized image of the leader depicted in the popular press. To the extent that they are effective means to image presentation, metaphors might be an important linguistic means that had influenced our respondents in their image portrayal of Burr.

A metaphor, as defined by the Random House Dictionary, is "the application of a word or phrase to an object or concept it does not literally denote in order to suggest comparison with another object or concept, as in 'A mighty fortress is our God'." Lakoff and Johnson, however, had a more general definition, which includes both literal and non-linteral metaphors.

Literal metaphorical expressions are those comparisons of two objects or concepts that are generally accepted and used as part of the normal literal language. Non-literal ones are novel comparisons that are figurative, the understanding of which requires some non-literal imagination. For example, using the metaphor "Theories are buildings," the sentence "He has constructed a complex theory" is a literal expression, whereas the sentence "His theory has thousands of little rooms and long, winding corridors" is a non-literal expression.

The non-literal type of metaphors seem to correspond with Random House's more restrictive definition of metaphor, and it was on these metaphors that our analysis focused. The reason for excluding literal metaphors was that, as part of normal langugae, they were much less distinictive and more difficult to pinpoint without controversy. The non-literal expressions, however, owing to their novelty, were relatively easy to identify and convey sharper imagery for comparison.

Lakoff and Johnson argued that one important function of metaphor is structuring, *i.e.*, using one concept (usually the known) to structure another (usually the new). Two key characteristics of structuring metaphors are stressed. One is that the conceptual structuring is partial. This is necessary because, if structuring is complete, the two concepts would be identical.

The partialness allows metaphor users or creators to relate certain aspects of one domain selectively to the corresponding aspects of the metaphorically defined or structured domain. Furthermore, partialness gives the metaphor user some freedom of downplaying or hiding certain other aspects of the defining domain. The second characteristic of metaphorical structuring is systematicity.

Despite the partialness, the authors argued, the selected aspects or the selection process is often systematic. So, or example, "organization," when conceived as an "organism," gives rise to a structured system of concepts: organization is analysed in terms of internal coordination and external adaptation; there are young and old organizations; and organizations have high or low birth or mortality rates, etc.

In analyzing metaphors about Burr, we did not assume systematicity in the fullest sense that the metaphors constituted one well-integrated conceptual system of leadership. Rather, we looked for more or less consistent interrelatedness among a variety of metaphorical expressions.

Given the license of highlighting and hiding in metaphorical structuring, we could observe how the overall conceptual structure of Burr's images would be modified through metaphors in accordance with the changing performance of his firm. Metaphor identification. A metaphorical expression was identified as a non-literal description of Burr if the description had to be understood and interpreted non-literally. For example, "Burr gave birth to People Express" is a metaphor because, interpreted literally, Burr has to be a female and People Express has to be a baby. We interpret the statement metaphorically and infer from the discourse context that it means that Burr was the founder of the company and that he endowed the business company with a human character. We screened, sentence by sentence, the same sampled journal articles that were presented to the respondents.

Those words, phrases, or clauses that metaphorically described Burr's personality, his behaviours, or his impact were identified as metaphorical expressions. Altogether, 46 such expressions were identified.

METAPHORICAL CONCEPTS AND SYSTEMS

The metaphorical expressions were grouped according to the performance periods in which they were printed. In each period, they were further classified into the metaphorical concepts that were conceptually similar to the respondents' image themes. Depending on whether or not a concept had multiple, interrelated expressions, individual concepts were labeled as a system concept or non-system concept.

A system concept consisted of multiple yet interrelated metaphorical expressions, whereas a non-system concept had only one single expression. System concepts, by definition, had higher frequency than individual, non-system concepts. The most frequent concept would be considered the dominant concept.

However, since all metaphorical concepts identified here, systems or non-systems, were about the same person, we looked for any possible structure that might interrelated them. We then compared and related all the concepts to discern a pattern of relationships. Finally, the metaphorical concepts were related to the image themes of the readers to assess the degree of correspondence.

RESULTS

Period 1. In the first period, Burr was compared to a preacher, a parent, a builder, a wizard Mr. Peanut, and a competitor. Of all the metaphors, the preacher metaphor stood out as the most salient, vivid, and elaborate.

Half of the metaphorical expressions about Burr were devoted to the preacher concept. Following is a sample listing of the preacher expressions: He could've been a preacher. They don't say "minister," or "reverend," or "clergy," they say "preacher" because it convyes exactly the right sense of sweat-in-a-hot-tent, evangelical fervour that makes the pulse race. Burr works hard when he talks. He paces, he sits; he stands; he throws out his arms; he condemns and praises, implores and jokes. The glue is Burr himself, who dashes about preaching his horizontal-management style with messianic zeal. Within the new structure, though, Burr will go on preaching his unorthodox management approach.

Then another question was posed and suddenly the evangelical fervour was back in his voice. "It takes almost a messiah," William Hambrecht says: "that's the glue that holds it together." The above expressions contained various aspects that constituted a system of the preacher concept.

Highlighted in this system were the specification of a message (horizontal-management philosophy), the unorthodox nature (not a minister or reverend or clergy), a strong sense of morality (he condemns and praises), the whole-hearted dedication and commitment (fervour, zeal, sweat-in-the-tent), and the spiritual hold (evangelic, the glue, the messiah) the preacher had on his followers. Other concepts did not have as many expressions for us to formulate separate conceptual systems. Nevertheless, comparing and relating them with the preacher metaphor one could discern that the latter concept was the most fundamental and was capable of incorporating and entailing the other concepts. The parent metaphor stressed that what Burr had created was not a company but a family, which was reinforced by the builder metaphor, pointing to the priority Burr gave to people.

The wizard metaphor referred to Burr's charismatic hold on his employees; Mr. Peanut characterized his unorthodox management style; and the competitor metaphor here referred to competition of doctrine more than that of business.

We therefore considered leader-as-preacher as the theme that unified various metaphorical expressions and that the various preacher qualities represented characteristics of an ideal leader.

Period 2. Metaphors in the second period described Donald Burr as a preacher, a father, a maverick, an entrepreneur, a Spartan, a visionary, a whiz, and a competitor. The preacher concept again was dominant. more than half of the expressions identified referred to Burr as a preacher. The preacher theme became more elaborate and systematic. The company was referred to as a "commune," "utopia," and "cult,; Burr's colleagues and employees as "disciples," "flock," and "band of renegades"; Burr as "teacher," "evangelist," "fervent," and "visionary"; his office as "pulpit"; and his speeches as "delivering sermons." The unorthodoxy concept was reiterated by the metaphors of maverick, Spartan, and entrepreneur. The preacher concept was systematically fleshed out by expanding from personal qualities to the organization: his office, his colleagues and subordinates, and the company as a whole.

In view of the great expansion of the company and the successful survival of crises, the highlighting and elaboration of the messianic features of Donald Burr could be expected. However, the period was also one of growing pains and internal tensions. Accordingly, a new aspect of the preacher concept was employed, namely, that of fanaticism. Hence, Burr was described by some as "Reverend Jim Jones" or "Guyana Jones," the religious cult leader whose followers committed mass suicide in Guyana in 1978. Here we witnessed an indication of the negative aspect of a preacher, which might prove fatal to his mission. As we progressed into the third period, despite the difficulty and failure the company was facing, the preacher theme persisted, as was evidenced in the following metaphorical description: "People Express sometimes seemed more cult than company.

Donald Burr, chairman and co-founder, was spiritual leader. The thousands of travelers who crowded its planes at unthinkably low fares were its flock." Yet, in addition to the preacher metaphor, there emerged another salient set of metaphors, namely those of fighting. While Burr's competitiveness was stressed in both the first and second periods, the fighter metaphor in the third period stresses his strong will and heroism in the face of adverse situations.

Donald Burr was depicted as a "fallen hero" and a "Luke Skywalker" (the protagonist of the science fiction movie, "Star Wars"); People Express was described as a "victim of the competition," its activities as a life-and-death struggle in the skies, and its failure as "plunging"; other airlines were referred to as "foes" and likened to "the dastardly Darth Vader" (leader of the evil empire in "Star Wars"); the airline industry was seen as the sky of "a Darwinian environment," characterized by "fare wars," and "dominated by giants."

The fighter metaphor was compatible with the preacher metaphor, in the sense that "heroism" in the face of failure could be construed as creating an important nuance in the connotative image of Burr as a preacher. We witnessed a confrontation of the preacher and the brutal reality of the Darwinian environment. The result was that Donald Burr and People Express failed. Nevertheless, Burr was portrayed as heroic fighter for what he believed to be the just cause.

That he was a preacher rather than a traditional business manager effectively explained both his great success in the first and second periods and his tragic failure in the third period. Compared with the first- and second-period descriptions of Burr, the metaphorical expressions in the third period highlighted the hostility and adversity faced by Burr. The supportive metaphors of parent, builder, wizard, maverick, and visionary were absent; the fundamental aspect of spiritualism, however, persisted.

In general, this analysis evidenced the metaphorical construction and reconstruction of Donald Burr and a conceptualization of managerial leadership in the popular press. In this case, the role of leader was consistently likened to that of an unorthodox preacher who was visionary, charismatic, and dedicated to his mission. What was emphasized about the mission was giving people (customers and employees alike) the first priority. Although this new type of leadership had weaknesses, such as the double-edged idealism and dedication, and failed to survive the more powerful orthodox forces, it nevertheless represented in its mission, as one journalist put it, "the future of management."

A comparison of images constructed through metaphors with those by readers revealed a high degree of correspondence. Most of the image themes in the analysis of readers' descriptions had their expressions in the metaphors; for instance, Ability in wizard or wiz; People in preacher, parent, and father, Innovation in maverick, visionary; Motivation in preacher, competitor, and fighter; Thrifty in Spartan; Profit in Mr. Peanut; Overdone in Guyana Jones.

The descriptions given by the respondents were to a large extent the literal version of the metaphorical expressions used in the original news articles. There was also a correspondence between the general structures of the images revealed in the two analyses.

As with the metaphorical concepts, the image themes were all positive in the first period; in the second period, negative image themes co-occurred with the metaphors of fanaticism; and in the third period, the determination aspect of the Motivation theme corresponded with the fighter metaphorical concept, and the emphasis on the ill-fit between Burr and the Darwinian environment was present in both the description themes and the metaphor concepts.

Over time, the most striking resemblance was the persistance of the People theme and the preacher concept. We have observed in this study how the image of Donald Burr was constructed and reconstructed as the performance drama of People Express unfolded.

Our content analyses revealed a number of complexities and subtleties regarding how Burr was portrayed in the popular business press and gave us a reasonable degree of confidence in the changing image it provided. The results of the analysis of the readers' leader descriptions showed that the image of Burr over time achieved a certain consistency with the past at the same time that it was modified to accommodate new and radically different information regarding the fortunes of People Express. In addition, a direct analysis of the metaphors collected from the news accounts about Burr buttressed the above finding.

The symbolic and partial nature of metaphors permitted significant reconstruction of Burr without creating discontinuities with the past. We discovered a consistent, dominant concept that ran across all three time periods. The way the metaphorical system around the preacher concept was elaborated in successive historical periods served to retain an essential commitment to Burr's leadership as a way to understand both the initial success and the ultimate demise of People Express.

This analysis can be used to make some tentative statements about the popular business press. One might consider that journalistic reports are a main product of this industry. In the effort to meet the demands of consuming publics, the reporting of hard, factual news is enhanced via soft constructions of various organizational processes and attributes, including images of organizational leaders. The production of these images is committing and thus exposes press organizations to risks that could damage their credibility. Such risks are present when the implications of hard facts are dissonant with the soft constructions that have been sold to consumers. Credibility is generated out of a consistency with past constructions and the ability of those constructions to accommodate current realities.

Stakes in credibility are, undoubtedly, common to many industries. However, unlike other industries, in which major revisions to products and services seem to carry the implication of innovation and, hence, more desirability for consumers, revisions to journalistic products seem, instead, to more easily carry the connotation of unreliability.

This point is poignantly illustrated in a recent ad campaign by Forbes magazine, which was run during the few months prior to the failed coup atttempt in the Soviet Union. The page-long ad was headlined "While the world has changed its opinion on Gorbachev, we haven't." To underscore the point, the ad cited four Forbes journalists at four points of time over eight months to illustrate the consistent position they all held on Gorbachev. What was highlighted was consistency across time as well as across individual reporters.

Our analysis also has the potential to offer some insights into the functioning of organizations in general. The commitment to images displayed by the popular press has its counterpart within organizational contexts, in the form of commitments displayed by various constituents to their own leaders. Issues of credibility, commitment, and reconstruction are a part of the process that determines the relative longevity of CEOs and other corporate executives in the face of lagging firm performances.

Not all constituents are in the position to form images of the leader to which they will be committed, and one plausible hypothesis is that evidence of initial soft-imaging of a CEO, on the part of various and powerful organizational constituents, may to some extent forecast the leader's tenure in office following indications of declining organizational performance.

The political viability of a leader riding a downturn in the fate and fortunes of a firm may depend heavily on the extent to which interested parties have been willing or able to construct a favorable image of the leader early one. Organizational constituents who have formed their own images of the leader may find them difficult to discard.

The effectiveness of public relations campaigns designed to keep incumbents in office may in fact depend on their ability to capitalize on this process: generating initial positive constructions during good times, fostering commitments to them, and causing them to be resistant to change during less fortuitous periods in the life of the organization.

Of course, dramatic performance downturns, as in the case of People Express, will put pressure on the initial constructions, and the commitments to them may eventually necessitate at least some image reconstruction in light of new and hard realities. Drastic organizational performance changes are themselves compelling enough to prompt the process of reevaluation and reconstruction of the leader image. Whether performance changes alone can significantly affect the content of subsequent images depends on their interaction with other forces.

In our case, the pressure of performance information was tempered by forces that favored continuity. By and large, the new images was continuous with the past but at the same time could account for the changed fate of the organization. This sort of continuity and conservative revision was in keeping with the constraining forces of self-consistency, values, and organizational routine.

We view this as a general process that could apply to different patterns of performances and initial constructions. Further research, however, should be conducted to test whether initial negative leader attributions follow a similar pattern of continuity.

With respect to leadership studies, it can be said that the static, one-shot attribution context in which previous performance-cue effects have been found does not approximate closely the on-going, continuous aspect of performance, attributions regarding it, and the resultant images of leaders that are constructed.

Simple performance-cue effects in isolation cannot adequately account for the dynamics and complexities of leader-image perceptions. Images of leadership are constructed and reconstructed within a context of organizational performance histories.

Accordingly, attributions based on performance must also have a history. While organizations may not perform consistently (always successfully or always poorly), organizations and members strive for consistency in their judgement of the leader to maintain credibility as well as a sense of control. Yet attribution consistency is not to be achieved at the expense of its power of accounting for the ups and downs of performance.

Part of the commitment to the success image of Burr, one might suggest, is linked to his embodiment of certain cherished values. Burr is an idealized representation of the American entrepreneurial spirit: a visionary, daring to dream and daring to pursue the dream until it comes true. Who would ever want or even dare to destroy such a spirit?

The positive leadership characteristics abstracted from the two separate analyses in our study showed great overlappings with the journalistic values identified by Gans. His research on national news media over two decades identified eight clusters of enduring values that reflect value preferences of journalists as a profession and, to some extent, also those of news sources and audiences. Of the eight clusters of values, we found the following four to be closely related to the leader-image themes in our study.

1. Altruistic Democracy: Politicians, officials and democracy are expected to be honest, efficient, dedicated to acting in the public interest, Spartan in their tastes, and citizens should participate to eliminate the need for government;
2. Responsible Capitalism: Moopoly is evil, smallness and family-owned business is viewed favorably; business officials are expected to be honest and efficient; business news is dedicated to entrepreneurs and innovators as well as able corporate managers' innovation and risk taking are seen as more desirable in business than in public agencies;
3. Small-town Pastoralism: a specification of the desirability of nature and smallness; bigness is impersonal and inhuman; the ideal social organization should reflect a human scale; and
4. Individualism: The ideal individual struggles successfully against adversity and overcomes more powerful forces; self-made men and women remain attractive; hard and task-oriented work is valued.

Three out of the four positive image themes about Burr, namely, People, Innovation, and Motivation overlapped greatly the above four clusters of values, and these were the themes that were stable across the performance periods. More specifically, the following information made salient in the press about Burr and his company showed close links to the journalistic values.

Burr was an entrepreneur (Responsible Capitalism), a self-made man (Individualism); People Express was the product of the Airline Deregulation Act and a challenger of the big monopolies (Responsible Capitalism, Small-town Pastoralism, and Individualism); at People, there was no corporate hierarchy—employees were owners, everybody was a manager, and Burr had no secretary (Altruistic Democracy, Responsible Capitalism, Small-town Pastoralism).

These overlappings provide evidence of the impact of values and ideology on the initial construction and subsequent maintenance of the positive leader images. In addition, a scan of recent business publications, from newspapers and magazines to best sellers, reveals that American business places similar values on transformational and charismatic leaders who are reputed to empower employees and achieve performance "beyond expectations."

To test directly the impact of values on image construction, future research can examine how news agencies with different value orientations report the same leader. For example, the present study could be redesigned to explore differences in reports of Burr by the general press (New York Times and Time) versus the business press, the more liberal versus the more conservative.

Alternatively, research can also focus on differing reports by the same news agency on different kinds of leaders: the entrepreneurs versus the big corporate executives, or charismatic versus non-charismatic leaders, such as Burr versus Frank Lorenzo, the technician-like CEO of Texas Air and Eastern Airlines. These kinds of studies would throw light on how value orientations influence people's conceptualization of organization and leadership.

The reconstruction of Burr's image, as we have been able to observe it, can be portrayed as a process that began with highly positive features but ended not with a denial or replacement of those endowments but with a revised image in which those very same endowments were portrayed as being responsible for his demise. The "downside" of Burr's idealism and motivation gradually came into relief for news readers and writers as the performance drama of his firm unfolded.

This particular sort of reconstruction is reminiscent of a theme in classic Greek tragedies, that of the fatal flaw of character. The early Bible-stumping imagery during Burr's ascension gradually turned into overzealousness during his fall from grace. Burr's magnificent endowments as a leader were tragically flawed in a way that accounted for his ultimate failure with People Express. In this respect, the reconstructed image of Burr's persona is similar to the likes of characters such as Oedipus and Medea.

Such constructive and reconstructive efforts seem to be consistent with the notion of the romance of leadership. The collective commitment to leadership represents perhaps another important constraint on the images of leaders that will be set forth by news press and tolerated by reading publics.

Whatever particular reconstructions emerge, their general themes must not diminish the significance of leadership as a way of understanding performance. The media—in the present case, the business press in particular—with its antideterministic bent, makes an important contribution to that kind of reassurance. Just as buyers and sellers, through their influence on supply and demand, determine prices in the marketplace, writers and readers, who traffic in images of leadership, influence each other to determine how leaders are talked about and, in the end, how these images are systematically reconstructed so as to preserve leadership as a concept.

4

Social Services in the Press

INTRODUCTION

When social workers recount their adversarial relationship with the news media, the critical precipitating event is usually said to be the 1973 criminal trial and official enquiry that followed the death of Maria Colwell and the subsequent official enquiry. Maria, aged seven years, was killed by her stepfather while she was in the care of the local authority.

The case attracted very extensive publicity both nationally and locally and established a template of news coverage which was applied again when three similar cases occurred over a short period in the mid-1980s. Essentially the deaths of Jasmine Beckford, Tyra Henry and Kimberley Carlile were represented as preventable, if only the departments concerned had been better managed and co-ordinated and the workers involved had been more expert, more experienced and better supervised. In short, social services should have intervened more. Yet the Cleveland crisis of 1987 (when suspicions of sexual abuse within families led to large numbers of children being taken into care) and similar events in Rochdale and the Orkney Islands resulted in the excoriation of social services for taking children into care by intervening too much.

In none of these cases was there any suggestion that the staff or departments had acted in other than good faith. By contrast, during the 1990s there has been real scandal: a series of court cases in which social services staff have been accused of serious, long-term, sexual abuse of young people in their care. Surely the combination of breach of trust, policy failure and sexual wrongdoing would attract the most vitriolic press coverage? In fact these dreadful events have been downplayed or ignored, particularly in those papers which social workers fear most, the mass tabloids. This may, at least in part, reflect the legal prohibition against naming either the perpetrators or survivors of abuse, but this neglect also suggests that it is not simply the intrinsic characteristics of an event that determine whether and how the news media will take it up. The explanation lies in the economics and politics of newspapers themselves.

NOT LOW PROFILE BUT NO PROFILE

The fact that all the instances mentioned above relate to social work with children is not haphazard, but fundamental. Social work becomes news because it is about the politics of the family as we can see from a major aspect of social services work that is almost entirely ignored by the press, even when mistakes are made, like the care of elderly people.

For instance, when the local government ombudsman criticised the London Borough of Hammersmith and Fulham for failing to meet the needs of a confused elderly resident, only the *Guardian* covered the story.

After a resident had lain dead for six weeks in her Wirral Borough Council sheltered home, the council ordered an enquiry but only the *Daily Telegraph* reported it. An 'important test case' in the High Court in which a group of residents in local authority homes tried to establish their rights seems to have been entirely ignored by the national press.

Why then, was the possible closure of several local authority elderly persons' homes the subject of a very high-profile campaign in the Nottingham *Evening Post* from late 1991 to mid-1992? Two aspects of the news treatment provide the key. First, that it was never placed within a 'social work' frame. The dispute was reported as a matter of local politics, while the staff were portrayed as quasi-family 'carers'. (Social services management hardly got a mention.)

Second, the elderly people at the centre of the furore were rendered almost entirely passive in the construction of stories, the use of language and in pictures: '"Tearful pleas from Beattie, 99"; "Why can't they leave us alone?"'- a resource to trigger an emotional response.

The 'address' was not to readers in the same situation but to younger people in their capacity as voters, employees or family members. When the issue re-emerged during the summer of 1998 the *Evening Post's* focus was on closure as an employment dispute. This time residents were almost invisible.

'He Let Her Die'

Social workers dread that, whatever the complex actuality, the death of a child in care will lead to sensational press coverage organised round 'the search for blame'. This belief has some foundation. Between 1985 and 1987 some of the newspaper treatment at the conclusions of three very highly-publicised trials represented the supposed errors of social workers as almost equivalent to the guilt of the convicted person.

Martin Ruddock, as the child's social worker, gives a paradigmatic account of being a key witness in the Kimberley Carlile case: massed photographers outside the court, the 'door-stepping' of his family, and 'fishing expeditions' for background information. At the end of the trial, he writes, the *Daily Star* published a seven-page shock issue in which his picture was placed alongside those of her stepfather and her mother with the caption 'He let her die'. Reports on the earlier death of Tyra Henry had attributed supposed blame in less personal terms, but nevertheless all sectors of the press assumed that there had been avoidable errors: 'Life sentence for Tyra's father' was the front page-lead in the *Daily Telegraph* with a subsidiary story headed 'Row over who was to blame'.

The *Daily Express* devoted its first three pages and entire editorial to the trial outcome, including an item headlined 'Probe reveals basic blunders'. The editorial talks of 'bumbling amateurism' and workers being 'fobbed off or fooled' while the *Sun* had a banner across pages two and three in white-on-black: 'Our deadly blunders'.

Like the Kimberley Carlile case, the interpretive frame in the Tyra Henry coverage closely matched that of the Jasmine Beckford trial in early 1985. This is not, however, to be understood simply in terms of lazy journalism or unimaginative editorial mind-sets.

The intensity and tone of the coverage was crucially linked to the political context of the mid-1980s, when the Conservative government under Margaret Thatcher was at its most confident and radical. Local government was the crucial terrain of conflict as a number of very vocal Labour-led local authorities were pursuing left-wing policies around issues of 'race', gender and sexual orientation. These 'loony left' councils provided a perfect ideological target to mask the more prosaic central government goal of reducing central government contributions to local authority spending in order that direct taxation could be reduced.

All three cases referred to above took place in left-wing London boroughs; in two of them the local politics of 'race' was central. Both Jasmine Beckford and Tyra Henry were African-Caribbean.

The professional and organisational conflicts and confusions surrounding their lives and deaths reflected intense controversy over how child protection practice should adapt to a multi-ethnic and multi-cultural population.

Antagonisms between elected members, senior officers and staff in the London Borough of Lambeth, culminating in a strike by frontline staff, enlarged the news value of the Tyra Henry case well beyond the trial, particularly in the broadsheets. In the tabloid sector the racialisation of the case took a variety of forms from the pseudo-analytical 'Are black power politics costing the lives of children?' to the crude 'Animal gets life', simultaneously illustrating the discourses of otherness and dangerousness then being mobilised to legitimate the reconstruction of local government and social policy. If professional 'failure' was the sole driver of newsworthiness, condemnatory press treatment similar to that recounted above might be anticipated every time a child in care comes to harm. The pivotal importance of the political context is demonstrated by cases where, though they were apparently similar to those discussed above, media attention was low-key, short-lived, or even non-existent. Charlene Salt died in Oldham, Lancashire despite multi-agency involvement. After the trial verdict in October 1985, although there was extensive coverage in 'how could this happen?' mode, responsibility was placed firmly at the door of Charlene's parents. Later that year, the parents of an African-Caribbean boy were tried for manslaughter at Nottingham Crown Court.

It was reported that his mother had unsuccessfully approached social services for help, but despite the potential 'race' angle, national press coverage consisted of small factual items on inside pages.

Sudio Rouse was in the care of the Conservative-held London Borough of Croydon when she died. The subsequent murder trial in 1991 was covered extensively in the national press (perhaps because of its geographical accessibility and some of the grim details of the child's death) but with no editorial comment and general acceptance of the director of social services' assurances that an internal enquiry had resolved any problems of practice.

'Simply a Terrible Botch'

Between March and September 1990 Rochdale Social Services took legal measures to protect seventeen children from suspected ritual abuse. In mid-September it was announced that there would be no prosecutions, for lack of criminal evidence. The social services committee asked for a report on practice from the central government Social Services Inspectorate (SSI). In March 1991, after a case in the High Court lasting three months, ten of the fifteen children still in care were returned to their parents. The court judgement contained very adverse comments on aspects of the social work intervention.

Nearly a decade later, many of the positions taken up during the Rochdale events seem less secure. While Jean La Fontaine found no evidence of links between Satanism and child abuse, the uncovering of the systematic sexual abuse of children and young people has occurred with ghastly regularity.

As Kitzinger claims, however, the contemporary hysteria about paedophilia has constructed it as 'stranger danger' rather than involving family members. In Rochdale parental rights were being challenged. The Rochdale events raised very complex issues of law and evidence. What is particularly notable about the press coverage is the drive to simplify and to accept 'common sense' attitudes and explanations, even in newspapers addressing a sophisticated professional audience, like the *Guardian*.

The coverage in the *Daily Telegraph* was more even-handed, providing a very detailed account of the legal judgement and allowing a 'voice' not only to aggrieved parents but also to members of the social work agencies involved. Two factors may account for this curious reversal. First, the *Guardian* was originally based in Manchester and still has a strong presence (and source of intelligence) in the north west through its sister the *Manchester Evening News*.

Over Rochdale, it adopted the style of a local paper, identifying with the local community. Consequently, second, it may have responded more sympathetically to several pressure groups representing parents which pursued a well-organised media relations strategy, possibly including the leaking of the SSI report. Its response to the High Court judgement was harsh and unequivocal 'Rochdale: simply a terrible botch'. The paper interprets the judgement as establishing that there had been no abuse. In fact social services were criticised for their failure to produce an evidentially sound basis for their actions in most (but not all) cases-hardly the same thing. The *Daily Mail* had no problems with complexity. From the start its accounts were inscribed with support for the parents and scorn of the local authority's actions: '"Satan case"' parents in clear, say police', another instance of treating lack of robust proof as equivalent to disproof.

The SSI report was represented as having been demanded by central government and being utterly condemnatory, whereas it was neither. On 8 March 1991 the High Court judgement was given most of the front page, supported by editorial drawing parallels with the 'scandalous oppression of innocent parents' which had previously occurred in Cleveland.

Alongside the editorial was a feature about allegedly Trotskyite councillors in the London Borough of Lambeth. Neither the *Sun* nor the *Daily Mirror* covered the case as extensively as the broadsheets and mid-market tabloids, nor in such partisan terms.

'Four pages of Utterly Compelling Reading'

After several separate police investigations over more than a decade, in 1991 Frank Beck was tried (with two other defendants) on sixty charges of rape, buggery and sexual assault against young people resident in the local authority homes that he had worked in and managed. His victims included staff as well as residents, women and men.

Beck was sentenced to life imprisonment (and died of a heart attack in prison). Leicestershire County Council had already set up an independent internal enquiry. At the end of the trial the Secretary of State ordered a national enquiry and a further internal investigation. The matter was also referred to the Police Complaints Authority.

The Beck case demonstrated that social workers could be not merely 'amateurish' but criminal wrong-doers and that their managers might have failed to stop them. Given previous denunciations of state social work in the press, the logical inference would be that the trial and its aftermath would be-literally-front-page news.

Moreover, earlier the same year investigative journalism for a television documentary and by the *Independent* had uncovered inhumane (but not criminally deviant) practices in Staffordshire children's homes, also accompanied by ignorance or tolerance on the part of managers and elected members. News of Alan Levy and Barbara Kahan's report on the 'pindown' affair had been extensive and, in a well-established pattern of news media operation, had 'sensitised' newspapers to similar controversies elsewhere in the UK. Residential social work was on the news agenda. In fact, the press treatment of the Frank Beck trial was relatively low-key in relation to its implications. While the ten-week case was in progress, national press interest was sporadic, triggered by Beck himself giving evidence and by allegations about a local MP.

Despite the sensational nature of the charges, there was more consistent reporting of the trial in the broadsheets than either mid- or mass-market tabloid newspapers. At the beginning of the Beck trial there had been legal restraints on reporting (as there had in Rochdale) the lifting of which was news in itself. As far as can be established, however, after the verdict and sentencing there was no reason not to print the kind of background and 'colour' stories typical of other major trials, like the cases of Charlene Salt and Rikki Neave.

In the Leicestershire scandal, moreover, much useful material was presented readymade to the news media by the publication of the Newell internal enquiry report, a detailed saga of management incompetence.

The *Leicester Mercury,* which had covered the case extensively almost every day under a linking logo, produced a pull-out supplement: 'Today we publish the secret report on the Beck years of evil; four pages of utterly compelling reading'.

In the national newspapers sampled, however, only the *Independent* put the case on page one, where it appeared as a descriptive 'hard news' item, without editorial comment. Nor did the *Daily Mail* make any explicit comment, although its page-two coverage gave more space to 'Blunders over Beck' than to the case itself. The *Daily Mirror*'s presentation was dramatic, but on page nine, while the *Sun* provided extensive text but also in hard news format only and on page seven.

TEN YEARS ON PROBATION

During the mid-1980s, when other agencies of state social work found themselves with a high and very unwelcome media profile, the probation service in England and Wales was almost invisible. In two of the instances of the death of a child in care referred to above the accused man was under the supervision of the service, but neither the work done, nor the effectiveness of probation itself were questioned.

Only once has a probation officer been subjected to media accusations of personal responsibility for an avoidable tragedy. The conviction of Colin Evans, in December 1984, for the sexual assault and murder of Marie Payne (aged four years) was given very extensive coverage in all the national newspapers. At the end of the trial the *Sun* devoted five pages to it and the *Daily Star* nearly six. At the trial it emerged that Colin Evans had a very long record of sexual offences yet his supervising probation officer had introduced him to a Christian voluntary organisation without informing them of his record. This conferred respectability with other social work agencies and users which allowed Evans to set up a babysitting organisation (unconnected, however, with Marie Payne's death).

All the newspapers criticised the probation officer in trenchant and personal terms; all but three printed a photograph of him. The case also reverberated politically, with members of parliament demanding that a register of sex offenders be set up.

While most of the national press followed up the policy and politics of the case, only the *Daily Mail* news and editorial treatment questioned the *idea* of probation work. It located the issue in a much wider frame: the 'scandalous leniency' of the whole apparatus of social control: 'Our courts, our probation and social services, our schools and education authorities cannot toy tolerantly with violators and corrupters of youth'.

In a classic example of the *Mail's* technique of imputing guilt by juxtaposition this editorial shared the page with a feature claiming that London supply (temporary replacement) teachers were left-wing failures and misfits. Condemning the probation service as practitioners of social work has been a unique theme in the *Daily Mail* which has been pursued relentlessly ever since. The paper is the most loyal in its support of the Conservative Party and a consistent advocate of conventional values, notably the patriarchal family and the strong state. According to the *Mail* almost all players in the criminal justice system are 'soft' and/or 'out of touch'.

Given the high political salience of law and order, the probation service's quiet life could not continue. Despite the Thatcher administration's well-cultivated reputation for toughness in relation to crime, Home Secretaries of the period favoured relatively liberal policies, including the wider use of 'community disposals'.

Consonant with the party's traditional position, however, a series of government policy documents and speeches from 1988 onwards required that probation work be more focused on concepts of punishment and control. No more 'clients', but 'offenders'. Both locally and nationally the probation service was directed simultaneously to toughen its image and to increase its visibility in the local community.

The Association of Chief Officers of Probation (ACOP) and the National Association of Probation Officers (NAPO) both responded by developing their media relations work. Given its greater financial resources and structural freedom as a trade union, NAPO had more success.

Among local probation areas the importance attached to promoting the service's work was very variable (and remains so). When it was actively pursued, though, it could generate just the kind of 'good news' in local media that had been demanded. In a three-month period of 1991, for example, a probation public relations officer working in the south west of England collected thirty-six items about his area, of which thirty-three were neutral or positive. When Michael Howard became Home Secretary, however, priorities changed dramatically.

From 1993 he played a key role in trying to re-establish Conservative credibility over law and order, under the slogan 'Prison works'. Clearly a policy centred on imprisonment has profound implications for the probation service, but Michael Howard's strategy was much more radical, not just uncoupling the probation service from social work, but eroding its autonomy by dismantling its training.

Inevitably his attempt to discursively reconstruct probation training and practice as flawed and the profession's response were pursued in part through the news media. Neither the Home Secretary nor probation professionals, ironically, gained the extent or type of press attention that they desired. 'More former soldiers and police officers are to be recruited to the probation service to dilute its "liberal do-gooding ethos"', reported the *Guardian* in response to a Home Office briefing, as the future tense construction clearly indicates. An announcement about the new form of professional training was expected by the autumn but did not appear. As subsequent events showed, the Home Secretary was finding that few interested parties shared his views about the probation service, so classic techniques of news management were deployed.

In the 'slow news' hiatus between Christmas 1994 and the New Year, the *Daily Mail* printed, across two pages, an 'exclusive' by the political editor headed 'Howard calls up the probation troops'. Doubts as to whether his proposals would gain public endorsement seem to have persisted.

As the *Guardian* pointed out the announcement was 'buried' by appearing on the same day (22 February) as the publication of a major policy document on Northern Ireland. Apart from the faithful *Daily Mail,* the only papers that reported the issue were *The Times* and the *Daily Express,* both in neutral hard news style, and the *Guardian* in a report dominated by dissenting voices.

Unfortunately for those in the probation service, this lack of press response continued during their campaign against the dismantling of their training system. Like the Home Secretary, NAPO and other stakeholders were attempting mobilise support.

Their hope was that the broadsheets would take up the issue and stimulate a response from politicians and other sections of the 'policy community'. Though unlikely, coverage in the tabloid press would be very welcome as it would confirm that probation training was a public issue that might result in political embarrassment. Even NAPO did not expect active support from the real 'public': as so often the press reaction was being used as a surrogate for public opinion. The campaign lasted for most of 1995, but neither a major House of Lords debate featuring three former Home Secretaries, and expressing almost unanimous hostility to the training proposals, nor a mass lobby of parliament by probation staff attracted significant national press coverage. The demonstration was widely reported in local media which, though important for morale, is not significant in terms of national policy and politics. NAPO's final tactic was to challenge the Home Secretary's proposals through judicial review but it lost the case in February 1996. As this deviated from a run of defeats for Michael Howard in UK and EU courts, it had a certain novelty value and was reported in all the broadsheets. The probation training saga was arcane, protracted-lasting over three years-and appeared to affect directly only a very small number of people. It was never going to be newsworthy for mass tabloid papers. According to NAPO, even the broadsheets seemed to find it 'dry', despite its significance for other professional groups in a close relationship to the state.

Looking back, it is likely that the real problem for the defenders of probation training was that it remained an abstract policy matter. It was never transformed into party politics, a domain deeply incorporated into the structures and daily routines of newspapers where, vitally, issues can be dramatised and personalised. The Labour party, then in opposition, resisted the Home Secretary's attempts to dismantle probation training without a House of Commons debate, but it maintained an ominous silence on the substance. In government Labour, far from reversing the training changes, carried out a review of the whole probation service.

The resulting consultation document appeared in August 1998 proposing far more swingeing changes than those pursued by Michael Howard, including making probation officers into civil servants and thus directly answerable to central government. The preoccupation with corporate profile persisted: a key part of the review process had been the search for a new, 'tougher' name for the service. Apparently Jack Straw had thought better of his earlier enthusiasm for 'reviving the old-fashioned title "corrections service"'. Instead, finding a name formed part of the public consultation process. It appears, however, that the probation service remains stubbornly lacking in news value.

Of the papers sampled on 7 August 1998 the government's announcement of the policy and consultation process was covered by the *Guardian* with a news items and adverse opinion piece, only as straight news by the *Daily Telegraph* (page 2) and the *Daily Mail*, not at all in the *Sun*, and on page 15 of the *Mirror* where a two-sentence box headed 'Name is on probation' opens 'Ministers are asking the public to think up a new name for the Probation Service, because they can't'.

Even the *Daily Mail*, under the heading 'Probation service gets a macho makeover' expresses an uncharacteristic mix of irony and scepticism. In the reflexive world of postmodern promotional politics, even senior ministers cannot guarantee a result.

APPLICATION OF SPECIAL PRESS PRIVILEGES

Professional journalists have a privilege under some state laws and, possibly, under the First Amendment, against being compelled in court to name sources. This privilege helps journalists to get information, and thereby bolsters the free press as a check on government abuse. The privilege was widely discussed in connection with a special prosecutor seeking testimony from reporters in his investigation of the leak of classified information that Valerie Plame was a CIA agent.

The question for present purposes is the extent to which amateur journalists should have any such privilege. This issue goes to the heart of the distinction between amateur and professional journalists.

If amateurs are likely to contribute inaccurate or otherwise low-value speech, society should not encourage their activities by making it easier for them to get information.

On the other hand, if, as argued earlier, amateurs are subject to reputational and other sanctions and supplement the information and views of professional journalists, the law should encourage their activities by giving them privileges and protections similar to those of professional journalists.

The journalist's privilege directly implicates the public choice considerations discussed earlier. Extending the privilege to include amateurs would arguably weaken it as to both professionals and amateurs.

This applies both to constitutional arguments and to efforts to enact a federal journalist's privilege. Journalists' only political hope for an absolute privilege may be a bright line between amateurs and the professional media, even if the better policy result is a weaker privilege that extends to both categories. A leading case on this issue is Apple Computer, Inc. v. Doe 1, which denied a blogger a protective order that would have prevented him from having to disclose sources in a trade secret suit brought by Apple. The blogger claimed he was privileged as a journalist.

The court denied the motion, noting that "[d]efining what is a 'journalist' has become more complicated as the variety of media has expanded." It quoted a dictionary definition of "journalist" as "a writer who aims at a mass audience." The court, however, said it need not decide whether the blogger "fits the definition of a journalist, reporter, blogger, or anything else" because "there is no license conferred on anyone to violate valid criminal laws."

If the court had recognized a journalist's privilege under these facts, the movant may have been held entitled to its protection. The blogger described himself as having "co-founded the first dedicated Apple Power Book User Group... in the United States... has contributed articles to MacWEEK, MacWorld, MacAddict, MacPower(Japan)... [and] written chapters for The Macintosh Bible." Some elements of the definition quoted above suggest the need for a "mass" or "public" audience. The movant was certainly more than a casual contributor. But this case leaves the question whether the privilege should be available to someone who blogs only to express himself.

Spurred largely by the Plame controversy, Congress is considering a federal shield law, the Free Flow of Information Act, that would protect journalists from revealing sources except under designated circumstances.

The bill would apply to a person who, for financial gain or livelihood, is engaged in gathering, preparing, collecting, photographing, recording, writing, editing, reporting, or publishing news or information as a salaried employee of or independent contractor for a newspaper, news journal, news agency, book publisher, press association, wire service, radio or television station, network, magazine, Internet news service, or other professional medium or agency which has as 1 of its regular functions the processing and researching of news or information intended for dissemination to the public.

Congressmen have expressed reservations about applying the bill to bloggers. Senator John Cornyn said he doubted "whether the proposed shield law should apply to the 'Internet blogger who has a cell phone with a camera, and maybe a laptop computer, and can publish with equal ease as a journalist,'" and Senator Richard Lugar, the bill's primary sponsor, said "bloggers should 'probably not' be considered journalists." The most important question in deciding whether to apply the journalist's privilege to bloggers is whether bloggers should be deemed to serve an information function similar to that of journalists.

As stressed throughout this Chapter, although individual bloggers lack the checks and balances of journalists, amateur journalism as a whole is capable of self-correction that can produce equivalent accuracy. Moreover, the openness of blogs avoids the biases that can infect professional journalism.

On the other hand, these considerations might not support the extraordinary protection of shield laws and constitutional privileges. Indeed, they may cut the other way. As long as amateur journalism thrives, it may be unnecessary to offer privileges to individual bloggers. Indeed, even a professional journalist's privilege may be unnecessary in a world that includes bloggers.

Moreover, extending the journalist's privilege too broadly may involve the special danger of broadly disabling investigation of harmful or criminal behaviour. Thus, it may be necessary to ensure that the privilege is available only to those who are subject to strong professional norms and reputational sanctions, even if this distinction risks reinforcing professional biases.

Shield law politics also matters in evaluating potential legal approaches. Republicans, though apparently reluctant to protect them through a shield law, have urged strong protection of bloggers from the election laws. In the case of the election laws, the relevant speech may favour a particular viewpoint. However, with respect to the shield laws no one can know who might be called on to provide information to prosecutors. This disparity of treatment indicates that the regulation of amateur journalists may be at least partly content-oriented rather than based on the method of speech. Whether this disparity raises First Amendment concerns, one should keep in mind these public choice considerations when considering how to approach legal regulation of amateur journalism.

These political and policy considerations suggest that the best result would be no federal law, leaving any protection to the laboratory of state law. Most states already have shield laws, which may or may not apply to blogs. National uniformity is unnecessary.

The applicable state shield law can supply a default contractual term in dealings between the media and the source. A source who wants anonymity can go to journalists who work in a state with a strong state shield law.

Without federal statutory law or constitutional constraints, states can decide on their preferred tradeoffs between the accuracy costs of protecting sources and the increased information that results from protection. Because the Internet facilitates quick dissemination of news from any source, the national interest in whether a particular state has a shield law is minimal except to the extent that newspapers based in a particular jurisdiction have a special role in gathering and disseminating particular news.

A related question is whether amateur journalists are entitled to any extra constitutional protection afforded by the "Press Clause" of the First Amendment. Paul Horwitz argues for protecting blogs under an "institutional" approach to the First Amendment that asks whether blogs play a role in furthering democracy that is comparable to that of the "Fourth Estate" of professional journalism. Horwitz reasons that this approach calls for an examination of the norms and characteristics of blogging as an institution.

The courts might give bloggers an extra journalist-type level of constitutional protection only to the extent that they participate in the collective accuracy-producing process discussed earlier, as by enabling comments and trackbacks, and adhere to the evolving accuracy-related norms of blogging. This approach might, however, encourage the development of professional-type constraints on the activities of amateur journalists that reduce the benefits of amateur journalism in avoiding the professionals' biases.

This discussion is intended only to indicate considerations that should be brought to bear in regulating blogs--in this case, determining whether amateurs should have the same privileges as professional journalists. These considerations involve balancing the lack of constraints on individual blogs against the information function of blogs in the aggregate. The difficulty of arriving at the proper balance across the vast range of blogs, together with the politics of regulating amateur journalism, suggest the propriety of a state rather than federal solution to the problem.

Election Laws

Campaign finance and other election laws may implicate considerations closely related to accuracy of information in assuring presentation of a diversity of views. Just as truth more likely emerges from many sources than from a single outlet, political decisions more likely reflect voters' preferences if voters and candidates can speak freely. Ability to speak, in turn, often depends on the ability to finance dissemination of one's views.

The application of the election laws to bloggers has been particularly controversial since the 2004 U.S. presidential election because of the perception that most bloggers supported the Republicans and affiliated causes.

Candidates might skirt campaign finance restrictions by coordinating with sympathetic bloggers. On the other hand, applying the election laws to millions of amateur journalists may require invasive regulation that could constrain amateurs' public access. The Federal Election Commission (FEC) attempted to avoid the issue by broadly exempting Internet activities. These exemptions were invalidated in Shays v. FEC. FEC Commissioner Bradley Smith then elicited a strong reaction when he suggested that political bloggers may be subject to the McCain-Feingold campaign finance law.

The main issue here concerns the "media exemption" from the definition of "expenditure" in the Federal Election Campaign Act:

The Term "Expenditure" does not Include

- Any news story, commentary, or editorial distributed through the facilities of any broadcasting station, newspaper, magazine, or other periodical publication....

Blogs may or may not be included in this definition depending on the emphasis on regularity in defining "periodical." Blogs raise at least three issues for regulation of campaign finance.

First, political campaigns might coordinate with bloggers who link to campaign web sites, thereby increasing the leverage of campaign expenditures. Second, corporations might establish and fund blogs and argue that the expenditures are excluded under the above provision.

Third, voters may not be able to determine when bloggers are paid for their opinions. Though this issue is potentially a problem in the professional media, it is harder to solve when readers must sort through millions of blogs.

One election law expert suggests that bloggers "should have to include on each blog page view a statement that the writing was paid for by the applicable candidate or committee."

As a policy matter, the election laws are supposed to address "corruption" of the political process by those with easy access to money. As a potential conduit of political money, blogs arguably are part of this problem. However, amateur journalists also can be viewed as part of the solution. When viewed on an aggregate rather than individual basis, the participation of many amateurs in political debate makes it harder for money to dominate. From this standpoint, any regulation must not discourage the proliferation of true political blogs. Requiring disclosures or imposing other restrictions and sanctions easily could reduce both the number and the diversity of political bloggers. Most political bloggers are motivated by the desire to express themselves rather than to make money through advertising or by selling their expertise.

They therefore generally may prefer not blogging to taking a significant risk of liability, paying for legal advice, or spending significant time complying with the law. Those who are not deterred may be a self-selected group with particularly strong views or links to campaigns. The market can solve some specific problems of coordination and bias even without regulation.

The large number of bloggers and low entry barriers to amateur journalism will guarantee that there are bloggers on all sides of political issues with significant self-expression incentives to expose cheaters. The risk of reputational harm may be enough to constrain the more influential bloggers, who also have the most reputation to lose, from damaging their credibility by maintaining excessive or secret connections with political campaigns.

These general considerations enable an evaluation of the FEC's recently proposed regulations of Internet activities, including blogging. An important issue the FEC grappled with is how the regulations should apply to corporate blogs. In general, little justification exists for restricting corporate contributions based on the need to constrain corporate "corruption" of the political process or agency costs within the firm.

Indeed, the real reason for regulating corporate campaign contributions is to protect corporations from "shakedowns." Blogs further complicate regulation of corporate campaign activities. Given the low-level incentives of many political bloggers, regulating" corporate" blogs could silence these voices and thereby give more power to, for example, large non-profit groups that so far are unregulated.

The FEC's final rules indicate a recognition of these costs of regulating blogs. The rules clearly exempt Internet campaign activities that involve "uncompensated personal services," "regardless of who owns the equipment and services" that the individual uses. This broad exemption avoids several questions that were raised by proposed rules that turned on whether the blogger was working "independently" and on who owned the computer on which she worked.

As with the other issues discussed in this Part, this analysis is intended only to indicate the considerations relevant to regulating amateur journalism. In particular, with respect to the campaign finance laws, one must keep in mind that proliferation of blogs may be part of the solution to any supposed "corruption" rather than part of the problem.

Media Ownership Restrictions

FCC limits on media ownership are intended to prevent undue industry concentration and ensure a diversity of viewpoints in every market. The FCC recently tried to rationalize these rules, but ran into a roadblock in Prometheus Radio Project v. FCC.

Regulation of media ownership in local markets is questionable, particularly given the many specialized information sources now available on the Internet, including the rise of blogs. As Judge Scirica, dissenting in Prometheus, noted: The FCC may want to reconsider how the Internet fits into the traditional concepts of measuring viewpoint diversity, especially the emphasis on local news. By nature, the Internet is uniform everywhere. Its content is not dependent on geographic or metropolitan boundaries. This fact should not undervalue this critical media as an important source for the dissemination of diverse information. In this respect, new modes to characterize diversity may be required. The Internet allows a dentist in Iraq to post a weblog with daily entries and photos from Baghdad for viewing anywhere in the world.

As with the campaign finance laws, blogs therefore can provide a solution to the perceived problem of big money corrupting public discourse, as long as they are not discouraged by excessive regulation.

Defamation Law

Amateur journalists, like other speakers, may be held liable for reputational injuries. The main question in this respect concerns the extent to which the First Amendment and laws protecting free speech insulate bloggers from liability and permit them to sue for defamation.

The most important case on many free speech issues relating to bloggers is Gertz v. Robert Welch, Inc., in which the Supreme Court held that states may permit defamation actions by a "private individual" based on negligence or other fault-based standards, whereas public officials or public figures must prove "actual malice." The Court reasoned:

Public officials and public figures usually enjoy significantly greater access to the channels of effective communication and hence have a more realistic opportunity to counteract false statements than private individuals normally enjoy. Private individuals are therefore more vulnerable to injury, and the state interest in protecting them is correspondingly greater.

An individual who decides to seek governmental office must accept certain necessary consequences of that involvement in public affairs. He runs the risk of closer public scrutiny than might otherwise be the case....

Those classed as public figures stand in a similar position For the most part those who attain this status have assumed roles of especial prominence in the affairs of society. Some occupy positions of such persuasive power and influence that they are deemed public figures for all purposes. More commonly, those classed as public figures have thrust themselves to the forefront of particular public controversies in order to influence the resolution of the issues involved. In either event, they invite attention and comment.

Amateur journalism may force rethinking of this distinction. For example, Gertz indicates that a blogger who is prominent among amateur journalists, even if not generally in society, would be deemed as a result of his blogging activities to have "thrust [himself] to the forefront" of a controversy. One who defamed the blogger would then be judged under the lax actual malice standard. Also, the blogger may be deemed to have "effective opportunities for rebuttal" through his blog.

Even amateurs arguably have access to a public forum to "counteract false statements" and have opened themselves up for attack by publicly posting comments. The availability of self-help was emphasized in the leading case on defamation specifically in the blogging context, Doe v. Cahill. The Delaware Supreme Court held that an Internet service provider need not disclose a blogger's identity in a defamation case, stressing the access for rebuttal discussed in Gertz: The internet provides a means of communication where a person wronged by statements of an anonymous poster can respond instantly, can respond to the allegedly defamatory statements on the same site or blog, and thus, can, almost contemporaneously, respond to the same audience that initially read the allegedly defamatory statements. The plaintiff can thereby easily correct any misstatements or falsehoods, respond to character attacks, and generally set the record straight.

This unique feature of internet communications allows a potential plaintiff ready access to mitigate the harm, if any, he has suffered to his reputation as a result of an anonymous defendant's allegedly defamatory statements made on an internet blog or in a chat room. Bloggers' public access, however, may be more apparent than real because it depends not just on being able to plug into the Internet, but also on the informal screening of Google and other search engines that enable readers to find the blog.

The courts might take blog rankings into account for purposes of determining public figure status and damages, or emphasize the blog's importance within a subcommunity that is relevant for reputation purposes. Additional questions remain concerning the extent to which amateur journalists are entitled to the same level of protection from defamation actions that professional journalists receive. The Press Clause of the First Amendment supports special treatment for the "press," but whether amateur journalists would qualify remains unclear.

Dun and Bradstreet, Inc. v. Greenmoss Builders, Inc. raised questions about a possible distinction between the journalists and other reporters that might be relevant to blogs. The Court held that a private individual could recover for defamation in a credit report, applying Gertz to a statement that was not a "matter of public concern." Justice White, concurring in the judgement, clarified that "the First Amendment gives no more protection to the press in defamation suits than it does to others exercising their freedom of speech."

On the other hand, Justice Powell's plurality opinion noted that the speech here, like advertising, is hardy and unlikely to be deterred by incidental state regulation. It is solely motivated by the desire for profit, which, we have noted, is a force less likely to be deterred than others.

Arguably, the reporting here was also more objectively verifiable than speech deserving of greater protection. In any case, the market provides a powerful incentive to a credit reporting agency to be accurate, since false credit reporting is of no use to creditors. Thus, any incremental "chilling" effect of libel suits would be of decreased significance.

This reasoning suggests that the Court might give a higher level of First Amendment protection to amateur than to professional journalists because the former have less robust self-expression motives for speaking. Distinguishing professional and amateur journalists for purposes of defamation actions may be particularly important in applying state statutes that provide protection from defamation lawsuits if the publisher retracts the allegedly defamatory statement.

For example, in Mathis v. Cannon, the Georgia Supreme Court applied the Georgia retraction statute to a posting on an Internet bulletin board. The statute covered a statement "in a regular issue of the newspaper or other publication." A lower-level Georgia court had held that the statute applied only to print media.

The Cannon court noted that the legislature had amended the statute to substitute "other publication" for "magazine or periodical." The court held that a "distinction between media and non-media defendants... is difficult to apply and makes little sense when the speech is about matters of public concern" and "fails to accommodate changes in communications and the publishing industry due to the computer and the Internet."

The court also observed that a broad reading of the statute would avoid having to make difficult distinctions about covered publications "at a time when any individual with a computer can become a publisher." The court cited Justice White's concurring opinion in Dun and Bradstreet as to the inappropriateness of distinguishing among types of speakers. The court concluded that its ruling "strikes a balance in favour of 'uninhibited, robust, and wide-open' debate."

Although the above reasoning generally would support giving full protection to all Internet speakers, including bloggers, some of the court's reasoning applies specifically to the retraction context.

The court noted that punitive damages may be fairer against the media than against an individual, who may reach only a small audience and whose retraction would likely target the same small audience. Finally, the extent of bloggers' liability for comments placed by others on their blogs is unclear. An advantage of blogs is interactivity, particularly blog posts' ability to evolve through comments and trackbacks.

Although professional journalism on the Internet has incorporated similar features, professionals' need to protect intellectual property rights might limit how much interactivity they can provide. Blogs' interactivity, however, may decline if amateurs are held liable for statements by others.

Bloggers and other journalists may have federal protection under section 230 of the Communications Decency Act against defamation liability for publishing material written by others. This provision has been held, for example, to protect America Online (AOL) from liability for statements by others it disseminates. A blog author may be a "provider or user of an interactive computer service" under the Act who is insulated from liability for a comment on her blog on the ground that the comment is "information provided by another information content provider."

The Act defines an "interactive computer service" as any information service, system, or access software provider that provides or enables computer access by multiple users to a computer server, including specifically a service or system that provides access to the Internet and such systems operated or services offered by libraries or educational institutions.

A blog that enables comments might fall within this definition as an "information service" or, through the blogging front-end, "access software provider" equivalent to an Internet hosting service. In either case, the blog would be "provid[ing] or enabl[ing] computer access by multiple users to a computer server." If a blog is within the definition, the author would be insulated from liability irrespective of knowledge or notice of defamatory content or other facts. The provision mainly has been applied to AOL-type internet service providers (ISPs) that provide a neutral medium. Broadening the application significantly beyond ISPs raises many questions about the law's potential breadth, and could make significant inroads on state defamation law.

On the other hand, broad application to web sites that incorporate comments or postings from third parties arguably would comport with Congress's stated purpose "to preserve the vibrant and competitive free market that presently exists for the Internet and other interactive computer services." Congress clearly sought to prevent this medium from being strangled by the potential for open-ended liability.

Imposing extensive responsibility for the accuracy of Internet posts could force firms like AOL, which serve millions of users, to sharply reduce the Internet's freedom. Bloggers who enable comments would not seem to face an equivalent mass-liability problem. But here again one must consider bloggers' low-level incentives.

Although bloggers derive enough value from self-expression to risk liability for their own statements, they may not want to take responsibility for others' statements. If bloggers are not protected, they thus might decline to take the liability risk of enabling comments. This outcome would reduce blogs' interactivity and perhaps even blogs' accuracy because comments enable corrections by disinterested readers. As with application to AOL, this would thwart the Internet's potential as a free and open market for information.

A case applying section 230 to bloggers' liability for comments, DiMeo v. Max, is consistent with this analysis. The court dismissed a suit alleging that the plaintiff was defamed by comments written by others on defendant's web site. The court held that the web site fit the definition of an "interactive computer service." The court also held that defendant did not lose his protection by exercising editorial control over comments on his site because such a result "would deter the very behaviour that Congress sought to encourage."

The point here as elsewhere in this Chapter is not to draw definitive conclusions as to the extent of amateur journalists' liability, but to suggest the considerations that courts should bring to bear in adjudicating legal issues concerning amateur journalists.

Most importantly, courts should take into account the low-level incentives of amateur journalists, and therefore the significant potential deterrent effect of liability. They should also evaluate accuracy in light of the self-corrective and interactive nature of amateur journalism. Finally, courts should assess bloggers' ability to self-protect based on whether they are likely to be noticed and not simply on their access to the Web.

Professional Regulation

Blogs may be subject to regulation as professional practice or advice. Although the following discussion focuses on lawyer licensing, it is generally applicable to other professions, such as medicine or investment advice. Blogs on legal subjects raise potential issues as to whether they:

- Constitute unauthorized law practice by a non-lawyer;
- Might be unauthorized practice in a state other than where the lawyer is licensed;
- May be regulated as impermissible lawyer advertising.

The first two types of problems seem remote with respect to the sort of amateur journalism that is the focus of this Chapter. In the Internet context, the courts have defined legal advice for purposes of unauthorized practice of law as involving individualized legal services rather than generalized information such as self-help kits. This suggests that an answer to a specific legal query on a listserve might constitute practicing law, but a web site that includes general legal discussions probably would not.

Even if courts extend unauthorized practice laws beyond individualized legal services, they should hesitate to cover general statements in lawyer blogs. This conclusion follows from the policies underlying lawyer licensing. The classic argument in favour of lawyer licensing is that the law should address information asymmetries between lay people and professionals in the rendition of professional services. States accordingly prescribe standards as to who is qualified to give this advice, and regulate the conduct of those who are licensed to give it. Licensing standards are only rough proxies for the quality of legal services and might skeptically be viewed as the product of the lawyer's cartel, serving mainly to hinder access to legal services by low-income people.

Even if some licensing laws are defensible, these laws should not be designed so as to deter speech that would alleviate information asymmetries in professional advice. Lawyer blogs can enable consumers of legal services to evaluate legal advice or inform them as to whether they need to see a lawyer.

To be sure, there is a danger that blogs might contain incorrect legal advice. This risk might be reduced by screening out those who do not have certain minimum professional credentials.

However, blogs are subject to correction by other blogs and by commentary. Moreover, applying licensing laws to blogs might lead to an adverse selection problem: practicing lawyers, whose blogs may be most valuable, are most likely to be deterred by the threat of unauthorized practice liability outside their home state, whereas non-lawyers, whose legal advice is least valuable, are least likely to be deterred by these laws. An alternative justification for lawyer licensing is to give lawyers the incentive to invest in the development of law by giving them a quasi-property right in the law of the state in which they are licensed. Applying licensing laws to blogs, however, is unnecessary to protect this investment.

Lawyer bloggers are mainly concerned with marketing their main business in the states where they are licensed, whereas non-lawyer bloggers' offhand legal-type statements are seriously unlikely to threaten lawyers' businesses.

An important aspect of applying professional licensing statutes to lawyer blogs concerns advertising restrictions. For example, Kentucky attempted to apply a rule charging fees for lawyer advertising to lawyer blogs. Whether or when blogs that do not directly advertise a lawyer or firm will be deemed to be advertising remains unclear.

As with the application of unauthorized practice laws to blogs, applying restrictions on professional advertising would be inconsistent with the analysis. Restrictions on lawyer advertising, like licensing laws in general, address laymen's inability to assess the quality of legal services. But enabling proliferation of blogs and comments, and the reputational constraints on bloggers, also can effectively address this asymmetry.

For example, a law firm's blog that discusses a legal issue in order to encourage readers to use the firm's services will expose the firm to commentary and refutation if its advice is erroneous. This exposure gives the firm an incentive to be careful about what it says.

As in the other legal areas discussed in this Part, the application of professional licensing rules to amateur journalism should take account of economics of blogging discussed in this Chapter. To the extent that licensing laws are intended to address information asymmetry, courts and regulators should consider blogs' aggregate information value and not just the potential inaccuracy of individual blogs.

Blogs as Commercial Speech

Regulation of blogs may involve significant First Amendment problems. For example, Kentucky's attempt to charge fees for lawyer advertising on blogs was criticized on this basis. The Supreme Court has applied the First Amendment in striking down overbroad regulation of attorney advertising, citing the information functions of these communications. For the reasons discussed earlier, this concern is particularly applicable to blogs.

The main First Amendment question regarding blogs is whether and under what circumstances they might be entitled only to the lower level of constitutional protection given "commercial speech." A blog might be "commercial" if it cross-promotes another business and thereby directly proposes commercial transactions, but not if it is primarily devoted to the author's personal opinions on politics and culture. The commercial speech doctrine provides little theoretical basis for drawing a line in marginal cases that have some commercial aspects. Indeed, the market for ideas arguably is constitutionally indistinguishable from other markets.

One feature of blogs ultimately may persuade the courts to take many of them out of the commercial speech category. Bloggers generally have low-powered reputational-type incentives rather than a strong profit motive, and therefore may be more deterred by regulation and the threat of penalties than conventional commercial speakers.

The Court's current distinction in Virginia State Board of Pharmacy v. Virginia Citizens Consumer Council, Inc. between commercial and non-commercial speech is based at least partly on the theory that profit-motivated speech is less likely to be chilled by regulation. This argument makes general economic sense.

However, it may not be useful in all cases, because many political speakers may have robust incentives, whereas many commercial speakers are agents who lack strong incentives to promote their firms' interests. But the chilling effect argument does apply generally to amateur journalists, who by definition lack strong economic incentives to speak and therefore may be easily deterred by regulation.

The fact that a blog carries advertising should not be enough to put it in the commercial speech category. Although the advertisements themselves are likely to be commercial speech, one who merely publishes the advertisements is not thereby proposing commercial transactions. Applying the commercial speech doctrine to all publications that carry advertising, including most newspapers and magazines, would swallow most First Amendment protection. Indeed, the media's ability to get paid to support its activities is arguably itself an important First Amendment right.

Thus, Judge (now Justice) Alito held for the Third Circuit Court of Appeals that Pennsylvania's attempt to bar alcoholic beverages ads in school publications was unconstitutional, reasoning in part that "[i]f government were free to suppress disfavored speech by preventing potential speakers from being paid, there would not be much left of the First Amendment."

Whether the blog carries advertising, however, may affect its level of First Amendment protection apart from the commercial speech issue. The potential chilling effect of regulation may matter on its own rather than as a rationale for applying the commercial speech doctrine. The Court's plurality opinion in Dun and Bradstreet cited as a reason for applying the lower level of Gertz protection to a credit report the argument from Virginia State Board of Pharmacy that for-profit speech is less likely to be deterred.

The credit report did not itself propose a commercial transaction, but merely had a commercial incentive. Following this reasoning, the Court may hold in a marginal case that, other things being equal, a blogger who sells ads is less likely to be deterred by speech regulation than one who blogs without direct monetary reward.

Distinguishing blogs based solely on whether they carry ads, however, may not be a sufficiently nuanced way to assess bloggers' incentives. Even non-advertising bloggers may reap financial rewards from cross-promoting their main businesses. Less directly, academic bloggers who do not have any "businesses" may receive tangible career rewards from blogging. Also, bloggers who are not currently selling ads may be exploring the market in preparation for doing so, or may eventually capitalize on their audience by selling their blogs. In general, the extent of constitutional protection of amateur journalism is a good example of how the regulation of blogs may depend on an understanding of the economics of blogging, particularly including bloggers' financial and non-financial incentives.

Fraud Liability

Misrepresentations on blogs may be subject to fraud liability, general consumer fraud statutes, or federal or state securities laws. The hybrid expressive/commercial nature of many blogs may raise reliance, materiality, and intent to defraud issues under these statutes. In other words, did the plaintiff, or would a reasonable person, rely on a statement casually made in a blog, and is it likely that the blogger intended to defraud? As with the commercial speech issue, the blogger's incentives may matter. For example, a reader may assume that a blogger who sells advertisements or is cross-promoting her main business is more motivated, and therefore should be taken more seriously, than a blogger whose postings are intended solely for self-expression purposes. Even if a statement in an individual blog satisfies the usual tests for fraud, the interactive nature of amateur journalism may matter to the scope of liability.

A statement that is false in isolation may not be materially false, or may not have triggered reliance, given immediate correction through comments and trackbacks and by other blogs. Again, the technology and economics of blogs should determine the extent of regulation. As has been the case for the other issues this Part addresses, this analysis is not intended to state a definitive rule, but rather to indicate some relevant considerations.

Vicarious Liability

A blogger might be vicariously liable for a statement of a co-blogger on a group blog. In particular, a group blog may be a partnership unless the bloggers have explicitly selected some other form. This categorization means that partnership default rules would apply to the relationship, including partners' personal liability for their copartners' wrongful acts. Liability for blog posts on the partnership's behalf might extend to intentional torts such as defamation. Such liability is significant to the extent that it may deter bloggers who have relatively weak self-expression incentives.

The resolution of this issue may partly depend on whether the blog is a "business," which is part of the definition of partnership under the partnership laws. That issue, in turn, may depend on whether the blog carries advertisements. Bloggers who generate a little income stream to help cover expenses probably lack the sort of high-powered incentives to maximize revenues and minimize costs that induce conventional partners to monitor each other.

Instead they may recognize that they have strong self-expressive reasons for blogging and therefore hesitate to interfere with each other's activities. Thus, even if courts characterize some group blogs as partnerships for vicarious liability purposes, they might require more evidence of control and other partnership indicia to compensate for the weaker profit motive.

A group blog whose writers share revenue from advertisements and expenses might be viewed as a profit-sharing relationship that is at least presumptively a partnership. On the other hand, the blog might be considered only a loose association created solely for promotional reasons, analogous to sole-practitioner lawyers who share a receptionist and office space.

Even this situation may create a liability depending on how the relationship was represented to clients. But given blogs' novelty and evolving nature and the lack of a common understanding as to the relationship among co-bloggers, it may be difficult to determine how co-blogging relationships are "represented" to the public. Group bloggers may argue that they had no interest in reviewing each other's posts and may even have a stated policy of not blocking posts they disagreed with. A court, however, might assume that the likely rationale for a group blog is to drive more readers towards each blogger's posts. This rationale requires some quality control, even if not in the strict hierarchical sense of a newspaper. If the blog also accepts advertising, it starts to look like a conventional profit-maximizing business. Courts therefore may deem group bloggers to have enough interest in co-bloggers' posts to have partner-like control.

A group blog also might be an agency relationship, as when a separate firm hires the bloggers and acts as the principal. This is probably the case for "corporate" blogs that have a blog-type format but in which, unlike the amateurs on whom this chapter focuses, the bloggers are full-time employees. In this situation the employing firm is liable for the bloggers' acts in the scope of employment.

Liability is more ambiguous when a separate firm such as Gawker or Weblogs aggregates previously independent bloggers into a group blog. These writers may not regard themselves as colleagues with common interests and may simply want to maximize their joint advertising revenue. They therefore may be only a loose federation of independent writers who have hired a common agent to sell advertising, similar to the group of lawyers that hires a common receptionist and shares office space discussed above.

The network also might be considered a separate employer, in which case the bloggers probably would be independent contractors rather than "servants" for whose acts the employer would be liable. That classification depends on whether, instead of the employer supervising the details of the writer's work, the blogger "commits himself to providing a specified output, and the principal monitors the contractor's performance... by inspecting the contractually specified output to make sure it conforms to the specifications." This description seems to fit a blogger who agrees only to contribute a general type of commentary but does not submit to detailed monitoring.

The argument for agency in the latter scenario is that the blogging network or aggregator is analogous to a newspaper, with the writers analogous to reporters for whose acts the employer would be liable.

Although the reporters resemble servant agents because they are employed and paid full-time rather than by the article, the problems inherent in a principal's supervising the work arguably are similar in both cases.

From an economics standpoint, the partnership and agency issues arguably depend on whether a blogger should be deemed to be in a good position as owner to monitor his or her co-bloggers. This general economic analysis of agency relationships, however, may not be appropriate in the context of blogging. The agency analysis assumes that the relevant monitoring occurs in the "vertical" or hierarchical relationship among the parties to the firm. But as stressed throughout this Chapter, blogs are monitored by other blogs through such interactive mechanisms as comments and trackbacks. Courts should take this characteristic into account in determining whether group bloggers should be liable for inaccuracies in each other's posts.

The extent to which vicarious liability may deter blogging depends on how easily bloggers may avoid this liability. They, of course, could simply decline to take on co-bloggers. But group blogs may be useful in attracting more readers to the posts of all group members. Group bloggers also might attempt to avoid liability by contracting explicitly that their relationship is not a partnership. But courts may hold in favour of partnership despite such provisions in which other indicia of partnership are present.

The group may deal with the above ambiguities and reduce the risk that their personal assets will be exposed to liability by purchasing insurance. However, insurance may not protect them from all liability, including liability for intentional torts. The bloggers might incorporate or form some other type of limited liability business association--a limited liability company, limited partnership, or limited liability partnership. The quality of the liability shield depends on whether the bloggers have maintained the appropriate formalities and facts that would support veil-piercing, including separation of business and personal affairs.

Even if the bloggers successfully limit their liability to the firm's assets, they may incur other costs from forming a limited liability firm, such as triggering the application of inappropriate partnership-type default rules. Thus, the availability of limited liability is not a complete solution to the risk of vicarious liability.

In general, as throughout this Part, this discussion is not intended to reach definitive conclusions on the law of amateur journalism, but only to show the considerations that courts should bring to bear based on the economics and technology of blogging. Given the social value of blogs, the opportunities that blogs present for self-correction and informal filtering, and bloggers' relatively low-powered incentives, courts should be wary about creating broad vicarious liability for co-bloggers. Even if a blog is technically a "business," its moonlighting and self-expressive nature mean that it should not be treated as the sort of business for which partnership-type vicarious liability is appropriate. Also, application of vicarious liability may constrain governance, as by deterring some types of monitoring that courts might view as partner-like conduct.

Harmful but Accurate Speech

Regulation of blogs that is intended to protect against harms other than those involving inaccurate speech may present problems distinct from rules intended to ensure accuracy. Speech that is obscene or infringes privacy or property rights in information can be harmful without being false. Permitting more of this type of speech will not necessarily reduce social harm by correcting error. Also, the harm in these situations can be done by any blogger, not just one who has garnered special access through trustworthiness.

This reality suggests that, for some types of harm, courts and regulators should distinguish non-professional bloggers from professionals. To be sure, professional journalists, like amateurs, care more about forfeiting their reputations for accuracy, which is an important value for many readers, than they would about other types of harm, such as invasions of privacy or abuse of proprietary information.

But professionals also must be concerned about their and their employers' reputations for respecting confidentiality and privacy in order to continue to have access to sources. Professionals and their employers thus have special incentives to protect their investments in information and to generally defend intellectual property rights.

Amateur journalists, by contrast, rely on commentary or on their own special sources of information. They are consumers, rather than producers, of the costliest and most valuable forms of intellectual property.

Conversely, as discussed throughout this chapter, the costs of regulating amateur journalists may exceed those of regulating professionals.

Because of their weaker economic incentives, amateurs may be more easily deterred than professionals by sanctions for infringing property rights and other harmful speech.

For example, a professional journalist could stifle criticism by amateurs by threatening to strictly enforce copyright against critics who excerpt or parody its work.

Special issues are raised by the application of copyright and trademark law to amateur journalists. As discussed above, blogs can serve as "remora" in adding value to professional media stories by checking on their accuracy and completeness.

Yet links and references to professional media raise questions concerning violation of copyright law. Los Angeles Times v. Free Republic held that posting Los Angeles Times and Washington Post articles on web sites constituted copyright infringement and was not protected as "fair use." This case illustrates the need to reach some accommodation with the professional press's property rights.

Although blogs may improve the health of the professional media, they also need the investigative reporting and other services that robust professional media provide. In other words, remora need sharks that are willing to invest in intellectual property. Professional media's incentive to invest depends on some legal protection from free-riding blogs. A reasonable compromise may be possible. Rather than reproduce the full article, the blogger can simply link to the article, which is the accepted practice. The source thereby can control and charge for access to the actual article. To be sure, linking may not be equivalent to copying. In particular, a writer who wants to "risk" an article or photo may rind no substitute for reproducing the entire document in the blog. Moreover, some outlets, such as the Wall Street Journal, charge for access, even free registration can be burdensome (as by opening the registrant to spam), and there are some copyright constraints on linking.

Professional media can decide whether blogs' parasitic function is worth encouraging by making the source material freely available. If blogs add value, and controlling or charging for access to the original material reduces that added value, professional media has an incentive to allow free linking or pasting. Larger media sources may have strong incentives to obtain competitive advantage by becoming nodes for networks of blogs. Blogs and other web sites that are motivated more by self-expression than commercial objectives may be willing to adopt Creative Commons licenses.

Some sites, however, may not adopt a formal policy. They may not be able to capitalize on the network advantages of blog commentary, or otherwise internalize the social benefits of making their material freely available. For these sites the private benefits of strict copyright protection may exceed the private costs.

This balance may leave a significant amount of intellectual property on the Web subject to the restrictions and uncertainties of copyright law. Because of their weaker profit incentives, amateur journalists may be reluctant to push the margins of copyright laws, particularly if they have substantial personal wealth and reputations to protect. This reluctance may significantly reduce the potential information advantages of blogs.

One possible solution is to raise the bar for default copyright protection. Alternatively, Congress might revise the fair use doctrine to better accommodate blogs, as by specifying that linking is not a violation unless the copyright owner clearly reserves linking rights. Either approach would place burdens on copyright owners to obtain strict protection. This condition would help ensure at least that this protection is reserved only for those owners who obtain the largest private benefits from protection.

As with the discussion of other legal issues in this Part, this analysis is intended to outline relevant considerations rather than to prescribe definitive rules. In particular, the interactivity of amateur journalism depends significantly on the ability to link and copy from other sources. This interactivity may require an accommodation of speech rights with protection of intellectual property. The relevant actors themselves may be able to work out the necessary rules. To the extent they cannot, the courts and Congress should do so, guided by the economics and technology of amateur journalism. Blogs are a relatively new medium that could have significant ramifications for several areas of the law.

In resolving these legal issues, it is important to consider the distinct technical and economic aspects of blogging. This Chapter is a modest beginning. It is important to keep in mind that the technology of the Internet and the Web in general and of blogs in particular is evolving rapidly. Amateur journalism may soon be very different from what it is today.

For example, authored blogs and authorless wikis might co-evolve into a hybrid that combines spontaneity and authorship. This potential development could have implications for the reputational bonding mechanisms emphasized in this chapter. Professional and amateur journalism might converge in ways that cannot now be predicted.

Thus, this Chapter can provide only a snapshot of amateur journalism's current phase of development. In order to be useful, an analysis of amateur journalism must focus on core principles that will continue to be relevant even if the technology changes.

The core of amateur journalism is open access and interactivity, in contrast to the more closed model of conventional bricks-and-mortar media firms. Open access has both benefits and risks that need to be taken into account in future regulation. In evaluating the risks, one must keep in mind that open access itself may serve as a self-corrective mechanism. Blogs, or whatever replaces them, therefore may be more an opportunity and a solution to the problems of bricks-and-mortar journalism than the problem Joel Klein's "pajamas" image suggests.

UNDERSTANDING SOCIAL WORK NEWS

National and local newspapers in the UK are run for profit and are free to be politically partisan. Indeed, the political sympathies of national daily papers are a crucial aspect of their identity and position in the market. The interplay of these two factors explains nearly everything about the press treatment of state social work. Obviously a newspaper needs readers. They pay directly for the product; the size and spending power of the readership determines advertising revenue.

No newspaper, therefore, can address itself primarily to sections of the population with little to spend. Even the mass tabloids, specifically pitched at 'ordinary folk' (a code for working class) are filled with news of and for people between young adulthood and middle age. They may not be well off but, typically, they are setting up households and having children.

Money is being earned and spent. Newspapers, in other words, have a powerful commercial interest in the family-based household which, by itself, explains their greater responsiveness to child protection work than to social work with elderly people or those with a mental illness.

As well as being economically crucial-and ever more so in a society driven more by consumption than production-the family is a key site of political cleavage, over the potentially competing rights of women and men, children and adults. This is the terrain on which state social work operates, so it is inevitable that professional practice will often be newsworthy, justified or not and skilful or not. The *Independent* is positioned as supporting children's rights and addresses a professional audience, hence the very extensive resources invested in the 'pindown' affair.

While the *Daily Mirror* concentrated only on the personal experience of those involved, it, too, implicitly supported a welfare system in which children are seen as having rights as well as needs.

Conversely, the *Daily Mail* powerfully and consistently promotes the conventional, patriarchal family where parents' (particularly fathers') rights prevail. The parents of the children subject to pindown did not feature as an organised voice in the controversy (unlike Rochdale) so the *Mail* showed little interest in this instance of social work failure.

If state social work were as accessible to families in difficulties as the NHS is intended to be for the sick, the cost would be commensurately huge. Most of the Conservative changes to the welfare state in the 1980s were intended to reconstruct welfare services as a minimal system of containment for failure and deviance, in which resources were concentrated on the 'dangerous'.

Apart from the struggles over local government and the politics of difference, already referred to, the cases of Jasmine Beckford, Tyra Henry and Kimberley Carlile were also politicised in this sense. Social workers were being accused of lack of expertise in identifying and controlling the 'other/them' on behalf of 'us'. Taken together with the very real drama and tragedy at the centre of the cases, extensive and melodramatic media coverage was not merely likely, but over-determined.

So social work with children will always be contested, but in recent years its significance as a political symbol and metonym has diminished. Cambridgeshire Social Services was heavily criticised during and after the trial in 1996 of Ruth Neave for the murder of her son Rikki (of which she was acquitted). It could not have been otherwise: social work's alleged failings were part of the defence case; the department had itself declared its practice as falling short; and further enquiries into its operation were ordered by central government.

Most press comment, however, did not target individual social workers, nor enlarge the issue any more than might be the case where, say, a health authority's failings were in the news. The *Daily Mail* devoted most of its two-page coverage to the allegedly obvious 'dangerousness' of Neave, including the curious accusation that 'By 16 she was having sex with men'.

Arguably, however, the Neave trial was big news because of other features of the case, notably allegations of drug use, witchcraft, threats and intimidation. At the conclusion of a much more brutal child murder case, the judge said 'The social services [Northeast Lincolnshire] have already instigated a wide-ranging internal enquiry into these matters-I don't think they are thorough enough'. Although all the papers sampled reported the verdict and sentence in the case, only the *Daily Mail*-'Boy of 4 taken off "at risk" roll killed by couple'-gave the social work and 'preventable death' motive prominence in its report.

The Rikki Neave trial also illustrates the different interpretive frame applied by local newspapers. While the national papers all reported the first and last day, there were only occasional reports during the intervening four weeks, ranging from six in the *Daily Mirror* to none in the *Daily Mail*.

The Peterborough *Evening Telegraph* covered the story every day, sometimes prominently and in detail. The outcome took up all of the front page and seven inside pages. A local paper, however, must appeal to the whole population, not a section defined by age, class and politics.

Accordingly, the editorial comment emphasises not individual blame but community responsibility for the events and for recovery: '...a shadow hangs over our city'. Everyone is given space to justify themselves, including social services. It is clear that Ruth Neave was a controversial figure: she pleaded guilty to five cruelty charges and was sentenced to seven years' imprisonment.

Nevertheless, the background features on her life and behaviour are complex and sympathetic. Similarly the material on Rikki Neave resists the 'tragic tot' reflex in favour of an account of a sad little boy from a difficult background.

Frank Beck's wrongdoing extended over many years beforehand, so the case failed to provide the staple materials for constructing satisfactory news stories. His victims had grown up and dispersed, making it very difficult to produce 'background' and 'colour' featuring either them or their parents. Nor did the young people comfortably fit the frame of innocent 'tragic tot'. One reason that it took so long for Beck to be challenged, according to the Police Complaints Authority report (1993), was that his victims had already been written off as deviants.

In the last analysis, however, the key to the mysterious silence over the Frank Beck case is that he raised too many questions about the solidity of the social and institutional order. This applied as much to the *Guardian,* with its investment in the possibility of professional trust and rational policy-making, as to the *Sun*. Cheeky irreverence cannot work without stable authority structures as both butt and boundary.

Deviance and conflict are central to news but newspapers' place in parliamentary democracy-to say nothing of their capitalist rationale-relies on social stability. That a well-respected local authority manager, local councillor and consultant on childcare methods could be behaving as Frank Beck did was too chaotic to be contained within conventional press narratives which, among other things, require a reassuring 'closure'.

Recent events have, unfortunately, simply verified this interpretation of the press response to the Frank Beck trial. A succession of similar cases, involving men working both in local authority and voluntary agency homes, has gone almost unreported in the national press, even though the Conservative government was worried enough to set up a tribunal chaired by a retired High Court judge. The Waterhouse enquiry began on 21 January 1997 (and heard evidence for a year and a half). As the *Independent* reported (22 January 1997) on its front page it was 'Britain's biggest child abuse enquiry: 650 cases, up to 80 staff involved at 30 homes'.

The other broadsheet reports were relatively low-key accounts of opening speeches, placed on inside pages. The *Sun* ignored it while the *Mirror* gave it three paragraphs and the *Daily Star* two. The *Daily Mail* devoted most of page 12 to the tribunal, foregrounding the possible culpability of social services management even though the remit covered the role of the Welsh Office and other agencies. The outcome of the Waterhouse enquiry will undoubtedly be a matter of profound public interest. As we have seen, though, this does not help us predict how the press will treat it.

That will be determined by a judgement as to whether it will interest their public. Politically and commercially it is safer to entertain and titillate, even to make readers indignant, than to take risks with their ontological security. Consequently, literally dozens of definitions for public relations exist in the literature. However, it is my contention that Bernays provided the best definition in his early writings. Bernays describes PR's key function as "the engineering of consent," or the ability to get diverse individuals with varying perceptions and values to come to a "consent to a programme or goal". Newsom, Scott and Turk have similarly referred to PR as a "broker for public support of ideas, institutions and people".

And there were plenty of opportunities for PR to attempt to build consensus among American publics in the late 1800s. Rex Harlow points out the mix of increasing industrialization (*e.g.*, the railroads) and "expansions in science, invention, commerce government, and communications" helped contribute to rising complexities. Then, Harlow makes an unmistakable allusion to how PR developed in great part to address fissions within American communities:

Under the impact of these swiftly moving... developments, individuals and institutions of all kinds were broken loose from their moorings and cast adrift upon a tide of uncertainty and uneasiness... the elements of fear and uncertainty made demands that brought public relations to the fore. Cutlip, Centre and Broom address how PR rose to the occasion:

To state that public relations has evolved from press-agentry, though a gross oversimplification (my emphasis), contains a kernel of truth. Systematic efforts to attract or divert public attention are as old as efforts to persuade and propagandize. Much of what we define as public relations was labeled press-agentry when it was being used to promote land settlement in our unsettled west. However, when addressing the push westward and the related need to build new western communities, PR faced an almost paradoxical situation; the westward move emphasized individualism. Says McDougall, "There was a struggle for existence, and the fittest did survive. Self-reliance... did flourish. Pioneers had to look to their own resources and efforts".

How could PR address the need for community-building in the new West, yet still respect individualism? One answer could be found in PR's attempts to further settlements near expanding railroad lines. PR's attempts to reach large groups of individuals and persuade them to move west would literally establish a public - a public of individuals. John Peters refers to this persuasion when he wrote, "...These representations can then invite [a dispersed people] to act as a unified body. This is where rhetoric comes in: it is the means of articulating common identity and belief".

It would be difficult to pick one moment where public relations established its presence and value within the railroad industry. However, one can make the case that the 1869 completion of the transcontinental railroad at Promontory Point, Utah, was PR's first high-profile opportunity. As guests and media were entertained with speeches, alcohol and the whistles of four locomotives, a golden spike was driven into the last tie.

The news was immediately telegraphed coast-to-coast. Notes Stover in The Life and Decline of the American Railroad, "A seven-mile parade began to move in Chicago, dozens of firebells rang out in San Francisco, and a magnetic ball dropped from a pole on top of the Capitol dome in Washington, D.C." Coming off of this success, PR was seen as a valuable aid to the railroads as they moved west and needed to sell government-granted lands to settiers. In fact, at one point shortly after the Promontory Point celebration, the railroads had full title to more than 133 million acres, the majority of it in states west of the Mississippi.

The railroads also understood, from earlier westward movements, that "many people traveled in caravans and settled as communities, although each family claimed its own plot of land". They also understood what historian Ray Allen Billington noted that these individual communities could be persuaded to act in an almost concerted manner: The migrations that peopled California and the Oregon country in the 1840s were induced not only by the usual impulses to escape an uncongenial homeland - but by one of the most effective promotional campaigns in history.

Historian J. Valerie Fifer refers to the same power of PR, when she says: Together the transport, tourist, and information industries played a crucial role in Western development... All brought new settlement... into the West... and stimulated the growth of a new spirit of American nationalism. Many of the early persuasive approaches taken by the railroads in the 1870s were covert.

The railroads used lobbyists and secret press agents to make their claims for routes and the related lands. Both the Burlington and Illinois Central railroads paid for books and newspaper and magazine articles that were to appear to be unbiased accounts. These lines would also pay for making reprints of the favorable articles and having them sent to thousands of media and VIPs - one mailing list had more than 30,000 "influentials."

A shift happened in the early 1880s. Because of the secrecy, efforts to reach key opinion leaders and media were highly complicated, and a little too narrow. So, it's no surprise that Railway Age, a trade journal, established a "Bureau of Information," that would send settlement-related information to both the targeted "influentials" and the general public. The railroads moved towards increasingly overt contact with the media and began setting up their own 30-to-40-person staffs to crank out stories, advertisements and pamphlets.

The desire to reach outward for as large an audience as possible slowly became the practice. Burlington's Charles Russell Lowell said, "We are beginning to find that he who buildeth a railroad west of the Mississippi must also find a population... We wish to blow as loud a trumpet as the merits of our position warrants."

Consequently, Burlington built a PR campaign through the writings of J. D. Butler, a newspaper correspondent and lecturer. Butler was a late-1880s version of Charles Kurault. He would travel extensively throughout Iowa and Nebraska and write about the common man's life. His letters were not only shared with the media in the eastern U.S., but also shipped over to the British press. Burlington also took his writings and turned them into pamphlets, circulars and posters. These writings were also given to advance men in England who shared the news about the good life in the American west with roomfulls of emigrants who "paid for their night's lodging by attending" the speech.

The Atchison, Topeka and Santa Fe (ATSF) took these approaches and added a few innovative touches. They worked with European colonization agencies, land companies and steamship lines to attract European immigrants. The ATSF started a branch office in London and distributed more than 300,000 pamphlets in various languages throughout Western Europe.

Stateside, pamphlets and brochures extolling Kansas were given to dozens of agents, who would distribute this info in Illinois, Iowa and other nearly states. ATSF would also hold "colonization meetings" where it offered free or low-cost trips to Kansas. In fact, ATSF was able to get a delegation of 225 journalists to proclaim the ATSF lands as the "Garden of the West."

Even more innovative was ATSF's use of the Philadelphia Centennial in 1876: The ATSF sent a large display of Kansas crops to the fair, and a new pamphlet was issued for circulation in Philadelphia. Forty-six pages long, "How and Where to Get a Living. A Sketch of `The Garden of the West'" sang the praises of the land grant.... President J.A. Anderson of the Kansas State

Agricultural College praised the land, and urged farmers to see it for themselves because it was "the best thing in the West".

Further north, the Northern Pacific (NP) Railroad was not going to fall behind. As early as 1870, the NP held a special promotional ride for 150 VIPs from New York to San Francisco. NP set up a small printing office on the train and, when local, general and world news was telegraphed in at a designated stop, the printing office would compose a small newspaper and hand it out to all on board. The NP also took the newspapers and mailed them to other influentials across the country, generating significant publicity.

Where ATSF had emphasized the natural attraction of their lands, NP preferred to focus on the need for colonization. When Congress, in 1871, passed a homestead act for veterans, NP set up a bureau of immigration. This bureau handed out pamphlets extolling the need to organize colonies.

NP also offered to assist veterans with reduced transportation rates, the selling of building materials at wholesale prices and even offered to build reception houses! Essentially, NP's promotional literature was designed to appeal to an individual's desire for a new beginning that would not only be a good move, but an economically smart move. NP's pamphlets emphasized the benefits of colonization; the Guide to the Lands of the Northern Pacific Railroad offered: The Boston colonists who are rearing their homes on the shores of beautiful Detroit Lake in Minnesota can ship their grain to market at as low rates as the farmers who live in Dubuque, 188 miles from Chicago.... With cheap transportation, with [fertile] soil... there must be a corresponding increase in the value of the land, and the settler who secures a farm of 160 acres now may be sure of an advance of several hundred per cent for his investment a few years hence.

Another major player in the growth of railroad PR was the Union Pacific (UP). UP took many of the same approaches as Burlington and ATSF within a "Go West" promotion. Its emphasis on affordable, productive land as the basis for new communities attracted many immigrants, including those seeking religious freedom, like Mennonites (Nelson, 21). UP also hired one of the best publicists of the westward movement Robert E. Strahorn.

A former Indian wars corespondent for the New York Times and the Chicago Tribune, Strahorn also had done some freelance publicity writing over the years for the Denver and Rio Grande railroads. UP's Jay Gould hired Strahorn to start a publicity bureau in both Denver and Omaha. Under Strahorn's guidance, the bureau put out The New West Illustrated, full of information tailored for westward emigrants. He also insured the bureau wrote publicity pieces to papers throughout the country - in one summer alone, the Omaha Republican printed 45 columns from his bureau. Strahorn's approach emphasized the new West as the place to build a new world, with resulting new wealth. Says historian Oliver Knight:

Strahorn's emphasis on guidebooks differentiated him from other publicists. His job was not to publicize the Union Pacific but the entire West, not to sell UP lands but to attract settlers who would create freight tonnages and passenger revenues. His propaganda... was the kind that contributed to the urbanization and industrialization through which the developing West was absorbed into the economic nationalization of America.

More than 2,000 muckraking articles appeared in magazines that reached a distribution of about 5 million copies (during a time when there were only 20 million families in the U.S.). Riding a wave of the disaffection, and the economic disenfranchisement, of the common man, muckrakers sought out more than corruption and malfeasance in the business world.

These journalists reflected a concern in the U.S. that the absolute power of the few was disintegrating society. Said Chalmers, "They described a condition in which all of the individual parts seemed to conspire against the whole.... The muckrakers seemed to be explaining... the moral disintegration of a whole society".

The railroads, with their extensive web of political and economic power, were seen as prime targets by the muckrackers. In fact, the muckrakers unveiled the seamy side of the railroads - the rate inequities, their setting rates for farmers' products their influence in setting land values and their bribing of politicians. Reporters for Leslie's, The Nation, The Arena and The Science Monthly also detailed scandalous problems concerning railroad accident rates. Ray Stannard Baker, writing for McClure's, found that the massive trusts built their wealth on the ownership of the highly profitable railroads. In fact, Baker believed that, unless Congress passed some effective restraints, the railroads might be ripe for government takeover as the only sure way to eliminate abuse.

In sum, the more the muckrakers looked, the more they discovered. Christopher Connolly, writing for Collier's found: That the railroads were involved in corruption. Where they did not cause it, they at least sought a share of the profits. They were everywhere exploiting mineral resources and seeking possession of public lands. In West Virginia... the Baltimore and Ohio railroad dominate the legislature.... The Southern Pacific was the real government of California. In the face of such massive exposes, the railroads were rightfully nervous. If the public continued to see only pictures of railroad corruption, could nationalization of their industry be far behind?

Accordingly, their use of PR changed. Gone were the days of using PR to disseminate information to the public in an attempt to build western communities. In its place came advocacy PR, best exemplified by the railroads' turning to the Publicity Bureau to fight off government regulation. The railroads retained this Bureau, considered the forerunner of the modern PR agency. The Bureau, which opened branches in several major U.S. cities, and also stationed employees in South Dakota and California, attempted to directly reach reporters and editors with railroad propaganda. This approach, say Cutlip, Centre and Broom, shows one of PR's first attempts to use "the tools of fact-finding, publicity, and personal contact to saturate the nation's press... with the railroad's propaganda".

Ivy Ledbetter Lee, considered by many experts to be the father of modern-day public relations, assisted in efforts to defend the railroad industries. While retained by Pennsylvania Railroad, Lee wrote a Declaration of Principles that clearly show the new advocacy approach. A key part of the Principles reads: We aim to supply news... In brief, our plan is, frankly and openly, on behalf of our business concerns and public institutions, to supply the press and public of the United States prompt and accurate information concerning subjects, which is of value and interest of the public to know about.

From this course of events we can see in action the adage "for every action, there is a reaction." In essence, the rise of the muckrakers, and their relentless attacks against the railroads, caused the railroad industry to seek out PR as a way of defending itself.

When this happened, PR as a community-building instrument became a secondary concern. Henry Adams, in 1902, writing on the railroad's dilemma, best summed up their thinking when he said, "The task of publicity is to allay [the public's] suspicion... Indeed for whatever point of view from which the trust problem is considered, publicity stands as the first step in its solution." Kruckeberg and Starck observe that:

Thus, what really prompted the birth of contemporary public relations... was the reaction against the muckrakers with their new power to communicate with the masses.... If publicity was being used to effectively to attack business, why could it not be used equally well to explain and defend business?

What of PR and Community-Building Today? In the case of the western expansion of the railroads, we've seen that PR helped attract settlers and build communities through widespread publicity techniques. We've also witnessed how railroad PR abruptly changed course towards corporate advocacy in the face of the muckrakers.

At this late date, is there a case that can be made for PR to once again assume a community-building role? There are some recent developments that point to that very possibility, especially if one looks at the recent rise of another phenomenon -public journalism.

First, the sense of community that was once known in this country is slowly crumbling, say Kruckeberg and Starck. Modern U.S. society, with its high premium placed on technology, is witnessing a corresponding isolating effect. Technological communications developments like the television, the computer and the telephone all tend to move individuals away from community interaction. Two-way communication, however, can help make sense of the information flowing within a community and can help develop a healthier social structure.

PR, with its firm grounding in communications approaches, is well positioned to take an active step in facilitating the two-way flow of communications within a community. Kruckeberg and Starck maintain that the modern PR practitioner can through being an effective communication facilitator - successfully overcome the weaker sense of community. However, for now, PR, according to Kruckeberg and Starck, hasn't recovered from the defensive "information-dispensing" role adopted in the face of the muckrakers' assault. They speak of this when they write:

The transmission view of communication connotes doing something communicatively persuading? advocating? - to someone else.

The competing model, which indeed probably predates the other, stresses the "communal" or "communitarian" aspect of communication.... This model connotes doing something with someone.... Public relations early adopted and has continued to apply - the transmission model of communication... rooted in persuasion and advocacy rather than principles based on social involvement and participation.

With PR abdicating the role it once played in mixing communication with community-building, another powerful entity has recently stepped forward to begin filling the gap. Communication historian Robert E. Parks has written that "the newspaper... is the great medium of communication within the city, and it is on the basis of the information it supplied that public opinion rests." However, other communication theorists, including John Dewey, have written that printed communication alone is but a precursor to community-building around an issue or event.

Hence the recent public journalism (PJ) movement among several newspapers in the U.S. With PJ, the newspaper attempts to be more than "information-dispenser." PJ is an attempt by newspapers to be part of the dialogue within a community, essentially facilitating discussion and helping to mold consensus and further decision-making. Recently, James Carey, professor of journalism at Columbia University, described PJ in this way:

If journalism is not actively engaged in enhancing and forming a democratic public in debate, disputations, arguments and... things done outside of the realm of surveillance - it's at odds with its original purpose (Klotzer). And Cole Campbell, the editor of the St. Louis Post-Dispatch, has identified a similar way of looking at PJ's role, which sounds very close to some of the opportunities Kruckeberg and Starck have identified for PR:

I like what Buzz Merritt of the Wichita Eagle has said about a successful community. He says a successful community is one whose members know what's going on and take responsibility for it. So to me public journalism is a way of making both of those things happen.... You also need to get below the event-driven news agenda to find out what's truly happening in a community (Bishop). How does one get a clear idea of just what PJ is? Campbell's definition seems to be mostly accurate. However, at this early stage, PJ is mostly visible through certain "event-driven" activities. The Akron Beacon-Journal asked readers to sign racial progress cards vowing to work for racial harmony. The Spokesman Review in Spokane enticed communities, by offering pizza, to have backyard gettogethers to discuss the issues that concern their neighbourhoods. Several California dailies promoted gang peace summits to try to find an answer to escalating violence.

Without too much imagination, one can easily picture a business, government organization or non-profit group offering any of these PJ activities as a PR programme (and many similar-sounding programmes have been offered through PR involvement - the award-winning gun buy-back programme held a couple of years ago in St. Louis immediately comes to mind). What is likely happening here is that PJ has identified both the continuing need for dialogue facilitation within a community, as the part this dialogue plays in community-building. In the meantime PR has not, in large part, made a turn off the road of "information-dissemination" first widely followed in reaction to the muckrakers. The earlier use of PR to build communities along the westward railroad development shows that PR can fulfill what Baskin and Aronoff describe as the third stage of development - mutual influence and understanding:

In this most recent stage, public relations accepts the responsibilities of [information dissemination], but also provides information and counsel to management of the nature and realities of public opinion and methods by which the organization can establish policy, make decisions and take action in light of public opinion (my italics). It's this interaction with the community (and the related community-building) that PR needs to investigate. Otherwise, PR might have to resign itself to continue primarily with information-dissemination. If so, the media, through public journalism, is already preparing to fill the need for dialogue facilitation and related community-building.

With an awareness of the numerous and widely varied sources of political violence, one should proceed cautiously to consider more narrowly why some individuals or groups choose terrorism as a form of political violence. A clear concept of what constitutes terror and how terrorism functions must be obtained at the onset. To illustrate, terror is a superlative form of fear, and fear is a human emotion that pertains only to the living. The helpless victims who were massacred by the Abu Nidal group at the Vienna and Rome airports in December 1985 were not terrorized. They were simply murdered.

Those who survived the massacre, either physically present at the airports or miles away learning of the atrocities through media depictions, were those who were perhaps terrorized. While the above illustration is overly simplistic, one is well advised to approach the study of political terrorism by recognizing that the "victims" of political terrorist atrocities are not normally the "targets." Herein lies an important distinguishing feature that separates political terrorism from other forms of terror such as psychopathic. The psychopath's victim is likely to be first terrorized and then killed, and is the principal object of the psychopath's atrocity. The terrorizing and elimination of the victim is both method and goal.

In contrast, the political terrorist's victim is symbolic. A victim is chosen who is representative of a target group that is strategically involved in the terrorist's political goals. When the Iranian-backed hijackers of TWA Flight 847 beat and killed U.S. serviceman Robert Stethem and threw his body on the tarmac at the Beirut airport, his death was not a direct objective of the terrorists. His demise was not their goal; rather, their goal was the elimination of U.S. influence in the Middle East in general and Lebanon in particular. Stethem was their victim, but not their target. Their target was the American public who observed the atrocity through the international media. The strategy for their target selection was based on the notion that the American public had the power to force a change in the Reagan administration's foreign policy for the Middle East and Lebanon.

CONSTRUCTING ALTERNATIVE PRESS THEORIES

Both Eastern and Western media researchers have tried to redress the deficiencies of the four-theory model by creating their own models. Three more theoretical concepts-development journalism, democratic-participant media, and the revolutionary media-were developed to accommodate the progress and changes in press systems and to supplement the dominant paradigm's four press categories.

Of the new theoretical concepts, development journalism has caused more controversies because the degree of press freedom varies greatly from society to society, and the very concept may imply a role for the government. The controversy also seems to stem from the fact that the deciding factor in creating the four press theories was the presence or absence of press freedom, which was defined mainly in terms of government control.

Based on such a criterion, how can one type of press system allow vastly different degrees of press freedom in different societies? When a new concept cannot be fit into the established paradigm, it becomes" controversial." Progressive, insightful, and creative as these new theories are, they are mostly supplementary to the established four press theories.

More ambitious efforts were made by Ralph Lowenstein, J. Henry Altschull, John C. Merrill, and Shelton A. Gunaratne, who constructed alternative models reclassifying press systems. Ralph Lowenstein developed a" progressive typology," according to which," press systems evolved from authoritarian to libertarian, to social libertarian or social centralist, and then to a big futuristic question mark". This typology seems to have the same tendency as the established four theories of basing its discussions mainly on the development paths of Western press systems, which makes it less relevant to the evolution of press systems elsewhere in the world. J. Henry Altschull proposed three basic media models - market, Marxist, and developing. To make the concepts value free, Altschull described them as market, communitarian, and advancing. In trying to reclassify media systems, Altschull brought in the element of culture and belief systems.

He explained that the market system emphasized the" individual" while the communitarian system focused on the" communal life" or the" collective." Altschull also analysed the role of the media - preserving status quo under both market and communitarian models and advocating change under the advancing model.

He explained that there were variations within each model, giving the classification much flexibility. With the exception of the advancing model describing press systems in the South, Altschull's models were also based mainly on the analysis of Western media systems even though he classified his models also as East, West, and South, where East refers to Marxism and the former Soviet communist bloc in Eastern Europe rather than to Asia.

The only Eastern society mentioned in the analysis was Japan. Altschull explained that despite the variations within the market model, the basic belief systems - hostility to a communitarian belief system - remain intact." Discord notwithstanding, the broad sweep of the first movement of the symphony is heard throughout the industrialized capitalist world, in Japan as in Denmark and Canada".

Despite Western influence, the Japanese society, steeped in Asian culture and Confucian traditions, has no such hostility. As discussed earlier in this chapter, the press club system in Japan dictates communal behaviour within the industry by discouraging competition and scoops and encouraging collective reporting. A mixture of the East and the West, Japan proves to be a difficult case to be classified.

John C. Merrill's circular model shows that individualistic press systems gravitate towards libertarianism and more collectivistic systems are at the authoritarian end. Merrill said,"... the basic model is a simple spectrum, with authoritarianism at one end and libertarianism at the other. All press systems fall somewhere along this continuum".

Merrill's model resembles Altschull's models without the" advancing" or" South" element. Men-ill's model has the merit of built-in flexibility. The classification of a press system depends on in which direction the system gravitates. But it is still difficult to place Japan on Merrill's model. The Japanese press is mostly free from government control, but it is not individualistic. The press club system emphasizes collective action, but it cannot be described as authoritarian. The models proposed by Altschull and Merrill represented major improvements over the four-theory model - AltschulPs model moved away from the exclusive emphasis on government control, and Men-ill's model had the merit of built-in flexibility to accommodate different types of press systems and changes within those systems.

Despite Men-ill's inclusion of the communitarian factor, the two models still seem to largely rely on Western philosophies, scholarship, and examples of Western media performances. Jiafei Yin called for the construction of a new model, which would be based on a broader foundation of both Western and Eastern philosophies and cultural influences, but did not produce an actual model.

Shelton A. Gunaratne brought in both Eastern and Western philosophical, religious, and cultural traditions in building his model-The Dao of the Press. There are two parts to Gunaratne's model: one part is the libertarian-authoritarian (L-A) continuum with varying shades of social responsibility across the continuum, and the other part is a centre-semiperiphery-periphery world system with individuals and groups, nation-states, and the world system at different levels. And all the three levels" autopoietically adjust the degree of free expression" along the L-A continuum. Gunaratne's model emphasizes both Eastern and Western cultural values in the definitions and interpretations of the term" social responsibility," giving the model much needed flexibility in accommodating different shades of social responsibility found in world cultures.

Merrill also addressed the relativity of the concept of responsibility among societies and even within a society. Similar to many of the previous press theories and models, Gunaratne's L-A continuum also focuses on the libertarian-authoritarian dichotomy, reflecting Western emphasis on freedom and liberty.

With the rich heritage of Asian philosophies and cultures, can a new model reflect diverse global cultural values and describe and explain press systems around the world without bias either from the West or the East?

After all, different cultures prioritize values differently. Therefore, press theories that are supposed to address global press systems should have a wider base to reflect a broader, more balanced global view. With adequate attention to factors such as world history, global cultures, and economic pressure, the problems inherent in the four established theories because of the authors'Western bias and their sole focus on governmental influences can be addressed.

For a new paradigm of press theories, the optimal balance between specificity and universality should also be considered. The four theories of the press have the beauty and elegance of a very simple but clear structure - four categories under a dichotomy, which aimed to describe and explain press systems in the whole world.

Conveniently general as they are, the four or five theories have difficulties in providing a reliable guide to the global press systems. The universality of the theories is limited. However, if categories are too specific and accurate in describing particular press systems, there may be too many categories for the model to be an effective guide. One other important factor that needs to be paid attention to in building a more reliable press model is that the model should be dynamic so that it can accommodate the changes in the press systems around the world. Obviously, press systems in the new democracies in Eastern Europe are very different from the press systems in the West even though they all operate under democratic systems now.

The press systems in the new democracies in Asia, such as Indonesia, Cambodia, the Philippines, Taiwan, and South Korea, vary from those in Eastern Europe despite the fact that they are all new democracies and share some similarities. And the press system in China today cannot be compared with the Chinese press system two decades ago, or the press system in North Korea. It would defeat the purpose of having models if every time any changes occur, new models have to be created.

A DICHOTOMY OF VALUES, EAST AND WEST

A new paradigm of press theories requires new ways of thinking in order to broaden the foundation. In this section, an examination is conducted of the dominant Eastern and Western cultural values, which are by no means exclusive to either the East or the West but rather reflect the quintessence of each.

To summarize Asian, or more particularly the Confucian, culture, leading Confucian scholar Tu Wei-ming said: "Industrial East Asia, under the influence of Confucian culture, seems to have developed a different kind of modern civilization, less adversarial, less individualistic, and less self-interested. One sees there the coexistence of market economy and government leadership, democratic parity with meritocracy and individual initiatives with group orientation."

THE INDIVIDUAL VERSUS THE STATE AND FAMILY (THE GROUP)

Western libertarian philosophy values the independence and rights of each individual. John Stuart Mill's On Liberty spelled out classic liberal individualism-it "set out the limits to the legitimate interference of collective opinion with individual independence". Mill wrote that the only warranted interference with the liberty of an individual is for mankind's self-protection, that is, to prevent harm to others, and that no power should be exercised over an individual for his own good. "Over himself, over his own body and mind, the individual is sovereign."

The Confucian thought, however, focuses on the state and the family. Confucius believed that only when the state and families are strong can the well-being of individuals be guaranteed. In the equation of the state, family, and individuals in Confucian societies, individuals are often encouraged and expected to sacrifice their own rights and interests for the sake of the state and family if contradictions should arise, which is in sharp contrast to Mill's belief that the individual is sovereign.

In Confucian societies, the state is sovereign. In Western culture, individualism is extolled, but in Eastern culture, people are taught to think about "us." In the West, ideal societies are composed of free individuals while in Confucian societies the individual "is not viewed as an isolated individual but as a centre of relationships".

The Chinese tradition has largely been influenced by a Confucian-based relational and social definition of person instead of by any concept of discrete individuality. "Under the sway of this relational understanding of human being, the mutuality and interdependence of personal, familial, societal, and political realization in the classical Chinese model can and has been generally conceded."

FREEDOM AND RIGHTS VERSUS RESPONSIBILITY

John Locke, an early libertarian, believes that freedom is essential to the full development of a human being. Merrill summarized Locke's philosophy as "Each person has a natural right to be free and not to be subjected to the will of another." Freedom, for Locke, is a "natural" right.

"Besides being bound by natural law, humans possess natural rights, in particular the right to life, self-defence, and freedom. They have also duties; in particular, the duty not to give away their rights". The Enlightenment in eighteenth century Europe led to the rise of classical liberalism and capitalism. It also led to the French and American revolutions, which uprooted the power of religion and the aristocracy in France and heavily influenced the most distinguished leaders of the American Revolution-Jefferson, Washington, Franklin, and Paine. "The language of natural law, of inherent freedoms, of self-determination, which seeped so deeply into the American grain, was the language of the Enlightenment..". "Give me liberty or give me death." Patrick Henry's rallying call meant that there was no compromise over liberty-to be free is the precondition to live. In the East, the emphasis is on being responsible and loyal rather than on being free. Western libertarian philosophers' focus of attention falls on the welfare of the individual, so it is only logical that these philosophers advocate that these individuals should be equal and free to pursue what they want. Confucian thought lays emphasis on the group; hence, there is the concern of being responsible and loyal to the group. In his research, Tu pointed out the Asian focus on the ethic of service and obligation.

INDIVIDUAL FREEDOM AND HAPPINESS VERSUS PUBLIC GOOD AND RESPONSIBILITY

Mill, a defender of personal and political liberty, said in his On Liberty:

"The only freedom which deserves the name, is that of pursuing our own good in our own way, so long as we do not attempt to deprive others of theirs, or impede their efforts to obtain it".

Mill's "sovereign self" echoed the U.S. Bill of Rights and the Declaration of Independence in upholding individual freedom and rights and the pursuit of happiness, not individual or collective responsibility.

So when President Kennedy demanded, "Ask not what your country can do for you; ask what you can do for your country," it was refreshing to the American youth as their civic education focused mostly on the value of equality, freedom, and rights embedded in the Constitution when they grew up. Confucius teachings emphasize a strong commitment to the world and encourage sacrifice of self-interest to be ethical. The Confucian concept of the ethical links up directly with the public good.

And Confucius believes "self-realization is fundamentally a social undertaking, therefore, 'selfish' concerns are to be rejected as an impediment to one's own growth and self-realization".

LEGAL VERSUS MORAL

In Western democratic societies, the legal system is very well developed as the law embodies the ideal that everyone is equal before the law. And citizens have a strong sense of the law, which sets the boundary of people's behaviour, including what parents legally can or cannot do in disciplining their children. In Asian societies, especially more traditional and less developed societies such as China, the legal system is much less well developed.

With the opening up of the country's economy, China's legislative body, the National People's Congress, has been busy making laws as conflicts in the past were resolved mostly through mediation based on judgements of who was right and who was wrong.

And a major part of Confucius's teachings comprises moral guidelines, which is why he was also considered a moralist. Confucius firmly believes that children are the responsibility of their parents and that aging parents are the responsibility of their grown-up children whether it is legally required or not. As a result, Chinese press occasionally exposes cases of mistreating aging parents by their grown-up children even though it is a private matter.

Likewise, Confucius believes that it is parents' fault if a child goes astray. Even today some immigrant Asian parents are surprised by the child abuse laws of the United States, where children are encouraged to call the police if they are spanked by their parents.

Such laws would shock Confucius. Confucius's teachings also place emphasis on being just and public minded. It would be unimaginable to Confucius that one country could have billionaires the same time it had a trillion dollars of national debt.

According to the moral teachings of Confucius, those who pursue only personal interests (Ii) are the "little men" (xiaoren), people of no character; only those who think about what is appropriate and beneficial to all concerned (yi) are the "gentlemen" (junzi), people of noble character.

TO BE FREE TO EXPLORE VERSUS TO KNOW RIGHT FROM WRONG

Western libertarians advocate for a free marketplace of ideas, where the public should be left free to explore and discover the truth on their own. In his pamphlet, Areopagitica, John Milton argues that truth would emerge victorious over falsehood should the two be locked in a grapple. John Milton also wrote about the importance of diversity of opinions and perspectives. In Asian societies influenced by Confucian thinking, especially in the case of China after almost 5,000 years of civilization, truth seems to be self-evident. In such cases, the focus is on teaching the people what is right and what is wrong rather than the freedom to explore what is right and what is wrong.

The real challenge becomes the task of convincing the people, or in an ideal Confucian way, for people to convince themselves, to always make the right choice. Confucian scholar Tu Wei-ming phrased the contrast as "the right to think" versus "right thinking."

In Western democracies, the emphasis is on the process-if decisions are made with public input. In Confucian societies, the emphasis is on the result-if the right decision is made. The process often is deemed less relevant.

DEMOCRACY VERSUS MERITOCRACY

The U.S. Declaration of Independence states unequi-vocally at the very beginning, "all men are created equal." The conviction in the equality among men forms the basis of Western democratic governments-government of the people, by the people, and for the people. Such libertarian thinking has deep roots in the history of Western philosophy. In Two Treatises of Civil Government, Locke maintains that before there were any states to make statutes, men were aware of a natural law, which taught that all men were equal and independent.

"These men, with no earthly superior above them, are in a state of liberty, but not a state of licence."In his book, A Theory of Justice, John Rawls promotes the adoption of a "veil of ignorance," which would ideally eliminate all the personal identifiers of each individual-male or female, black or white, rich or poor, intelligent or not-and return everyone to his or her original position of being equal with everyone else. "Rawls believes that justice will come forth from a discussion by rational and equal people concerned with their own interests but without anyone being advantaged or disadvantaged". Western societies are democratic and horizontal, emphasizing public participation in the government, while Confucian societies are hierarchical and vertical, believing in meritocracy instead of democracy.

For more than a thousand years in the history of China, only top scholars after rigorous national exams became government officials. In Singapore today, the brightest young people are selected for education in world's top universities supported with government funding so they will become the next generation of worthy leaders. "Statecraft is an integral part of Confucian learning". The ideal Confucian officials are people with "inner sagehood and outer kingliness."

Equality in human relations is a foreign concept in Confucian thinking as he decreed three sets of subservient relationships: subjects should obey their kings, sons should obey their fathers, and wives should obey their husbands. Confucius was not a democrat as some Confucian scholars tend to believe.

CIVIL LIBERTIES VERSUS SOCIAL ORDER AND STABILITY

The concept of human rights was developed during the Enlightenment. The Bill of Rights as amendments to the U.S. Constitution marked a milestone in mankind's fight for civil liberties. Western democratic societies keep a watchful eye on the government to prevent it from encroaching upon those rights. The most recent example was the heated U.S. Congressional debate on the Bush administration's domestic spying programme.

In contrast, a salient feature of Confucian thinking in government is the primacy of political order. In China, the traditional assumption has been that personal order and the order of a society entail each other. Thus, in Confucian societies, governments expect respect and obedience to keep social order.

Social stability often takes precedence over civil liberties and is regarded as vital to the strength of a country and the welfare of its people. The Confucian order was built on traditional values and norms. Confucius's unwavering focus on social order and stability might have been the result of the endless wars China was embroiled in during his lifetime.

Thousands of years later, some Asian leaders could not agree more with the ancient Chinese philosopher. Fighting back criticism about too much control in his country, Lee Kuan Yew, first and former prime minister of Singapore who led the city-state for thirty-one years, said, "Without order and stability, nothing can be achieved". Lee was responsible for turning Singapore from a fishing village at the end of the Second World War into one of the cleanest and richest countries in the world today.

COMPETITION VERSUS HARMONY

Capitalism thrives on free competition on the market, which is supposed to drive economic growth even though such growth may be achieved at a social cost. Competition presupposes freedom and equality, but competition spawns conflicts as well-disputes between management and labour, hostile business takeovers, smearing political campaigns, fights in sports arenas, and even the constant race to be the most popular teen in high school. As a result of competition, people are labeled as winners and losers. And the rule of competition decides that there are often more losers than winners, resulting in many unhappy people. In some Asian societies such as China and Singapore, and even in some European countries such as Germany, comparative advertising is banned. In Japan and South Korea, state-guided capitalism softens real competition. "Harmony is at the core of the Chinese culture". Preferred methods of resolving conflicts are building consensus and making compromise rather than many voices competing.

"A pertinent contrast can be developed between the western liberal commitment to many voices and the traditional Chinese concern for a communitarian consensus as a social good". One values pluralism; the other harmony. The "promotion of harmony and goodwill among individuals and their families and community in the context of the five constants: ran, yi, li, zhi, and xin (humanity, righteousness, decorum, wisdom, and trust) is a social responsibility from the Confucian point of view". However, the ancient Chinese sage would be flabbergasted to witness the transformations China is going through today. Since China ushered in the market economy and private enterprise, competition is becoming a new way of life, bringing relentless assault on traditional values and leaving the conservatives lamenting the decline in moral standards.

ADVERSARIAL WATCHDOG

Press in the West takes pride in being a watchdog of the government. The uncovering of the Watergate scandal has inspired young journalists to follow the footsteps of Bob Woodward and Carl Bernstein. Dan Rather's dogged pursuit of the truth in Bush's service in the National Guard cost his career. To deal with an enquiring press, government officials hide behind press secretaries.

In traditional societies, people tend to be in deference to their governments. In Confucian societies, the government is supposed to take care of the people, and the people are expected to respect the government. "Confucianism holds that man is born for uprightness, and that people's goodwill is essential for good government in the context of an intellectual democracy headed by a benevolent ruler".

Chinese "benevolent despotism" fascinated Western thinkers. In Confucian societies, the press becomes a tool for nation building. Even in Japan and South Korea, both democratic societies, press tends to keep cozy relationships with the government and is, thus, reduced to a lapdog.

The dichotomy of dominant Western and Eastern values does not imply that there are no overlapping areas between Western and Eastern cultures. There are Western philosophers such as Plato and Rousseau who put emphasis on the state and the collective rather than the individual and preferred rule by the elite, which is very close to the Confucian ideal of government.

In The Social Contract, Rousseau promotes public good and common interest instead of interests of individuals. In the East, there are also philosophical schools such as Taoism that focuses on individuality and extols the virtue of being free, free from the constraints of governments and institutions for the full and free development of the potential of each individual.

But these philosophical schools in the East or the West have not become the dominant influence in their respective cultures. By and large, contemporary Western societies extol freedom and individuality, while Asian societies emphasize interests of the collective and the concept of responsibility regardless of political systems.

Some critics may contend that few Asian societies today including China can be described as Confucian societies because of the influence from the West. Indeed, modernization has inevitably had an impact on Asian societies, especially the young, who are much more accepting of what is Western.

Tu Wei-ming said: "The Westernization of Confucian Asia, including Japan, the two Koreas, mainland China, Hong Kong, Taiwan, Singapore, and Vietnam, may have forever altered its spiritual landscape. But its indigenous resources, including Mahayana Buddhism, Daoism, Shintoism, Shamanism, and other folk traditions, have the resiliency to resurface and make their presence known in the new syntheses."

Confucianism is neither a political system nor a religion; it is a way of thinking and a way of life. It is deep-rooted in the cultures of Confucian societies, and it is reflected in the decisions people make in their everyday lives, including the value of family ties, education, and hard work. A recent media farce in China provides a glimpse of the undisputable respect Confucius still enjoys in China today.

A Peking University professor was quoted in the media as saying that Zhang Ziyi, an internationally known Chinese actress, who was featured on the cover of an issue of Newsweek in 2005 and at the Oscar award ceremony in 2006, was greater than Confucius.

The statement, perceived as an insult to the Chinese culture, sparked a public outcry on the Internet condemning the professor. Bombarded with interview requests from the media, the professor had to post an article on his blog, claiming that he was misquoted by the media for sensationalism.

He explained that Confucius represented China's elite culture, while Zhang Ziyi represented its pop culture. The professor hoped that with the actress's international appeal, she could attract more worldwide interest in Confucianism.

An examination of dominant Eastern and Western values helps provide a more balanced foundation for building a new press model. A New Model: The Two-Dimensional Freedom Responsibility Coordinate System

THE SYSTEM

Based on earlier press models and on an analysis of the salient values of the Western and Eastern cultures, a new press model is proposed here, which is a two-dimensional coordinate grid with the horizontal axis denoting the degree of freedom in a press system and the vertical axis indicating how responsible a press system is. The system illustrates that a free press can be responsible or irresponsible, and that a press that is not free can also be responsible or irresponsible. Merrill also believes in the possible existence of responsible authoritarian systems and responsible libertarian systems.

THE TWO-DIMENSIONAL MODEL

The major difference between what is proposed here and most of the theories and models before it is that this proposed model has departed from the traditional one-dimensional models, which focus mainly on the degree of freedom in a press system, reflecting Western philosophical emphasis on the concept of freedom.

The proposed two-dimensional model, instead, has broadened the foundation of theory building to include a key Asian cultural emphasis on the concept of responsibility. The Asian emphasis on the concept of responsibility is not only a result of Confucian moral influence, but also a result of the socio-economic realities of Asia, where development journalism originated and is still being pursued and where guerrilla warfare or religious and ethnic rivalries can flare up as a result of provocative news articles.

And even in Hong Kong, where dominant discussions tend to focus on the survival of press freedom, Chief Executive Donald Tsang encouraged journalists to think about what was important to society rather than what was popular to readers at the 2005 News Awards ceremony.

Confucius's teachings mesh well with the aspirations of development journalists in Asia, who see the role of the press as agents for social change. Through their work, they want to improve the quality of life of their people. Pakistani media researcher Owais Aslam AIi (undated) analysed the major differences between Western news values and Asian news values, which he summarized as elitist press versus press for national development.

He pointed out the futility of Western news values in "the monumental uphill struggle" of the Third World towards economic progress. Given the diverse economic and social realities of the countries of the world, it is not difficult to see why different philosophies of journalism and news values exist around the world. Some Western libertarian thinkers also addressed the issue of responsibility, rationality, or limits in exercising freedom. Locke gave impetus to the concept of "responsible individualism," predicated on a love of reason and the importance of natural law. According to Locke, individuals live in a social context and need order, not anarchy, for their own well-being.

"Therefore, reason serves as an automatic limitation on freedom. In order to guide themselves in living an orderly and moral life, which is the essence of humanity, rational people voluntarily give up much freedom". Even though well known for his libertarian ideas in his pamphlet On Liberty, Mill held an elitist view on entitlement to freedom. "Mill felt that his freedom principle was appropriate only in societies of relatively high educational standards in which people could rationally exercise freedom". In the field of journalism, debates on press responsibility and accountability have never stopped, such as the work of the Hutchins' Commission, which gave rise to the social responsibility press theory, and the ongoing experimentation with civic or public journalism in the United States. If there is public concern over press responsibility, the concern should be addressed in building a new theoretical model.

The newly added dimension of press responsibility adds balance to existing press models by bringing in cultural values important not only to the West but also to the East, presents a fuller description of a press system, and helps address an important public concern over press responsibility and accountability.

Defining and Measuring Press Responsibility

The immediate question that arises is the definition of responsibility as what is considered responsible in one culture may be viewed as irresponsible in another culture. The notion of responsibility is always culture-specific. Similar to the argument that all concepts of responsibility are relative, the concept of "a free press" is also relative, as there is no absolute freedom of the press in this world, not even in the United States. Addressing press freedom worldwide, Merrill said, "... in fact, there are no free-press nations".

Because of the challenges in setting the standards of a responsible press that can be universally accepted and in deciding who should have the authority in setting the standards, and because of media's aversion to the concept of "a responsible press" imposed from the outside as illustrated by the fate of the Hutchins' report and by the "survey methodology" section of the 2005 Freedom House report that practically equates press responsibility with government control, discussions about press responsibility often hit a dead end.

They do not have to be. AIi (undated) emphasized the watchdog role of the media in development journalism, warned against the discussions on Asian values in journalism being hijacked by government officials as justification for the control of the media, and urged Asian journalists, "who have been struggling to reduce government involvement in the media," to create a form of journalism relevant to the needs of their societies. Only then will the concept of Asian values have credibility, AIi wrote.

UNIVERSAL VALUES IN JOURNALISM

A starting point in exploring the standards of a responsible press can be the search for universal values in journalism, and the Hutchins' report can serve as a helpful reference, such as being accurate and providing balance and diversity of opinion in news coverage, acting as a watchdog of the government, businesses and all other powerful social institutions, addressing issues of public concern, covering all sectors of the society instead of just the prominent, and avoiding invasion of privacy and sensationalism.

If the list continues to include the elimination of hate speech, which is banned in Germany, and pornography, which is banned in the Muslim world, most of the Asian countries, and perhaps some African and South American countries as well, the exploration for universal standards of a responsible press will soon become controversial. And questions such as what is balanced to one may not seem to be balanced to another remain.

CURRENT COMMUNITY STANDARDS

To deal with such tricky issues in setting the standards of a responsible press, the standards used for deciding what is obscene can be borrowed-current community standards. If the majority of readers believe their press is responsible, then they have a responsible press. Vice versa, if the majority of readers believe their press is irresponsible, then they have an irresponsible press. As the concept of responsibility is highly cultural-specific, the best solution is to let the local population decide instead of imposing standards from the outside.

INDEX OF PRESS RESPONSIBILITY-A COMBINATION OF UNIVERSAL VALUES AND LOCAL STANDARDS

Based on accepted universal values in journalism, which may include truth, accuracy, and balance, and results of public opinion surveys on press responsibility, an index of press responsibility can be compiled for each country to help media researchers and students better analyse the characteristics of a particular press system. If survey results distort reality such as in a controlled society, where a survey of honest public opinion is not feasible, universal values in journalism can serve as primary checkpoints.

In the meantime, despite the fact that they sometimes serve as a helpful reference, the criteria of the Freedom House in determining the ratings of press freedom in each country should be revised to add balance to the current standards, which do not take into account media content. The current methodology examines the legal, political, and economic environment of the media, but not the results of those environments-media content.

The survey questions are predominantly negative. Data are not collected through systematic or scientific method but through arbitrary answers by a small group of hand-picked interviewees, including "correspondents overseas, staff and consultant travel, international visitors," and "specialists in geographic and geopolitical areas." Such data collection methods raise serious questions about both the reliability and validity of the results.

THE FOUR CORNERS AND FOUR QUADRANTS

If a pair of dotted diagonal lines are superimposed on the coordinate grid, four corners of the grid will appear, representing four extreme types of press systems-free and responsible, free but not responsible, not free but responsible, and not free and not responsible. As the four corners indicate maximum or minimum degrees of freedom and responsibility, very few press systems fall exactly on those four corners; most of the press systems will fall somewhere within the four quadrants.

FREE AND RESPONSIBLE

While it may be hard to find a perfect example of a free and socially responsible press, some media endeavors are definitely directed towards that goal, such as public broadcasting in Britain and the United States, the civic and public journalism in the United States, and community and development journalism in India and Pakistan. Even though these types of journalism do not represent the mainstream media in their respective societies, they are the free press's attempts to be responsible and relevant to its readers.

The press in this group is mostly free and chooses to avoid sensationalism and play a positive role in society on its own. With or without public funding, it provides mostly quality information and often a public servicefighting crime in neighbourhoods, boosting voter turnout, and educating and empowering the poor rural population.

Depending on events of the day, its content can be a mixture of negative and positive stories. In well-developed and free media markets, the press can afford to choose to be responsible because such a press would be assured of market support if there is public demand for a free and responsible press. Even in underdeveloped societies such as those in South Asia, press responsibility in the form of development journalism can exist because of support from the vast rural audience. For the press to be free and responsible, the market has to demand it and has to be well developed enough to finance it.

FREE AND NOT RESPONSIBLE

It is not very difficult to find free but irresponsible press around the world, press that chases profits or power under the name of press freedom.

Under such press systems, the press is free to pursue whatever story sells on the market with little concern for the consequences of such reporting. In the race to be the first on the market, accuracy in reporting and ethical standards are often compromised. If criticized for their low professional standards and lack of accountability, journalists in such media environment often invoke the defence of freedom of the press. Such press systems tend to exist in intensely competitive media markets, such as new democracies in Taiwan, Indonesia, the Philippines, and some East European countries, where media outlets mushroom and bring immense pressure on the media market and where new regulations are still taking shape.

Even in China where the press is becoming increasingly commercialized, tabloids, sensationalized news, or even made-up news stories are not hard to find. Such press systems may also exist in well-developed, saturated and consolidated media markets where it is very challenging to expand market share such as Hong Kong and Thailand. Because of the profit-oriented nature of such press systems, media companies are regarded as moneymakers, regulated by market demand only. Circulations and ratings become the only measure of success.

Whatever sells is repeated in the media, resulting in over-coverage of some topics and events, such as celebrity journalism and press conferences, and the undercoverage of other less glamorous topics and events, such as poverty. Under such systems, the media spend far too much time covering and far too little time uncovering.

As they become pure businesses, such media are financed mostly with advertising dollars and subscriptions. Another form of press irresponsibility is the partisan press or political patronage of the press, in which case some press allows itself to be used as political tools especially when the democratic system is still young.

With a political power vacuum as a result of the dismantling of control mechanisms, political families, parties, or organizations often rush to take control of the media and use the media to advance their particular agendas, often employing such tactics as personal attacks or smear campaigns. Such a press tends to exist in free but less developed media markets as political patronage provides much needed financial support for the media.

Under such press systems, media content is often negative, full of political attacks in partisan press, or sex and violence in tabloids instead of stories about progress, which is often a long and less dramatic process. Tabloids and partisan press are typical products of such a press system.

RESPONSIBLE BUT NOT FREE

The very term seems to be an oxymoron. Critics may ask how a press can be classified as responsible if it is not free. The answer can depend on the definition of responsibility according to local community standards.

Such press systems tend to exist in more traditional societies where the emphasis is on the group rather than the individual and where cultural traditions or religions have a major impact on public life. Press in this group tends to stress the importance and interests of the country, society, community, and families rather than freedom and rights of individuals. It tends to follow moral or religious principles and societal goals in news coverage rather than follow market demand because to publish what is perceived to be responsible is more important than to publish what sells.

The emphasis is on publishing what is right versus the right to publish, which is the difference between what is ethical and what is legal.

The goals of such a press may vary from country to country, including social order and stability, economic development, or reinforcement of religious values. The press in this category tends to support these societal goals under government or public pressure, or both.

For example, in Saudi Arabia and much of the Islamic world, newspapers devote sections to the teachings or discussions of Islam while criticism of Islam is forbidden. And in most of the Islamic press, the content is very clean, free of pornography. Elsewhere in the world, many of the developing countries in Asia, Africa, and South America see national development as the top priority and expect the media to serve as a tool for nation building.

In Singapore, because of the fear of ethnic and religious riots and the importance of its relations with its neighbours, the press cannot report on issues concerning race, religion, or its neighbours to maintain order and stability.

If the majority of the people in these societies support those goals, then the press is responsible. However, in some cases, especially when a country is involved in a war, current community standards may prove unreliable when the public is caught up in a patriotic frenzy. When that happens, it would depart from the universal values in journalism, such as accuracy and balance.

Because it has special roles to play in society, press in this group may obtain financial support from the government, public or social institutions, or the church even though a major part of its income may still come from the market.

NOT FREE AND NOT RESPONSIBLE

The press in this group does not enjoy much freedom of operation, and the controls applied unilaterally by the government are most likely not supported by the people. The most typical examples are perhaps the press in North Korea and Turkmenistan, where there is very little information but plenty of glorifications of the state leaders in the press. Hardships endured by the people can hardly be found in the news media.

The press in this group is also prohibited from criticizing the government or exposing corruption. The press in this group does not have the freedom to make its own editorial decisions, and public opinion is suppressed. After a review of the different types of press systems, where should the Japanese press be plotted on the coordinate grid? It should perhaps be placed somewhere close to the origin of the coordinate grid as being partly free and partly responsible.

It is free from government control but not free from industry control. And if the press refrains from uncovering high-level scandals in the government or big corporations, it cannot be described as socially responsible.

But until the Japanese people start to reject their press, which is opposite to the fact that Japanese newspapers enjoy the highest circulations in the world, the press in Japan cannot be described as irresponsible either. A responsibility index as discussed earlier plus a more accurate press freedom rating can help determine the position of the Japanese press on the grid and the positions of the press in other countries.

A Dynamic Model

The proposed two-dimensional Freedom-Responsibility coordinate system attempts to provide a more balanced press model in explaining press systems around the world, measuring not only the degree of press freedom but also the level of press responsibility. The validity of the new model will be determined by how many press systems in the world it can satisfactorily describe and explain. But societies are constantly changing, and so are their press systems. One of the advantages of the new model is that it can accommodate such changes in the system.

For example, the American press seems to be trying to be more responsible and relevant to its readers while having some of its freedom curtailed because of the War on Terror. Comparing with the press elsewhere in the world, the American press is best known for being free but not necessarily for being responsible.

The low credibility of the news media in repeated public opinion polls shows public dissatisfaction with media performance. Civic and public journalism seems to be pushing the American press towards more press responsibility when the press tries to be more relevant to its readers and more conscious of the role it can play in society, such as helping crime-fighting and boosting voter turnout.

And in the age of war on terror, the Bush administration is tightening up press access to information, citing national security concerns. It also launched an investigation into the leaking of the National security Agency's domestic spying programme to discourage such disclosure of information.

During the war in Iraq, the government controlled reporters' access on the battlefield with a system of embedded reporters. And the concentration of ownership also reduces the independence and freedom the press once had.

The press in China seems to be moving slowly in the opposite direction-freer but messier even though sometimes more relevant to its readers. The press in China used to follow only Party lines. Now it also has to follow market demand by addressing public concerns.

Some local papers target rural poverty by providing tips on how to grow better crops or how to generate cash by engaging in non-farming businesses.

Competition, unheard of before the economic reforms, has given rise to diversity in the media. The Internet has provided a channel for news stories turned down by the traditional media. These changes are clearly pushing the Chinese press towards more freedom and responsibility.

However, competition also drives down the quality of news coverage and the ethical standards of journalists as sensationalism and bribery are prevalent. The Chinese press is in a state of flux as different factors are pulling it in different directions with deepening economic reforms. The most important factor, however, is still government policies. The press in Russia presents perhaps the most intriguing case for study as the degree of press freedom and responsibility shifted dramatically with the changing political climate of the country. Described as the prototype communist media, the press in the former Soviet Union was a political tool, following Lenin's ideal of press's functioning as collective agitator, propagandist, and organizer.

After the fall of communism, the press in Russia changed overnight from not free to completely free. Then under the presidency of Putin, press freedom in Russia was once again being curtailed. With a new president coming into the Kremlin, the status of press freedom in Russia is yet to be determined.

The proposed new Freedom-Responsibility model is dynamic not only because it can accommodate the changes within particular press systems, but also because it can reflect changes in the structure of the model. In the debate on press freedom and press responsibility in the West, the concept of press freedom often trumps the concept of press responsibility.

The same is true on the global scene as free news media in the West dominate the global information flow. The call for the New World Information and Communication Order from developing countries was drowned out in the West's battle cry for the free flow of information.

And the Freedom House measures press freedom, not press responsibility. Given the dominant position of press freedom in the coordinate system, the press freedom axis represents the yang arm of the coordinate system while the press responsibility axis stands for the yin arm of the system. The yang and yin axes complement each other, forming a balanced system.

However, the pendulum of history never stops swinging. Laozi, an ancient Chinese philosopher, sees reversal as the way the natural order operates: "everything that has gone far in one direction will move in the opposite direction, and to be in a low or weak position is to be in a state in which one will thrive".

That is the law of the dialectics. If the abuse of press freedom becomes a global issue and the world's press is forced to be more responsible because of public pressure, there can be a paradigm change within the coordinate system with the concept of press responsibility becoming the dominant feature of the model and thus, the yang axis of the system, and the concept of press freedom becoming the yin axis of the system.

But that may take a long time to occur even though such changes will never stop. Confucius advocated the "middle path" and Aristotle promoted the "golden mean," each avoiding the extremes at either end. The same principle applies to press performance-there is neither absolute press freedom nor absolute press responsibility. The desirable middle path would be the optimal combination of press freedom with press responsibility, a blend of the West and the East.

The two-dimensional system proposed in this chapter is an attempt at exploring a more balanced model in studying press systems around the world. The major challenge in the application of the model would be the measurement of press responsibility in a press system. So far no effort is ever made in that regard, given the expected controversies it is bound to draw.

If media observers and researchers can agree that development journalism and press responsibility do not automatically translate into government control of the press, measuring press responsibility does not have to be a forbidden task. The compilation of a global press responsibility index can provide a helpful guide in studying the characteristics of a press system.

A good starting point can be the identification of universal values in journalism as discussed earlier. The more universal values societies can agree upon, the more reliable the index can be. "Current community standards" in the form of public opinion surveys offer a way of accommodating values specific to local culture.

Debates on universal values in journalism can be messy, but the results can be crystallizing and enlightening. With more research, media researchers from the East and the West may find more common ground than they expect. One weakness of the model is perhaps that Western and Confucian philosophies and values tend to dominate the discussions even though there are so many other religious and philosophical influences in the world. Therefore, this study is only exploratory in nature. It can be enriched and improved with perspectives from more cultures or serve as a starting point for future research.

In future research, alternative concepts or dichotomies can be explored in building new models, such as an observer-interventionist/activist dichotomy, or commercial-ideological dichotomy. The point of departure will depend on the angle of analysis and on the perspectives and approaches of researchers.

5

Trust in the Culture of Journalism

INTRODUCTION

An association between perceived audience trust and journalistic professionalism is expected not only given social psychological knowledge regarding felt trust, but also granted that trust is a central element in the professional ideology of journalism. The centrality of audience trusts to journalistic professionalism can easily be noticed when one looks at journalists' codes of ethics. Such documents often mention the trust of the audience as the rationale for many journalistic decrees, such as neutrality and objectivity, and even for not accepting gifts.

Audience trust is often mentioned and referred to as "an asset" presently enjoyed by journalists, but potentially threatened by ethical misconduct. Conditional sentences such as "without the trust of our readers, we will be unable to adequately perform our mission of providing news" are prevalent in formal codes of journalistic ethics. Such sentences, along with the frequent use of terminology referring to the "retaining" and "maintaining" of trust, all point to the fact that journalistic professional discourse treats trust as something enjoyed at present, and at the same time as the raison detre for journalistic professionalism.

The centrality, or even sanctity, of audience trust for journalistic professionalism can also be inferred from the reaction of the journalistic community to events potentially damaging for audience trust, such as the Janet Cooke scandal, or more recently the Stephen Glass or Jay son Blair affairs. In such cases, most journalists respond to the violations of the norms of credibility and factualness by stressing the centrality of audience trust to the profession.

As Eason argues, journalists felt "assaulted," "humiliated," and "befouled" in the wake of the Janet Cooke scandal because the violation of trust potentially reflected upon what journalists see as a profession with "only one credential": credibility.

As columnist Ellen Goodman put it in the aftermath of the affair: "This is a society running short on trust... Most journalists deal with this fact every day. We're assigned the role of public trustee. So we are all affected by any single reporter who fuels the public wonder: Is this true? Do I believe them?... It makes our jobs harder. It makes our lives harder. We feel it."

In sum, audience trust plays a vital role in the occupational culture of journalists. This trust is an aim, an important tool, an asset, and the rationale behind most professional credos. Journalists adhering to professional norms do so partly because they wish to maintain audience trust. Those less committed to professional norms might rationalize that these principles are unimportant, since the audience does not trust media reports anyway.

However, in recent years journalists have had reasons to doubt the validity of the professional assumption regarding the trust of the audience. Survey data in the United States point to the fact that public trust in the media is eroding. While there has not been much academic research into journalists' reactions to survey data tracking the declining trust of the audience, abundant professional discourse reacting to such reports can be found in professional magazines and conventions.

Some journalists have dismissed survey findings about diminishing audience trust as representing nothing more than responses people give to pollsters, bearing no relation to reality. Others have pointed to the various methodological problems that might impair the validity of such surveys. Others still simply argue that it should not matter for journalists whether a growing number of citizens do not trust the press.

As Ben Bradlee, former editor of the Washington Post, argues, "We journalists are not there to be loved. And I don't know that other professions are getting more respect. Not Congress. Not politicians. Not businessmen." As Brace Sanford maintains, however, journalists may simply be resisting survey findings about dwindling audience trust by saying that they are not in the business of being popular.

In sum, some reports indicate that journalists ignore survey findings regarding shrinking audience trust. However, social psychological research about trust seems to indicate that when trustees feel mistrusted, they tend to betray trust. This leads to the contrary expectation, that when journalists sense audience mistrust, they might become less committed to the audience.

The central role of audience trust in journalistic professional ideology also suggests that perceptions of audience trust should be correlated with journalistic professionalism; but in this case, audience trust is such an essential part of the professional culture that it is impossible to speak of a causal direction.

Given this conflicting reasoning, it seems sensible to ask: RQ1: Will perceptions of audience trust or mistrust be related to identification with professional journalistic norms? This will be the main research question examined in the following pages. Because this is the first exploration to date of journalists' perceptions of audience trust, it seems warranted to ask who those journalists who feel trusted are. Are they demographically or professionally different from journalists who feel mistrusted?

Therefore, the second research question seeks to explore the demographic and professional characteristics of journalists who feel trusted by the audience: RQ2: What is the profile of journalists who feel trusted, based on demographics, professional ascription and status, and the evaluation of the audience?

THE CONTEXT: JOURNALISM IN ISRAEL

Since its inception in 1948 and for more than three decades, Israel, a state with a centralist governmental structure and a social-democratic tradition, had a media map dominated by government-controlled public radio (and since 1968, television), accompanied by party-controlled newspapers, with virtually all political parties owning newspapers.

As a result of the collapse of the social-democratic ethos, as well as the rise of privatization and globalization, and the strengthening of neo-liberal tendencies, the nature of the media market has completely changed. Since the 1970s, party newspapers have lost their status and their readership, and three independent papers have come to dominate the scene: two tabloids (Yedioth Ahronoth and Maarw) and the highbrow Haaretz.

Television broadcasting has been transformed from a system based on one monopolistic public channel (Channel One of the Israel Broadcasting Authority, or IBA), to a multi-channel structure, with the launch of the commercial and privately owned Channel Two and Channel Ten (the former commenced operation in 1993, the latter in 2002).

Radio news is still dominated by the state owned Kol Israel (Voice of Israel, operated by the IBA) and the military-operated Galey Tzahal. Since the 1980s, local newspapers, mainly syndicated and privately owned, have flourished in many localities. Local television news, broadcast through cable only, began operation during the 1990s.

As in other settings, the Israeli mainstream national and local media are supplemented by "small," alternative media outlets, owned and operated by members of minority groups and co-cultures, and made for their consumption. These include a variety of newspapers and (mostly pirate) radio stations targeted at populations such as Arab Israelis, Ultra-Orthodox Jews, extreme right wing ideological groups, and Mizrachiyim (Jews of Middle Eastern origin). Unlike the United States, where the main reason for fragmentation was the desire of producers and advertisers to reach a clearly defined niche for selling their products, in Israel the motivating force was the development of identity politics, and the desire of co-cultural groups to express themselves, largely due to the fact that as "mute communities," they had been excluded from the national media. These alternative media are mostly small-scale, underfunded and understaffed news productions. While some of these channels are very popular among their target audiences, most of their audiences consume alternative media in addition to, rather than instead of, mainstream news channels.

A thriving journalistic professional community has evolved in Israel over the years, especially since the 1960s, with the establishment of formal journalists' associations. The most prominent of these, the Israel Press Council (IPC), was able to acquire semi-formal acknowledgement by the legal system.

The professional community of Israeli journalists has codes of ethics, ethics courts, and various publications dedicated to professional discourse.The journalists' associations have been somewhat effective in combating legislation that sought to curb the freedom of the press, but much less effective in preventing the erosion in salaries, and the move from employment arrangements based on tenure and uniform wages to those based primarily on personal contracts.

Despite the legacy of "mobilized journalism," loyal to national or party causes, recent studies seem to point out that most Israeli journalists at present adhere to the objective "gatekeeper" journalistic model, rather than to alternative models of advocacy, public, or "new" journalism. Interestingly, survey data show that the Israeli public maintains moderate levels of trust in the media.

Perhaps the Israeli public is more trusting of news institutions due to the ongoing IsraeliPalestinian conflict: institutional trust is known to be higher during times of crisis, due to "rallying" effects.

Method

Data: The research questions will be examined in survey data collected from a sample of Israeli journalists between September and December 2002. As in previous survey research, a journalist was defined as a person who makes decisions directly affecting hard-news content.

This category includes reporters and editors, but excludes camerapersons, graphic editors, copy editors, and the like. Also excluded were journalists who concentrate on soft news, for example, sports, entertainment, travel, and fashion. Stratified sampling was used to build a diverse sample of reporters and editors.

Journalists were sampled from every Hebrew language national news outlet (including print, television, and radio), and from a sample of local newspapers. Each outlet was further stratified by respondents' seniority to ensure that the sample included senior reporters and editors, on the one hand, and more junior reporters, on the other.

A separate stratum was created for journalists from alternative media targeting specific populations (including news outlets in Arabic, English, and Russian, and news media targeted at religious and right-wing groups). The list of Israeli journalists that was used as a sampling base was obtained from the Ifat Media Information Centre. This list was updated and completed using bylines and credits, and in a few cases using lists of journalists obtained from editors of the various news media.

Some of the questionnaires were sent by mail to journalists who had previously been contacted and had agreed to participate in the study. Other journalists were interviewed by telephone. The Dahaf Institute for public opinion research conducted the interviews for this portion of the study.

Of the 389 journalists contacted, only 13 (about 3 per cent) refused to participate. However, an additional 167 journalists (about 43 per cent) who had agreed to participate in the study did not return the questionnaire by mail (even after they were re-contacted by the research assistant).

The rest, 209 journalists, completed the questionnaire by either phone or mail. Hence, the overall response rate was 53.7 per cent. This response rate is comparable to those achieved by other scholars using questionnaires to investigate journalists worldwide.

The sample included 201 Jews and 8 Arabs (about 4 per cent). The average age was 39. Approximately 79 per cent of the respondents defined themselves as "secular," 8 per cent as "religious," and an additional 12 per cent as "traditional." About 90 per cent of respondents were Israeli-born, 45 per cent identified themselves as Ashkenazim (Jews of European or American origin), and 14 per cent identified themselves as Mizrachiyim (Jews of Middle Eastern origin). The rest of the Jewish respondents stated that neither category applied to them, or that they were of mixed origin. Approximately 61 per cent had an academic education, 20 per cent had studied in schools of communication or journalism, and an additional 20 per cent had degrees in fields of study related to the subjects they covered (political science, economics, Middle Eastern studies, etc.).

The sample somewhat over-represented male journalists (71 per cent, while estimates of the proportion of female journalists in the Israeli media range from 35 per cent to 40 per cent), probably because it over-represented senior journalists (101 of the 209 respondents were "senior").

Measures

Identification with Professional Norms. Respondents were asked to rate the importance of a series of professional journalistic norms. The question was worded, "Please indicate whether you think each of the following is an important principle of journalism." Response categories ranged from 1="not at all important" to 4="very important."

The items included "always remaining neutral," "getting the facts right," "not publishing rumors," "getting both sides of the story," "providing at least two sources to corroborate a story based on anonymous sources," and "keeping some distance from the people you cover." The items were averaged to create a scale.

Perception of Audience Trust was measured using two items. Respondents were asked whether they agree with the statements, "The Israeli audience trusts the Israeli media" and "My audience is very trusting of my journalistic work and the journalistic work of the news organization I work for."

The latter question was intentionally doublebarreled to allow the inclusion of relatively anonymous reporters and editors in the study (who would probably not be able to respond to questions about audience trust in their particular work). Response categories ranged from 1="do not at all agree" to 4="strongly agree."

The correlation between the items was only moderate. Hence, results will be reported for two separate measures [one measuring perceived general trust in the Israeli media as a whole, and the other tapping perceived particular trust, as well as for a joint perceived trust measure calculated as the sum of both items.

Evaluation of the Audience. Respondents were also asked whether they agree with the following statements: "The Israeli audience cares only about sensationalism" and "The Israeli audience is very interested in news". Response categories ranged from 1="do not at all agree" to 4= "strongly agree." The correlation between both items was moderate ($r = .29$, $p < .001$, after reverse-coding the first statement), and hence they will be treated separately, as well as jointly, in the following analysis. The joint measure, calculated as the sum of both items, had a mean of 6.08, and a standard deviation of 1.14.

Results

Israeli journalists perceived low levels of audience trust in the Israeli media in general, but high levels of trust in their own news organizations. While only 5.4 per cent strongly agreed with the perceived general trust statement, 35.2 per cent strongly agreed with the perceived particular trust statement. Only one respondent (.5 per cent) strongly disagreed with the perceived particular trust item. In comparison, 16.6 per cent of respondents strongly disagreed with the perceived general trust statement.

A paired sample f-test was used to test for the statistical significance of the difference between the answers to the particular and general trust items. Results showed that the perceived general trust scores were significantly lower than the perceived particular trust scores. RQ1 asked whether journalists who perceive audience trust would adhere to professional norms relating to audience trust.

To examine the association between the constructs, the perceived trust items were correlated with the professional identification scale. Significant correlations were found for both perceived general trust, perceived particular trust, and the joint perceived trust measure. That is, the more the journalists sensed that audiences trusted the Israeli media in general and their own news organization in particular, the more they thought that journalistic values such as neutrality and verification were important. Bivariate analysis, however, is not sufficient in order to demonstrate a connection between perceived trust and identification with journalistic norms. The bivariate association could be spurious, *e.g.*, caused by potential correlates of both constructs.

To negate the possibility that the association between perceived audience trust and adherence to professional norms is entirely caused by an association between both and a third variable, multivariate analysis is required. For this purpose, Ordinary Least Squares regression was run, with the professional identification index as the dependent variable. Factors potentially related to professional identification were entered as covariates.

These included formal training in communication or journalism, working for local vs. national media, working as a senior or junior journalist, journalists' perception of the audience, their own trust in the Israeli news media, and a range of demographic variables. The model explains 22 per cent of the variance in the professional identification scale. Age was associated with the professional identification scale. Older journalists exhibited a tendency to identify more with professional norms such as factualness and balance. Personal trust in the media was significantly associated with professional identification: the more journalists trust the media, the more they tend to identify with trust-related journalistic norms.

Formal training in journalism or communications, seniority, and education were all positively, though not significantly, related to professional identification. Religious journalists identified less with professional norms, and females identified slightly more. Again, both latter effects were not statistically significant.

Our main interest here is the coefficient for perceived trust. Even after controlling for all other variables, the association between perceived audience trust and professional identification remained statistically significant. That is, the more journalists identified with professional norms, the more they felt trusted.

The same regression model was run twice more, with the particular and general trust items instead of the joint perceived trust measure (all other variables were kept as covariates in the model). Results show that the general pattern reported above holds for both perceived general trust and perceived particular trust separately.

The more people perceived particular trust, the more they identified with professional norms. The same was true for perceived general trust, though this time the coefficient was only borderline significant. Who Feels Trusted? Since this is the first exploration of journalists' perceptions of audience trust, it seems worthwhile to ask what characterizes journalists who feel trusted.

For this reason, the association between the perceived trust variables and other phenomena was examined. Perceived audience trust was statistically unrelated to most demographic variables. The differences between males and females on both perceived trust items (particular and general) were not significant. Both perceived trust items were not significantly correlated with age, education, or ethnic origin. The only demographic variable departing somewhat from this pattern was religiosity, which correlated positively and significantly with perceived particular trust. More religious respondents felt that their audience had more faith in their news media outlet than did secular respondents.

Perceiving audience trust was also uncorrelated with variables relating to respondents' seniority in the journalistic community. Senior reporters and editors did not differ from more junior journalists in the levels of perceived general and particular audience trust.

Journalists working in national media outlets did not differ from journalists working in local media outlets. There were also no significant differences in the perceived trust items among journalists working in different types of broadcast media-print, radio, television, Internet, and news agencies. In sum, it seems that perceived trust could not be predicted by any type of occupational or demographic variable, except for religiosity.

For this reason, the correlations between the perceived trust items and additional variables were tested. The perceived trust items were positively correlated with journalists' own trust in the Israeli media. This item was worded, "Personally, I am very trusting of the Israeli media." Perceived audience trust was also correlated with journalists' evaluations of the audience.

The more the journalists felt trusted, the more they agreed with the statement, "The Israeli audience is very interested in news". The more the journalists felt that Israelis trusted the media, the less they agreed with the statement, "The Israeli audience cares only about sensationalism". The correlation between the joint perceived trust measure and the joint audience evaluation measure was $r = .25$.

Discussion

This study was designed as a preliminary and exploratory investigation of journalists' perceptions of audience trust. Results show that feeling trusted is correlated with the identification of journalists with professional norms relating to trust-principles such as telling both sides of the story, remaining neutral, getting the facts right, and not publishing rumors.

When interpreting this finding, we should keep in mind that the correlation between perceived audience trust and adherence to journalistic norms does not imply causation. Social psychological research and theories about trust advance the interpretation that felt trust leads to greater professional identification. However, it was argued that audience trust is embedded so strongly within journalistic professional ideology that we cannot determine what causes what. Arguably, the direction of the association could even be reversed, with professional identification leading to perceptions of trust, rather than the other way around.

The association between perceived audience trust and identification with journalistic norms remained significant even after controlling for potential intervening variables. This was true especially with regard to perceived particular trust. However, it is important to note that the absolute size of this association was not very strong.

The difference between journalists perceiving the most and the least audience trust translates to a difference of.40 on the 1-4 journalistic identification measure. Still, perceived trust was one of the strongest predictors of identification with journalistic norms, second only to age, and stronger than some more likely determinants of professionalism, *e.g.*, formal training, seniority, and demographics.

The findings are, of course, limited to Israeli journalists, and hence cannot be generalized to other contexts, given enormous cultural differences between Israel and other developed societies. Though slightly more trusting of the media, Israelis are less trusting in general, and therefore probably less likely to feel trusted than Americans.

Thus, they might dismiss perceived mistrust more easily by thinking that trust is not important. More research needs to be carried out in order to determine whether Israeli journalists are the exception, or whether the association between perceived mistrust and professional identification is the rule.

As the first exploration of journalists' perceptions of audience trust, this study provides us with an opportunity to probe into these potentially important perceptions. The data revealed that Israeli journalists sense a low level of audience trust in the Israeli media in general, but a high level of trust in their own news organizations and in their own journalistic work.

This finding, perhaps similar to Davison's thirdperson perception of the audience, should probably be interpreted as a "self-preserving bias." Psychologists tell us that people tend to perceive the world in ways that preserve their own self-evaluation. For journalists, perceiving that "I am trusted," while "other journalists are not," is certainly human.

Feeling mistrusted was associated with believing that the audience was uninterested in politics and sought only sensational stories. This attitude could also be a self-preserving bias: "If the audience is mistrustful, then the audience is probably shallow."

The study also explored other potential sources of journalists' perceptions regarding audience trust in addition to their evaluation of the audience. However, both measures of perceived trust were not associated with most demographic variables, with the reporters' rank in the journalistic hierarchy, with the medium in which they operate, or with their employment by a national or local media outlet. The only significant predictor of perceived trust, outside religiosity and the evaluations of the audience, was the journalists' own trust in the media. When journalists had faith in the Israeli media, they exhibited a tendency to think that audiences trusted the media, and vice versa for journalists mistrusting the Israeli media. We tend to think that others see the world as we do.

This "looking glass effect" is probably the explanation for the associations between journalists' perceptions of audience trust and their own trust in the Israeli media. As one top producer told Gans in his seminal study of news organizations, "The conception of our audience is a reflection of ourselves."

Additional potential sources for journalists' perceptions of audience trust in their news organization or in the Israeli media in general were not measured in this study. Some editors and journalists probably read market research that frequently reports on audience trust.

Others may be aware of academic research documenting audience trust in the media, especially research that has been quoted by news outlets. Journalists' sense of audience trust or mistrust may also be influenced by informal feedback.

Journalists probably vary in their exposure to formal and informal audience feedback, and the content of such feedback varies between and within news organizations. These differences, which were not measured in the current study, may account for the differences among journalists regarding perceived audience trust.

More religious journalists sensed a higher level of audience particular trust. This finding is interesting given the fact that among the Israeli population in general, religious audiences tend to mistrust the news media.

Perhaps religious journalists simply do not feel the antagonism and alienation of religious audiences towards mainstream media because these sentiments are targeted mostly at secular journalists, in addition, some religious journalists probably do not personally feel audience mistrust, since they work for alternative niche-targeted media, and hence they enjoy their religious audience's trust (while their audience's mistrust is targeted towards mainstream news media).

A major limitation of this study has to do with measurement problems in both main constructs. The reliability of the professional identification scale was rather low, and the correlation between the two components of perceived audience trust was only moderate.

However, the main findings were replicated when analyzing general and particular trust components separately and by and large when separating the professional identification scale into single items. Furthermore, when interpreting the results, one should consider the fact that measurement error typically biases correlation estimates downward.

If weak measures worked in the above analyses, then the associations reported could probably be replicated with more accurate measures. In sum, this study demonstrated that journalists' perceptions of audience trust are correlated with their identification with professional norms, their general evaluation of the audience, and their own trust in the media. The design of this study limits our ability to reach conclusions with regard to the causal mechanism explaining these associations.

Future research should explore these mechanisms using a superior (perhaps longitudinal) design and improved measures. The results of the current exploration suggest that doing so should be worthwhile. On the afternoon of April 11, 2007, attorney James Cooney, who represented one of the "Duke Lacrosse case defendants," spoke to a group of students, family and supporters of the defendants, and the news media.

Just minutes before, North Carolina Attorney General Roy Cooper, after an exhaustive investigation in the case, dropped all charges and declared the defendants, Reade Seligmann, Collin Finnerty, and David Evans to be "innocent of all charges." While excoriating the performance of the Durham Herald-Sun in its coverage of the case, Cooney then declared that one cannot win by suing "people who buy ink by the barrels." In other words, while the attorneys and defendants clearly were unhappy with the newspaper, there would be no libel suit forthcoming.

The decision by the attorneys not to sue the Herald-Sun, as well as other media outlets, such as CNN's "Nancy Grace Show," which especially had been quick to pronounce guilt for the Duke Three has its roots in a series of decisions made by the U.S. Supreme Court more than four decades ago. The first of these decisions, Times v. Sullivan, which was decided in March, 1964, in essence rewrote all of state law regarding the libeling of "public officials."

In subsequent decisions, the High Court added most government employees and later included "public figures" as well. There is no doubt that modern libel law is a product of what the court led by Earl Warren decided during the tumultuous Civil Rights Era and did much to change the landscape there.

In a 2004 report, the Media Law Resource Centre noted that over the past 25 years, the media firms have been increasingly winning libel lawsuits filed against them. Media firms are winning more trials, and even the number of libel trials is falling, according to the report1 Furthermore, even large jury awards often are substantially reduced on appeal, the report noted.

It would seem that these developments would bode well for the freedom of the press, and many people have given the U.S. Supreme Court much of the credit for this change in the legal landscape. The U.S. Supreme Court under Chief Justice Warren was well known for its decisions that changed much of the legal landscape in this country.

From Brown v. Board of Education to the Miranda case, the high court reshaped the direction of government policy in its issuances from the bench, triggering a debate on "judicial activism" that resonates to the present day. Although the Warren Court was not known to be particularly friendly to private enterprise, it did act decisively to protect one set of private firms - newspapers and other print media companies - from the ancient tort of libel.

Beginning with its landmark 1964 decision, Times v. Sullivan, to its 1967 decisions of Associated Press v. Walker and Butts v. Curtis Publishing Company, the court in effect rewrote libel law for the entire nation, setting down new and extensive burdens that "public officials" and "public figures" had to overcome in order to win libel suits.

The litigation that began the Sullivan chain of events came from the South during the turbulent Civil Rights Era. A police commissioner from Montgomery, Alabama, claimed that an advertisement in the New York Times libeled him, and a local jury agreed, awarding him $500,000, at that time, according to Lewis, the largest libel judgement in Alabama history. Other officials in southern states were also seeking damages from the Times and other media outlets they considered to be "unfriendly."

The Warren Court overturned that decision - and much of state libel law - and permanently changed the legal environment for libel. For the most part, the court's action is portrayed as an ideological attempt to expand the bounds of freedom of speech and to affect public discourse in this country.

Yet, we believe that this is a rather short-term view that does not take into account the interests of the various players in the courtroom dramas. Indeed, the issue was not simply about free speech, but also how the courts were to deal with what essentially was a strategy by southern politicians to win large libel judgements against northern-based news organizations.

As we see it, there were gains from trade to be obtained from the court's decision: the court protects the newspapers, which simultaneously help to protect the courts from adverse public opinion. James Buchanan and Gordon Tullock began the Public Choice revolution in which researchers have examined government through the lens of interests of the participants. For the most part, the analysis has been of legislatures, since it is rather easy to do statistical analysis using votes.

Examination of the courts via analysis other than one of the "public interest," on the other hand, has been almost non-existent. Timothy Terrell took a Public Choice approach to the issue of standing for environmental groups, but little else has been written on this subject We attempt to add to this literature.

We add that a relatively new journal, the Journal of Empirical Legal Studies, does apply statistical analysis to the courts. It does not pursue a particular point of view but rather examines cases as they occur. For example, the November

2004 edition was devoted entirely to the trend towards civil settlements and criminal guilty pleas, but did not attempt to place it in anything like a Public Choice or interest group framework.

Besides raising questions about the intentions of the Supreme Court in these libel cases, this chapter also examines some of the changes brought about by the high court's decision, looking at the frequency of libel verdicts being reversed on appeal.

Our study shows that (1) the Sullivan decision and others following decidedly changed the patterns of libel awards and appeals, and (2) one can give an alternative explanation to the Gertz v. Welch decision, which we believe was decided, at least in part, because of the unpopular political positions of the John Birch Society.

In the end, we raise the interesting question as to whether or not the Supreme Court was more interested in protecting the "civil rights" and other "progressive" movements, as well as so-called mainstream news media, than it was actually protecting and promoting universal free speech.

Libel and Liability

Libel suits are occupational hazards of journalism, even in the wake of the landmark U.S. Supreme Court decisions. While the First Amendment protects the press from most government censorship, the peril of multimillion dollar losses through libel judgements can threaten the financial and reputational well-being of media organizations, along with reporters who write the offending stories.

Overbeck points out that "the fear of libel suits often leads journalists to suppress newsworthy stories they would otherwise publish, thus engaging in a form of self-censorship that is rarely in the public interest". Even if the libel claims are not legally valid, Overbeck says that "hostile juries sometimes hand out enormous punitive damage awards against newspapers, magazines, and broadcasters...."

He adds that a "single libel suit can be financially devastating even to a powerful media corporation". (In many cases, however, these damage awards are either severely reduced or overturned altogether on appeal, although Overbeck warns that courts do not overturn all multi-million dollar libel judgements.

We argue that the Sullivan and Walker decisions greatly reduced the likelihood of actual payment of huge libel judgements.) Even though newspapers carry libel insurance, the legal fees that newspapers must absorb, even if they win in court, can damage the firm, even in a post-rimes v. Sullivan legal climate.

The possibility of losses due to even the successful defence of a claim of libel can serve as a warning to residual claimants to monitor the content of their newspapers. If a media firm loses a libel case, the payout can be expensive, even if the firm has libel insurance. Furthermore, there is also the loss of "reputational capital" that a news firm can suffer, and it can have a negative impact on the value of the firm's assets. Thus, one can expect residual claimants to set up a system that will attempt to intercept stories that might be regarded as libelous. Editors, publishers, and attorneys are the barrier to libel, an important line of defence set up by owners of the media firm.

Historical defence of libel has rested upon:

1. Truth: If a statement is true, no matter how harmful or hurtful it may be, it cannot be considered to be libel.
2. Privilege: "Fair and accurate" accounts of what happens during an official government proceeding (including legislative bodies and the courts), along with an accurate report of a government document.
3. Fair Comment: This is a statement of opinion regarding the performance of someone considered to be in the "limelight," including politicians, actors, or sports celebrities.

The U.S. Constitution is not the only legal document protecting freedom of the press. State constitutions also restrict civil authorities from suppressing news stories. Most libel suits have been filed in state courts, and libel cases rarely were overturned by U.S. Supreme Court review before Times v. Sullivan. In 1964, however, the U.S. Supreme Court changed the bounds of freedom of the press dramatically.

The court, led by Chief Justice Warren, continued its activist legacy in Times v. Sullivan, which Editor and Publisher declared to be "one of the most important decisions upholding freedom of the press in our time." It was perhaps the single most important court ruling on libel since the John Peter Zenger decision of 1735 in New York.

Literature on Libel

As one might expect, the legal literature on libel is immense and cannot be covered in a meaningful sense in this brief chapter. However, we use for our background two law journal pieces, including Logan and Franklin; communications law books; and communications books, including Overbeck and Nelson, Teeter and Le Due. However, the legal literature on libel fails to deal with the economic effects that libel cases have had on media firms.

The economics and business literature, unfortunately, is quite scant on this subject Anderson has covered the effects of libel upon asset values of newspaper firms, but most libel literature tends to deal either with the laws themselves or approaches the subject from an ideological viewpoint

According to Franklin, Times v. Sullivan along with Walker did, indeed, change the libel landscape. He writes about libel cases since 1964 that "From an overall perspective, the most striking conclusion is that plaintiffs win such a low percentage of appeals (5 per cent) compared to the success rate of 66 per cent for defendants." Although there have been numerous high dollar judgements given at the trial court level, they rarely stand, Franklin writes.

Logan is even more enthusiastic. Of the post Times v. Sullivan era, he says: Several decades later... we can now fully evaluate the Court's handiwork: few libel claims filed; many dismissed before trial by judges (both state and federal); a handful of trials; some plaintiff victories, but because of the close appellate oversight, only the occasional full affirmation of a jury award, especially punitive damages; and eventual payouts of only cents on the dollar. These are indicia of a significant victory for those who hoped to rein in, but not destroy, the deterrent effect of the law of libel.

As shall be shown at the end of the next section, one can argue that the Sullivan verdict proved to be very important for news organizations that were engaged in libel defences, especially at the appellate level We first describe the case and then look briefly at its effect on libel verdicts.

Case of New York Times v. Sullivan

On March 29, 1960, the Committee to Defend Martin Luther King and the Struggle for Freedom in the South, a civil rights group, ran a full-page advertisement in the New York Times. Entitled "Heed Their Rising Voices," the advertisement alleged police brutality against civil rights demonstrators in several southern cities, including Montgomery, Alabama.

Nelson, Teeter, and Le Due write that "there were errors in the advertisement" The New York Times admitted in court that it had not checked the text of the advertisements against its own news stories, which gave conflicting accounts of the events. As Nelson, Teeter, and Le Due note, die controversy centered upon the following statement:

In Montgomery, Alabama, after students sang "My Country 'Tis of Thee" on the State Capital steps, their leaders were expelled from school, and truckloads of police armed with shotguns and tear-gas ringed the Alabama State College Campus. When the entire student body protested to state authorities by refusing to re-register, their dining hall was padlocked in an attempt to starve them into submission.

Actually, while police were present in large numbers, they did not surround the Alabama State campus. Furthermore, no one padlocked the dining hall. Although his name was not mentioned in the advertisement Montgomery Police and Fire Commissioner L.B. Sullivan took exception and claimed he was libeled by implication. He sued the Times in Alabama state court for $500,000 in damages. While only about 39 copies of the Times circulated in the Montgomery area (394 in the state of Alabama), according to Lewis, the trial judge in Montgomery ruled that that was a significant enough number for the case to be heard in Alabama Circuit Court. Judge Walter B. Jones instructed the jury panel that Sullivan did not have to prove that he had suffered any financial damages due to the advertisement He said jurors only had to consider whether or not the statements in the advertisement were false and, if false, it they had adversely affected Sullivan's reputation. The jury returned a verdict for $500,000 in favour of the plaintiff.

The Times appealed to the Alabama Supreme Court which affirmed the lower court ruling. The court said that the verdict did not violate Alabama law, and that the amount of the judgement was fair, even though Sullivan did not prove financial damages. The Times appealed to the U.S. Supreme Court, which agreed to hear the case.

Indeed, the verdict was popular in the South at a time when the region was in the midst of the struggles of what now is called the Civil Rights Era. Even though a fellow newspaper had been financially damaged, the nextday editorial in the Alabama Journal, the Montgomery evening paper, declared that the decision "could have the effect of causing reckless publishers of the North... to make a re-survey of their habit of permitting anything detrimental to die South and its people to appear in their columns".

Emboldened by the decision, a number of other government officials from southern states filed libel suits against news media organizations. By 1964, according to Lewis, local and state officials "had brought nearly $300 million in libel actions against the press," or more than $1.7 billion in current dollars.

Overbeck writes that the U.S. Supreme Court historically had been reluctant to hear state libel cases, but this was no ordinary libel case, nor was this an ordinary Supreme Court. In the January 6, 1964, hearing, Sullivan's attorneys told the court that "the Constitution has never required that states afford newspapers the privilege of leveling false and defamatory 'facts' at persons simply because they hold public office. The great weight of American authority has rejected such a plea by newspapers."

Benjamin J. Stein writes that the court's decision was more about the social and political climate of the day, not about the law: There were two distinctive aspects to this advertisement. First it was largely false in its descriptions of brutality and repression, which turned out to be often made up (emphasis Stein's). second, the advertisement changed history.

He further writes: Legal realism has to be understood, at least glancingly, before one can even start to understand what happened when the Supremes got the appeal on New York Times v. Sullivan. The justices in their black robes were faced with an awesome legal realism problem. On the one hand, cleariy the lower courts were correct in Sullivan.

The advertisement had been not only false, but wildly, irresponsibly, cruelly false. A man had been called a lawless "violater" (sic) when many of the specifics of his bad acts were simply made of whole cloth. libel was a crucial part of the legal structure of America....As recently as 1952, the Supreme Court, per Justice Frankfurter, had said there was no First Amendment protection for libel.

The Supreme Court, Stein writes, was in a quandary. He says: all of the weight of authority stood for the proposition that Sullivan had been defamed falsely, had lost reputation, and collect. Note to author Is something missing in the quote, since "and collect" doesn't fit in Plus, the decisions of the lower courts are presumed to have some weight just because they saw the evidence and the witnesses with their own eyes.

On the other hand...the appellee, Mr. Sullivan, was a segregationalist, an official of George Corley Wallace's Alabama, and all of his friends and supporters were racists and bigots too, presumably. The appellants, and the libelers, so to speak, were kindly black clergymen allied with Martin Luther King, Jr. They were for racial justice. Also, one appellant was the New York Times, by far the most powerful newspaper in the world, a voice of enlightened racial harmony, a strong, important backer of the Warren Court in its most controversial decisions.

It certainly is true that the New York Times was a strong ally of those in the "civil rights" movement, and was on record as editorially supporting many of the controversial Warren Court decisions like Brown vs.

Board of Education. Furthermore, as already pointed out, the strategy of public officials and other outspoken opponents of civil rights for blacks suing New York-based news organizations for libel was proving to be a huge financial threat to these firms, and a decision that would have preserved the established pattern of leaving libel decisions to the states would have left newspapers and broadcast entities open to even more lawsuits.

In hindsight, it is not surprising that the court "saved" the Times, given the situation at that time and the activist nature of the Warren Court. On March 9, 1964, the High Court handed down a 9-0 reversal of the verdict, creating a whole new standard for libel when "public officials" were involved. Furthermore, the justices did not order a new trial, but rather closed the case in order to keep the suit from returning to Alabama.

Justice William J. Brennan wrote the decision for six members of the court (Three other justices, while agreeing with the majority, published their own decisions.) Brennan wrote that the Alabama verdict could not stand for three reasons. First, it gave public officials too much leverage in fighting newspapers with which they disagreed.

Second, it would truncate the "national debate" on controversial issues. Third, public officials voluntarily move into an arena that opens them to more public criticism than is given to private citizens. Brennan's decision declared that "debate on public issues should be uninhibited, robust, and wide-open."

While he agreed that such debate "may well include vehement, caustic, and sometimes unpleasantly sharp attacks on government and public officials," the First Amendment protected such debate, said Brennan. The court raised the burden of proof for public officials who sue for libel, making them prove that a defamatory statement "was made with 'actual malice', which is knowledge that it was false or given with reckless disregard of whetiier it was false or not," according to Justice Brennan's opinion.

"Times malice" requires that public officials who wish to win a libel suit must be able to demonstrate successfully in court that those who published the falsehood either knew the information they were publishing was false, or that the defendants acted recklessly in searching for the truth. Armed with its decision, the court expanded the "Times malice" requirement to nearly all government employees. In its Curtis Publishing Company v. Wallace Butts and Associated Press v. Edwin A. Walker decisions in 1967, a unanimous court extended libel protection to stories written about people who were "public figures." The court's decision granted extra protection to media firms, and potentially saved newspapers and broadcasters millions of dollars in libel judgements.

The Walker case was similar to that of Sullivan. Former U.S. Army Gen. Edwin Walker, who had been accused of circulating John Birch Society literature to his soldiers in the 24th Infantry Division stationed in Germany, later organized protests to the admission of James Meredith, an African-American., to what was then the all-white University of Mississippi in 1962 after Walker's resignation from the army.

Like Sullivan, Walker sued the Associated Press for its admittedly inaccurate coverage of his activities during the protests, which became so violent that President John F. Kennedy sent National Guard troops to enforce a desegregation order from the federal courts. And like Walker, he was awarded $500,000 by a sympathetic jury, a decision that was upheld until the Supreme Court overturned it by its decision to apply the "Times malice" standards to Walker, whom it determined to be a "public figure."

The numbers bear out the success of the Sullivan and Walker decisions in reducing libel claims. While the average verdict at the trial level rose significantly in the years following the decisions, the appellate courts clearly took the high court's rulings to heart and were much more likely either to reverse the lower court decisions or to substantially reduce the awards amounts. While jury awards did rise during the post-Sullivan era, the appeals courts were much more likely to overturn the jury decisions or at least shrink the judgements that juries awarded people they believed to be victims of libel. The Walker decision seemed to have settled the libel question, but the Warren Court also had generated much controversy.

First, jurists like William Rehnquist and Warren Burger believed the high court had erred in taking much of the libel authority from the states in the way that it did in Sullivan and beyond. Second, one can argue that the "liberalism" of the Warren Court also helped to energize conservative political groups who were against the court's decisions against prayers in public schools, school desegregation, the rights of criminal suspects, and criminal investigations. Thus, when Republican Richard Nixon became President of the United States in 1969, conservatives hoped that he would make appointments that would push the courts in other directions. (Whether the Supreme Court under the leadership of Nixon appointee Chief Justice Burger was more "conservative" is a matter for discussion, but it is clear that Nixon and other conservatives wanted the court to change some of its ideological and legal directions.)

The case of Gertz v. Welch ultimately was a challenge to the earlier Warren Court libel rulings for two reasons. First, it offered the court the alternatives of either to continue its expansive rulings regarding libel or to scale them back; second, it offered the court another opportunity to examine the separation of powers between states and the federal government However, as is demonstrated in the next section, the high court took a third option: it relied upon what one might describe as a "legal technicality."

The Gertz v. Welch Decision

Gertz is similar to Butts and Walker in that Elmer Gertz, a Chicago attorney, was prominent in his profession. However, unlike those two, the high court ruled in a 5-4 decision that Gertz was not a "public figure" and, therefore, did not have to meet the "Times malice" standard in order to win his lawsuit against American Opinion, which is published by the John Birch Society.

(Gertz, an attorney, successfully represented a family that brought civil action against a Chicago police officer who shot and killed their son. An article in American Opinion called Gertz a "Leninist" and a "Communistfronter," among other things and claimed the lawsuit was a "frame-up" against the police officer.)

As the numbers demonstrate, not all of the court agreed. Justices William O. Douglas and Brennan argued for expanding the "Times malice" standard to everyone, not just public officials and public figures in the course of public discussion. As in the situation of Sullivan and Walker, one of the parties in the lawsuit opposed the imposition of civil rights laws and policies.

However, unlike Sullivan and Walker, this time the anti-civil rights party was the plaintiff, not the defendant The John Birch Society was and is known for its "ultraconservative" views and was vehemently opposed to the Warren Court and many of its decisions, although, ironically, it was using one of that court's most famous decisions on libel as die basis for its appeal. If the standards used in the Butts and Walker decisions had been applied in Gertz, it is clear that the court would have deemed Elmer Gertz a "public figure."

Gertz, after all, had been involved in a number of prominent cases, including the winning of parole in 1958 of the notorious killer Nathan Leopold, and he ultimately succeeded in having the death penalty overturned for a famous client, Jack Ruby (who shot Lee Harvey Oswald to death on national television). Nor was the High Court united, as it had been with Sullivan and Walker, both of which were unanimous decisions, while the Gertz vote was 5-4.

Justices who were on all three courts included William O. Douglas, William Brennan, Potter Stewart and Byron White. Of these justices, only Stewart voted with the majority in Gertz. The four other votes came from justices appointed by presidents Lyndon B. Johnson and Richard M Nixon.

Public discussion in the aftermath of Gertz centered on the question of whether the high court was "giving back" protections that the Warren Court had given to the press. In his dissent, Douglas argued that the decision amounted to an "erosion of First Amendment protection" of journalists. While Chief Justice Warren Burger also dissented, he and White "argued that the Court had gone too far in the direction of protecting the press, and that common law rules should be left intact in libel cases involving private individuals."

Yet, the court ultimately based its decision on a small point: it ruled that Elmer Gertz was not a "public figure," so the court's rules established in Walker did not apply. However, as pointed out before, Gertz was well-known in legal circles around the country, not to mention in Chicago itself, and certainly was as much a "public figure" as others to whom the courts had given that designation.

The real difference was not in the nature of the plaintiff, but rather in the common thread of each of the defendants: they held to very different views on race and racial integration than did the majority of the Supreme Court-and the plaintiffs. American Opinion was not a mainstream publication, but rather an arm of the very conservative John Birch Society, which not only had called for resistance to the civil rights movement but also had been at the forefront in calling for the impeachment of Earl Warren during the 1960s.

The court clearly was not in favour of offering protection to an entity which-unlike the New York Times a decade earlier-was not on the same page with the Supreme Court when it came to civil rights issues. The Supreme Court not only upheld Gertz's claim that he was not a "public figure," but also remanded the case back for another trial. This time, instead of the $50,000 verdict which came from the first trial, the jury ordered the John Birch Society to pay Gertz $500,000.

Moreover, it is clear that the court's decision and the trial that followed afterwards was popular with at least some advocates of press freedom. Perhaps the most telling example comes from the former New York Times columnist and reporter Anthony Lewis, who already has been cited at length in this chapter for his book that strongly supported the U.S. Supreme Court's Sullivan decision. Writes Gertz (1992):

Congratulatory letters and calls poured in following the extensive publicity of the (second) jury verdict....Anthony Lewis, the much-quoted columnist and Supreme Court reporter whose book Gideon's Trumpet is a classic in narrating a case in understandable terms, had been calling me from time to time during the long years of delay to learn the latest developments in my case. "You did it for many others besides yourself," he wrote.

This is the same Anthony Lewis who wrote the following about Times v. Sullivan and its aftermath: in the years following the Sullivan decision, the court resoundingly vindicated the promise of the First Amendment that in the United States there shall be "no law... abridging the freedom of speech, or of the press."

However, Lewis was willing to make an exception in the Gertz case, and if one has read Lewis' columns over the years, it is clear that he has a special dislike for people whose political positions are anywhere to the right of his, and, thus, he would not be sympathetic to the John Birch Society.

Furthermore, he claims that Elmer Gertz had his reputation "damaged" by the American Opinion piece, yet Gertz clearly was open about his left-of-centre political viewpoints and certainly would not have minded being called a "Leninist" or anything else by people on the right In fact, it would seem that in Gertz's circles,praise fromAmerican Opinion would have been much more damaging to his reputation than condemnation.

Moreover, Lewis specifically condemned the use of libel as a bankrupting tool elsewhere in Make No Law, yet when it was clear that the half-million dollar verdict was aimed at doing severe financial damage to the John Birch Society, that was acceptable to him.

Upon pocketing his award, Gertz took his wife and friends on an around-the-world cruise and sent "wish-you-were-here" postcards to the JBS headquarters from various ports of call.

Yet, if one gains a sense of the First Amendment, which Lewis claimed to be supporting, it was written to protect unpopular speech by unpopular people, and one would hope that includes members of the John Birch Society. In judging Lewis's post-Gertz actions, however, one gains the sense that it could be an example of what Nat Hentoff called Free Speech for Me, but Not for Thee.

The editorial response of the New York Times to the Gertz decision also gives us pause as to the newspaper's views on free speech. The June 26, 1974, a front-page article in the Times began with the following:

The Supreme Court ruled today that an ordinary citizen elevated to sudden prominence by news events can sue any newspaper or radio or television station that circulates a false and defamatory account of his role in those events....The high court left standing however, the protection of newspapers and broadcast stations against such libel suits when their reports deal with "a public official" or a "public figure," even if the articles are untrue and damage his reputation.

As noted earlier, Elmer Gertz hardly was an "ordinary citizen," given his penchant for representing high-profile clients, nor did American Opinion's information, as inaccurate as it might have been, damage Gertz's reputation in any meaningful sense of the word. Furthermore, an editorial in the New York

Times dated June 27, 1974, fully supported the Supreme Court's decision: In a five-to-four decision, the Court made what impresses us as a sensible adjustment in its rules permitting private individuals, as distinct from public officials or other public personalities, to sue newspapers or television stations for libel. Under some past decisions it has appeared virtually impossible for ordinary citizens projected into sudden prominence by a particular event to protect themselves against false and defamatory reports.

Civil libertarians, not to mention organizations representing newspapers, had a much different opinion than did the Times, which apparently was all-too-happy to see the court backtrack when the defendants were of a different political persuasion than the Times editorial board.

As Gertz himself acknowledges, a number of organizations, including the American Newspaper Publishers Association, American Society of Newspaper Editors, Association of American University Presses, and the Authors League of America, among others, formed the Libel Defence Resource Centre in 1981 in part to deal with potential libel problems that arose, in part, because of the Gertz decision.

Whether or not ideology or a commitment to "fairness" drove the Times to take its supportive position of Gertz v. Welch is beyond the scope of our research. However, one does have to look somewhat askance at a journalistic organization that was willing to sacrifice "robust" speech because people whose political beliefs were inimical to that of the Times editorial board were in the dock.

The Impact of Sullivan and Gertz

By changing the ground rules of libel during the 1960s, the High Court lowered the risk newspapers face in publishing stories, as many news stories involve either public officials or public figures. Thus, the decisions significantly lessened the probability of someone successfully suing media firms. While media companies would still have to spend money for legal fees if someone chose to sue for libel, Times v. Sullivan reduced the chances of newspapers and broadcasters having to pay large judgements and also would be seen to be a deterrent to new lawsuits.

Even though libel insurance many pay a large portion of the judgement, the lessening of the chances of losing a libel suit would also serve to enhance the firm's "reputational capital" because a news outlet suffers in the public esteem after a jury returns a guilty verdict.

The court's actions fit an event study because because in hindsight this decision was not surprising, given the activist nature of the Warren Court and its sympathies for those in the Civil Rights Movement However, at the time the ruling was a bombshell. Even the attorneys for the New York Times, who had hoped the court at least would overturn the libel verdict never expected the justices to effectively rewrite libel laws for all 50 states. It was not just the new standards set by the court that turned libel law upside down, but also the fact that the High Court once again had trumped what once had been in the states' domain.

Up to the court's disposition of that case, many in the media believed that the Supreme Court had all but abolished state libel laws. Gertz, while reaffirming the court's public official/public figure position, left the libel door open for "private persons" to successfully sue by requiring less than the "actual malice" or "Times malice" standard in their case, yet one wonders if the application of "private person" status to Elmer Gertz was made arbitrarily because the justices on the U.S. Supreme court, as well as many of their political allies, did not wish to be seen as standing up for an organization like the John Birch Society..

But, as noted earlier, while private individuals did not have to prove the actual malice standard to win a judgement, they did have to prove actual damages, according to the court despite the small gain for those suing for libel, there was no returning to the pre-Sullivan legal climate. Thus, the case both kept vital protection for newspapers, but also left other media outlets vulnerable.

For example, on the same day, June 25, 1974, the high court struck down a Florida law that required newspapers in that state to print replies by people who believed they had been unfairly criticized by that particular paper, a newspaper version of the "Fairness Doctrine" that at the time applied to broadcasters. The unanimous ruling was an important victory for newspapers, and it further raises questions about the protections the court afforded established newspapers versus the publication of an unpopular political organization.

In examining the aftermath of the court's decisions on libel, one first must keep in mind that the court did not employ these rulings in order to provide financial benefits to newspapers. We contend that it was trying to protect certain news outlets from being sued into bankruptcy by segregationalist politicians and activists, and the court was trying to protect its own civil rights legacy by helping to ensure that news organizations that supported its actions were not silenced.

Thus, while it is clear that the decisions conferred at least some economic benefits upon newspapers, that hardly would have been the court's main purpose. Likewise, when the court in 1974 ruled that Ebner Gertz was a private figure, one result was that it created a temporary loss in the stock value of newspapers, and one doubts that the court meant to cause financial damage to all newspapers.

There is no doubt, however, that the Gertz decision did cause serious financial loss to the John Birch Society. Not only did the organization lose money, but it had to pay court costs and other expenses. As noted in the previous section, the immediate results also suggest that the limited nature of the court's decision in Gertz gives evidence that the action was not necessarily a backward turn on libel, but rather another example of the court protecting the civil rights legacy that it and others had established.

THE CULTURAL SPACE OF JOURNALISM

Many journalists today feel that the boundaries between news and entertainment are blurring, particularly in the television medium. In this book, I examine these boundary concepts and attempt to answer a few complicated questions, such as: Why and how are journalism's boundaries socially constructed? How are they negotiated by different groups of people with interests in mass communications? And—perhaps most importantly—how do journalists breach these boundaries and then respond to the breaches through boundary-maintenance exercises? I hope to recover some of the messiness of the boundaries through this enquiry.

The impetus for this study are the numerous observations and arguments that network television news and tabloid television entertainment programmes are converging in style and content into a new genre called "reality-based programming."

This study will examine some of these arguments, looking for how this phenomenon is described, the explanations given for it, as well as the ex planations for why it has become an issue. As analyst, I will not be in a position to reach a definitive conclusion about the boundaries of these categories. Rather, I will describe how interested players draw the boundaries. It is important to note that boundary work is committed within the day-to-day work of journalism as well as in the latter representations and reconstructions of journalism content and practice.

To accomplish these goals, I will examine three case studies—specific instances of boundary construction, negotiation, and maintenance in journalism. Most of the emphasis will be on how these boundaries affect television journalism, but other journalism media are also examined. According to Justin Lewis, television is arguably the greatest culture-producing machinery on earth. For that reason, and because many conceive of television as primarily an entertainment medium, most of the attention in this study will be focused on television journalism boundaries.

SIGNIFICANCE OF THE PROJECT

As Peter Dahlgren says (perhaps understatedly), "Journalism's centrality in politics and culture, as well as its vested economic and occupational interests, make questions regarding its boundaries, uses and contingencies of more than idle concern".

Some of the questions along this vein that demand our attention include: How have journalists been able to demarcate their area of mass communication from other types of mass communication? What do they gain from such work? Do journalists maintain control over the production and evaluation of news? How are journalists able to maintain the public perception that they are authoritative or credible? How do journalists convert cultural authority into other opportunities, such as jobs, political influence, and prestige? How do journalists respond to threats or challenges to their cultural authority? Admittedly, this study is just a start in this line of research.

Journalists assert that they have the authority to perform an important function in our democratic society: to truthfully report the news and to inform the public. This authority depends on the trust of the publics that the news media serve. American journalists say the defining characteristics of their work are that it is true, accurate, and in the interest of the audience—yet these are irrelevant unless audiences believe in the truthfulness and accuracy of journalistic accounts. If the public believes in the accuracy of journalism, then journalists gain authority—the authority to tell the news.

Other culture-producing mass media institutions, such as the advertising, public relations, and entertainment industries, also communicate to the masses. When these institutions and industries produce messages that appear similar to journalism, journalists interpret these events as threats to the boundaries and authority of journalism. The cultural authority of the institution of journalism depends on the ability of people to distinguish between it and other kinds of mass communication.

It is useful for us to examine what sociologists of science call *boundary-work rhetoric*: the rhetorical strategy of one group wishing to distinguish itself from another. For example, medical doctors draw a boundary—within their discourse and routine practices—between what they do and what faith healers do. Likewise, journalists who consider themselves mainstream draw boundaries between what they do and what other mass communicators do. As I will show, these other communicators include people such as entertainment talk show hosts and tabloid journalists.

When the public does not notice the difference between a faith healer and a doctor, either the doctor, the faith healer, or both will engage in boundary-work rhetoric; socially constructing a boundary in order to protect the authority to do their work. Likewise, journalists engage in boundary-work rhetoric because they want the public to be aware of the differences between news work and entertainment work.

RESEARCH QUESTIONS

The main questions I examine in this study are: How and why have television journalists and others defined "television news" and the goals, norms, and ideologies of television journalism as they have? How have the boundaries between entertainment and news been constructed and negotiated as they have;

and what rhetorical moves do journalists and others make to distinguish between the two? What are the differences in the uses of distinguishing characteristics between those within the journalism profession and those outside the profession?

In effect: Who does boundary work, and how do different groups do it differently? And finally, how do the interests and strategies of boundary-work rhetoric along the news/entertainment boundary compare to the interests and strategies of rhetoric uncovered along other boundaries, such as science/non-science; and what is it about the news/entertainment boundary that makes these strategies different—or similar?

To understand the significance of these questions, we must first examine some of the concepts that seem to be at stake here, such as authority, jurisdiction, and autonomy.

THE AUTHORITY AND SELF-DEFINITION OF JOURNALISM

The institution of American journalism has earned a mantle of authority in American society. The mere fact that many historians rely on newspaper and magazine accounts as primary source material indicates in a small way how journalism and the work of journalists become authoritative. As purveyors of facts and interpretation, journalists use this authority to describe events and everyday life to the public.

Gieryn and Figert describe this kind of authority as social power: "'Cognitive authority' is the legitimate power (in designated contexts) to define, describe or explain bounded realms of reality". The public entrusts journalists with this cognitive authority to the extent that they believe in journalists and their work. When the authority is threatened, journalists respond to consolidate their power.

Paul Starr, in his studies of the medical profession, calls this power *cultural authority*. He says "cultural authority entails the construction of reality through definitions of fact and value". Starr distinguishes cultural authority from social authority, which he says "involves the control of action through the giving of commands."

Cultural authority, on the other hand, is derived from performing a service and from the ability to determine the *needs* of clients. If journalists perform the service of informing public debates, then they determine which cultural conversations people need to be aware of and engaged in. The cultural authority of journalists, therefore... is based on the dependence of the public on the ability of journalists to present important information in a coherent and reliable fashion, or at least make it seem that way.

This authority is reproduced in and through the everyday practices of journalists as well as later through boundary work rhetoric. Starr says the cultural authority of medical doctors rests on three aspects of legitimacy:

collegial, cognitive, and moral. For journalistic cultural authority, these same aspects of legitimacy are appropriate:

- The collegial legitimacy of the journalist—the acceptance by others in their profession;
- The cognitive legitimacy of the journalistic product—it is perceived to be based on rational, objective methods; and
- The moral legitimacy of the journalist—journalists' judgements are expected to be oriented towards altruism and public service.

Threats to cultural authority of an institution or profession do not always come from outside the institution or profession. A well-publicized case of fraud or fakery is perhaps the prime example of an internal threat to the cultural authority of a social institution or profession. Such turmoil is publicly discussed and thereby constructed as an issue or problem. The discussion of the issue occurs as discourse within journalistic media by journalists who control the content and topics of the medium.

For example, in 1980, *Washington* Post reporter Janet Cooke fabricated a news story about an imaginary eight-year-old heroin addict and was on the verge of accepting a Pulitzer Prize for it when the deception was revealed. The *Post*'s subsequent analysis of the deception argued that the problem was not organizational, the problem was that Cooke was an aberration—a compulsive liar.

As Dahlgren notes, one of the distinctive aspects of turmoil within the institution of journalism is that those within the institution "strive to maintain discursive control over such turmoil. Among other things, this helps to consolidate and legitimate professional practices and identity (by)... retain(ing) definitional control of the field, its problems and potential solutions".

Definitional control of the boundaries of journalism is also accomplished by journalists when they do things like formulate definitions of news and news work. It is also accomplished through the selection of news topics.

Defining news is not a simple task. A 1965 textbook for journalists admits, "To recognize news is easier than to define it". Yet the primary role of journalists is to determine what is newsworthy, that is, to define news. In defining news, journalists also define what it is they do. This study shows how journalists often define journalism in relation to its neighbouring professions.

SOME BACKGROUND ABOUT "THE PROBLEM"

Many journalism critics have recently argued that American journalism is undergoing a profound change because it now regularly mixes entertainment with the news. Critics typically argue that this entertainment is in the form of sensationalistic celebrity-scandal.

In fact, there is a long history of sensationalism in American journalism, a fact documented by several journalism historians.

But the main point of contemporary critics is that sensationalism and tabloid-style techniques, which were always present on the fringes of journalism, are now becoming the norm in American journalism, and are being adopted by so-called "mainstream" media as part of economic survival strategies in the cutthroat business climate of American mass media.

These contemporary critics typically argue that there should be a rigid boundary between mainstream journalism and other kinds of mass communication such as tabloid journalism. The critics imply that one kind of communication is more legitimate in certain contexts than the other, and even that tabloid journalism is not journalism at all but is instead entertainment. As noted above, one of the claims made by mass media critics is that journalism just recently got worse. But this may be a perennial complaint.

A quick review of journalism criticism reveals that the argument that journalism used to be better but just recently got worse is common throughout the history of journalism. The critiques usually say that journalism used to make bold distinctions between news and entertainment but now combines the two. These critiques construct the logical conclusion that journalism has steadily decreased in quality over many years.

Taken together, the criticisms add up to the conclusions that the people who used to do journalism were better and had higher standards than those of today and that the distinctions between news and entertainment used to be greater. Examples of this critique can be found in even the earliest discussions of American journalism.

For instance, critics panned Benjamin Day New York Sun of the early 1830s because it often contained humour and sensational news of suicides. Similarly, some critics hated James Gordon Bennett New York Herald of the mid- to late-1830s because it contained entertaining, satirically written police court reports, as well as in-depth crime stories. Bennett pioneered the "human-interest story" or feature story, when he wrote in vivid detail in 1836 about the grisly murder of the prostitute Helen Jewett, quoting her madam and describing Jewett's apartment in minute detail.

Bennett's day-by-day narrative of the ensuing sensational trial reminds us of how journalism and entertaining literature have been combined for many years to make newsworthy stories "more palatable for consumption." Bennett was soundly criticized by his competitors and others for blurring the boundary between journalism and entertainment.

His detractors, many of them his competitors, waged what they called a "Moral War" in the late 1830s against Bennett and his enjoyable but sensationalistic newspaper. They maintained that Bennett was a "deviant" journalist because he blurred the boundaries of journalism by making his newspaper entertaining and popular. Those running the "Moral War" against Bennett were unsuccessful at running him out of the journalism business, but they did seriously wound his business. In the 1920s, many journalists were labeled "yellow journalists" because they sensationalized and twisted the news by appealing to prurient interests and base instincts. In 1962, philosopher Jürgen Habermas argued that the boundaries between news and entertainment are blurring because people prefer "entertaining" news and its immediate rewards: Public affairs, social problems, economic matters, education and health... 'delayed reward news'—are not only pushed into the background by 'immediate reward news' (comics, corruption, accidents, disasters, sports, recreation, social events, and human interest) but, as the characteristic label already indicates, are already read less and more rarely.

In the end the news generally assumes some sort of guise and is made to resemble a narrative from its form down to stylistic detail (news stories); the rigorous distinction between fact and fiction is ever more frequently abandoned.

News and reports and even editorial opinions are dressed up with all the accouterments of entertainment literature, whereas on the other hand the belletrist contributions aim for the strictly 'realistic' reduplication of reality "as it is" on the level of clichès and thus, in turn, erase the line between fiction and report. The integration of the once separate domains of journalism and literature... brings about a peculiar shifting of reality—even a conflation of different levels of reality. Under the common denominator of so-called human interest emerges the mixtum compositum of a pleasant and at the same time convenient subject for entertainment that, instead of doing justice to reality, has a tendency to present a substitute more palatable for consumption and more likely to give rise to an impersonal indulgence in stimulating relaxation than to a public use by reason.

Habermas, in making the observation that literature and news were "once separate domains," is doing, in 1962, journalism/entertainment boundary work. An example of a similar critique of journalism boundary-degradation—but attributed to a different root cause—is the melodramatic opening paragraphs of Ron Powers' 1977 book *The Newscasters*, which says the sea-change in journalism happened in the 1970s: The biggest heist of the 1970s never made it on the five o'clock news.

The biggest heist of the 1970s *was* the five o'clock news. The salesmen took it. They took it away from the journalists, slowly, patiently, gradually, and with such finesse that nobody noticed until it was too late.

By the 1970s, an extravagant proportion of television news—local news in particular—answered less to the description of "journalism" than to that of "show business." This transformation, carried out by the sales-oriented station managers in an unbounded quest for profits, bore the profoundest implications in the way Americans were to receive information and perceive political choices. Many local newscasts ceased serving the public (at best, they served the public only incidentally) and bequeathed their primary allegiance to the advertisers.

Powers blames the quest for profits, instead of journalistic values, for the swing towards show business techniques and content.

Similarly, Edwin Diamond, in 1975, notes that the potential for profits associated with high ratings points for news programmes led to the downfall of journalistic control in local television newsrooms around the country.

The responsibility of controlling the news process was relinquished to news consultants who had no knowledge of journalism but who were well-versed in audience survey techniques and behavioural psychology. In other words, they knew how to design a local news programme that would attract a mass audience but not one that would inform it: Up until a few years ago, television news was in the hands of professional news directors and producers, traditionally trained in newspaper or magazine work or broadcast journalism.

It still is at the networks. But local station management has not had the same professional approach, especially since the local stations began discovering that their news times could be highly salable, often cheaper to run than straight entertainment shows, and attractive to many advertisers. Not only has television news become longer... [it] has become too important to be left to the newspeople. Audience research has been perceived as the key to ratings success.

For Diamond, "professionals" are those trained in journalism, especially in newspaper and magazine journalism, areas where audience research has not been pursued as thoroughly as in television.

In taking control away from the professionals, journalism has taken a back seat to superficiality, and news judgements are now made by managers skilled in audience research. Powers' and Diamond's critiques of television journalism are quite similar to the critiques that were raised throughout the early history of the television medium. They seem to argue for a monopolization of authority and protection of autonomy for journalists. In other words, Powers and Diamond would like to see journalists maintain control over all aspects of journalism and keep others from controlling any aspects of it.

Recently, Steven Stark, a commentator on popular culture for National Public Radio, wrote that the root cause of increased sensationalism in radio and television news is the advent of all-news channels in the 1980s, such as CNN. He says the increased demand for news around the clock has caused journalists to become irresponsible:

Unlike the old days, when there were, at most, two news cycles a day, there is now a 24-hour demand for information. That means the network news and newspapers have to provide a different product than they once did, because they assume people get their headlines elsewhere.

The result has been a considerable broadening of what is considered reportable news and analysis—much of it far less objectively verifiable than in the past. We now have fields of news that didn't exist 15 years ago, such as entertainment reporting. News from the tabloids is considered fair game. Call-in shows can put forward any "expert" they can drum up, while encouraging callers to speculate and gossip. Some TV commentary itself is close to staged: Crossfire and The McLaughlin Group are to James Reston and Edward R. Murrow what pro wrestling is to sports.

Because of the incessant demand, news is also presented more quickly to the public, with the inevitable result that there's a far thinner line between fact and rumor—one reason why personal details about celebrities get reported more quickly, if not falsely—than before.... This is all part of a far larger cultural pattern—the babble of a postmodern age that has seen feeling gain pre-eminence over thought, while elites collapse.

Stark's theory that journalists responded to the increased frequency of news "cycles" and an increased demand for news by lowering their standards for newsworthiness implies that journalists are not doing their jobs, and are, in fact, remiss in their responsibility to decide what counts as news. This is not a new critique, though the root cause selected by Stark may be a new idea.

Many other examples could be cited of journalists and others arguing that journalism is changing, moving towards more entertainment and less information. The critique is indeed perennial. As shown above, examples of it can be shown from the very beginnings of American journalism right up to the present. Journalism professor and historian Mitchell Stephens puts this kind of criticism in context:

Some of the criticism television journalism inspires is... shortsighted.... News and entertainment [did not] meet and mate for the first time on often giggly, often frivolous, local television newscasts in the United States; their affair dates back at least as far as criers and minstrels. Television news, in other words, did not inject a foreign substance—playfulness—into the news; news has been enjoyed for as long as it has been exchanged.

Like the penny papers of the 1830s, the yellow journals of the 1880s and 1890s and the tabloids of the 1920s, television has succeeded in attracting a new audience to the news. Once television sets became affordable, news became available to audiences of many millions, including even those lacking the energy, skill or maturity to read a newspaper or concentrate on a radio narrative.

If the critique is perennial, then there must be a reason for it being so persistent. Perhaps these critiques serve an important purpose. Instead of evaluating the legitimacy of these claims and critiques, the constructivist approach to this debate focuses on how self-interested stakeholders (relevant actors) construct a conception of journalism that makes sense to them and that helps to consolidate their power and prestige.

These stakeholders believe that the cultural authority of their institution depends on distinct boundaries, which, in turn, rest on concepts such as the perceived credibility and objectivity of their work. This constructivist approach to the issue helps us understand how the boundaries of journalism are constructed, negotiated, and maintained, giving us insights into what journalism means to people. To say that these boundaries are *constructed* implies that they have no firm, absolute contours. Instead, they are contextually contingent, local, and episodic, with the *potential* to become stable and widespread.

To give a brief example of boundary-work analysis, let us examine the words of the authors cited earlier in their arguments about the blurring of the news/entertainment boundary. They all imply that "real" journalism is something different from what we have now. The characteristics of "real" journalism that the various authors mentioned earlier in this section cite include distinctions such as: News is meant to inform, not entertain; it presents facts, not fiction; it does not include speculation or gossip; and it is controlled by professionals who serve the public, not by advertisers who seek only profits.

These are demarcation criteria that help journalists "construct" their role in society—and help them understand the shape and contours of the *cultural space* in which journalism resides. Looking at the claims more closely, it appears that the authors mentioned earlier in this section cite the *functional* differences between news and entertainment: One informs, the other entertains. They also note *epistemological* differences: One is a factual kind of knowledge, the other contains fiction.

They also cite *methodological* and *organizational* differences: One uses gossip and speculation, the other does not; and one is controlled by professionals who serve the public, the other serves less-altruistic goals. Instead, I look at how others solve them. In particular, I examine the apparent goals of boundary debates; how interested parties pick out the essential elements of the boundaries; and whether and how their work achieves any results.

The goal is to analyse how the boundaries between news and entertainment are "constructed" by relevant actors. To accomplish that goal, I look at several examples of constructions of monopoly, deviance, and autonomy as "social issues" with stakeholders in journalism. The constructivist approach to questions about what is journalism and what is not replaces the answer with the question as the thing to be studied.

In other words, I do not try to find a definitive-necessarily essentialist—answer to the question "What are the boundaries of journalism?" Instead, I analyse and examine how journalists and others have attempted to answer this perplexing question, particularly when they claim that certain acts and practices are not journalism but are entertainment. In these kinds of claims, we gain valuable in sight into the ways journalists make sense of what they do, and about the role of journalism in society.

Journalism, like all social institutions, is socially constructed. Questions about where journalism ends and entertainment begins are a viable field of study that up to this point, has been largely ignored. This project should begin to remedy this situation by examining what many call journalism ethics issues from a constructivist point of view. The way journalists make distinctions about acceptable behaviours, intentions, and content says a lot about culture production and how society creates and defines itself.

Throughout this study, cartographic metaphors—mapping images-are used as a way of thinking about the relationships between different institutions in American culture.

Journalists map out the cultural space of journalism by specifying where the boundaries are located. As Gieryn notes, cartographic metaphors are useful when discussing the idea of a cultural space—territorial markers that people use to make sense of the world around them.

He says, "cartographic metaphors offer a robust language for thinking about relations among cultural phenomena," particularly the relations between adjacent phenomena. In the cultural space of mass media, news and entertainment appear to be adjacent phenomena.

Gieryn suggests thatwe consider using cartographic terms such as "contours, landmarks, scale, orientation, coordinates, points of interest, and legend". These terms compel us to examine how this cultural space was slowly carved out of the cultural landscape rather than privilege journalism-as-it-is as the only logical outcome.

Some of the boundaries of journalism may be moving and flexible or perhaps blurry and indistinct. In other places they may be uncontested and easy to see.

In any case, it is the players on either side of the alleged boundary (or in the middle of it) who are the primary stakeholders in constitutive rhetoric that attempts to delineate borders. That is why the primary site of this study is in the rhetoric of journalists: They have the most to gain or lose by such rhetoric about the boundaries of journalism.

This chapter is an ethnographic analysis of the process whereby anomalous journalists who are perceived to be a threat to the institution are ritually "relocated" to the outer edges of the boundaries of journalism. It is an examination of a case of journalistic misconduct that was discussed in great detail within the institution of journalism. Dateline NBC, a network news division-produced weekly newsmagazine, broadcast a story in 1992 about General Motors pickup trucks; it contained a fiery simulated crash scene, which was staged by the program's producers.

This staging was not disclosed to the audience. Michael Gartner, then president of NBC News, was held responsible for the misconduct, which was labeled an act of journalistic fraud. The rhetoric by journalists that followed this example of journalistic deviance resembles what Harold Garfinkel calls a successful status degradation ceremony, whereby deviant members are expelled from an institution (in this case, the institution of journalism) in order to minimize harm to the institution as a whole.

Garfinkel has had a profound impact on sociological theory. As the founder of the ethnomethodology movement, his social constructivist emphasis on the way members of a group “make sense of, find their way about in, and act on the circumstances in which they find themselves” has opened up a vast new territory within sociology.

This chapter utilizes Garfinkel’s theory and methods to examine one way in which journalists demarcate the realm of journalism within the cultural landscape. This rhetorical analysis scrutinizes the naturally occurring discourse among journalists following the *Dateline* broadcast, focusing attention on the elements of status degradation ceremonies described by Garfinkel.

This is an examination of the rhetorical strategies of journalists reacting to accusations that the NBC News division used fraudulent methods in presenting the news and that Michael Gartner failed his profession by allowing it to happen. Deviance in American journalism is defined and confronted by the official agents and apologists of the institution of journalism--namely, other journalists who discuss the practices of journalism as an interpretive community.

This chapter is an examination of how members of a public institution produce cultural meaning and reproduce social structures by engaging in rhetorical discourse designed to map out the cultural space of a social institution.

The "universe" sample for this chapter included all the articles listed in the NEXIS database containing the words "Dateline NBC" and "General Motors" appearing in major American newspapers, magazines, and wire services between November 1, 1992, and June 30, 1993 (some 521 articles). Also examined: a videotape of a conference of journalists who examined the Dateline scandal; a lawyer's report commissioned by NBC and released March 21, 1993; as well as some earlier articles about Gartner and NBC News that were examined for historical context.

SOME BACKGROUND ON THE DATELINE NBC/GM "EVENT"

Dateline NBC was a weekly network newsmagazine programme that began in April 1992. On November 17, 1992, Dateline NBC broadcast a report entitled, "Waiting to Explode?," which criticized the design of General Motors full-size pickup trucks built between 1973 and 1987, alleging that they were more susceptible to dangerous explosions when involved in side-impact vehicle collisions. The news report included a powerful visual demonstration of the problem: footage described as an "unscientific crash demonstration," which included a fiery explosion.

General Motors Corporation investigated the charges made in the story and then filed a defamation lawsuit against NBC. GM took the unprecedented step of announcing their lawsuit via a two-hour globally televised press conference on February 8, 1993. During the press conference, GM lawyers alleged that Dateline's producers allowed "incendiary" or "sparking devices" (model rocket engines) to be attached to the underside of the trucks to ensure that any gasoline spilled during the simulated accident would ignite--and that Dateline then failed to publicly disclose this fact in the programme.

NBC responded with an on-the-air apology the next night, read by Dateline anchors Jane Pauley and Stone Phillips. GM dropped its lawsuit shortly after the apology. Michael Gartner resigned on March 2, 1993. Three producers responsible for the GM pickup story segment were forced to resign on March 19, 1993. NBC President and CEO Robert Wright publicly apologized to viewers and to GM on March 22, 1993.

The news media covered the story of NBC's fraud in detail, and many journalism critics discussed it in various newspapers, magazines, professional journals, and on television programmes. The Poynter Institute for Media Studies in St. Petersburg, Florida, sponsored a conference entitled "When Good Journalists Do Bad Things: Truthtelling and the Public Trust." The conference included a twohour discussion of the Dateline scandal by professional journalists and journalism professors, which was televised live on C-SPAN on April 15, 1993, recordings of which Poynter now sells on videocassette.

RESPONDING TO DEVIANCE

The very public outcry by journalists and journalism critics in this case--people who believed they were part of the "mainstream" American journalism institution--was a signal that a boundary line was crossed by Dateline NBC. The line was described as an epistemological boundary between different kinds of knowledge (truth and fiction), as a functional boundary between news and entertainment, and as a methodological boundary between disinterestedness and agency. The Dateline story was portrayed as a violation of professional norms that threatened the distinction between mainstream and tabloid journalism, or between news and entertainment.

This public discourse served several purposes:

- To distance the methodology, content, and apparent function of the Dateline episode from commonly accepted journalism standards and to signal that this kind of behaviour is deviant.
- To reassure the public that professional journalists are able to police their ranks.
- To maintain the social boundaries between journalism and entertainment (or between mainstream and tabloid television news) by showing that deviant behaviour that results in products that resemble these other genres of communication will not go unpunished.

To demonstrate the contours of the boundaries of journalism, Gartner and his associates were labeled as deviant journalists. There are both costs and benefits to revealing deviant behaviour: "the basic dilemma of social control: to publicize or not to publicize deviant behaviour". Such publicity is negative and can serve to undermine public confidence in the institution--especially in the short term. A pattern of unpunished violations of norms, however, could be more damaging to the perceived integrity of the profession in the long run.

Durkheim says the public sanction of deviance is a healthy exercise for a group or institution because it helps to show group members how to recognize the area between acceptable and unacceptable behaviour. In his study on the sociology of deviance among the Puritan settlers of America, Kai Erickson notes that "the interactions which do the most effective job of locating and publicizing the group's outer edges would seem to be those which take place between deviant persons on the one side and official agents of the community on the other".

The official agents of the journalistic community are fellow journalists, who operate together as an interpretive community, "united through their collective interpretations of key public events. The shared discourse that they produce is thus a marker of how they see themselves as journalists". One of the distinctive aspects of turmoil within the institution of journalism (probably much like turmoil in other institutions) is that those within the institution "strive to maintain discursive control over such turmoil. Among other things, this helps to consolidate and legitimate professional practices and identity (by)... retain(ing) definitional control of the field, its problems and potential solutions".

The site of this chapter is in the symbolic actions of journalists-their communicative acts--as they respond to threats to the cultural authority and boundaries of the institution of journalism in America. These rhetorical actions are interpreted and evaluated as components of a successful status degradation ceremony. Such a ceremony consists of "communicative work directed to transforming an individual's total identity into an identity lower in the group's scheme of social types".

The individual in this case is Michael Gartner, former president of NBC News. The other three Dateline workers who were fired over the controversy--executive producer Jeff Diamond, senior producer David Rummel, and field segment producer Robert Read--were also denigrated somewhat by their peers, but Gartner received the major blame for the controversy because he was ultimately responsible as head of the NBC news division.

Because he served as a lightning rod for criticism, most of the attention here will be given to Gartner and the rhetoric directed at him. It is clear that--to his detractors--Gartner symbolized everything that was wrong with NBC News and everything that was wrong with American television journalism.

Throughout the 1980s and 1990s, Michael Gartner was one of the most well-known and outspoken personalities in the journalism profession. Gartner--with his trademark bow tie--was an icon for First Amendment absolutism. A third generation journalist, his father and grandfather both worked at newspapers in Iowa. Some of his previous accomplishments include: page one editor, Wall Street Journal; editor and co-owner, Ames Iowa, Daily Tribune; general news executive, Gannett Co.; president, Des Moines Register and Tribune Co.; editor, Louisville Courier-Journal and Louisville Times; member, Pulitzer Prize board; and president, American Society of Newspaper Editors.

A New York University Law School graduate, Gartner is known as a strict interpreter of First Amendment press rights. For instance, Gartner once argued that "there is no right to privacy--except from the government". This stance led to some controversial decisions, such as NBC's decision to identify the alleged rape victim in the William Kennedy Smith trial. Gartner is also known among journalists for his strict stand on the use of anonymous sources.

He says it is wrong for reporters to use anonymous sources "in all but the most delicate of stories," because it damages the credibility of all journalism. Gartner is also known for his business and financial expertise. In 1984, he managed to get the Gannett Co. into a bidding war for control of The Des Moines Register, and reportedly pocketed more than $3 million from the deal.

THE STATUS DEGRADATION CEREMONY

Garfinkel theorized that there are eight sequential stages of a successful status degradation ceremony, consisting of specific "effects that the communicative tactics of the denouncer must be designed to accomplish". These eight types of arguments must be put forward by people within a community or institution that wants to banish deviants and at the same time, minimize harm to the institution itself.

The eight stages of this rhetorical ceremony are:

- Both the event and the perpetrators are made to look unusual.
- The perpetrators are compared to bad stereotypes—implying that they are not just accidentally bad.
- The denouncers show that they belong to the community and that they are speaking for the community or institution, not just as private individuals.
- The denouncers show that the values of the community are salient, and that they are correct and justified.
- The denouncers show that they speak for these values.
- The denouncers show that they have support from the community.
- The deviants are banished.
- The deviants are ritually separated from the community so that the community may go on as before.

Next is a detailed examination of each of the steps in the status degradation ceremony. Journalists made arguments before, during, and after the *Dateline* fiasco that seem to resemble each of the stages described by Garfinkel 40 years ago. The charges against NBC first came to light when GM staged its global press conference to announce its lawsuit. Harry Pearce, executive vice president and general counsel of General Motors Corp., said: "We now face a poisoned environment spawned by the cheap, dishonest, sensationalism of NBC's programme 'Waiting to Explode?' and its aftermath." GM's attack was quickly reported by journalists who seemed shocked that NBC had apparently used "other than standard" newsgathering techniques.

Journalists argued that *Dateline* used methods journalists don't normally use—they hired a biased subcontractor who staged a news story. NBC had hired The Institute for Safety Analysis (TISA) as a subcontractor to conduct the "unscientific crash demonstration." TISA is commonly hired to provide evidence for plaintiffs in personal injury lawsuits.

GM argued that the Institute had an agenda to promote, and *Dateline* did not disclose this fact, nor did it attempt to balance TISA's views with those of disinterested sources. It appeared that *Dateline* had crossed an epistemological and methodological boundary into the realm of agency, fiction, and entertainment. The information was gathered using entertainment-style methods, so it was fictional—designed to shock or entertain.

NBC was also charged with stonewalling—for not quickly admitting guilt but instead trying to rationalize its methods and its story. Stonewalling is one thing journalists particularly despise—but love to publicize. Eventually, Gartner realized that he should come clean: "I realized that we were just plain wrong.... We were stonewalling them, using all kinds of excuses and rationalizations. What we had done was just plain dumb, and wrong. And I was raised to admit you're wrong when you're wrong". Gartner did not come to this realization, however, until after GM initiated its multimillion dollar lawsuit.

Michael Gartner, *Dateline NBC*, and NBC News were made to appear strange, and their offences were made to look like elementary violations of common sense.

Howard Rosenberg of the *Los Angeles Times* delivered a potent insult: "A high school journalism student knows that staging or faking or fabricating or falsifying news is, under any circumstances, absolutely forbidden. The big lie, the ultimate corruption.

Sweep that ethic under the rug, and a news organization becomes morally barren". Rosenberg's rhetoric implies that *Dateline*'s producers were not journalists at all because they apparently did not receive (and do not reproduce) the methodological training common to all journalists (even high school journalists); they were made to seem unusual.

Even before the *Dateline NBC*/GM event, critics charged that NBC was unable to launch a successful newsmagazine or other types of news programming, implying that NBC had an inferior network news division.

NBC News was also criticized for inadequate checks on accuracy and journalistic standards. Peter Herford, a 26-year veteran broadcast journalist from CBS, said the *Dateline NBC*/GM event would have never happened at ABC, where someone is in charge of standards. Herford, who now heads the broadcasting programme at Columbia University Graduate School of Journalism, said,

At ABC, they had a full-time person, a vice president for news standards, who had a staff, who did nothing but review every investigative piece that went on the air, every major magazine piece that went on the air. He read all the scripts, etc., etc., etc.... At ABC, that ['Dateline'] piece never would have gotten past him. Thus, the NBC News division was portrayed as an unusually inferior organization, with no one doing the normal task of enforcing journalistic standards.

In some of the rhetoric following the event, Gartner was portrayed as an outsider to broadcast journalism. For instance, Jonathan Alter noted that a few years before he went to work in broadcast journalism Gartner once told some ABC News producers that he thought

TV News is nothing more than a "shallow comic book"... a superficial medium incapable of complex ideas. Today Gartner is in danger of being fired as president of NBC News, in essence for living down to his low expectations for the medium in which he works.... Ultimately he looked down his nose a bit at what he did for a living—and it showed. That both loosened his own standards and left him without allies below him.

Alter thus argues that Gartner's outsider attitude towards television journalism carried on during his tenure at NBC News and could be one of the causes for this scandal. Alter also criticized Gartner for being more of a money manager than a journalist. This is a familiar charge among journalists who bristle at the thought of money managers— "bean counters"—invading their ranks (penetrating their jurisdictional boundaries) and controlling journalistic output. It is an attempt by journalists to equate the journalist/manager organizational boundary with a "good" journalism/"bad" journalism boundary.

In the rhetoric examined here, Gartner, NBC News, and *Dateline*, were all made to seem unusual—as deviants who lacked knowledge of basic journalistic standards and thus operated outside the realm—the boundaries—of journalism.

One of the ways journalists made sense of the *Dateline NBC*/GM event was to stereotype it as similar to other well-publicized instances of journalistic deviance. The 1980 Janet Cooke/*Washington Post* scandal and the 1989 scandal following ABC News's re-enactment of the Felix Bloch suspected spy case were mentioned by several journalists as examples of similar lapses in journalistic standards.

In the infamous Janet Cooke case, a *Washington Post* reporter fabricated a story about an eight-year-old heroin addict and then passed the fiction off as reality. In the Felix Bloch case, ABC's World News Tonight showed a tape that it identified as suspected spy Felix Bloch, passing a briefcase of secrets to a Soviet spy. The people in the video were actually actors hired by ABC, and the video was doctored to make it look like a surveillance tape.

By stereotyping the practices of *Dateline NBC* as similar to those of other well-known journalistic scandals, journalists were able to quickly make sense of the event, understand its significance, and formulate responses to it. Four authors mentioned the Cooke scandal and one mentioned the Bloch scandal as stereotypical examples of the same kind of fraud.

Another author implies that the *Dateline NBC*/GM event is stereotypical of news values used in other countries where simulations, staging, and non-disclosure are not taboo in journalism:

If NBC is looking for some consolation, it can find plenty of company in Japan. Staging the news is so commonplace that the Japanese have a word for it: *yarase*. "In America, it's the exception rather than the rule," says *Newsweek*'s Tokyo Bureau Chief Bill Powell. "Here, it's just standard operating procedure. There is much greater latitude given to producers to set things up if it doesn't work out." Adds Dorian Benkoil, an Associated Press editor who researched Japanese media on a Fulbright journalism fellowship: "In the U. S. the lines between entertainment and news are blurring recently. In Japan they never developed." The implication of this rhetorical claim is that the way *Dateline NBC* operates is completely foreign (literally and figuratively) to American journalists.

Another of the rhetorical claims made by journalists following the *Dateline NBC*/GM event was that the "unscientific crash demonstration" was methodologically similar to things done on tabloid television programmes, and that there were organizational similarities between *Dateline* and the tabloids. Others noted that some of the people who worked on the *Dateline NBC* programme had previously worked at the tabloids.

Ironically, tabloid producers used the *Dateline NBC* event as an opportunity to argue that their standards were higher—if anything-than NBC's network news standards. John Terenzio, executive producer of A Current Affair, was quoted in a *New York Times* article: "We would not have re-enacted a car crash using little rockets to blow up the car.... We would have felt that was not correct, and our legal department would not have allowed it". Terenzio thus delivers the fatal rhetorical blow to *Dateline NBC*: Its standards are even lower than those of tabloid television programmes. Rosenberg makes a similar point about NBC News's standards when he notes that none of the tabloid shows identified the alleged rape victim of William Kennedy Smith, though NBC's Nightly News did.

Stereotyped as anomalous, Gartner, NBC News, and *Dateline NBC* are rhetorically "moved" outside the realm of journalism to the cultural space where tabloid television, "reality-based programming," and entertainment television programmes reside.

Journalists demonstrated that judgement on Gartner and the *Dateline* scandal was only to be passed by fellow journalists—who understood the nuances of journalism—and who alone had the jurisdiction to police their ranks and control the boundaries of their profession. The Poynter Institute conference in which the actions of NBC in the GM truck incident were debated was filled almost exclusively with members of the journalism community—reporters, editors, producers, and journalism professors.

Lawyers were notably absent from the field of invited participants. Lawyers did get involved when NBC hired "outside" counsel, Robert Warren of Gibson, Dunn and Crutcher in Los Angeles, and Lewis Kaden of Davis, Polk and Wardwell in New York, to conduct an investigation of how the exploding truck story came to be broadcast. This concerned some journalists who felt threatened by the fact that people from outside the institution of journalism were going to judge the performance of journalists:

Some NBC News staffers have questioned why the network hired lawyers to investigate the case rather than... asking a respected journalist to conduct an internal enquiry. NBC's [spokeswoman Peggy] Hubble said that management felt outsiders would provide the most impartial investigation. [But]... one source speculated that hiring attorneys may be in part to protect lawyer-client confidentiality and to protect the network [from] lawsuits.

In the final analysis, journalists quickly assumed the role of jury in this case, undercutting any attempts by General Motors to have the trial go to a real court. Later, at the Poynter conference, Michael Gartner said that he wanted to settle the case quickly and get it behind them, and this is why the on-air apology was broadcast the day after GM filed its lawsuit. He also said that he had complete authority on the wording of the apology, and whether to accept the conditions of it or not.

6

New Media Techniques for Social Change

INTRODUCTION

Social Movement Media has a rich and storied history that has changed at a rapid rate since New Media became widely used. The Zapatista Army of National Liberation of Chiapas, Mexico were the first major movement to make widely recognized and effective use of New Media for communiques and organizing in 1994. Since then, New Media has been used extensively by social movements to educate, organize, share cultural products of movements, communicate, coalition build, and more. The WTO Ministerial Conference of 1999 protest activity was another landmark in the use of New Media as a tool for social change. The WTO protests used media to organize the original action, communicate with and educate participants, and was used an alternative media source.

The Indymedia movement also developed out of this action, and has been a great tool in the democratization of information, which is another widely discussed aspect of new media movement. Some scholars even view this democratization as an indication of the creation of a "radical, socio-technical paradigm to challenge the dominant, neo-liberal and technologically determinist model of information and communication technologies." A less radical view along these same lines is that people are taking advantage of the internet to produce a grassroots globalization, one that is anti-neo-liberal and centered on people rather than the flow of capital. Of course, some are also stepchild of the role of New Media in Social Movements. Many scholars point out unequal access to new media as a hindrance to broad-based movements, sometimes even oppressing some within a movement. Others are stepchild about how democratic or useful it really is for social movements, even for those with access. There are also many New Media components that activists cite as tools for change that have not been widely discussed as such by academics.

New Media has also found a use with less radical social movements such as the Free Hugs Campaign. Using web sites, blogs, and online videos to demonstrate the effectiveness of the movement itself. Along with this example the use of high volume blogs has allowed numerous views and practices to be more widespread and gain more public attention. Another example is the on-going Free Tibet Campaign, which has been seen on numerous web sites as well as having a slight tie-in with the band Gorillaz in their Gorillaz Bitez clip featuring the lead singer 2D sitting with protesters at a Free Tibet protest. Another social change seen coming from New Media is trends in fashion and the emergence of subcultures such as Text Speak, Cyberpunk, and various others.

NATIONAL SECURITY

New Media has also recently become of interest to the global espionage community as it is easily accessible electronically in database format and can therefore be quickly retrieved and reverse engineered by national governments. Particularly of interest to the espionage community are facebook and twitter, two sites where individuals freely divulge personal information that can then be sifted through and archived for the automatic creation of dossiers on both people of interest and the average citizen.

INTERACTIVITY AND NEW MEDIA

Interactivity has become a key term for number of new media use options evolving from the rapid dissemination of Internet access point, the digitalization of the media, and media convergence. In 1984, Rice defined the new media as communication technologies that enable or facilitate user-to-user interactivity and interactivity between user and information. Such as Internet replaces the "one-to-many" model of traditional mass communication with the possibility of a "many-to-many" web of communication. Any individual with the appropriate technology can now produce his or her online media and include images, text, and sound about whatever he or she chooses. So the new media with technology convergence shifts the model of mass communication, and radically shapes the ways we interact and communicate with one another. Vin Crosbie described three communications media in "What is new media?". He saw Interpersonal media as "one to one", Mass media as "one to many" and, finally New Media as Individuation Media or "many to many".

When we think of interactivity and its meaning, we assume that it is only prominent in the conversational dynamics of individuals who are face-to-face. This restriction of opinion does not allow us to see its existence in mediated communication forums. Interactivity is present in some programming work, such as video games. It's also viable in the operation of traditional media. In the mid 1990s, filmmakers started using inexpensive digital cameras to create films. It was also the time when moving image technology had developed, which was able to be viewed on computer desktops in full motion. This development of new media technology was a new method for artists to share their work and interact with the big world. Other settings of interactivity include radio and television talk shows, letters to the editor, listener participation in such programmes, and computer and technological programming. Interactive new media has become a true benefit to every one because people can express their artwork in more than one way with the technology that we have today and there is no longer a limit to what we can do with our creativity.

Interactivity can be considered as a central concept in understanding new media, but different media forms possess different degree of interactivity, even some forms of digitized and converged media are not in fact interactive at all. Tony Feldman considers digital satellite television as an example of a new media technology that uses digital compression to dramatically increase the number of television channels that can be delivered, and which changes the nature of what can be offered through the service, but does not transform the experience of television from the user's point of view, as it lacks a more fully interactive dimension. It remains the case that interactivity is not an inherent characteristic of all new media technologies, unlike digitization and convergence.

Terry Flew (2005) argues that "the global interactive games industry is large and growing, and is at the forefront of many of the most significant innovations in new media" (Flew 2005). Interactivity is prominent in these online computer games such as *World of Warcraft*, *The Sims Online* and *Second Life*. These games, developments of "new media", allow for users to establish relationships and experience a sense of belonging, despite temporal and spatial boundaries. These games can be used as an escape or to act out a desired life. Will Wright, creator of *The Sims*, "is fascinated by the way gamers have become so attached to his invention-with some even living their lives through it". New media have created virtual realities that are becoming mere extensions of the world we live in. With the creation of Second Life people have even more control over this virtual world where anything that a participant can think of in their mind can become a reality in Second Life.

New Media changes continuously due to the fact that it is constantly modified and redefined by the interaction between the creative use of the masses, emerging technology, cultural changes, etc.

THE INDUSTRY

The new media industry shares an open association with many market segments in areas such as software/video game design, television, radio, and particularly movies, advertising and marketing, which seeks to gain from the advantages of two-way dialogue with consumers primarily through the internet. The advertising industry has capitalized on the proliferation of new media with large agencies running multi-million dollar interactive advertising subsidiaries. Interactive web sites and kiosks have become popular. In a number of cases advertising agencies have also set up new divisions to study new media. Public relations firms are taking advantage of the opportunities in new media through interactive PR practices.

CREATIVE SERVICES

Creative services are a subsector of the creative industries, a part of the economy that creates wealth by offering creativity for hire to other businesses. Examples include:

- Design and production agencies.
  - Studios
  - Software development firms
  - Temp agency.
- Marketing firms.
  - Public relations agencies
  - Advertising agencies
  - Promotional agencies
  - Branding agencies.
- Entertainment Industries.
  - Talent agency
  - Guilds.

Like lawyers and accountants in the professional services sector, creative services firms sell a specialised technical service to satisfy the needs of companies that do not have this expertise themselves.

ENTERTAINMENT AND FINE ARTS

In addition, multimedia is heavily used in the entertainment industry, especially to develop special effects in movies and animations. Multimedia games are a popular pastime and are software programmes available either as CD-ROMs or online. Some video games also use multimedia features. Multimedia applications that allow users to actively participate instead of just sitting by as passive recipients of information are called *Interactive Multimedia*.

In the Arts there are multimedia artists, whose minds are able to blend techniques using different media that in some way incorporates interaction with the viewer. One of the most relevant could be Peter Greenaway who is melding Cinema with Opera and all sorts of digital media. Another approach entails the creation of multimedia that can be displayed in a traditional fine arts arena, such as an art gallery. Although multimedia display material may be volatile, the survivability of the content is as strong as any traditional media. Digital recording material may be just as durable and infinitely reproducible with perfect copies every time.

SPECIAL EFFECT

The illusions used in the film, television, theater, or entertainment industries to simulate the imagined events in a story are traditionally called special effects. Special effects are traditionally divided into the categories of optical effects and mechanical effects. With the emergence of digital film-making tools a greater distinction between special effects and visual effects has been recognized, with "visual effects" referring to digital post-production and "special effects" referring to on-set mechanical effects and in-camera optical effects.

Optical effects (also called photographic effects), are techniques in which images or film frames are created photographically, either "in-camera" using multiple exposure, mattes, or the Schüfftan process, or in post-production processes using an optical printer. An optical effect might be used to place actors or sets against a different background.

Mechanical effects (also called practical or physical effects), are usually accomplished during the live-action shooting. This includes the use of mechanized props, scenery, scale models, pyrotechnics and Atmospheric Effects: creating physical wind, rain, fog, snow, clouds etc. Making a car appear to drive by itself, or blowing up a building are examples of mechanical effects. Mechanical effects are often incorporated into set design and makeup. For example, a set may be built with break-away doors or walls, or prosthetic makeup can be used to make an actor look like a monster.

Since the 1990s, computer generated imagery (CGI) has come to the forefront of special effects technologies. CGI gives film-makers greater control, and allows many effects to be accomplished more safely and convincingly – and even, as technology marches on, at lower costs. As a result, many optical and mechanical effects techniques have been superseded by CGI.

CONTEMPT OF COURT AND MEDIA

The right to a fair trial, uninfluenced by extraneous pressures is recognized as a basic tenet of justice. The Constitution of India and the Contempt of Courts Act, 1971 contain provisions aimed at safeguarding the right to fair trial. Restrictions are imposed on the discussion or publication of matters relating to the merits of a case pending before a Court.

The problems raised by trial by media involve a tug of war between two conflicting principles free press and free trial. The freedom of the press stems from the right of the public in a democracy to be involved on the issues of the day, which affect them. People cannot adequately influence the decisions that affect their lives unless they can be adequately informed on the facts and arguments relevant to the decisions. Much of such fact-finding and argumentation necessarily has to be conducted vicariously, the public press being a principal instrument. This is also the justification for investigative and campaign journalism. At the same time, the right to fair trial, uninfluenced by extraneous pressures is recognized as a basic tenet of justice. The Constitution of India and the Contempt of Courts Act, 1971 contain provisions aimed at safeguarding the right to fair trial. Restrictions are imposed on the discussion or publication of matters relating to the merits of a case pending before a Court. A journalist may thus be liable for contempt of court if he publishes anything which might prejudice a fair trial or anything which impairs the impartiality of a court to decide a cause on its merits, whether the proceedings before the Court be a criminal or civil proceeding.

In relation to freedom of speech and expression, there are three types of contempt of court:

(a) One kind of contempt is scandalizing the court itself;
(b) There may likewise be a contempt of court in abusing parties who are concerned in causes in the court;
(c) There may also be contempt in prejudicing mankind against persons before the cause is heard.

However, the above classifications are by no means exhaustive. Very broadly speaking, the conduct may refer to anything that tends to bring the administration of justice into disrepute or to obstruct or interfere with the due course of justice.

PRE-TRIAL PUBLICITY

Sensationalized journalism has also had an impact on the judiciary. For example, in upholding the imposition of the death penalty on Mohammed Afzal for the December 2001 attack on the Indian Parliament, Justice P. Venkatarama Reddi stated, (t)he incident, which resulted in heavy casualties, had shaken the entire nation and the collective conscience of the society will only be satisfied if capital punishment is awarded to the offender. A media trial began almost immediately after Afzals arrest. Only one week after the attack, on 20 December 2001, the police called a press conference during the course of which Afzal incriminated himself in front of the national media. The media played an excessive and negative role in shaping the public conscience before Afzal was even tried.

Similarly, S.A.R. Geelani, one of Afzals co-defendants in the Parliament attack case, was initially sentenced to death for his alleged involvement despite an overwhelming lack of evidence. Large sections of the Indian media portrayed him as a dangerous and trained terrorist. On appeal, the Delhi High Court overturned Geelanis conviction and described the prosecutions case as at best, absurd and tragic.

PROTECTION OF THE RIGHTS OF THE ACCUSED

Taking exception to the media interviewing witnesses and commenting on cases during trial, the Law Commission has recommended changes in the Contempt of Courts Act, 1971 to protect the rights of the accused and ensure the proper conduct of trial in its latest report titled *Trial by Media*, headed by Justice M Jagannadha Rao. It has also emphasised the need to sensitise journalists through proper training in certain aspects of the law. What is going on in the media may indeed be highly objectionable. Merely because it is tolerated by the courts, it may not cease to be contempt, the Commission noted in the report. The Commission said: In our country the lack of knowledge of law of contempt currently shows that there is extensive coverage of interviews with witnesses. The panel said that this is highly objectionable even under the current law of contempt if such interviews are conducted after the chargesheet is filed. We are of the view that there is considerable interference with the due administration of criminal justice and this will have to remedied by Parliament, the report said.

In its report submitted to the Government, the Commission said, Today there is a feeling that in view of the extensive use of the television and cable services, the whole pattern of publication of news has changed and several such publications are likely to have a prejudicial impact on the suspects, accused, witnesses and even judges and in general on the administration of justice. The report said, according to our law, a suspect/accused is entitled to a fair procedure and is presumed to be innocent till proved guilty in a court of law. None can be allowed to prejudge or prejudice his case by the time it goes to trial.

It said that publications, which interfered or tend to interfere with the administration of justice would amount to criminal contempt under the Contempt of Courts Act, 1971 and if in order to preclude such interference, the provisions of that Act impose reasonable restrictions on freedom of speech, such restrictions would be valid.

The report noted that at present, under Section 3 (2) of the Contempt of Courts Act, 1971 such publications would be contempt only if a chargesheet had been filed in a criminal case. The Commission has suggested that the starting point of a criminal case should be from the time of arrest of an accused and not from the time of filing of the charge sheet. In the perception of the Commission such an amendment would prevent the media from prejudging or prejudicing the case.

The United States and Australia both have stringent provisions regulating media trials, and the solutions that are envisaged to the damage caused to the right to a fair trial of the accused range from sequestering of the judge/jury for the duration of the trial, to transferring trials to more neutral jurisdictions, to declaring mistrials and acquitting accused persons, and in extreme cases, even barring further criminal complaints against an accused whose character has been so tarnished by media scrutiny that it would be impossible for him to be given a fair trial. In India, the Press Council of India does have regulations concerning reporting of *sub judice* matters, but a violation of these norms will only call for sanction against the media organization and will not necessarily ensure justice to the accused. At present, in India, the impossibility of a fair trial for an accused can possibly be a ground for transfer of cases to another jurisdiction. The Supreme Court has come down on trials by media, especially in dowry cases, where public sympathy is clearly with the victim and her family, and out pours of public outrage against the errant husband and his family easily find place in local publications.

In *M P Lohia v. State of West Bengal,* Justice Santosh Hegde of the Supreme Court felt compelled to note the disturbing factor. The case concerned the death of one Chandni in February, 2002 and the complaint in this regard was registered, the investigation was in progress and the application for grant of anticipatory bail had been disposed of by the High Court of Calcutta when an article has appeared in a magazine called Saga titled Doomed by Dowry written by one Kakoli Poddar based on her interview of the family of the deceased. Justice Hegde remarked that all material narrated therein are those that may be used in the forthcoming trial, and was convinced that they would certainly interfere with the administration of justice.

THE NEED FOR OPENNESS

There is a concern that the above regulations may result in the restricted reporting of important cases. In the interests of ensuring fair trials, the media in UK for instance have restricted the reporting of terrorist trials for long periods. Conviction following a fair trial is a major weapon to combat terrorism. The case with family courts is also similar. There is a feeling that the workings of, and the decisions made in family courts are too secretive. The argument runs that without increased openness there can be no confidence in the workings of the family court, and therefore no confidence in the process or the outcomes. To a consultation in the UK on the issue, the Newspaper Society wrote that:

We fully support the proposal that the media should be allowed to attend ALL family courts as of right and the principle of a general presumption of openness must be the established if public confidence and accountability is to be achieved. The role of the media as representative of the public particularly in relation to attendance at court proceedings is well established and understood. Media groups argue that the solution lies in letting journalists in as of right to act as a proxy for the public. To restrict them would be to deny the public and mean that miscarriages of justice could go unrecognised and unreported.

The contempt law is as old as Common Law itself. The Court, however, will act only where justice is jeopardized by a gross and/or unfounded attack on the Judges, where the attack is calculated to obstruct or destroy the judicial process. The judiciary cannot be immune from criticism. Judges and courts are alike open to criticism, and if reasonable argument or expostulation is offered against any judicial act as contrary to law or the public good, no Court could or would treat that as contempt of court. It is only the scurrilous abuse on a Judge in his character as a Judge, which would be actionable under the Contempt of Courts Act.

The freedom of the press and the independence of the judiciary are two of the most important indices of democracy in a country. It is essential to preserve both. Pliable press and subservient judiciary are the first step in the process of extinguishment of democratic lights.

SOCIAL RESPONSIBILITY OF MEDIA

An important consideration in doing ethnographic research in the study of new electronic media is the social presence attributes of the technology itself.

Short, Williams, and Christie were apparently the first researchers to conceptualize the construct they called social presence, which they defined as being a quality of the communications medium itself. As they elaborated, social presence "varies between different media... affects the nature of the interaction... and interacts with the purpose of the interaction to influence the medium chosen by the individual who wishes to communicate".

Media perceived as high in social presence are generally judged (on Semantic Differential Scales) by users as warm, personal, sensitive, and, sociable; those low in social presence as cold, impersonal, insensitive, and unsociable. Chief among the reasons for differentiating media in their degree of social presence is the medium's ability to restrict stimulus-conveying information. More specifically, media that are less able to convey non-verbal elements are more likely to be judged as being low in social presence.

In another sense, social presence is the degree to which a medium is perceived as conveying the "presence" of the communicating participants; it is dependent not only on the words involved in the communication but on the full range of verbal and non-verbal cues, and the communication context.

Thus CMC technologies typically would be judged lower in social presence than face-to-face communication (FTF) because of the lower bandwidth of information conveyed by the former (vis-a-vis verbal and non-verbal messages). This notion of the bandwidth of the medium is closely related to media richness, a construct developed by Daft and Lengel. Rice describes the term as the:

Extent to which media are able to bridge different frames of reference, make issues less ambiguous, or provide opportunities for learning in a given time interval, based on the medium's capacity for immediate feedback, the number of cues and senses involved, personalization, and language variety. The essential underlying element in both of these notions is that a good match between the medium's characteristics (high in social presence or media richness) and the intent of the communication activity (getting to know someone, strategic decision making) should lead to higher performance and satisfaction. The importance of all of this to ethnographic research is, how can one adequately do participatory research with media that are judged low in social presence or media richness?

Stated another way, how will the ethnographic researcher be able to make adequate sense out of communication that restricts important cues such as non-verbal behaviours? in their study of e-mail in organizations, Garton and Wellman have discussed the consequences of e-mail's exclusion of non-verbal cues: E-mail does not supply non-verbal interactional cues to group members, such as eye contact, gestures, nodding approval, frowning, or hesitating before replying.

There are no contextual cues, either: Participants cannot use seating arrangements to identify coalitions and cleavages, or choose meeting sites to identify the importance of sponsorship of meetings. Because e-mail users typically are identified by name only, people are not constantly reminded of the social roles cues others have beyond the narrow confines of the task group.

Users may not be aware of another group member's gender, race, expertise, or organizational position. One approach to this dilemma is to take account of the ways participants do compensate at times for the restricted bandwidth of the medium by providing clarifying cues in their messages.

Social role cues can be transmitted in e-mail (either implicitly or explicitly) by adding status information to their "signatures," by their writing style, or by forwarding communications to (or from) important persons. Baym also found the standard components of Usenet posts for a soap opera news group—*e.g.*, "from" line, "subject" line, "organization" line (site of message's origin), and the quotation system, in addition to signatures—to provide subtle contextualizing cues about the sender's interests and status.

Other examples of clarifying cues are:

- Emotions used to pictorialize emotional states (*e.g.*, the computer "smiley face"),
- Meta-messages included to communicate physical states (*e.g.*, using " " to designate jocularity),
- Acronyms used to designate degree of emotion (*e.g.*, "FOTFL" to represent "failing on the floor laughing," or a greater degree of merriment beyond a mere smile or grin).'

As Walther, Anderson, and Park noted in their meta-analysis of computer mediated interaction, the interpersonal effects expected to accrue rapidly in face-to-face interactions can (and do) occur in CIVIC, but these interpersonal cues require extended time interactions.

That is, interactional, contextual, and social cues that provide immediate feedback in FTF communication have to be stated explicitly in CIVIC and require more time to develop. Deep knowledge of an organizational culture may also enhance the participants' hermeneutic ability to embellish an e-mail with meaning. Of course, social cues do more than merely clarify or boost informational richness in FTF or CMC encounters; they also mark a person's identity (*e.g.*, gender, age, ethnic, class, sexual, cultural, occupational, etc.) as being of a certain moral or political character. Gender norms, for example, are a powerful means of designating the inappropriate or disvalued behaviours of men and women in specific contexts and vary widely from ideologically dominant expressions to the communication contexts and media of subaltern groups.

Thus, women ethnographers learn very quickly how their bodies—not only skin colour and body shape, but also aspects of clothing, adornment, hair style, and facial, gestural, and speech styles—affect the way they are perceived in the field, and the roles and motives attributed to them.

Embodiment in all of its forms is not a condition that can be controlled independently or somehow neutralized. Rather, it is through the ethnographic body performing with other cultural members that one learns the schemes of cultural valuation. Practical problems of "fitting in" are of a piece with issues of acculturation which are enormously important to understanding the scene being studied. In CMC environments, where perceptions of identity derive almost totally from what and how one writes, the notion of representational reality collapses and the ambiguity of action becomes foregrounded. Multiple identities are tried on, and specific traits or behaviours may be expressed more boldly in the widespread use of aliases, aptonyms, and role-playing domains in which players build characters for themselves. By detaching self-expression from the politics of the body, CMC liberates its users from certain kinds of discriminatory practice and promotes a low-risk, often playful, exploration of skill sets.

Certainly, the texts one writes may unwittingly leak signs of personal identity which could be attributed by readers to the author's embodied self.

As long as there are other users supervising the actors and the threads of their discourse, standards of plausibility, coherence, and trustworthiness will still apply to the textual contributions. Ultimately, the CMC ethnographer should be prepared to confront the ambiguity of identity performance as a central fact of virtual life, worthy of study on its own terms.

Concerns about testing the informational richness, or the authenticity, of virtual action against criteria of embodied action may be much less important to the project of ethnography than issues of how computing worlds are socially constructed, what recognizably human purposes they serve, and how they relate to a range of other "possibility spaces." Reduced social presence also affects the way in which researchers enter virtual scenes. Interaction management seems to function similarly in FTF and CMC in the opening and closing phases of encounters, but in CMC the choice of names and the use of attention-getting strategies are critical decisions.

The risks of field entry may be lessened by learning the norms of such strategies in advance. Thus the "outsider" designation one usually expects in the first stages of an FTF project may be less of a problem in entering a virtual space once the right level of competence has been gained via observation.

On the other hand, veteran members often do not suffer novices gladly, and the ethnographer may need to ask for the cooperation of the group (or its influential members) in order to be heard, or to engage them in directed queries or tasks. Researchers face subtle differences in the social makeup and interactional preferences of virtual scenes, which may require them to devise different strategies for entry and field positioning than in FTF situations.

SOCIAL STRATEGIES

Matters of self-presentation and scope of action are critical to the relations built among researchers, the virtual "places" populating the Internet, and the cultural membership. Correll, for example, was able to convey the location, look, and meanings of the "furniture" of the Lesbian Cafe mostly from her observations of electronic postings, but also from interviews. Compared to Leal's analysis of the relation of TV sets to the domestic material culture in working-class Brazilian homes, the mise-en-scene of the Cafe is not nearly as dense, tactile, and sensuous.

Despite this possibly unfair comparison, "the sense of a common reality [in the Lesbian Cafe] was used by patrons much like physical settings are used by co-present conversationalists—as a source of mutually relevant topics". Like the dialogue one hears in a radio play, conversationalists in the Lesbian Cafe must include many more references in their ordinary talk to objects, the current status of the objects, and the presence or absence of people in and around those objects in order to maintain orientation and sustain a convincing sense of as-if reality. The lean exposition Correll offers would likely be unacceptable in other forms of ethnographic work, but it turns out to be the one that matters to the women who "drink" and socialize there.

Media ethnographers begin their on-line presence in a variety of ways. One mode used by some is that of the unknown, unobtrusive observer. Over a three-year period, Harrington and Bielby collected and printed messages posted on two soap opera BBS's by subscribers to two commercial on-line computer services. They do not report interactions of any kind between themselves and the posters.

Presumably, the computer services were not notified of the initiation of the research activity, nor were the BBS system operators. Interestingly, while the authors appear unconcerned about their own lurker posture, they note the suspicion held by many of the BBS users that their conversations were being overheard by "industry insiders". Scodari also relies on transcripts of fan BBS discourse in interpreting critical reactions to changes in the soap, Another

World, although she aligns her own interests much more closely with the fans she quotes than Harrington and Bielby. Open participation characterizes the approach of several other studies and more closely resembles normative field practice. Baym started as an unabashed soap fan and news group contributor and found it easy to continue openly as an analyst of the group:

My position in the [rec.arts.arts.soaps, or r.a.t.s., newsgroup] is that of a participant at least as much as a researcher. As a long-time fan of soap operas, I was thrilled to discover this group. It was only after I had been reading daily and participating regularly for a year that I began to write about it. As the work has evolved, I have shared its progress with the group members and found them exceedingly supportive and helpful. They have acted as research participants as well as subjects and have treated me more as an ambassador than a researcher.

The confidence each party had in the other paved the way for Baym to obtain other forms of data besides the news group's messages, especially electronic mail correspondence with several participants and responses to open-ended questions she posted to r.a.t.s. Similarly, Correll's membership in the Lesbian Cafe, and the approval she got from the bar's founder, assisted her in posting queries and interviewing several of the patrons both by e-mail and in person.

Some researchers actually run the facilities that enable computer users to "find" the research project. In an early study, Myers operated a university BBS for two months and set up a number of networked research tools in order to investigate the perceived social context of CMC: on-line surveys, a focus group, and a role-playing game. More recently, Lindlof et al. launched a Web home page for X-Men fans that offered graphic content (thus participating in the X-Men array of more than 60 Internet locations), links to other X-Men sites, a survey to capture data, and a solicitation for dialogues with on-line X-Men users and page producers.

Like the Baym and Correll studies, the research purpose was stated openly in order to invite cooperation; however, its sudden appearance and the research team's initial contacts with users were sometimes met with suspicion, critique (of their knowledge of X-Men), and humorous skepticism. It became clear that the World Wide Web page of hypertext URLS's (Uniform Resource Locator) that linked to other pages related to the X-Men topic constituted the study's "gatekeeper" in the traditional sense of enabling an initial contact.

The study also hints at the possibilities of participatory design in which ethnographers may act as the interpreters of diverse voices, usage interests, and aesthetic tastes in the design of networked systems.

A final strategy for consideration moves the researcher physically alongside the user in order to "read" his or her real-time decision making and styles of engagement.

The user's dyadic interplay with a computer forms a focal interest, but included in this arena would be the material context of computing (*e.g.*, its location in a room, the CD-ROM's on hand), the institutional culture (*e.g.*, considering open viewing of sex sites as sexual harassment), interpersonal resources or constraints (*e.g.*, informal rules for sharing URL's), and the specific reality of what it means to "do computing" that these signify for users.

Models for this approach exist in the literature on social television viewing and family computer usage. However, since Internet usage is typically a solitary venture, the more promising route would seem to lie in some version of the "shopping with consumers" protocol from the field of consumer behaviour.

Accompanying users on their way through the kinetic pathways of virtual space and eliciting talk on a wide range of subjects, either retrospectively or on-the-spot, enables the researcher to understand the more embodied dimensions of CMC. In effect, the researcher shadows the user's on-site computing. The advantages of the approach are its close proximity to the user and setting, and the ability to comprehend computing performance as an activity that has a rich, localized back stage—that is, as more than lines of type scrolling down a screen.

In ethnographies of embodied social scenes, the researcher must continually negotiate with the culture membership and convince them of the value of the study and the reasonableness of the person doing the research. It is not unusual for ethnographers to have to adjust their persona somewhat differently as they pass through a scene, or disclose different versions of the project, since the members of a group often relate asymmetrically or even conflictively to each other.

CMC ethnographies, as we have shown, also involve some degree of negotiation when anonymous observation is not the method of access. Virtual spaces offer a limited window in which to explain one's purpose, and electronic text is not the most suitable medium for engaging in a sensitive interaction.

Trust tends to be a heightened concern where entry and exit and unbridled information disclosure are easily accomplished. Mistakes, once made, can have disastrous results, and be very hard to rectify. Institutional principles for informed consent are now being formulated for research on the World Wide Web, but it will take longer for ethnographers themselves to develop a consensus around protocols for responsible virtual space entry and ways to insure the fair treatment of those they study without compromising very seriously the conduct of enquiry.

TECHNICAL UTILITIES

In this section, we discuss the use of technical utilities for accomplishing research tasks. Some computer systems allow asynchronous communication interactions to be studied either by saving the individual messages, or archiving all postings for later perusal. Most of these have been around for some time. The ones we discuss here are electronic mail, news groups over Usenet, and list servers. Electronic mail is asynchronous (users generally are not communicating in realtime), quick (in terms of transmission and reply), text-based, and configured for dyadic or multiple connections (can be sent one-to-one, one-to-many, or many-to-many). Moreover, e-mail can be stored and manipulated. As Garton and Wellman noted in a recent review:

E-mail can be stored in external memory for future retrieval, searching, editing, and forwarding to others. People can edit their own or other's messages to change their meaning. The historical record of interaction may be used for surveillance of individual and group interactions, to review past decisions (as Oliver North belatedly learned), and to bring new members up to date.

What makes this modality particularly suitable for ethnographic research are its personal-contact and archival functions.

For example, in his 9-month participant-observation study of "Zytech," a computer systems firm, Workman utilized e-mail in the following ways:

- Being placed on the company's various distribution lists, which on a daily basis delivered internal documents, minutes of meetings, meeting agendas, and announcements;
- Scheduling interviews;
- Accessing hundreds of BBS's, including Zytech correspondence going back several years;
- Communicating with informants, including follow-ups to FTF interviews.

Though the staggered progress of e-mail interviewing does not promote the same qualities of rapport or spontaneity as personal interviews, it does permit a more elastic time frame for both interviewer and participant to think carefully about the meanings of questions and replies.

In another organizational study, special software was used to automatically save the headers (but not the message content) of all departmental e-mail to a designated file whenever a user read or transmitted a message, yielding a non-reactive means of learning who communicates with whom, when, and about what. For ethnographic purposes, the value of this procedure lies in its capacity to augment such methods as interviews or on-site observation.

However, the ability to retrieve and store this information without the users' permission (or below their conscious awareness, even when permission is granted) carries the potential for ethical abuse at worst, and suspicion on the part of participants at best. Usenet is a protocol that describes how groups of messages can be stored on and sent between computers, many of which lay outside of the Internet. In actuality, Usenet forms a "virtual forum" for the electronic community that is divided into a plethora of news groups dedicated to varied areas of interest. News group articles are read and written through programmes called newsreaders that keep track of articles that have been read, allow users to edit what has been read, and enable readers to reply to previously posted messages in the aforementioned study, Baym reported her participant-observation of a news group made up of soap opera aficionados.

Even though some Usenet sites can archive messages off-line, Baym herself saved the messages posted on the r.a.t.s group while she was an active member. Even working with a medium often described as low in social presence or media richness, she was able to develop a "thick" description of the personalities of this community based on features of their postings:

- Signature files (files automatically attached to postings containing identifying information about the sender),
- Humour in the messages,
- Self-disclosure,
- Comments made about personal lives.

By capitalizing on the features of Usenet news groups, variations of focus group interviewing become possible. During a two-month period of operating a public BBS, Myers set up a computer-mediated focus group "to determine what motivated frequent and active BBS use". As an alternative to a simple discussion, a focus group consisting of a theoretically interesting set of users could work on a virtual task. MacGregor and Morrison describe an editing-group protocol in which groups of people were given the opportunity to re-edit existing news reports (including video footage) in order to produce a more "ideal" version, thereby enabling them to understand viewers' journalistic values more concretely.

It is not difficult to see how this task could be adapted to computer news groups and the multimedia capabilities of high-end work stations, although techniques for training and monitoring the users in their editing-group activities would need to be developed.

Listserv groups (managed by listserver software) are similar to news groups in that they are discussion groups, but they operate in a completely different way by using the Internet e-mail system to exchange messages. Once a person subscribes to a Listserv group (or Listproc group, as they are called on networks other than the early Bitnet), their name is added to a mailing list that receives postings from everyone else subscribed to the list.

Many listservers offer features that allow users to search and retrieve files that are archived, and search the archives using keyword searches. Thus, anyone from a remote site can access archived messages for study from the host computer.

This capability raises interesting ethical issues: How does one receive consent to study the stored communications of users of a particular listserver? Is open access to a person's communications implied in the use of this service? Are the archived files considered the property of the individual subscribers, or are they "owned" in some form of fiduciary relationship by the listserv operator? Because the Internet has developed so rapidly, many such legal and ethical questions have yet to be resolved.

The CMC technologies mentioned above have been in place for a while and are generally well known to most researchers. Most of the communication from these sources is asynchronous, *i.e.*, it is archived for later review and becomes an excellent database. However some of the newer systems allow for the actual observation of synchronous, or real-time, communication behaviour. It is to these we now turn.

Some of the more recent real-time technologies are:

- Internet Relay Chat (IRC) systems, or" chat lines";
- The entire gamut of multiple-user technologies, *e.g.*, MUDs (Multiple User Domains, formerly known as Multiple User Dungeons), MOOs (MUD Object-Oriented), and MUSHes (Multi-User Shared Hallucination);
- Groupware,
- Desktop videoconferencing over the Internet. All of these systems operate synchronously and as such more approximate face-to-face communication.

Internet Relay Chat (IRC) is a multi-user synchronous communication capability available worldwide to users with Internet accessibility.

These real time" chat lines" provide for mutithreaded conversations from more than two users in something very similar to an" electronic cocktail party". In these" chat rooms" users are able to don bogus" personas" (false identities) and communicate with interactants from all over the globe. These chat lines are very popular on commercial services like America Online and are now available through various web browsers (*e.g.*, students can" chat" with the president of a university via its Web site).

One step up from IRC is a whole family of computer programmes that allow more than just written conversation in real time. These are multi-user programmes that, in addition to providing text, allow the additional depiction of a physical environment. Multiple User programmes are designed to offer a pseudo-physical dimension via its object orientation. In MOOs, for examples, individuals" virtually" move through" rooms," interact with virtual" objects" such as chairs, doors, and the like, and have virtual conversations with others. As Reid has remarked, in MUDs," text replaces gesture and has even become gesture itself".

A third, more recent technology is found in a generation of software called" groupware." Unlike MUDs, MOOs, MUSHes, MUCKs, and the like that are used more for entertainment and amusement, groupware is being developed mainly for business and professional uses. Most of the newer groupware programmes use Web-based technology and allow not only for sharing e-mail but for conducting synchronous multiuser conferencing. The promise for ethnographers in this technology lies in the" common thread" that runs through all these programmes--*i.e.*," the construction of shared memory" and recording of group discussions.

In essence, groupware allows for observing the" virtual office," *i.e.*, electronic mail, conferencing, scheduling, shared documents, electronic" whiteboards," and so on, and recording these interactions. All of this can function in real time or be archived for later study.

Appearing now on the horizon is the capability to use the desktop computer for real time videoconferencing. Using fairly inexpensive video cameras attached to desktop computers, and software such as CU-SeeMe technology, mediated FTF interactions are now available for study. As soon as compression capabilities for full-motion video are perfected, these dispersed FTF interactions, mediated by the computer, can be recorded and used in data analysis. When considering all these new technologies, the type of research done may have to be dictated by the characteristics of the medium. That is, for asynchronous media, the type of research conducted would be more akin to that for studying other forms of written communication, while synchronous media enable types of research more equivalent to naturalistic observation--*i.e.*, observing the unfolding of communicative events in real time.

It was inevitable that interpretive analysts would turn their attention to the profusion of common culture now moving through the Internet. Forms of ethnographic enquiry are being applied to many of the events that occur in virtual space, although questions remain about how well these approaches engage CMC phenomena.

One such question is the appropriateness of" community" as a conceptual device. The conventional idea of community as a stable locus for the practice of ritual, custom, and moral obligation applies to cyberspace groups, albeit in the context of a shifting sense of commitment.

When members can easily come and go, when many" members" do not even post, and when identities cannot be verified beyond the current situation, the power of a community ethos may be weakened considerably. The structural properties of the Internet also raise questions about how far a user community extends. For example, can any array of Web sites found by a search term be considered a" community," and if not, what criteria do we use for including a site in the community set?

Finally, what is the relationship of computer-mediated action to local social networks? It has been suggested, for example, that the growing reliance on computer technology for communicating with distant others may undermine the vitality of public life in so-called real communities or play a role in their economic and social fragmentation. Answers to these and other important issues about virtual community await further and more inventive empirical studies.

If there is one theme that runs through the differences between FTF (embodied) and CIVIC (virtual) ethnography, it is the problem of participation. CIVIC ethnography moves us into questions of what it means to engage in and explain" experience" without being co-present with others. Screen-life is a social sphere of its own with vocabularies, motives, and expectations that increasingly re-interpret the meanings of off-screen-life (*e.g.*, mail becoming known as" snail mail").

Objectifications of life in the screen world are also a part of that world. Computer users do act as textual performers and analysts, and knowingly comment on the skills of other text-makers. The use of symbolic codes like" FOTFL" and the real-time deployment of a character in a MUD are operations that create the affect of participation for users, and it would be unusual for ethnographers; not to consider their situated usage.

However, the sites of semiotic action in CMC are not the texts, but the persons who produce them. The text-threads from a Usenet news group or a stack of e-mail messages exnominate the moments in which they were created and read, and the influences of local institutions on their users' action are seldom seen in the messages themselves. In the years ahead, ethnographers will be struggling with basic questions of what it means to" participate" in simulated worlds as well as with developing tactical ways to participate as researchers.

Closely related to the problem of participation are issues of trust and ethical conduct to which we have alluded at various points in this chapter. These issues assume even more importance than usual in research practice due to the greater potential for engaging in covert surveillance of CIVIC social life and the still-unsettled distinctions between" public" and" private" behaviour across the range of cyberspace contexts.

The problem of the stable identifiability of persons who post in Usenet news groups, respond by e-mail, or visit a Web site may also confound the principle of informed consent as a precondition for engaging a human subject's participation. Generally, there is little debate about the need to provide as much disclosure as possible about research procedures to those who are asked to participate, and to shelter them from the possible harmful consequences of participation and subsequent publication.

However, as King notes, extremely wide ranges of" group accessibility" and" perceived privacy" exist on the Internet. The highest accessibility characterizes those public BBS groups that are unmoderated and unregulated, while the least accessible community is" a private, closed e-mail group where the subscription address is not published and there are enforced requirements to join".

Perceived privacy varies in terms of both the sensitivity of the information (in which, for example, a substance abuse support group would seek a very high level of privacy) and the need to disseminate information to the widest possible client group (the National Communication Association's CRTNET would seek a low measure of privacy). Yet a great many Internet conversations can in fact be monitored with relative ease, which complicates the understanding of what is permissible to study and whether observation is truly" covert" if no barriers are erected to keep one from observing.

Of course, it probably does matter to many virtual groups whether it is a naive visitor who is stopping briefly at their fora, or a person whose goal is to cast a long-term, analytic eye on their activities and publish the result. The conventional view holds that any research of on-line participants should" strive to obtain some degree of informed consent whenever possible.... Most importantly, researchers should negotiate their entry into electronic communities, beginning with the `owner' of the discussion, if one exists".

Preserving the dignity and empowerment of the persons being studied, even if their" real" identities and locations are unknown, demands that the researcher take steps to explain all of the elements of the study that may bear on their decision to participate voluntarily. Taking a different view, Jones argues that the highly elusive, evanescent presence and essentially unknowable identity of most of the subjects in cylberspace obviates the need in most cases for pursuing consent formally:" If the research does not involve identifiable subjects, there is no risk to subjects, and therefore the protection of these rights and interests no longer applies".

Jones goes on to argue that the strict application of conventional human subject protections would be especially detrimental to the study of cyberspace, which exists as an arena in which individuals can enjoy the freedom of withholding, revealing, and even fabricating information about themselves.

Somewhere between these positions is King, who states that" the perceived level of privacy with which most members of cyberspace forums post notes is the level that researchers are obligated to protect".

At the stage of publication, she advocates the removal from messages of all headers, signatures, references to the name and type of the group (e-mail, Usenet news group, etc.), and references to any person's name or pseudo-name. It may be that the evolving use of networked systems will alter the customs and arguments for what constitutes" privacy" and" autonomy," in turn informing the ethical practice of ethnography.

Finally, the implications of computer networks for the construction of the research text are of great importance. One can adapt the same hypermedia programming tools used in other scholarly efforts to the production of ethnographies that would in turn be fully compatible with the World Wide Web's system architecture. An example of such an effort is the Survivors of the Shoah Visual History Foundation, which has set out to videotape oral histories of all living Holocaust survivors and digitize them in hypermedia format along with maps, documents, photos, and written texts of the interviews.

The files, perhaps numbering 150,000 by the end of the decade, will be fully cross-referenced and accessible for on-line searches by key words. Similarly, ethnographies of CMC culture can be envisioned which would provide the discursive threads that underpin an analysis, along with field notes, full-text interviews, generations of Web page design, graphic material, and URL's to the ethnographic sites themselves and related research projects. Presumably the author would also be" available" in a rather immediate sense to readers via the research text's Web site or e-mail.

What distinguishes an archive a reader can navigate at will from a research text is that the latter usually embodies arguments, claims, and evidence in a style conventionalized within the discipline. While readers have always had non-linear access to a text, it is the linear narrative designed by the author that academic communities recognize as the only one subject to critique.

The capabilities of hypermedia threaten this formulation of the research product and the concept of authorial control that stands behind it.

If readings of an ethnography are neither the ones an author intended nor the ones deemed important or legitimate by a discipline, then its use-value becomes as widely distributed among communities of practical interest as the Internet itself. The move to modular, multi-threaded (but not necessarily plotless) research texts not only reduces the researcher's story to the stature of one among a potentially limitless number, it also accelerates the epistemological decentering of enquiry that began with the challenge to objectivist ethnography nearly twenty years ago.

NEW PERSPECTIVE OF MEDIA PLANNING

In India, we are experiencing an economic slow down. Consumer buying is on the decline. Ad spends are curtailed Agencies are becoming learner. Clients are becoming more discerning about media usage. Though they are cutting and budgets, they want more effectiveness. In common parlance, this is called 'more bang for the buck.' Clients have become extremely vigilant on how agencies spend their money on media. Intuitive media decisions and exploratory tactics are out.

Everything has to be substantiated. It is necessary to stretch every media rupee more and more. Though the broader media mix is planned annually, media planners are continuously shuffling the actual vehicles they choose channels or programmes in case of TV and publications in case of print. Clients want to know how involved their target audience is with a particular programming. Even though demographics cover the reach objectives, the target audience may be a passive viewer. Research on the involvement of the target groups is getting more attention. Agencies are making use of proprietary consumer involvement tools that help them measure media preferences of target audiences. There is a shift from planning based merely on reach to planning based on awareness/

involvement. The client wants to know whether his target audience has actually seen the campaign. He wants to know whether the client was at home when the commercial was telecast. Media planning goes beyond media buying. It has to focus more sharply on consumer decision-making process and the importance of media in that process. Media has to make accountable. Media planners have started using more efficient media evaluation matrices. Audience involvement scores are now weighted while arriving at ROI on media spends.

MEDIA PLAN

1. The first step in media planning is the collection of useful information about the people or the market to be reached through advertising. The more detailed and specific the target market data available on geography, age group, sex, income, attitudes, interests, etc., the more appropriate the media selection would be. However, it is well understood that the available advertising budget is an important guide to the media selection. The task is to select a medium most suited to the target market at a given budget cost. This concept of "what-can-you-afford?" in media planning is equally relevant to small as well as large companies, for they do have something like a budget or an appropriation of fund for promotion. Irrespective of the size of the company, it finally settles for how much money it can afford to put in for a particular market for advertising and/or for promotion.
2. The second significant step in media planning is to decide upon the nature of the message to be conveyed to the target market. However, this decision necessarily follows a thorough understanding of the consumer profile. The message or the copy, by which name it is more accurately called, is decided in the light of the aspect of consumer behaviour or motivation which is intended to be influenced.
3. Having gathered this significant information, the next logical step is to search for an ideal match of the audience characteristics of media with the target market profile and, at the same time, check for the perfect adaptability of the message (copy) requirement with the media. Following the media planning decision process, we have to take into account the other media concepts explained in the following paragraphs.
4. Reach is expressed in terms of the number of households or individuals reached by a given medium over a period of time. This is usually expressed in terms of per cent of total households or individuals in the target market. Sometimes, there is a possibility of duplication, *i.e.*, two media may reach the target audience. National magazines have a different reach from that of the regional' ones or other media, such as TV, radio, etc. National readership surveys

provide information about published materials, whereas several other conducted studies may provide the reach per cent of other media. One can buy reach with print in a specific geographical market by taking a combination of newspapers or magazines.

Frequency refers to the average number of times different households or individuals are reached by a medium in a given period of time. The frequency of advertisement exposure of the target market depends upon the amount of reinforcement of the image required or the amount of reminding required having sustaining patronage from the target customers. The greater the frequency, the greater the probability of the advertisement message making a deep and lasting impression.

To understand these concepts dearly consider the following illustration. A sample of viewers represents 10 TV Households (HHs)-Q to Z who watch a programme A over a four week period.

THE CORPORATE STRUCTURE OF THE MASS MEDIA

It was Walter Lippman who coined the phrase "the manufacture of consent", enjoining it as a means of population control. Lippman's concept may indeed be in effect today. In this regard, the status of the mass media and its faithful propagation of the established opinion that Western policy is fundamentally benevolent in intention, is an issue of paramount importance. What role has the media played in clarifying the real principles and motives of Western policy to the public, and what does this entail for the nature of Western democracy and the role of the population in the formulation of policy? The mass media is clearly one of the most powerful institutions in society; it is, for most of the public, the ultimate source of all their information.

The structure of the mass media will therefore have fundamental implications for the political and cultural orientation of the public. Hence, an understanding of the mass media will throw considerable light on the structure of Western society, the relationship between the public and those who possess power, as well as the ideologies produced by the media and their impact on the public.

All scholars generally agree that the media do have the capacity to set the agenda of public discourse about political affairs, and it is widely recognised that the media has a significant role in actualising the diffusion of Western ideology and culture throughout the world. However, they differ over the degree to which the media limits the public's understanding of current affairs and the overall consequences of this.

Nevertheless, the vast extent of the manipulation of the media under the sway of business interests has been harshly revealed in the statement of John Swainton, Chief of Staff of the *New York Times*. "There is not one of you who would dare to write his honest opinion," he reprimanded his colleagues at his retirement party in September. "The business of a journalist now is to destroy the truth, to lie outright, to pervert, to vilify, fall at the feet of Mammon and sell himself for his daily bread. We are tools, vessels of rich men behind the scenes, we are jumping jacks. They pull the strings; we dance. Our talents, our possibilities and our lives are the properties of these men. We are intellectual prostitutes."

The Independent Media: A Myth

It is generally clear that the media has failed to generate genuine public awareness of the actual nature of Western policy. Majid Tehranian, for example, who is Professor of International Communication at the University of Hawaii and Director of the Toda Institute for Global Peace and Policy Research, points out that:

"In their scholarship, William Appleton Williams, Noam Chomsky, Richard Falk, Ramsey Clark, Ali Mazrui, and other critics of US foreign policies have provided an abundance of evidence to support the charges on the counter-democratic role of the United States in much of Asia, Africa, and Latin America."

British historian Mark Curtis, former Research Fellow at the Royal Institute for International Affairs in London, similarly confirms:

"Mutual Anglo-American support in ordering the affairs of key nations and regions, often with violence, to their design has been a consistent feature of the era that followed the Second World War... Policy in, for example, Malaya, Kenya, British Guiana and Iran was geared towards organising Third World economies along guidelines in which British, and Western, interests would be paramount, and those of the often malnourished populations would be ignored or further undermined. Similarly, US interventions overseas-in Vietnam, Nicaragua, the Dominican Republic, Cuba, Chile, etcetera-were designed to counter threats to the Western practice of assigning the Third World to mere client status to Western business interests. British and US forces have acted as mercenary-and often extremely violent-mobs intended to restore 'order' in their domains and to preserve the existing privileges of elites within their own societies."

Development specialist Dr. J. W. Smith, who is Director of Research for the California-based Institute for Economic Democracy, is even more explicit: "No society will tolerate it if they knew that they (as a country) were responsible for violently killing 12 to 15 million people since WW II and causing the death of hundreds of millions more their economies were destroyed or those countries were denied the right to restructure to care for their people. Unknown as it is, and recognizing that this has been standard practice throughout colonialism, that is the record of the Western imperial centres of capital from 1945 to 1990... While mouthing peace, freedom, justice, rights, and majority rule, all over the world state-sponsored terrorists were overthrowing democratic governments, installing and protecting dictators, and preventing peace, freedom, justice, rights, and majority rule. Twelve to fifteen million mostly innocent people were slaughtered in that successful 45 year effort to suppress those breaks for economic freedom which were bursting out all over the world... All intelligence agencies have been, and are still in, the business of destabilizing undeveloped countries to maintain their dependency and the flow of the world's natural wealth to powerful nations' industries at a low price and to provide markets for those industries at a high price."

That the media has failed to accurately portray the real nature of Western foreign policy to the public, playing instead the subservient role of a propaganda machine for elite interests, is therefore quite obvious. The question that then remains is, why does the media – conventionally believed to be critical of the establishment-behave in a way that conforms to the false picture presented by the government and corporate elite of their own policies? The anwer is simple: in a nutshell, the mass media *is* the establishment.

To begin our analysis then, we will discuss a propaganda model of the mass media. It is thus useful to begin with what is arguably the most thorough model of the media-that proposed by Edward Herman (Professor Emeritus of Finance at Wharton School in the University of Pennsylvania) and Noam Chomsky (Institute Professor of Linguistics and Philosophy at MIT), both of whom are leading critics of US foreign policy.

There are particularly pertinent reasons to begin with their model-the primary one being that it is arguably the most thoroughly researched and empirically verified model available. Herman and Chomsky's landmark study, *Manufacturing Consent: The Political Economy of the Mass Media*, comes under the recommendation of America's leading national media watchdog and research group, Fairness and Accuracy In Reporting (FAIR). It is also recommended as an essential resource for media literacy by the Grand Rapids Institute for Information Democracy (GRIID), affiliated with the US-based Community Media Centre (CMC). The Oxford-based research and publishing group Corporate Watch (not to be confused with the US-based organisation of the same name), which works in cooperation with a variety of other human rights and environmentalist organisations, describes the study as "one of the most incisive critiques of the media's role in society". The respected journal *Publisher's Weekly* gives the following review of *Manufacturing Consent*:

"Herman of Wharton and Chomsky of MIT lucidly document their argument that America's government and its corporate giants exercise control over what we read, see and hear. The authors identify the forces that they contend make the national media propagandistic-the major three being the motivation for profit through ad revenue, the media's close links to and often ownership by corporations, and their acceptance of information from biased sources. In five case studies, the writers show how TV, newspapers and radio distort world events... Extensive evidence is calmly presented, and in the end an indictment against the guardians of our freedom is substantiated. A disturbing picture emerges of a news system that panders to the interest of America's privileged and neglects its duties when the concerns of minority groups and the underclass are at stake."

Indeed, according to the leading American media scholar Robert W. McChesney, Professor of Journalism and Mass Communication at the University of Illinois, any significant attempt to comprehend the structure and operation of the mass media must begin with Herman and Chomsky's study. He further observes that:

"This book promises to be a seminal work in critical media analysis and to open a door through which future media analysis will follow... Edward Herman and Noam Chomsky are certainly well qualified to provide a simple yet powerful model that explains how the media function to serve the large propaganda requirements of the elite. Together and individually, they have written numerous articles and books which have chronicled the ways in which the US media have actively promoted the agenda of the elite, particularly in regard to US activities in the Third World. Manufacturing Consent is a work of tremendous importance for scholars and activists alike... Each chapter is meticulously researched and most draw heavily on the authors' earlier works in these areas."

All this provides us with ample reason to begin with Herman and Chomsky's model. Contrary to the claims of the mainstream critique of radical media analysis, a propaganda model does not entail a grandiose conspiracy theory. Rather, this model is based on analysing the politico-economic influences on the mass media, and considering the extent to which those influences both have the potential to condition the media's reporting tendencies in accord with the interests of those who possess power. In other words, the model constitutes a 'guided free market' model, advocating that the media's reporting is influenced by the same factors that dominate corporate activities-the maximisation of profit and therefore the market. The next step is to document the occurrences where this potential is actualised. In this sense, according to the propaganda model the media is conditioned by the profit-orientated considerations of corporate elites. As Professor McChesney observes:

"Herman and Chomsky quickly dismiss the standard mainstream critique of radical media analysis that accuses it of offering some sort of 'conspiracy' theory for media behaviour; rather, they argue, media bias arises from 'the preselection of right-thinking people, internalized preconceptions, and the adaptation of personnel to the constraints' of a series of objective filters they present in their propaganda model. Hence the bias occurs largely through self-censorship, which explains the superiority of the US mass media as a propaganda system: it is far more credible than a system which relies on official state censorship."

7

Mass Media and Modern Society

INTRODUCTION

In political behaviour, opinion leading tends to correlate positively with status, whereas this is not the case in consumer behaviour. So for political behaviour, the general conclusion that the media merely fixes (confirms) people's opinion is not supported. Hovland, using experimental psychology, found significant effects of information on longer-term behaviour and attitudes, particularly in areas where most people have little direct experience (*e.g.* politics) and have a high degree of trust in the source (*e.g.* broadcasting). Since class has become a less reliable indicator of party (since the surveys of the 40s and 50s) the floating voter today is no longer the apathetic voter, but likely to be more well-informed than the consistent voter-and this mainly through the media.

There is also some very persuasive and empirical evidence suggesting that it is 'personal contact, not media persuasiveness' which counts. For example, Trenaman and McQuail (1961) found that 'don't knows' were less well informed than consistent voters, appearing uninterested, showing a general lack of information, and not just ignorance of particular policies or policies of one particular party. During the 1940 presidential election, a similar view was expressed by Katz and Lazarsfeld's theory of the two-step flow of communication, based on a study of electoral practices of the citizens of Erie County, Ohio. This examined the political propaganda prevalent in the media at the time during the campaign period to see whether it plays an integral role in influencing people's voting.

The results contradict this: Lazarsfeld et. al. (1944) find evidence for the Weberian theory of party, and identify certain factors, such as socio-economic circumstances, religious affiliation and area of residence, which together determine political orientation. The study claims that political propaganda serves to re-affirm the individual's pre-disposed orientation rather than to influence or change one's voting behaviour. Thompson does not see 'mediated quasi-interaction' (the monological, mainly one-way communication of the mass media) as dominant, but rather as intermingling with traditional face-to-face interactions and mediated interactions (such as telephone conversations). Contrary to Habermas' pessimistic view, this allows both more information and discussion to come into the public domain (of mediated quasi-interaction) and more to be discussed within the private domain (since the media provides information individuals would not otherwise have access to).

FREE ENTERPRISE SOCIETY

Although a sizeable portion of mass media offerings-particularly news, commentaries, documentaries, and other informational programmes-deal with highly controversial subjects, the major portion of mass media offerings are designed to serve an entertainment function. These programmes tend to avoid controversial issues and reflect beliefs and values sanctified by mass audience. This course is followed by Television networks, whose investment and production costs are high. Jerry Mander's work has highlighted this particular outlook. According to him, the atomised individuals of mass society lose their souls to the phantom delights of the film, the soap opera, and the variety show.

They fall into a stupor; an apathetic hypnosis Lazarsfeld was to call the 'narcotizing dysfunction' of exposure to mass media. Individuals become 'irrational victims of false wants'-the wants which corporations have thrust upon them, and continue to thrust upon them, through both the advertising in the media (with its continual exhortation to consume) and through the individualist consumption culture it promulgates. Thus, according to the Frankfurt School, leisure has been industrialised. The production of culture had become standardised and dominated by the profit motive as in other industries. In a mass society leisure is constantly used to induce the appropriate values and motives in the public. The modern media train the young for consumption. 'Leisure had ceased to be the opposite of work, and had become a preparation for it.'

MASS MEDIA, MASS CULTURE AND ELITE

The relation of the mass media to contemporary popular culture is commonly conceived in terms of dissemination from the elite to the mass. There are periods when this process is reversed. During the 18th century it was the utmost chic for the aristocrats of the French Court to assume the guise of shepherds and peasants in their restive outings.

The long-term consequences of this are significant in conjunction with the continuing concentration of ownership and control of the media, leading to accusations of a 'media elite' having a form of 'cultural dictatorship'. Thus the continuing debate about the influence of 'media barons' such as Conrad Black and Rupert Murdoch. For example, the UK Observer reported the Murdoch-owned HarperCollins' refusal to publish Chris Patten's East and West, because of the former Hong Kong Governor's description of the Chinese leadership as "faceless Stalinists" possibly being damaging to Murdoch's Chinese broadcasting interests. In this case, the author was able to have the book accepted by another publisher, but this kind of censorship may point the way to the future. A related, but more insidious, form is that of self-censorship by members of the media in the interests of the owner, in the interests of their careers.

AUDIENCE IN MEDIA STUDIES

Texts need audiences in order to realise their potential for meaning. So a text does not have a single meaning but rather a range of possibilities which are defined by both the text and by its audiences. The meaning is not in the text, but in the *reading*. (Hart 1991, 60)

Andrew Hart is among many writers, theorists and researchers who identify and value the existence of the audience in relation to the media. At the most basic level, audiences are vital in communication. It is for the audience that the media are constructing and conveying information, and, if it were not for the audiences, the media would not exist. The exact relationship between the media and their audiences has been the subject of debate since the media were first seriously studied and emphasises the importance of the audience and of their relationship with the media. The Frankfurt school, set up in 1923, were concerned about the possible effects of mass media. They proposed the "Effects" model, which considered society to be composed of isolated individuals who were susceptible to media messages.

The Frankfurt school envisioned the media as a hypodermic syringe, and the contents of the media were injected into the thoughts of the audience, who accepted the attitudes, opinions and beliefs expressed by the medium without question. This model was a response to the German fascists use of film and radio for propaganda uses, and later applied to American capitalist society. The followers of the hypodermic model of Effects adopted a variant of Marxism, emphasising the dangers of the power of capitalism, which owned and controlled new forms of media. Researchers in the fifties also supported the Effects model when exploring the potential of the new medium of television. Researchers were particularly concerned over increases in the representation of violent acts on television, which correlated with increases in violent acts in society. In the nineties, there was considerable concern over what were called "video nasties". The tabloid papers created a moral panic over whether particular violet films could influence child behaviour – and whether *Childs Play 3* influenced the child killers of Jamie Bulger.

However, theorists since have thought that media could not have such direct effects on the audiences they serve, and consider the media as a comparatively weak influence in moulding individual beliefs, opinions and attitudes. Other factors present in society, such as personal contact and religion, are more likely to influence people. The Effects model is considered to be an inadequate representation of the communication between media and the public, as it does not take into account the audience as individuals with their own beliefs, opinions, ideals and attitudes:

Audiences are not blank sheets of paper on which media messages can be written; members of an audience will have prior attitudes and beliefs which will determine how effective media messages are.

Supporters of the Effects model assume the audience is passive in the receiving and interpretation of media texts. Great emphasis is placed on the text itself and its power to directly influence the audience. Meanings in the text are readily available and easy to find. The impossibility to measure media effects is as a result of not being able to isolate the media from all the other potential influences at work in society. This leads to the Effects model generally being disregarded when considering the audiences response to the media.

A new approach to the dynamics of audience/text relationship was suggested in the Uses and Gratification model. In this model, theorists were not asking how the media effects audiences, but how were the audiences using the media. They suggested that audiences had specific needs and actively turned to the media to consume various texts to a satisfaction of these needs. The audience in Uses and Gratifications were seen as active, as opposed to passive audience in the Effects model. Uses and Gratifications acknowledged that the audience had a choice of texts from which to chose from and satisfy their needs. Blumler and Katz (1974) suggested that there were four main needs of television audiences that are satisfied by television. These included – Diversion (a form of escaping from the pressures of every day), Personal Relationships (where the viewer gains companionship, either with the television characters, or through conversations with others about television), Personal Identity (where the viewer is able to compare their life with the lives of characters and situations on television, to explore, re-affirm or question their personal identity) and Surveillance (where the media are looked upon for a supply of information about what is happening in the world).

While acknowledging that the audience are active and chose what to watch, the Uses and Gratifications model as a model for understanding audiences also has its limitations. The model still implies that messages are packages of information that all the audience will read as the same. It does not consider how the messages are interpreted or any other factors affecting the audience's interpretation. Another criticism is that of the tendency to concentrate solely on why audiences consume the media rather than extending the investigation to discover what meanings and interpretations are produced and in what circumstances, *i.e.* how the media are received. The Uses and Gratification model assumes that the audience's wish for satisfaction results in a media output to fulfil their desire, rather than acknowledging that audiences have to enjoy whatever is produced by the media.

Both the Effects and the Uses and Gratifications model ignore to some extent the audience and their social backgrounds, how they form their interpretations of the media messages and their specific relationship with the media text. In the 70s, the academic journal *Screen* suggested that audiences were positioned by the media text. Theorists started to take an approach influenced by semiotics and structuralism, to discover what meanings were made from texts and how this meaning was achieved. Great emphasis was placed on the text, particularly film. *Screen* thought that the position of the viewer of Hollywood film was determined for them through the use of camera shots. For example, the shot/reverse shot commonly used during dialogue enabled the viewer to position themselves as one of the characters. Another example is a close up of somebody who then looks offscreen. The next shot of the object that the character is looking at is shown, again placing the viewer in the position of the character. Writers, such as Laura Mulvey considered the "gaze" in Hollywood film to be a masculine gaze, where the camera shots adopt the male gaze and constructing the female as the object of that gaze.

Screen theory suggested that all media texts have a "mode of address" – a term used by semioticians which proposes that media texts address its intended audience in a particular way, establishing a relationship between the producer of the text and the media's audience. The mode of address is dependant on the particular medium. For instance, cinema rarely addresses the audience directly. Films are usually shot to suggest the film is reality. In comedy characters occasionally look into the camera. Recently there has be a trend in which films have become self-reflexive, drawing on and manipulating the conventions of the audience's expectations of the medium. The "Scream" films are a good example of this. Television differs from cinema, as the audience are not expected to pay the attention which cinema demands, so television has to work to attain and maintain the audience's attention.

The medium employs a wide range of techniques to address its intended audience. Youth programmes constantly have unusual camera angles and short shots to capture and keep children's attention. Quiz shows often address the audience ("who are playing along at home."). It is assumed that television viewing is done in family groups in a domestic setting. The scheduling highlights this view of the television audience; as the television output is regulated so that there is minimal "adult" material, such as strong language, sex scenes and violence, before the 9o'clock watershed. Whenever sport is on television and the national team is participating, such as the World Cup, the usual objective and neutral commentary changes to a more patriarchal and emotive mode of address. Newspapers clearly have a particular mode of address, reflected in the headlines and phrasing of the article. Broadsheet papers like *The Times* and *The Guardian* have a more impersonal and formal mode of address when compared with the tabloids *The Sun* and *The Mirror,* which are more emotional and often xenophobic.

The limitations of focusing on audience in media studies can clearly be seen in the mode of address made by the media. Different audiences use different media; both the audience that is assumed to be using the media and the particular type of media that is being consumed determines the mode of address.

The mode of address will be vital in constructing audiences' thoughts about an issue raised in media. However, previous models of audience reception do not take into account what actual audiences are going to do to the media texts. *Screen* theory, Uses and Gratifications and Effects models suggest that meaning is embedded within the text, which audiences can access easily and accept without questioning these meanings. Just because producers of media texts have a certain opinion and meaning does not mean that this meaning is obvious in the text, that, in turn, does not mean that the audience will read these meanings or agree with them.

The Centre for Contemporary Cultural Studies at Birmingham during the 70s again used a semiotic approach to understanding an audience response to media texts. David Morley studied audiences of an early evening news programme and argued in his paper *The Nationwide work* that audiences actively decode meanings from a media text. The Centre for Contemporary Cultural Studies, working under Stuart Hall, expanded on Morley's hypothesis and suggested that meanings were encoded by the producer into the media text and the audiences decodes the meaning from the text. This theory acknowledges that there is a preferred meaning in the text – the meaning made by the producer.

This meaning is encoded by the codes and conventions of the particular medium to hide the texts own ideological construction. The audience then read, listen or watch the media text and interpret the message. The audience's interpretation is dependant on a number of frameworks outside the text. These include socio/economic frameworks such as class, gender, age education and ethnicity. They include the individual's past experiences and also include previous knowledge and experience of the medium.

This current theory on audience reception in media studies takes into account the individual members of the audience. It realises there is a preferred meaning in the text, but also places emphasis on the audience in the process of constructing a meaning. Hall's encoding/decoding model draws upon two extreme ends of a spectrum, what Abercrombie (1996) refers to as the dominant text view and the dominant audience view. Researchers who give the text priority support the dominant text view, wherein the text is monolithic, there is a well marked preferred meaning and is difficult for other meanings to be read. The audience is seen as passive and heavily influenced by the text. Hall and his colleagues took the dominant audience view, which acknowledges the presence of a strong preferred meaning, but also saw texts as polysemic – they have a number of possible meanings, and that is up to the audience to analyse and interpret the text.

The advantage of the Encoding/decoding model is that it realises that the meaning made by the audience is affected by various other factors – including socio/economic frameworks and past experiences, but also involving the context in which the media message is consumed. Meanings constructed by the individual watching televisual news at home with two distracting siblings will be different to meanings constructed while concentrating on the television alone. These meanings will be different to those formed when the individual is reading news articles in the newspaper in a quiet room.

The Centre for Contemporary Cultural Studies also proposed a model for the types of audience decoding. The audience member assumes the dominant hegemonic position when they recognise and agree with the full-preferred meaning offered by the media text. The oppositional hegemonic position is established when the audience member understands the preferred meaning, but disagrees with it due to their own set of attitudes and beliefs. The negotiated hegemonic position is established when the audience member opposes or has to adapt the preferred meaning. The forth type of audience response is referred to as aberrant decoding. This is where the audience member reads the text in an unpredicted way, producing a deviant meaning. There are still a number of limitations to this model of audience reception, as David Morley (1989) notes: The extent to which the model tries to conceive of language merely as a conveyor belt for preconstituted meanings or messages; the way in which it tends to confuse textual meaning with the conscious intentions of broadcasters; and the tendency to blur together under the heading of "decoding" what are probably best thought of as separate prosesses along the axes of comprehension/ incomprehension, as opposed to agreement/disagreement with the prepositional content of messages. Furthermore, the concept of the preferred meaning, which is of course central to the encoding/decoding model has a number of criticisms.

The preferred meaning is a difficult concept to understand, and is simpler to identify in factual texts, such as newspaper reports, television news and documentaries. In fiction-based texts there are more likely to be different readings of he preferred texts. Additionally, it is unclear whether the preferred meanings are embedded in the text, or whether it is something agreed on by the majority of the texts audience. By considering the audience in the interpretation of the media text, it is clear to see that the process of media communication is not a simple concept. Meaning is considered to be what the audience make of the text, taking away most of the power of the producer and the text.

Abercrombie (1996) emphasises the importance of the producer, text and audience and reiterates Hall's opinion that all three, and the relationship between them, are vital in the process of media communication. By reviewing the past theories on the way audiences receive and interpret media messages, we can see that there are various ways in which the audience can be viewed. The emphasis on audience in the encoding/decoding model is advantageous for a number of reasons. As Andrew Hart states "...the meaning is not in the text, but in the *reading*". This illustrates the possibilities of the media. Emphasising audiences in this way insists that the media are not as manipulative as they were thought to be. By understanding how the audience construct meaning and make sense of texts, producers can change their texts so that audiences will read whatever meanings the producers want. Ultimately, it is the audience that controls the output of the media, and thus the content of popular culture:

The audience, regardless of the medium, has not been historically passive or inconsequential in shaping its participation in, or the content of, popular media. The producers of media texts often work with an image of the audience and what it wants. Therefore, a focus on audience is advantageous, as the media must work to satisfy the audience.

Assuming that meaning is only constructed by the reading of the text by the audience highlights the polysemic nature of texts and ambiguity of meaning. One sequence of pictures on the television will mean a number of meanings, depending on the individual in the audience. The phrasing of a newspaper could connote any number of meanings considering the experiences and background of the reader. The focus on audience in media studies illuminates the richness and potentials available in the media. As the audience construct meaning from a media text using frameworks already present in culture, it is...only by understanding the meanings constructed by the audiences that we can understand how that (cultural) form functions within the larger culture.

By understanding how audiences read meanings in the text, we are also able to gain a closer understanding of the culture to which that audience belongs.

The main limitation of a focus in audience has been highlighted by the various ways in which past theorists have thought audiences receive media messages. There are many different ways to conceptualise the audience and the way in which they work with media, but there appears to be no "right" way. This is complicated by the very nature of actual audiences. There are many different audiences for many different media.

Newspaper readers and radio listeners are two types of audience, but some newspaper readers will also be part of the radio audience. People who watch one type of programme on television will also watch another type of programme, and will be part of another audience. There is a tendency to think of audiences as masses, but a Williams (1998) observed, there are no such things as "the masses", only ways of imagining people as masses. Audiences are "unstructured groups...with...no social organisation...merely an aggregate of demographic characteristics." Different media will attract audiences which will consist of a mix of people who formed audiences of other media.

There are no effective ways to measure audiences, or to measure all the individual's responses to the media. The existing ways of measuring audiences seem inadequate. For example the equipment that monitors a sample television audience notes which channels are being watched. This method is ineffective as it does not take into consideration how audiences are watching the television, for example, if they are carrying out other activities while watching they will pay less attention compared to when they tune in especially to watch a programme dealing with issues close to their hearts.

The realisation that audience is not adequately explained by researching either the people of the audience or the texts they like, but that audience is distinctively inflected by the nature and cultural significance of the interaction between audience activities and textual character (understood in the widest possible sense) causes a reconsideration of the very nature of audience.

The existing methods of studying audience do not measure how and why the audiences differ in their viewing. For instance the audience watching one episode of a serial will not necessarily watch the following episode or, indeed, any of the other episodes. Additionally, the existing methods do not consider what meanings the actual audience is constructing. Questionnaires are limited by the questions that they ask and audiences will be trying to answer what they think the researcher is trying to find. There is no exact or easy way to study or compile accurate details of the particular aspects of the audience. Hart notes the difficulty in judging and representing audiences when he asks:

It is impossible to set up controlled or laboratory experiments with the media and their audience, as if you change the way in which the media is usually received you will undoubtedly change the interpretations made by the audience of the media text. The key issue about media is that exists as a comment and as a part of our culture and cannot be examined easily due to this.

The methods used for audience research (including ethnography, survey, experiment, text analysis or social commentary) result in class groups or "life style" groups – in which all the members of the audience of one media text are categorised together. This type of classification seems inadequate as the categories can be broad and there seems no benefit in categorising people in this way. The main limitation of a focus on audience in media studies is that the research and techniques used to research the audience are not effective.

A focus on audience is important in media studies. There have been many different theories on how audiences respond to and interact with the media. This shows clearly the complexities of focusing on the audience and the ways in which audiences can be visualised. By giving a focus on audience researchers are able to see the complex process of the construction of meaning made by the audience as a response to media text. No audience member will interpret the media message in the same way. This alerts uses of the various media to the ambiguity of meaning and the richness inherent in the medium, aspects that producers need to be aware of in the construction of their texts. The limitations of a focus on audience derive from the impossibility of investigating and measuring audiences and their responses. Existing methods of audience research are inappropriate, as they do not consider how the medium is being used and what the various responses are of audiences to the specific texts.

COMMUNICATING DEVELOPMENT THROUGH THE MASS MEDIA

This chapter paints development agents as part of an industry, one with its own dynamics and agenda that in turn belie the philanthropic claims made by, or on behalf of, this institution. Just as we need to acknowledge and deal with these great unspoken, so to it is valuable to recognise that the media is at the end of the day also a business. For the development industry to relate to the media industry, it needs to understand that industry.

The media business, generally speaking, deals with information in a very special way. News is a very particular way of identifying, selecting, arranging and presenting particular information. It makes one blind to other kinds of information at the same time as placing a straitjacket around that with which it does work. On the good side, news is clear, to the point, factual, concise, interesting.

On the bad side, it is event based meaning that underlying and unfolding slower trends are missed by news, and this is vital for reporting development which is a process. Long breaking stories are difficult to conceive, recognise and to research within the parameters of news. This is vital, however, for focusing on the sustainability of development. Another problem is that news is dead in a day usually, and it is an unfortunate, but strongly entrenched, custom that current news always sidelines older news and even precludes decent follow up news.

DEVELOPMENT COMMUNICATIONS

On the bad side, too, news depends typically on elite newsmakers, whereas most development communications want to tell about ordinary people as well, to report their real development relevant activities. Also on the bad side, news is often negative whereas one wants to highlight achievements as well as the problems, failures, corruption, and so on in development. This negativity is not because journalists are inherently disagreeable individuals. It is rather because negative news interests people and not surprisingly because it impacts on them severely. Good tidings are a bonus to people's lives: bad news can mean a setback.

For these reasons, it is more important for the public to hear about corruption in the school feeding schemes, than when things are running smoothly. Action is required to halt the deterioration and to remedy the situation. Negative events are also characterised typically by that other key ingredient of news: drama and conflict. These are the part of the language of (admittedly Western style) journalism a mode of communication to which the public is accustomed, and which has such an important place in a democracy. From the point of view of the press, people in development need to understand and accept these characteristics.

A further point from the press gallery would be that when complaining of negative press coverage, development communicators need to be clear on the distinction between criticism by the press itself, and reportage of public criticisms. To blur the two is to begin to blame the messenger for the message, and to embark on a strategy in which the logic is to deal with the manifest symptom, while ignoring the more profound causes.

In addition, a further necessary distinction is between the press's responsibility for what is carried, and the part played by the source of that content. If the RDP sends contradictory signals by saying on the one hand that it is not a pot of gold, and on the other presents the President's projects which suggest there is money to dish out, the press cannot be blamed for public confusion.

Finally, to the extent that the press sees itself as a watchdog, seeking out bad news rather than good, it is important to acknowledge where this comes from. It arises, of course, out of an historical, and very widespread, liberal ideology of the press combined with the special circumstances of fighting the extreme authoritarianism of the apartheid state institutions. We should welcome this as being of benefit to our new democracy, and indeed of being in the interests of clean governance and good development. Many people in politics and development have great frustrations with the media, and these have increased in proportion to growing frustrations with the slow pace of transformation in society and the implementation of the Reconstruction and Development Programme.

The complaints about the mass media thend to be of commission and commission. There is the claim that development is ignored, underplayed or inadequately reported.

There appears to be some substance in this. Why is it so? Even apart from staff shortages in the mass media, existing staffs are very poorly trained. Compounding this problem are the demographics of much South African journalism (and indeed professional life in general). Most media owners are still disproportionately white, most journalists are still disproportionately white, most experts cited in the media are still disproportionately white. Little wonder that there is a lack of media sensitivity to different life concerns and experiences in much of the media in contrast to the situation in the political and developmental world. There is escalating change in this unfortunate situation, although not fast enough for many.

The media then is undeniably vulnerable to criticism of the quality of its coverage. In the light of this, of the problems of having one section of the community trying to report on concerns alien to their experience, not to mention vast array of extremely complicated and specialist kinds of information, a question arises. Could not development experts themselves, then, do a better job than the journos? Perhaps so. Yet it is also precisely the value of the journalist as an experienced communicator that needs to be fostered, rather than bypassed. Although officials prefer to see stories in the press on their own terms, there is value in their handing over control to journalists. "It is the responsibility of the reporter... to translate the activities of the agency into pertinent information for the reader." (Hage et al, 1983). The example is given of reporters having to translate terms like "comprehensive modalities of treatment" into simple English like "a range of methods" in a story on health issues.

So, the message is: don't bypass the media supplement it by all means, but use it as well. Remember that some of the blame for poor press coverage must also be laid at the door of government as well. Inefficient and slow press liaison, like unstructured rambling press conferences, press statements issued on Friday afternoons, poor access to the actors involved are all areas about which journalists could talk a lot.

How to have better media liaison then? The major point to recognise is that the media industry is an industry and one in the business of producing and selling certain kinds of commodities. Some of these commodities have scarcity value, and exclusivity: a good media liaison side to development will recognise this and exploit it. "Stop shouting at the news media and start whispering to increase the newsworthiness of that which is to be conveyed." An example of astute media manipulation is recorded by Gaber (1994) who describes the case of a major speech by a party leader: "Several days beforehand judicious leaks from 'sources close to the leader' (not infrequently the leader himself) will start to spin 'watch for the vision thing' or 'he'll be stamping his authority on the Party' are two well known refrains.

On the day before the speech his press secretary will brief the media officially about the text, and sub text, of the speech; after the official briefing new lines will emerge in one to one conversations. After the speech, which the journalists would have been following with the aid of an advance copy, but before they will have had time to consider and reflect upon it, they will have received yet another briefing, either from the leader or his aides, at which the spin will have been re spun, the nuances re nuanced, and the whole message re packaged." The same example could easily be applied to the launch of any major development project. It would be simplistic to work on the assumption that the press is solely in a watchdog role, only looking for corruption scandals and improper conduct. There is also, at least, the role of performance monitor where the verdict is not necessarily negative, and the role of service provider where simply useful information is supplied.

The development industry could do well to ask how much reactive and how much proactive media liaison it gets involved in. Are its officials doing the kind of sustained press out reach and liaison required to provide their news to increasingly overstretched (and under trained) journalists? The potential for success is much higher than they might think.

Part of media liaison must include a policy definition about the level at which information can be released. Usually holding briefings or issuing statements is the prerogative of senior officials or public information officers. But lesser people banned from speaking to the press may resort to anonymous leaks, notwithstanding all manner of controls and surveillance mechanisms not to mention the develops themselves getting in on the act. A policy where each individual may speak to the media (provided he or she takes responsibility for what is said), seems preferable. Such a policy is strengthened when effective internal communication with government and state empowers all levels of officials with understanding of the issues. To the extent that the development industry hopes to utilise the mass media, it needs to exploit the strengths and dodge the weaknesses of the system.

To use the media effectively requires training relevant specialist officials. And this is not just training in efficient operational skills, but in understanding the nature of news and deadlines, and the social value of an independent press even when the relationship is an adversarial one. That means understanding that the media are not free agents, but industrial and business institutions limited by things like their need to be topical, news values which include impact and drama, dependence on events rather than processes. And it means acknowledging the distinct social functions between development agents and the mass media.

THE ROLE OF THE MASS MEDIA IN NATIONAL DEVELOPMENT

Herman and Chomsky (1988) attribute to the mass media the role of inculcating individuals 'with values, beliefs and codes of conduct that will integrate them into the institutional structures of the large society.' They postulate that in societies which are characterized by major social conflicts and concentration of wealth, the mass media can fulfil this role only by systematic propaganda.

They continue: 'In countries where the levers of power are in the hands of a state bureaucracy, the monopolistic control over the media, often supplemented by official censorship, makes it clear that the media serve the ends of the dominant elite'. Herman and Chomsky's propaganda model focuses on inequality of wealth and power and its effects on mass media interests and choices, and how these 'are able to filter out the news fit to print, marginalize dissent, and allow the government and dominant private interests to get their message across to the public'.

Riegel (1977) cautions that 'the objective of governments in communications is not to promote 'world-mindedness' or education in the sense of increased understanding and appreciations of the ideas and cultures of other nations and peoples in a world community, but rather to preserve and strengthen the sense of nationality and the national status quo.' Expropriation of the media of mass communication was a major feature of the newly-independent countries in Africa, even though these countries had neither a sense of nationhood to preserve, nor national institutional structures to which the mass media could integrate citizens.

The disparate peoples in former European colonies that gained independence as African nations with full status at the United Nations had no consensual values in culture, politics, or economics, nor was there agreement on the mode of political leadership and how those leaders were to be chosen and changed. As Riegel (supra) says, 'Bringing emerging nations into the twentieth century in communications usually translated into providing governments with tools to combat differences and tribal and other fragmenting loyalties for the purpose of promoting national unity and discipline.

Bluntly stated, this translates into turning nomadic Africans into soldiers'. Discounting Riegel's sarcasm and overstatement, he aptly captures the essence of the problem. Most African countries explicitly stated that it was the role of the mass media to create national unity and foster development. In fact this was deemed so important that many governments became the mass media through nationalization.

Journalists suddenly became civil servants and government spokespeople. Most journalists did not object to this development and actively supported government nationalization in the belief that this was being done for patriotic reasons, and that politicians would play their traditional role of leadership and leave journalist to play theirs of watchdog and sentinel. Some were effusive in their support.

For instance, Tanzanian journalist Ng' wanakilala (1981) argued that what was crucial was whether the media were used for liberation or oppression of the popular masses. He enthused: 'where a government is committed to the development of all the people, media takeover by the government is an act of liberation and emancipation.'

Others such as Kenyan editor and publisher Hilary Ng'weno (1969) were willing to accept a certain amount of limitation of press freedoms associated with democratic societies. He suggested that the media should impose limitations upon themselves rather than have the government impose censorship, and that such action was justified because: 'The challenge to the press in young countries is the challenge of laying down the foundations upon which future freedoms will thrive...

Under some of the conditions (of poverty, illiteracy and disease) in which vast numbers of Asians, Africans and Latin Americans live, it would be sacrilegious to talk about press freedom, for freedom loses marring when human survival is the operative principle upon which a people live... In such countries, the first duty of the press, as indeed fany other institutions or individual, is to encourage greater national unity.'

Some politicians like the late president of Ghana, Kwarne Nkrumah, a former journalist who used his paper to whip up support for his political party 'during the struggle for Ghana's independence, rejected the idea of an independent press. He argued that 'Within the competitive system of capitalism the press cannot function in according with strict regard to facts' (Nkrumah, 1965). Nkrumah believed in activist journalism, insisting that journalistic practice involves choice of topics and arrangements of facts in a way that fits in with the preferences of the owners. He argued that, in privately-owned media, the journalist often 'finds himself rejecting or distorting facts that do not coincide with the outlook and interest of his employer or the medium's advertisers. Under the pressure of competition for advertising revenue, trivialities are blown up, the vulgar emphasized, ethics forgotten, the important trimmed to the class outlook.

Enmities are fanned and peace is perverted.' Nkrumah believed that a journalist should have high ideals, be a political act visit and party member, and 'His newspaper a collect be organizer, a collective instrument of mobilization and a collective educator, a weapon first and foremost for the overthrow of colonialism and imperialism and to assist total African independence and unity.

The true African journalist often works for the organ of the political party to which he himself belongs and in whose purpose he believes. He works to serve a society moving in the direction of his aspirations. ' Ng'weno and Nkrumah's arguments remain the two most powerful inspirations and justifications for African's mass media policy. They also provide the utilitarian underpinnings of development journalism as an occupational self-perception and a theory of the press.

In the decade of the 1960s, arguments such as these provided the rationality for government action. Radio and television stations were nationalized where they existed because, after all, they had been mouthpieces of colonial authorities.

The broadcast facilities were required, so the argument went, for the education of the masses, creation of a sense of national identity, and to unify the new nations. In some countries such as Tanzania, for instance, not only was the broadcast system put under the powerful ministry of information, but newspapers were also nationalized and turned over to the ruling party. In others, such as Kenya, only the broadcast networks were nationalized and made a part of government bureaucracy; some independent (foreign-owned) newspapers remained.

But many governments or the political parties in power established their own newspapers as well. Kenya's first Minister for Information and Broadcasting, Rarnogi Achieng Oneko, justified government involvement in newspaper publication on egalitarian grounds. He said the government would establish rural newspapers because 'commercial newspapers aim primarily at making profits, so they are not likely to undertake the publication of newspapers for small linguistic groups' (quoted in Mytton, 1983).

Oneko's reasoning makes sound social policy and business sense. But it should also be borne in mind that the political strengths of a vast majority of African politicians are in their rural homes where they return every election time for votes, not in the cities where they live. More importantly, the other thing Oneko did not say was that the government aimed to fill the vacuum left by private investors with newspapers through which government officials could talk down to the small linguistic groups. Through UNESCO support, the Kenya government has established a network of rural newspapers which, by and large, have become just another voice of the government whose information officers publish them.

It is hard to argue against the principles behind government participation and control of the mass media in Africa given the fact that in some of these countries the only newspapers present were those established by government, there being no able individuals or private sector interests that could invest in newspapers, leave alone broadcast systems. There were no models for cooperative ownership of mass media, and this has not been encouraged to-date.

As Ng'weno (1969) put it, the need for self-restraint by the mass media in fragile democracies will always be there given the forces at play in their politico-economic arenas. But such arguments ring hollow in an environment of flagrant neglect of responsibility by the people in power.

It is a truism that a cowed and subservient press has served African dictators superbly and no politician or soldier in power would wish to change the status quo. It can no longer be legitimate to urge restraint by journalists who daily witness wanton profligacy from government officials and politicians some of whose only qualification to leadership is that they bombed their way into power. And neither is it legitimate to ask the media to look the other way when some elected leaders betray their vows to defend the constitution and instead tinker with it constantly. Bagdikian (1983) says that there are moments in history when all established power becomes uneasy. He says such are usually 'times of social change when those in control are operating with an obsolete picture of the world and are alanned at suggestions of flaws in the system they govern. (But) their hostility at such times may be directed at what they most need to recognize.'

Most of the established powers in Africa today are operating with obsolete pictures of the world. Here's the most salient picture they see: constant threats to their governments from armed bandits lurking to seize power on behalf of some hostile foreign government; for this they blame everyone else but their own policies and actions. The rest of the world, on the other hand, sees this: Sudan = hunger, war; Liberia = mass murder, breakdown of civil society; Mozambique and Angola = civil war, communist threat; Kenya = corruption, tribalism; Tanzania = benign neglect of economy, communism; Nigeria = military dictatorship, tribalism; Zaire = corruption, political thuggery, tribalism; and just outright medieval societies in many parts of Africa.

These pictures may be distorted. But consider these other pictures that are not seen: the linkage between the endemic political instability in Third World nations and their poverty; the linkage between poverty and the integration of the global economy; and the linkage between an integrated global economy and the history and perpetuation of empire. By some inexplicable conjuncture of bad luck and sheer circumstance, we are often told, the private interests of local and international political economic elites so merged that Africa's development must now be negotiated with endogenous multilateral and bilateral agencies. This is hardly surprising given the fact that colonial structures in government and the economy remained largely intact at independence 'for stability and continuity.' But where 'revolutionary' governments undertook measures to alter neo-colonial superstructures, the result was often military take-over of government, drying up of economic aid coupled with a blitz of negative foreign media propaganda and, invariably, very well financed and armed 'liberation' wars. Against this backdrop is a vast majority of African people who feel that the trust which they placed on their politicians had been betrayed.

Thus, lacking popular support, many African governments have fallen; others have resorted to increasingly authoritarian methods to contain all stripes of criticism, often interpreted as dissent Even patriotic journalists like Ng'weno (1969:4) began to grumble that the trouble with most African countries is that 'governments tend to treat themselves as the sole judges of what constitutes the national interest.' Many independent journalists have been hounded out of town, arrested, tortured, or jailed to reveal 'their foreign paymasters.' Many of the remaining journalists have been cowed through the calculus of survival and economic necessity.

Another conjecture of local and international opinion in the 1980s held that there was need for change in Africa. The international media had just 'differed' that millions of people were dying in Ethiopia and Sudan as a result of drought and civil war. Suddenly philanthropists in the west were at hand to marshall aid for the victims. Pressmes for structural changes of African economies were also stepped up and the international media began to report atrocities of African governments and guerrillas engaged in bush combat as though these were new. Yet most African civil wars have been fought since the early 1970s! 'The root process of peaceful change begins with the right of the aggrieved to be heard. Thus presenting the best evidence of the need for change,' says Bagdikian (supra). 'And the voice of the aggrieved, being heard by the general citizenry can create consensus for a remedy. The media are crucial to this process.

It may be argued that in an integrated world such as we have today. The role of the mass media in social change is an international cooperative effort, and that reporting Africa's developmental problems requires resources which its media institutions cannot afford. Moreover, as we have seen, governments are the mass media in many African countries and this does not allow for the necessary criterion that governments require for the development of democratic institutions. Regrettably however, the narrow ideologises of international media would seem to make them unlikely supporters of popular structural and democratic change in Africa. In addition, there is little likelihood that they will shed in a hurry their cold-war approach to news gathering so well documented by Herman and Chomsky (1988) and Aronson (1990).

Moreover, Bagdikian (1990) tells of 'private ministries of information and culture' in western industrial democracies. He says these private ministries are media monopolies, endless mass media chains which manufacture public information as industrial by-products for sale worldwide. We are told that money from such sales finance the purchase of oil, mineral and agricultural concessions throughout the world; the media chains also have interests in the armaments industry and reap hefty profits from fratricidal wars in Africa and the Middle East We are also told by Aronson (1990) that these private ministries of information played a leading role in fuelling the hysteria that came to be known as the cold war through disinformation and propaganda that same cold war which has transfixed Africa in a dance of hunger unto death, and in a macabre ritual of fratricide.

We see many such 'objective' reports about African hunger, African inhumanity to fellow Africans, and African corruption. What we don't see are the causes of such miseries and the linkages between these things and the events that have shaped the destiny of Africa throughout the nineteenth and twentieth centuries. Africa played no active role in the events of this century. It might all together become invisible at 'the end of history' as the rest of the world simply becomes too ashamed to acknowledge its existence. The capitulation of African journalism to local bullying and international calumny is the more regrettable because there is no one that will be sentinel and watchdog of this unhappy continent; no one to amplify 'the voice of the aggrieved:) Hence there are reduced chances for peaceful social change in the continent.

THE ROLE AND INFLUENCE OF MASS MEDIA

Mass media is communication—whether written, broadcast, or spoken—that reaches a large audience. This includes television, radio, advertising, movies, the Internet, newspapers, magazines, and so forth.

Mass media is a significant force in modern culture, particularly in America. Sociologists refer to this as a mediated culture where media reflects and creates the culture. Communities and individuals are bombarded constantly with messages from a multitude of sources including TV, billboards, and magazines, to name a few. These messages promote not only products, but moods, attitudes, and a sense of what is and is not important. Mass media makes possible the concept of celebrity: without the ability of movies, magazines, and news media to reach across thousands of miles, people could not become famous. In fact, only political and business leaders, as well as the few notorious outlaws, were famous in the past. Only in recent times have actors, singers, and other social elites become celebrities or "stars."

The current level of media saturation has not always existed. As recently as the 1960s and 1970s, television, for example, consisted of primarily three networks, public broadcasting, and a few local independent stations. These channels aimed their programming primarily at two-parent, middle-class families. Even so, some middle-class households did not even own a television. Today, one can find a television in the poorest of homes, and multiple TVs in most middle-class homes. Not only has availability increased, but programming is increasingly diverse with shows aimed to please all ages, incomes, backgrounds, and attitudes. This widespread availability and exposure makes television the primary focus of most mass-media discussions. More recently, the Internet has increased its role exponentially as more businesses and households "sign on." Although TV and the Internet have dominated the mass media, movies and magazines—particularly those lining the aisles at grocery checkout stands—also play a powerful role in culture, as do other forms of media.

What role does mass media play? Legislatures, media executives, local school officials, and sociologists have all debated this controversial question. While opinions vary as to the extent and type of influence the mass media wields, all sides agree that mass media is a permanent part of modern culture. Three main sociological perspectives on the role of media exist: the limited-effects theory, the class-dominant theory, and the culturalist theory.

MODERN MASS MEDIA

During the recent years mass media has invaded the life of a common man in a big way. Upto seventies, mass media mainly remained confined to cinema, newspaper and radio. It was in the early eighties that audio-visual electronic medium in the form of television invaded the Indian scenario in a big way. The

Government created huge infrastructure for spread of television network in the country. During this decade itself, advent of computers and Video Cassette Recorders (VCR) also supplemented the audio-visual media, putting well established medium of cinema to shade. During the early nineties, satellite television revolutionised the audio-visual media by reaching most of the households in the urban areas.

The latest invasion of audio-visual electronic media has suddenly increased the demand for professionals in journalism, technicians and other service individuals. These careers not only offer excellent opportunities, salaries, challenge and satisfaction of work, but also provide an opportunity for self-employment in various fields.

MASS MEDIA AND WOMEN'S STATUS IN RURAL INDIA

Cable and satellite television have grown rapidly throughout the developing world. The availability of cable and satellite television exposes viewers to new information about the outside world, which may affect individual attitudes and behaviours. This paper explores the effect of the introduction of cable television on gender attitudes in rural India. Using a three-year individual-level panel dataset, we find that the introduction of cable television is associated with improvements in women's status. We find significant increases in reported autonomy, decreases in the reported acceptability of beating and decreases in reported son preference.

We also find increases in female school enrolment and decreases in fertility (primarily via increased birth spacing). The effects are large, equivalent in some cases to about five years of education in the cross section, and move gender attitudes of individuals in rural areas much closer to those in urban areas. We argue that the results are not driven by pre-existing differential trends. These results have important policy implications, as India and other countries attempt to decrease bias against women. The growth of television in the developing world over the last two decades has been extraordinary. Estimates suggest that the number of television sets in Asia has increased more than six-fold, from 100 million to 650 million, since the 1980s (World Press Review, 2003). In China, television exposure grew from 18 million people in 1977 to 1 billion by 1995 (World Press Review, 2003). In more recent years, satellite and cable television availability has increased dramatically. Again, in China, the number of people with satellite access increased from just 270,000 in 1991 to 14 million by 2005.

Further, these numbers are likely to understate the change in the number of people for whom television is available, since a single television is often watched by many.

Beyond providing entertainment, television vastly increases both the availability of information about the outside world and exposure to other ways of life, particularly in otherwise isolated areas. Previous work has demonstrated that the information and exposure provided by television can change attitudes and behaviour. Gentzkow and Shapiro (2005) find effects of television viewership on attitudes in the Muslim world towards the West, and Della Vigna and Kaplan (2006) show large effects of the Fox News channel on voting patterns in the United States. In the developing world, Olken (2006) shows that television decreases participation in social organizations.

India has not been left out of the satellite revolution: a recent survey finds that 112 million households in India own a television, with 61 per cent of those homes having cable or satellite service (National Readership Studies Council 2006). This figure represents a doubling in cable access in just five years from a previous survey.

The study also find that in some states, the change has been even more dramatic; in the span of just 10-15 years since it first became available, cable or satellite penetration has reached an astonishing 60 per cent in states such as Tamil Nadu, even though the average income is below the World Bank poverty line of two dollars per person per day.

Most popular satellite television shows in India portray life in urban settings; further, a wide range of international programmes are now available. The increase in television exposure, therefore, is likely to dramatically change the available information about the outside world, especially in isolated rural areas. Indeed, anthropological case studies in India suggest that exposure to television in rural areas has an effect on behaviours as disparate as latrine building and fan usage.

In this chapter we explore the effect of the introduction of cable television in rural areas of India on a particular set of values and behaviours, namely attitudes towards and discrimination against women. Although issues of gender equity are important throughout much of the developing world, they are particularly salient in India. Sen (1992) argued that there were 41 million "missing women" in India women and girls who died prematurely due to mistreatment resulting in a dramatically male-biased population. The population bias towards men has only gotten worse in the last two decades, as sex-selective abortion has become more widely used to avoid female births. More broadly, girls in India are discriminated against in nutrition, medical care, vaccination and education. Even within India, gender inequality is significantly worse in rural than urban areas.

Given this, if satellite television increases the exposure of rural areas to urban attitudes and values, it is plausible that it could change some of these attitudes and behaviours. It is this possibility that we explore in this chapter. The analysis relies on a three-year panel dataset covering women in many Indian states between 2001 and 2003. These years represent a time of rapid growth in rural cable access. During the panel, cable television was newly introduced in 21 of the 180 sample villages. Our empirical strategy relies on comparing changes in attitudes and behaviours between survey rounds across villages based on whether (and when) they added cable television.

Using these data, we find that cable television has large effects on attitudes and, to the extent we have information, behaviours. After cable is introduced to a village, women are less likely to report that domestic violence towards women is acceptable. They also report increased autonomy (for example, the ability to go out without permission and to participate in household decision-making). Women are less likely to report son preference (the desire to give birth to a boy rather than a girl). Turning to behaviours, we find increases in school enrolment for girls (but not boys), and decreases in fertility (which is often linked to female autonomy). These results are apparent when using regressions with individual fixed effects and when using a matching estimator.

In terms of magnitude, the introduction of cable television dramatically decreases the differences in attitudes and behaviours between urban and rural areas between 45 and 70 per cent of the difference disappears within two years of cable introduction in this sample.

The effect is also large relative to, for example, the effect of education on these attitudes and behaviours: introducing cable television is equivalent to roughly five years of female education in the cross section. These effects happen very quickly; the average village has cable for only 6-7 months before being surveyed again, which implies a rapid change in attitudes. However, this is consistent with existing work on the effects of media exposure, which typically find rapid changes (within a few months, in many cases) in behaviours like contraceptive use, pregnancy, latrine building and perception of own-village status.

A central concern with the results is the possibility that trends in other variables (for example, income or "modernity") are driving both cable access and attitudes. We argue that this does not seem to the case. Changes in attitudes between the first two survey waves are not predictive of cable introduction between the second and third wave.

Further, among villages that add cable during the survey period, initial attitudes are not predictive of which year (2002 or 2003) they get access. It is difficult to identify the mechanism behind the effects in this paper precisely. However, we do find some suggestive evidence that the mechanism alluded to at the start of the paper {increased exposure to circumstances outside of the village {is operating.

In particular, we find that the effects of cable are largest in areas with initially worse attitudes towards women, *i.e.*, those for whom cable is providing information most different from their current way of life. Although certainly not conclusive, this evidence is consistent with a model in which television changes the weight individuals put on the behaviours of their immediate peer group in forming their attitudes. The results are potentially quite important for policy. Gender discrimination in India is a significant issue, and has been a consistent source of concern for policy makers and academics. A large literature in economics, sociology and anthropology has explored the underlying causes of discrimination against women in India, highlighting the dowry system, low levels of female education, and other socioeconomic factors as central factors.

Changing these underlying factors is difficult; introducing television, or reducing any barriers to its spread, may be less so. From the policy perspective, however, there are potential concerns about whether the changes in reported autonomy, beating attitudes, and son preference actually represent changes in behaviours, or just in reporting. For example, we may be concerned that exposure to television only changes what the respondent thinks the interviewer wants to hear about the acceptability of beating, but does not actually change how much beating is occurring. This concern is likely to be less relevant in the case of fertility or education; the former is directly verifiable based on the presence of a baby in the household, and the latter is listed as part of a household roster.

The fact that we find effects on these variables provides support for the argument that our results represent real changes in outcomes. Without directly observing people in their homes, however, it is difficult to conclusively separate changes in reporting from changes in behaviour. However, even if cable only changes what is reported, it still may represent progress: changing the perceived "correct" attitude seems like a necessary, if not sufficient, step towards changing outcomes.

HISTORY OF TELEVISION IN INDIA

State-run black and white television was introduced into India in 1959, but the take off was extremely slow for the first several decades by 1977, only around 600,000 sets had been sold. In 1982, however, the state-run broadcaster (Doordarshan) introduced colour television, which dramatically increased interest in, and viewership of, television. Even with colour, however, most programming remained either government-sponsored news or information about economic development. There were a few entertainment serials, which were watched with intensity. In the early 1990s CNN and STAR TV first introduced the possibility of access to non-government programming via satellite.

There was a large demand for this cable (satellite) television, which was, and continues to be, filled primarily by small entrepreneurs who buy a dish and a subscription and charge nearby homes to connect to it. This is especially true in rural villages, such as those in our sample. As we show in the data later, this means that cable access is more common in villages that are wealthier and have a higher population density, where more people can afford to pay for service and where it would therefore be more profitable to start a cable business. However, dramatic declines in the prices of both the equipment and satellite service subscriptions (due in part to reduced tariffs and increased competition), coupled with income growth, have allowed cable to spread over time to more and more villages. In the 5 years from 2001 to 2006, about 30 million households, representing approximately 150 million individuals, added cable service (National Readership Studies Council 2006). And since television is often watched with family and friends by those without a television or cable, the growth in actual access or exposure to cable may have been even more dramatic.

The programme offerings on cable television are quite different than government programming. The most popular shows tend to be game shows and soap operas. As an example, among the most popular shows in both 2000 and 2007 (based on Indian Nielsen ratings) is "Kyunki Saas Bhi Kabhi Bahu Thi," (Because a Mother-in-Law was Once a Daughter-in-Law, Also) a show based around the life of a wealthy industrial family in the large city of Mumbai. As can be seen from the title, the main themes and plots of the show often revolve around issues of family and gender. Among satellite channels, STAR TV and Zee TV tend to dominate, although Sony, STAR PLUS and Sun TV are also represented among the top 20 shows. Viewership of the government channel, although relatively high among those who do not have cable, is extremely low among those who do (and limited largely to sporting events).

The introduction of television in general appears to have had large effects in Indian society.

In contrast to the West, television seems to be, in some cases, the primary medium by which people in rural villages in India get information about the outside world. For example, Johnson (2001) reports on a man in his 50's in a village in India who says that television is "the biggest thing to happen in our village, ever". He goes on to say that he learned about the value of electric fans (to deal with the heat) from television, and subsequently purchased one. The same author quotes another man arguing that television is where they learned that their leaders were corrupt, and about using the court system to address grievances.

On issues of gender specifically, television seems to have had a significant impact, since this is an area where the lives of rural viewers differ greatly from those depicted on most popular shows.

By virtue of the fact that the most popular Indian serials take place in urban settings, women depicted on these shows are typically much more emancipated than rural women. For example, many women on popular serials work outside the home, run businesses and control money. In addition, they are typically more educated and have fewer children than their rural counterparts. Further, in many cases there is access to Western television, with its accompanying depiction of life in which women are much more emancipated.

Based on anthropological reports, this seems to have affected attitudes within India. Scrase (2002) reports that several of his respondents thought television might lead women to question their social position and might help the cause of female advancement.

Another woman reports that, because of television, men and women are able to open up a lot more." Johnson (2001) quotes a number of respondents describing changes in gender roles as a result of television. One man notes, "Since TV has come to our village, women are doing less work than before. They only want to watch TV. So we [men] have to do more work. Many times I help my wife clean the house."

Although television overall seems to have had large effects, cable television in particular may be even more significant. This is both because it dramatically increases television viewership, and because the content is very different (again, since popular serials mostly feature urban life). Scrase (2002) reports on respondents who note that prior to cable there was almost no entertainment, and very little current affairs, whereas the offerings on cable were broad.

There is also a broader literature on the effects of television exposure on gender issues in other countries. Many studies find effects on a variety of outcomes: for example, eating disorders in Fiji, sex role stereotypes in Minnesota and perceptions of women's rights in Chicago. Telenovelas in Brazil have provided a fruitful context for studying the effects of television. For example, based on ethnographic research, La Pastina (2004) argues that exposure to telenovelas provides women (in particular) with alternative models of what role they might play in society.

Pace (1993) describes the effect of television introduction in Brazil on a small, isolated, Amazon community, arguing that the introduction of television changed the framework of social interactions, increased general world knowledge and changed people's perceptions about the status of their village in the wider world. Kottak (1990) reports on similar data from isolated areas in Brazil, and argues that the introduction of television affects (among other things) views on gender, moving individuals in these areas towards having more liberal views on the role of women in both the workplace and in relationships. Interestingly, the studies in Brazil also suggest that the patterns of television viewing shortly after it is first introduced may be quite different than what is seen later on.

The evidence suggests that in the first years after introduction, interactions with the television are more intense, with the television drawing more focus (both at an individual level, and community-wide). It is during this early period that Kottak (1990) and others argue that television is at its most influential.

Most of the villages in our analysis are at this early stage of television exposure, suggesting this may be an ideal period to look for effects. The evidence described above, of course, is drawn primarily from interviews and case studies, and obviously does not reflect a random sample of these populations. Nevertheless, the overall impression given by the anthropology and sociology literature is that the introduction of television had widespread effects on society, and that gender issues are a particular focal point. Our data and setting provide an opportunity to test this hypothesis more rigorously.

8

Public Relations and Online Media

INTRODUCTION

Public relations has become a significant and powerful industry, particularly in recent decades. This industry and its actors mainly work through the media to spread information, persuasion and opinions to the public on behalf of their clients. Publicity is the predominant goal. Networking, relation-building, news production and activities intended to be published in the media are thus part of the everyday work of PR agents such as information officers, PR consultants and spin-doctors. The PR phenomenon needs to be examined and scrutinised as a new party and power in the democratic process. In recent years, some international studies have taken on this mission, but there is scope for more studies on different aspects of the phenomenon, not least in the Nordic countries.

This stage is focused on the relation between the PR industry and the news media. The main themes and questions are: What characterises the relation between the PR industry and the media or between PR agents and journalists? And, how do the characteristics of that relation affect journalism? The stage starts by outlining some of the pertinent circumstances concerning the relation between the parties as well as their view of each other. Suggesting that PR actors aim for a close and continuous relation with journalists in order to secure publicity payback is hardly controversial. The findings of this study support that assumption. The study is furthermore conducted under the assumption that news journalists have a sceptical approach to counterparts such as PR actors and that they are reluctant to publish such actors' material, fully in line with journalistic norms and professional journalistic work conduct. The outcome of this study shows that the first assumption about journalistic views is mainly correct, while the second is not.

THEORETICAL STARTING POINTS

The news media are the most outstanding, common, and important channel for interest groups to get their messages out and influence their surroundings.

Several researchers argue that a focus on media has, in fact, grown in importance to these agents, especially concerning those active on the scene of policy shaping in the broader sense. Manning means that media work has become a more central part of political activity in recent years; earlier, Franklin discussed 'packaging politics' and Blumler found that publicity advisers, public relations experts and campaign consultants "immerse journalists in what appears to be an increasingly manipulative opinion environment". In addition, Cottle among others also notices an increased interest on the part of commercial groups in strategically mobilising communicative power and attaining media space. Studies of the relation between the PR industry and the news media show that PR actors and journalists often establish close relations in order to fulfil a mutual need.

The situation is similar to what research has shown about the relation between the media and institutional representatives such as politicians and government leaders. The influence of the PR industry appears in many different shapes in daily life. It involves anything from traditional press conferences and press releases to various more or less successful long-term agenda-setting-related activities. Among other things, strategies for controlling the news agenda are based on producing and serving the media with material that promotes the instrumental purposes of the senders' interests.

This type of media influence and strategies for controlling the news agenda are today often referred to by the concept news management. Meanwhile, news material from sources outside the media may also be seen as a contribution to journalistic work and as a way of cutting costs. Observations in line with this point of view have made way for the theory of information subsidy, meaning "efforts by policy actors to increase the consumption of persuasive messages by reducing their costs", in the words of Gandy. Several studies have shown that a reasonably large proportion of published articles originates from external sources - in fact, most of the studies conducted in relation to the subject area show that more than half of the studied published articles stem from material originating from outside sources.

There is reason to argue that, in recent times, the theory of information subsidy has increased its relevance to the everyday journalism reality as a consequence of the financial and personnel cutbacks many news organisations have undergone. Some analysts claim that this type of contact and exchange has forced journalism to become increasingly dependent on, and more easily affected by, outside influences – a transformation of professional conduct that has resulted in a more alienated journalism. The cutbacks are one explanation of the fact that PR practitioners have come to strongly influence today's news agenda. He argues that the material they present has become extremely successful in passing itself off as 'real news', and thereby, to a great extent, PR people have "worked to erode the autonomy of journalists at the micro level".

Other researchers follow this line:

- What passes for news of politics is often an inextricable mixture of messages from different sources. Advertising, public relations, reports of opinion polls, and propaganda become mixed up in the news product along with facts and editorial opinions. It certainly tends to undermine any simple faith in the reliability and independence of news.

The view of media professionals as manipulated by representatives of the PR industry easily leads to questions concerning the media's position as the fourth estate.

The media's role as a public utility in this regard might be discussed, as a consequence of the activities conducted by, among others, PR practitioners:

- The liberal description of the fourth estate media, based on an image of independent autonomous journalists seeking out news, has been severely undermined.

In accordance, Street reasons that "journalists are the lapdogs of partial interests, not the watchdogs of the public interest". However, contrary to this view, McNair argues that editorial staffs are fully capable of evaluating and disregarding material sent to them by the PR industry.

SOCIAL MEDIA AND PUBLIC RELATION IN SOCIETY

The news media are the most prominent instrument for disseminating information in society. In the present study the interviewees claimed generally that the media have become an increasingly important stage for organisations' external communication.

During the interview sessions, some of them also talked about the media as a prominent marketplace, as did this editor of a business magazine:

- Today, the media are the most important marketplace – all important deals are settled in the media sphere.... And as everyone is squeezed together on the same media scene, it becomes very loud, very crowded and very short of oxygen. That's where the PR business comes in.

The media, however, do not constitute a platform with actors of equal importance to PR practitioners. Rather, the media sphere appears as a media hierarchy. Typically, the largest radio and television stations along with the large national newspapers constitute the most important targets for PR activities.

Within television, news programmes are especially sought after, followed by talk shows and entertainment programmes. For PR activities directed at the print media, the editorial and debate pages of the daily morning newspapers are essential targets. When it comes to activities such as product promotions and launches, trade magazines and other types of specialised press increase in ranking and become a high priority. For opinion-generating campaigns, regional and local media are also of interest. However, the latter types of media organisations pick up PR-related information mostly through news agencies, and thus their journalists experience little direct connection with PR agents. The features of the relationship between PR agents and news journalists vary with the type of organisation or consultancy they represent. Journalists often claim a sceptical approach to those representing commercial interests, as journalistic norms have long deemed textual product placement despicable. Representation in the interest of political organisations, on the other hand, sets a different tone because of these organisations' position as being fundamental to a democratic society and therefore considered to be legitimate opinion leaders.

Their actions thus become "in the interest of the public". Public authorities are also by their nature obvious targets of media observation. Between the corporate interest groups and the political groupings stands a middle-category - the non-profit organisations. Non-profit organisations with a clear social ideology are often treated much like a party or public authority by the media. Furthermore, representatives of non-social ideology groupings often aim for publicity by trying to pass off their PR-activities as relevant to policy or community matters, regardless of whether this is actually the case. In other words, they attempt to move the characterisation of a specific organisation and its activities from the commercial sphere up to the societal political one. In short, however, one can say that the media's perceived understanding of the potential social impact of the organisations the PR-agents represent largely determines the conditions for the relation.

One editor used as an example the publicity demands of an organisation defending the needs of disabled individuals:

- It's an organisation that uses us for its own purposes. But I see no problem as long as we make our own journalistic judgement. We are aware of the fact that we are subject to persuasion, but I don't feel we avoid it as we would with attempts of product launches.

FREEDOM OF WISE SOCIETY

This chapter in vokes something that is not generally appealed to in contemporary philosophy: the idea of a wise society. One of its aims is to stimulate exploration of this idea, which is pertinent to several branches of the subject. These include both political philosophy and epistemology, in particular social epistemology. The idea of wisdom, in general, is a longstanding part of the philosophical repertoire. The very word "philosophy," as is well known, comes from the Greek for "love of wisdom."

That is not to say that there is general agreement on what wisdom is. Nor is it to say that latter day philosophical discourse is peppered with references to "wisdom," Paradoxically perhaps, it isn't. It is even less common to find references in this discourse to the wisdom of a society as opposed to that of an individual person. The same is true of the frequent contemporary philosophical references to knowledge, belief, and other close cousins of wisdom. There are incomparably more discussions of the knowledge and beliefs of individuals than of the knowledge and beliefs of societies.

Outside the circle of professional philosophers-and, indeed, within it-discussion of the latter topic may recently have been stimulated by a popular work in which James Surowiecki argues that the wisdom of a crowd-"loosely defined"-may be superior to that of an expert on a given subject. As will emerge, a society, as I understand it, is a subtype of "crowd" in Surowiecki's sense. I take it that if a society can be wise, it will be better for being so, all else being equal. It is therefore important to consider both whether a society can be wise, and, if so, what that wisdom entails. For instance, given what it is, does a society's wisdom militate against its having some other valuable feature or features?

This paper addresses one aspect of the question just mooted: can a wise society be a free one? One's first response to this question is likely to be "Of course!" or at least "Why on earth not?" My main aim in this paper is to show how one can argue for a negative answer.

More precisely, it is to show how one can argue that, in plausible senses of the pertinent terms, the wiser a society is, the less free it is.

For the sake of a label, I call the argument I present the negative argument. It is essentially conceptual. It raises various evaluative questions but does not itself proceed at the level of evaluation. Given its focus, the paper might be categorized as an essay in political philosophy. Given that a good deal of time is spent elaborating an account of a wise society, however, it might also be categorized as an essay in social epistemology.

Before setting out the negative argument I must explain how I am interpreting its key terms. They are all open to, and have received, a variety of interpretations. Thus some degree of clarification is necessary. It is possible that the negative argument works for interpretations other than those I offer here. It is also possible that it fails to work for one or more plausible construals. For present purposes I set these possibilities aside.

I take a society to be a kind of social group, where paradigmatic social groups include informal discussion groups, army units, sports teams, and labour unions. To give a rough and partial characterization of such a group one might say, echoing Rousseau, that its members are unified in such a way that they constitute more than a mere aggregate of persons.

Typically a society, in particular, includes many smaller social groups. Thus within a given society there may be many families, labour unions, sports teams, and so on. A society is therefore relatively large, in contrast with a family, say, or a sports team. For now, this brief characterization of societies will suffice.

PERSONAL FREEDOM AND A FREE SOCIETY

The freedom of a society, as I shall construe that, is closely tied to the personal freedom of the individual members of that society, understood in a certain way. A concern for personal freedom in some sense of the phrase is central to a number of evaluative stances in political philosophy.

Thus, on one account of it, anarchism involves "a concern for preserving individual freedom and a distaste for the coercive measures of governments...." A government coerces by "threatening to use force or impose punishments if a person does not follow its laws". Now, in what I take to be the central sense of the term, punishment requires a special standing or authority. As I understand it, to have the authority to punish is not necessarily to be justified in doing so, but it does away with a possible objection to its use by a given agent. It cannot be objected "It is not for you to do that."

Indeed, anarchism is often characterized in terms of distaste, not so much for the coercive measures governments take but rather for government itself. Here government is construed as a matter of the authority to command, to demand or insist on compliance when non-compliance is threatened, and, where appropriate, to punish. The problem of government is posed in terms of the loss of personal autonomy inherent in the authority of one person over another, whether they command, demand conformity, or punish. That is the tenor of the well-known brand of philosophical anarchism that was advocated by Robert Paul Wolff, for instance.

The anarchist's concern is often couched in terms of the authority of one person, or of a body of persons smaller than the society that is in question. I take it, meanwhile, that there can be whole societies-even societies reasonably thought of as political societies or polities-without such a ruling person or body. Even in such "acephalous" societies, there are issues of personal autonomy. Such societies are likely to have a variety of rules. Each member will then have the authority to insist on any other's conformity to a given rule and to rebuke any other for not conforming to it.

Evidently, I take it that one cannot rebuke someone without a special standing or authority. One can, of course, speak in a rebuking manner without such authority, just as one can speak in a demanding manner, without the authority actually to demand.

Rebukes and demands may be unaccompanied by physical force or by threats that such force will be applied unless what is demanded is done. There is, nonetheless, something forceful about any rebuke, just as there is something forceful about demanding. Indeed, in The Concept of Law, Hart suggests that rebukes lie at the informal end of a spectrum at the formal end of which lie punishments imposed through due process of law.

Penal sanctions may sound-and may be-worse than informal demands and rebukes, but most people do not relish such forceful interventions from others.

Most would prefer not to incur the reproofs of strangers, the rebukes of colleagues, or the reprimands of friends and intimates. Mill, the great philosophical champion of liberty, saw this clearly. And verbal chastisement can be the precursor of physical violence.

Suppose, now, that there is a rule in my society that women are not to contradict men. I know that if I, a woman, contradict a man on some point, the other members of my society have the authority to rebuke me for doing so. Accordingly, I may regularly decide not to make some point though I desire to do so. In other terms, my freedom is limited in an important way: there is something I want to do, but I risk an authoritative forceful negative response should I do it. The account of a society's freedom that I shall make use of in developing the negative argument reflects the idea that the standing threat of such a response is an important limitation on personal freedom. In speaking of a "threat" here I do not mean to imply that the response is imminent, or even probable, but rather that it is "in the cards." If someone has the standing to rebuke me for doing something, I know that, should he speak to me in a rebuking manner, I cannot dodge the issue by saying "It's none of your business." If he has the standing to rebuke me, it is his business.

I shall say that a given member, M1, of a society S, is personally free to perform a given action, A, in face of another member, M2, if and only if M1 is under no threat of an authoritative forceful negative reaction from M2 should M1 perform A or, indeed, should M1 propose to perform A. For the sake of brevity, I shall generally refer in what follows to being under no threat of a rebuke. It should be understood that all forms of authoritative forceful negative reaction are included under this heading.

Now, a given member, M1, of a society S, may be under a threat of rebuke from another member, M2, where these rebukes are not grounded in his membership in S as such. For instance, M1 promised M2, and no one else, that he would not do A. I am not concerned with such grounds here. The definition of personal freedom just given should be interpreted accordingly. What is at issue is rebukes whose ground is some aspect of the membership of M1 and M2 in society S.

I take it that a society itself can be "personally free" in the defined sense, insofar as it can be a member of a society of societies. Meanwhile, the type of societal freedom with which this essay is concerned relates to the personal freedom of a society's members as just defined. This might be referred to as the society's internal freedom. My focal case continues to be a society whose members are individual human beings as opposed to other societies.

I shall assume that, as a matter of definition, a society becomes less free as particular personal freedoms are subtracted from those its various members already have. This is clearly only a partial account of societal freedom. It concerns only a single condition under which a society can be said to become less free than it was. Nonetheless it is of interest to ask whether a society's relative freedom in the respect at issue is altered by one or another factor.

I shall not attempt to offer a full account of a free society. Given the notion of personal freedom with which I am operating, however, a plausible account will not allow that a society is free when its members have little personal freedom. Nor will it demand that a free society be maximally free, where a maximally free society is one in which, for any action whatever, each member of the society is personally free to perform that action in face of any other member. It may reasonably be questioned whether a maximally free society, as just defined, is possible. As will emerge, it can be argued that it is not, given what a society is.

A WISE SOCIETY

Some may be inclined to deny that there is such a thing as a society that is wise to any degree. They may point to the fact that wisdom involves or is closely connected to knowledge or, at least, good judgement and argue that a society is not the kind of thing that can be wise. Individual human beings can be wise but societies are not sufficiently like them for a wise society to be possible.

When it is presented, this argument may look plausible. Yet people regularly talk about a society's beliefs, judgements, decisions, and knowledge. Thus a particular society may be said to have made a wise (or unwise) decision, wrongly to consider itself superior to other societies, and so on.

When people talk about the belief of a society or other social group, they think of themselves as speaking literally rather than metaphorically. Rather than assuming that they are misguided, one might do well to consider what phenomenon on the ground, so to speak, they have in mind.

Perhaps because they think along the skeptical lines mentioned above, contemporary political philosophers have not paid attention to the idea of a wise society. Following John Rawls, they have considered the key quality of a good society to be its justice and focused on that.

In the Republic, Plato also focused on a society's justice. This did not lead him to neglect the idea of a wise society. Indeed, he thought of a society's wisdom as necessary to its justice. Notoriously, he did not think this way about its freedom. Plato does talk about freedom. His picture of what he called "democracy" in Book of the Republic is perhaps the closest to true anarchy-and maximal personal freedom-that one can imagine. It is not clear, indeed, how consistent a picture this is. There is some talk of "laws" and "courts" of law, yet-he says-one can do anything one pleases. Those condemned to death or exile walk about as if they are heroes and nobody cares.

This is not Plato's favored scenario. In the type of political society he favours, the laws are taken seriously. Most important for present purposes, the rulers are few in number and carefully selected and trained. Those with the right natural aptitudes go through the rigorous training necessary for one who loves wisdom-a philosopher-to reach his goal, knowledge of the Good.

Before the details of this training have been developed Plato considers what it is for a political society to be wise. What he says is open to different interpretations, and I shall not attempt carefully to probe it here. At a minimum, it seems fair to characterize his opinion as follows. The judgements of the rulers, in making rules and decisions for the society, must, in a phrase, track the Good.

I shall work with an account of a wise society that has something of the same spirit. I shall not require that such a society is ruled by a particular person or body of persons, however-let alone a body of persons trained from birth for the purpose. Thus I shall allow that in principle an acephalous society can be wise. I shall not attempt carefully to explore either the idea of wisdom in general or the idea of a wise society in particular. The account of the latter that I shall work with has something to be said for it, but it may well be that an alternative account is more plausible. I hope that my discussion will help to stimulate consideration of precisely this issue. In the meantime, it is important to see that on the account of a wise society proposed, the negative argument is sound. A wise society, on this account, is a society possessed of features that, whatever their relation to wisdom in particular, would appear to be desirable, all else being equal.

The working account I shall adopt appeals, simply, to a society's true value judgements, in particular those relating to the goodness and badness of human and societal features and actions. Such judgements may be very general-as in the judgement that wantonly destroying a human life is a very bad thing-or quite specific-as in the judgement that Hitler was an evil man. They may not lead to specific decisions or actions or they may. If one judges that wantonly destroying another's life is a very bad thing to do, for instance, one is likely to avoid such destruction.

A true value judgement evidently tracks the Good at least to some extent. It may be plausible to argue that if a value judgement fully tracks the Good it must not only be true but it must also have been made on good grounds. It is not, then, "fortuitously" true. That said, I focus here on the simpler condition. I shall assume that, by definition, the true value judgements of one who is wise will be relatively numerous.

This, along with the following points, is intended to apply both to individual human beings and to human societies. I shall assume one who is wise, as a matter of definition, does not make false judgements. If the truth on some matter of value is hard to discern, one who is wise will if necessary act on working assumptions understood to be such. These are relatively stringent conditions. They are not, however, as stringent as they might be. At the upper limit of wisdom, one would get everything right. I shall take the stated conditions to be both necessary and sufficient for one to be wise. I shall make the following comparative judgement about one who is wise on the above account. Any new true value judgement one makes in addition to those one has already made amounts, by definition, to an increase in one's wisdom. This is only intended to be a partial account of what makes for an increase in wisdom, but it suffices for presentation of the negative argument. It is now time to turn to the core of the negative argument. This is the pertinent account of what it is for a society to endorse a particular value judgement.

A SOCIETY'S VALUE JUDGEMENTS

I have elsewhere developed an account of what it is for a group to believe that such-and-such. I have also proposed a related account of what it is for a group to make a particular value judgement. Here I shall do little more than sketch the account, saying only what I take to be needed to make the negative argument. I proceed in terms of an illustrative value judgement, which may or may not be true: marriage is a valuable social institution. I shall refer to this judgement as V. Obviously any other particular judgement might stand in its stead.

According to my account of such matters, in terms that will be explained, a society judges that V if and only if its members are jointly committed to judge as a body that V. I have argued at length elsewhere that the concept of a joint commitment is a fundamental part of human life, embedded in many of those central concepts with which human beings approach their interactions with one another. I must now say something about what a joint commitment amounts to.

A joint commitment, as I understand it, is a commitment of two or more parties. It is not a combination of commitments, one of one party, one of another, and so on. Given their joint commitment, each party has sufficient reason to act accordingly, just as one has sufficient reason to act according to a personal decision one has made. As I understand the phrase, if one has sufficient reason to do something, then one is rationally required to do it, all else being equal.

Any joint commitment is a joint commitment to "do" something as a body, in a broad sense of "do" that includes judging that V. To say that certain people are jointly committed to judge that V as a body means something like this. They are jointly committed as far as is possible together to constitute a single body-or person-that judges that V. I say more about this shortly.

How do people become jointly committed? Failing special background understandings-in the basic case-a given joint commitment can only be created by all of the parties together. The same is true of its rescission. Here is a rough account of the conditions under which such a commitment is created in the basic case.

Each of the would-be parties must express his readiness to be jointly committed with the others in a particular way, and the fact that these expressions have taken place must be open to all or, in something like David Lewis's sense, common knowledge. Though I shall not attempt to elaborate on this point here, this account does not rule out joint commitments on a large scale. I take it that people can enter joint commitments in situations of strong pressure. Just as you can make a decision under pressure to do so, you can enter a joint commitment in such circumstances. To say that is not, of course, to contest the desirability of one's making decisions and entering joint commitments in the absence of such pressures.

Special background understandings allow for non-basic cases. Thus all of the members of a given population, large or small, may create an open-ended joint commitment such that one person or a smaller population of persons is in a position to create new joint commitments for the population as a whole. For example, the members of a labour union may jointly commit to conform as a body to any fiats issued by Jones under certain conditions. In that case when Jones issues a fiat under the relevant conditions, the union members are jointly committed to conform, as one, to that fiat. To keep things simple here, I am going to focus on societies where no such special background understandings prevail.

For the purposes of the negative argument the most important feature of a joint commitment is this. If I am jointly committed in some way with another person, I am answerable to him with respect to my proposed or actual non-conformity to the commitment. Not only do I owe him an explanation of any proposed or actual non-conformity, I also owe him actions that conform to the commitment. I owe these to him insofar as he participates in the joint commitment.

I have said that the negative argument is essentially conceptual rather than evaluative. The point just made may seem to refute that. However, it relates to what a joint commitment is, as opposed to its value or the value of any related actions.

One way of amplifying the point is as follows. There is a sense in which, by committing each party to act in certain ways, a joint commitment in and of itself creates in each party ownership of the actions in question. Being in the future, the actions are owned but not currently possessed: in that sense they are owed. Evidently this puts each of the other parties in a special position in relation to me. If I propose not to perform an action the commitment requires, he has the standing or authority required in order that he demand it.

He can say, in effect, "Give me that! It's mine-qua party to the joint commitment!" He also has the standing to rebuke me. After the fact, he can say, in effect, "How could you not have given me that! It was mine!" Thus those who either propose to violate a standing joint commitment or who do violate one lay themselves open to the authoritative forceful negative reactions of the other parties.

So much, then, for the nature and implications of joint commitment. I turn now to the relationship of joint commitments to social groups. I have argued elsewhere that those who are jointly committed in some way constitute a social group in a central sense of the phrase. This accords with the rough characterization of a social group offered earlier in this chapter: its members are unified in such a way that they constitute more than a mere aggregate of persons.

Given this amplification, if certain persons are jointly committed to judge that V as a body then they constitute a social group. Indeed, they constitute a social group that judges that V. As I have argued elsewhere, to say that under these conditions people constitute a social group that judges that V answers to a standard everyday concept of a social group that judges that V.

In sum, the present account of a society's value judgement is not merely stipulative. It accords with entrenched, everyday understandings of the component ideas. On the account proposed, then, a society judges that V if and only if the members are jointly committed to judge that V as a body. That is, they are jointly committed as far as possible to constitute a single body that judges that V. How might this commitment be fulfilled?

When people are acting in conformity with the commitment, they might confidently state that V when talking to one another. They would refrain from calling V or obvious corollaries into question without preamble. In short, they would suggest by their actions and emotional expressions that V. They would refrain, therefore, from acting contrary to V and from reporting contrary actions with bravado.

Thus one would not say out loud, with an air of bravado "I've managed to avoid getting married again!" or, critically, "Marriage? That's for the birds!" I do not say that in order to act in conformity with the commitment people must personally judge that V. There are several reasons for this, but for now I simply state my understanding that a joint commitment to judge that V as a body does not require the parties personally to judge V. Should one judge that not-V, however, he is committed not to say this without preamble. Rather, he must say, for instance, "Personally, I don't think marriage is such a wonderful thing." This indicates that he is speaking not from the perspective of the group as a whole but from his personal perspective.

So much for the definitions and assumptions in terms of which I shall present the negative argument. They all have some plausibility, and it is worth considering what follows from them for the question: can a wise society be a free one? I am supposing that, by definition, a wise society endorses a fair number of true value judgements and eschews false ones, and that a new true value judgement added to its current stock of such judgements increases its wisdom. The negative argument can be put as follows. Suppose that society S is wise. Suppose now that it adds a new true value judgement J to its current stock of true value judgements. By definition, it becomes wiser. Given the nature of societal value judgements in general, J provides the members of S, as such, with a ground for rebuking one another for a new range of possible actions, R. R includes speech acts as well as actions that do not involve speech. Thus S becomes less free.

A query may arise as to this conclusion. What if there was already a joint commitment in S-one distinct from that underlying S's new value judgement J-such that members of S have a ground for rebuking one another for the very same range of actions R covered in the case of J? Assuming for the sake of argument that this is possible, it is still fair to say that S becomes less free on making J, for now there is a new ground for rebukes in relation to R.

People can certainly have the standing to rebuke one another for performing a given action on more than one ground. Perhaps, for instance, several of us agreed not to do something, and I made a special promise to you that I would not do it. Then you can upbraid me both on the ground that we agreed not to do it and on the ground that you promised me not to do it. It seems fair to say, generally, that the more grounds for rebuke there are for one's performing a given action, the less free one is.

Now it is true, of course, that if S were to add a false value judgement to its current stock of value judgements, it would also become less free. The striking thing about the negative argument, however, is this: something that on the face of it is a bonus-S's increasing wisdom-turns out to have a specifiable cost-a corresponding loss in S's freedom. That assumes, of course, that a lessening of societal freedom, in and of itself, is a bad thing, while an increase in societal wisdom is a good thing. As said, at least on the face of it, this is so.

I should emphasize that the negative argument does not render problematic the idea that, all else being equal, it is better for a society to replace a false value judgement with a true one, if these are the alternatives. It implies, however, that it would make for more freedom in a society with a false value judgement if that judgement were simply abandoned-if the society were left with no view on the matter-rather than replaced by the corresponding true judgement. True judgements, just like false ones, reduce the freedom of society.

The negative argument raises or highlights several important questions. Before concluding I note and discuss a number of these without attempting fully to answer any.

It may be proposed that the loss of personal freedom entailed by a wise society's increasing wisdom will make no practical difference if each member was happy to enter the relevant joint commitment. It may be added that it will matter even less if at the time they happily entered the joint commitment they personally endorsed the society's value judgement.

This seems not to be so. Suppose Qiong was happy to enter the joint commitment at issue in my focal example, personally believing that marriage was an excellent social institution. Suppose that through personal or vicarious experience she later changes her mind. Her change of mind is one thing; her society's change of mind is another. The joint commitment may still stand. She is then still subject to it.

At this point Qiong may well find none of her choices attractive. She can baldly make concordant statements she believes to be false and act in ways she takes to express a false value. She can cause herself to stand out from the crowd by saying, as the joint commitment permits," Personally, I think marriage as an institution is problematic." She can publicly violate the commitment and lay herself open to authoritative forceful responses. One may well shrink from any of these options, and from others that might be available-such as giving up one's membership in the society in question.

Knowing all this, one who is simply contemplating a personal change of mind may turn away from that option. Or the very movement towards such contemplation may itself be suppressed.

Note that Qiong's option of prefacing her antimarriage statement with" Personally" may do more than make her stand out from the crowd. (Some people might find that outcome relatively attractive.) Another possible outcome is likely to be less attractive. Though the joint commitment does not require her personally to endorse the value judgement in question, when she says or implies that she personally doesn't endorse it, she puts herself in a problematic position. People have reason to wonder if she can be relied upon to fulfill the commitment in the future. Might her contrary opinion not soon break out untrammeled? Might she be a spoiler? She may find herself shunned, though she did not violate the commitment.

In sum, even if each one of a number of people is happy to enter a given joint commitment, and each one's personal judgement at that point accords with the societal value judgement thus created, its providing a basis for rebuke makes a practical difference. It allows, in general terms, for a tension to arise between a given member's joint commitment, on the one hand, and his personal judgement on the other.

Some are inclined to think that if any human being violates a moral rule, any other human being has the standing to rebuke him for this. Moral rules, in turn, may be conceived of as existing independently of all actual societies, and as corresponding to the subset of true value judgements at issue in the present discussion. It may then be argued that the standing to rebuke another member of one's society that one gains from a new, true value judgement of that society does not make much practical difference to anyone's situation.

Irrespective of our status as members of one or another society, we are all always open to rebukes from others for the violation of any moral rule. The fact that with an increase in a society's wisdom some people have a new ground for some such rebukes is of interest, to be sure.

However, it would not seem to make much difference from a practical point of view. I have argued elsewhere against the idea that human beings as such have the standing to rebuke one another for violations of moral rules. If they do not then the argument in the previous paragraph must be rejected: its central premise is false.

At the least, the truth of its central premise is not immediately obvious. Given that this is so, people who attempt to rebuke others" because what you are doing is morally wrong" may be given short shrift by those to whom they speak. These latter may simply, and sincerely, respond that" It's none of your business." Thus even if rebukes were automatically in order by reason of the existence of moral rules as such, the practical impact of an increase in societal wisdom could be considerable." This runs counter to our values" may well be received as a more pertinent explanation of rebuke than" What you are doing is morally wrong."

Rather than attempting to curtail a society's wisdom-perhaps by making sure it does not address particular issues-is there a way of keeping its wisdom intact, and, indeed, increasing it, while reducing its impact on the society's members? The full spectrum of true value judgements may, indeed, include some that will lead a society that makes them to minimize the impact of its own value judgements. I have in mind here value judgements associated with when and how to tell people off for violating a given joint commitment. It may be that it is best to start in a kind and non-forceful manner.

A maximally wise society, at least, will take this value judgement on board. It will then be incumbent upon its members to act appropriately if someone baldly says something contrary to a value judgement of the society. For instance, he might mildly observe "That's not a very democratic sentiment!" or "I'm surprised to hear someone from these parts saying that!" or "I take it that you are simply expressing your personal opinion?" If the person addressed answers the last question affirmatively, the joint commitments to which he and his interlocutor are parties will offer little basis for rebuke.

A society's embracing the value judgements currently under consideration-those advocating an initially kindly approachwill most likely reduce the frequency of rebukes. If a rebuke is considered acceptable in face of a recalcitrant interlocutor, however-one who will not say the expressed opinion is his personal one, or take it back in the light of gentle suggestion-they may well sometimes occur.

Moreover, as all will understand, the members of the society will at all times have the standing to rebuke provided by the joint commitment that underlies any of that society's value judgements. Thus should one forego an initially kindly approach and immediately offer a rebuke, the person rebuked will not be able to respond, "It's none of your business." The parties, then, are still threatened with rebuke, in the sense in question here. What if forceful responses, though authoritative, never occurred? What might the effects of this be? How necessary to the very existence of a society's wisdom is the imposition, at least after gentler responses, of rebuke?

This question recalls Patrick Devlin's argument for the very strong thesis that a society risks disintegration if at least its core value judgements are not supported with the weight of the criminal law. His idea was, roughly, that the very existence of the society depends on the persistence of those core judgements as its judgements. If action contrary to those judgements was permitted by law, this would be liable to increase such action and would lead, eventually, to the demise of the society's value judgement as such. The general question is: what is necessary to ensure that a given true societal value judgement will persist? I shall not attempt to answer this question here.

That it can be raised suggests, at least, that there may be a cost to mitigating the effects of a society's wisdom to the point that even informal rebukes are disallowed. The cost in question is the loss of the society's wisdom.

EVALUATIVE QUESTIONS

Many evaluative questions arise. How good a thing is it that a society makes true value judgements as these have been understood here? Is it better, all things considered, that a society minimize its evaluative judgements or sticks only to certain areas of value judgement? Is a society that is good overall one that looks the other way as far as values, or some kinds of value, are concerned-irrespective of its capacity to get things right? If so, why is that? Personal freedom is likely to be invoked at this point. Invocation alone, however, is not enough.

Given that a diminution in personal freedom is always a loss, how is it to be weighed against an increase in the wisdom of a given society? All else being equal, is it indeed better for a society to make a true value judgement rather than no judgement on the topic or a false one? These questions are important and timely. They press us to think further about the wisdom of a society, its implications and its value.

IMPACT POTENTIAL OF THE NEWS MEDIA

The impact potential of the news media is of course a crucial factor in why journalists are a prioritised target of actions taken by the PR industry. However, there are at least two additional reasons for why media publicity is considered the best way to reach the public – and thereby to achieve a desired image and swing public opinion or parts of it in a favourable direction. First, publication in the media has a higher level of credibility than other communication channels do. Second, compared to advertising, media publicity is a cost-effective method.

It should be added that today's senders, whether they are professionals within an organisation or hired consultants, find it fairly easy to get material published in newspapers. The prevailing conditions are the result of decreases in editorial staff in recent years and increasing demands for raised production goals for each journalist. "Today, we are so pressed by shrinking advertising revenue and diminishing circulation rates, that we try to save, we cut back wherever we can", said one editor. The work climate has created an increasingly stressful situation and resulted in less time for journalistic fieldwork, especially with regard to investigative efforts. That, in turn, has created an increased need for access to raw material from sources outside of the news desks.

The senders – or agents promoting a specific interest – are well aware of the situation and use it consciously:

- The everyday work of a journalist is very stressful So they often consider contacts with PR agents as useful, if we practice serious work conduct and do no gold digging. Because we know exactly what journalists want.

The information flow directed towards the editorial staff has thus allegedly increased, partly as a result of a much more flexible attitude towards promotion-related activities from the communications sector. In addition, those who aim to influence today know how to get through the editorial filters: "If you can bring in something that looks like news material, you can have a great deal of influence", as one journalist from a nationwide morning newspaper put it.

During the interviews for this study, editorial staff members repeated the change in conditions and claimed it has brought about problems:

- Today the news desks experience an in-flow of information never seen before, especially from the corporate sector. The input is overwhelming – if previously it was a stream, it's now more like a river... Handling this flood of information is problematic, and there is a risk that journalists will get caught up in it and thereby decrease their ability to control the news agenda.

This raises questions of whether the media may become dependent on this subsidy of information and material. Some journalists reflecting over their own work situation suggested there is a risk that reporters will become dependent on the influence of different activist experts. Even journalists with special beats sometimes experience a lack of knowledge, especially those within technical, medical and natural-science-related subject areas: "

While we become too specialised we also become too dependent", said one public service TV journalist.

- PR people call both openly and under cover to try to sell an idea to us. It's presented in a very feasible way and then we're under extreme pressure to put together a paper for the next day... They know our work situation and they know exactly what things to pull.

By serving the media with news material, the activities of PR actors have caused their industry to move towards taking on the shape of a news desk located outside the media. In this study, one interviewed managing director of a PR consultancy in fact went so far as to suggest that PR firms "really are about being a satellite news desk".

PUBLIC RELATION AGENTS' AND JOURNALISTS'

The PR experts' and journalists' views of each other differ a great deal. It seems that, in principle, many representatives of the PR industry have great respect for journalism and the media's role in society. They underline the media's obligation to review the PR sphere just as they expect journalists to do with other social phenomena. "There should be a strong journalism – and there is a strong belief among us in the crucial role of journalism in society", said a junior consultant. One colleague stated that "it's extremely important to respect the media's integrity". At the same time, some of the PR actors in reality showed less respect for the media's professional task, as attempts to manipulate or steer the media in a favourable way seemed acceptable. Even among those who claimed a profound respect for the media, instrumental aims became discernible at times during the interviews.

Hardly any of the interviewed journalists expressed a corresponding respect for the PR agents. In principle, PR experts, especially consultants, were described as opponents, in line with the general normative thinking of journalism, which supports the view that PR people are to be kept at a distance. They are "my most important opponents," claimed one journalist of a national newspaper and continued by saying that the group has become so "unbelievably much more clever with what they do".

As PR agents inevitably exist in the media professionals' work context, journalists are forced to respect them in the same matter as one has to respects an opponent:

- I dislike the phenomenon PR consultants terribly. But I do realise that 'this is the way it is' and what am I to do? They're a part of today's society. And an influential part too.

Journalists' mainly sceptical approach to PR is familiar to those working in the PR sphere. It is mirrored in the strategies of the latter – how to present material as well as how to present themselves in order to establish contact – and perhaps also in their professional self-image. Some of the interviewed consultants pointed to the fact that they are always straightforward in their contacts with the media and always explain whom or what interests they represent. Others commenting on the matter said, on the contrary, that they are careful not to give away that they are consultants, because then "they usually hang up the phone".

Some also reasoned about the ambivalent approach they feel journalists have towards them:

- Journalists have a type of love-hate approach towards PR agents. On the one hand, there's a contempt for us for our well-paid work, on the other hand, there's many times a use for our service in journalistic work.

In their comments on PR agents, the interviewed journalists tended to group information officers and consultants. Both groups were viewed to have the same task and thus to be "of the same breed", as some journalists expressed themselves. The journalistic approach seems to be that there is actually no need for any PR agents. Meanwhile, in reality, the relation in itself may function differently depending on whether a PR person is placed inside or outside an organisation - the latter case often making it more restrained. Still, some journalists claimed to make use of consultants in terms of information overviews and ideas for suitable sources. In addition, while they also fill a censoring role, information officers admittedly seem to be useful in negotiating contacts higher up in the organisations. Journalists, however, often find these officers annoying, as they want to speak with the person in charge; they do not to wish to get the answers "filtered through representatives one has to go by".

In this specific matter, journalists and PR consultants actually seem to agree. The latter claimed they should never be the voice of the organisation they represent. Rather, their work is to organise the contact set up. It is always the client who should talk to the journalists, and "it would be absurd to have a consultant between the journalist and the corporation ". Yet many journalists claimed that they are constantly subject to in formation flows controlled by PR consultants. The discrepancy in the perception of the situation is likely to be a result of opposing relational perspectives on who controls the terms for the contact and in whose interest it is taken.

Journalists' mainly sceptical and negative approach to PR experts was accompanied by an attitude of rejection towards them when discussions during the interview sessions lead to the topic of what the relationship is actually like in reality. When the PR agents, on the other hand, voiced their opinion about the same reality, it was largely through opposite understandings of good and well-working relationships, common interests and sometimes collaboration.

RELATION BETWEEN PR AGENTS AND JOURNALISTS

Perhaps the best answer to the question of what characterises the relation between PR representatives and news journalists is one provided by an interviewed radio journalist: "it seems they have a better relation with me than I do with them". Overall, the interviewed PR agents claimed to have well-functioning relations with journalists and news desks. "We have a great relationship", was a typical attitude. None of the journalists expressed themselves in even a remotely similar manner. Very few spoke of such a relationship unless provoked to do so – it is obviously a sensitive topic from a normative perspective. Some journalists claimed to have no connection to PR people at all or that they avoid and reject such contact. Others had a more distanced approach to the relationship, saying that it constitutes "a role-play; they do their work and we do ours", or that the relation is completely neutral:

- The relationships are zero, neutral. They are neither positive nor negative. Not on my part. They sometimes bother me.
- I have no relationships with them at all actually. These very open-minded consultants that call me... my reaction is – no thanks, instantly. I want nothing at all to do with them.

Rather than describing a relationship, most journalists did claim to be in contact – a less loaded word from a normative perspective – with PR agents. The contacts, mostly initiated by PR agents, may occur frequently, especially for news editors and reporters at newspapers with specialised beats. This generally consists of a daily information exchange, and in some cases, "certainly 10 to 15 calls a day". One trade press editor stated that "I can no longer have my cell phone turned on without it being bombarded with phone calls". The interviewed PR representatives generally agreed with the journalists on this. However, specific ideas about the perceived situation varied somewhat with seniority, as many of the more experienced communications strategists are more frequently in contact with the media.

The perception of the information exchange also varied with the relevant topic and the client.

- I have a lot of contacts with journalists. It consists of everything; the ones I e-mail every day, talk to, have lunch with and the ones I get ideas from or talk to for updates. I give information to them as news in the same way as I advise clients.

Establishing relations with the media is crucial to the success of a PR agent. It is decisive to create and maintain well-functioning relations with relevant editorial staff. The "fundamental objective is to make sure to build personal relationships with 'your' editorial staff", as one of them stated. Maintaining the relationship is a constantly ongoing process, where the aim is to "create a long-term relationship with journalists so they will know exactly where I stand in relation to them and so they can trust that I will give them conclusive information".

Meanwhile, PR agents cannot constantly pursue journalists' attention, as that would run the risk of straining the relationship.

- Many journalists feel that PR consultants are extremely annoying. It depends on whether you call them and terrorise them indiscriminately and try to shower them with information they don't want – then things can take a wrong turn. If you, on the other hand, respect them and try to be of help to them in their work, you serve the purpose you're supposed to.

Well-functioning relations with editorial staff are, of course, of crucial importance to PR agents who work with topics related to social issues and politics. However, as brand awareness has arisen as a pronounced goal for actions within the PR industry, these relations have become more important for those focusing on marketing-related communication. "It pertains to the whole thinking process in terms of brand awareness and recognition", as the CEO of one consultancy firm stated.

It is essential for a PR agent to not only make contact, but to establish 'the right' connections. This means aiming for media that fit clients' ideas or products in terms of content and audience. In addition, consultants have to identify individual journalists who might be interested in the specific topic they are seeking publicity for. This also means finding out what the editorial staff are momentarily interested in so as to prepare for consultation on suitable actions. The consultancies direct special resources to map out where to turn in order to maximize media coverage for exclusive news announcements and which individuals to contact for attaining best results.

As one interviewed information officer put it, this is the ability and knowledge – or professionalism – that PR consultancies offer their clients.

- The first thing is to make connections with the right people. To know which journalists write about which topic and who covers a particular industry. Thus you conduct media analyses – analyse which journalists write about which type of questions.

The relationship-building activities of the PR industry serve several purposes. Apart from, for example, aiming for publicity for one particular opinion project, a second purpose is to be recognised among the editorial staff as the consultancy – and as the individual – with the best in-depth and general knowledge of a certain topic. If such status is achieved, the hope is to lead journalists to initiate contact in their search for general knowledge or standpoints and comments when reporting on the topic. Several interviewed consultants claimed that they receive these types of phone calls fairly often, but none of the journalists participating in this study mentioned that type of contact. One of them said, however, "I try to use them as administrators in bookings interviews with corporate representatives to facilitate my work". In other words, the consultant is used as an in-house spokesperson.

But there are consultants who do not focus at all on media relations or media influences, but concentrate on strategic and planning management.

They are primarily senior and well-established consultants with their own businesses, which allow them to choose and direct their tasks much more freely:

- I have no media relations of that type to constantly try to affect. I don't call and nag at them all the time... Besides, you destroy the relation by nagging all the time. It's not adult behaviour. But I can get things into papers when I need to.

The information exchange between the two parties seldom consists of direct personal contacts in the sense of meetings, as often is the case for contacts between journalists and political or institutional representatives. Rather, the communicative exchange between journalists and PR agents largely concerns phone calls or e-mail correspondence – of which especially the latter has grown to be a very common method in recent times. "I have relations with the media but I know no journalists, I have no personal relationships with them", stated one of the PR agents who was very representative of the collective. The interviewed journalists agreed more or less categorically with the statements and dismissed all talk about a colleague-like relationship. However, one common tactic among PR agents is to "try to establish a friendly relationship even though the two parties have never met". In this lies the risk of becoming too friendly with each other; "the danger lies in friendship corruption", as one journalist at a business magazine put it. Meanwhile, as the most senior of the interviewed journalists stated, after years or perhaps decades of exchanging information "developing a pretty close relationship can't be avoided".

Agents belonging to the division of the PR industry that acts as lobbyists or works with lobby-like activities, however, do meet journalists in person, for example, at political party and labour union events.

One consultant described how the work can involve spending a whole week at a party convention, registered as an 'observer':

- It is very much a networking event to me – being around, getting to know people, finding new business opportunities and making new connections, interpreting the atmosphere and talking to representatives I know or get to know... The most important thing is to observe the debate on general matters and matters of relevance to my clients' interests. Finding out what that makes the agenda and if there are any opponent representatives to my clients' interests. And you might as well admit it's a lot about talking to journalists.

A close and well-working relation with media professionals and an in-depth understanding of journalistic professionalism are, as we have seen, prerequisites of and a basic strategy for influencing experts in their aim to set the agenda. Although the attention to a client's interests is often obtained through contacts around specific campaigning, long-term success is best secured through on-going everyday relations and networking. Therefore, their work incorporates continuous updates and questioning and appearances at press conferences as well as attempts to spend time with journalists at different events that bring media professionals together – like seminars, breakfast meetings, entertainment happenings and sports-related events. Journalists, for their part, are well aware of the strategy:

- A clever PR person should network and talk to people around just about anything, that's how you establish a relation you can use later on. If you have established a relation you know the journalist will return to you to ask about more things... We do the same thing.

Journalists also network for the purpose of building a relation we can make use of in a longer perspective.

- Personal connections are really important to their businesses. If they can produce something that fits into the media logic and its plot, it will result in coverage regardless of whether they have had lunch with a journalist or not.

Common travels and dinner parties arranged by corporations – which used to be a common way of socialising – have largely disappeared, if one is to believe the interview responses of both parties. In general, today's editorial staff say they decline such offers, and corporations are allegedly restrictive about such activities. However, travels that include seminars, field trips and interview opportunities with powerful leaders still seem to occur, even if they occur less often today and have taken on a different form. Corporate management still orchestrates such events, but today the media organisations often seem to cover the journalists' expenditures.

During one of the interview sessions, a former information officer remembered travelling in the US a couple of years ago:

- Oh yes, journalists were on trips where we had seminars and further training for them along with visits to facilities. They didn't write about it then, but they might have written about it six months later, in total agreement with how we had laid out the situation. It's obvious there were elements of bribing or of an in-between zone.

A particular type of relationship pertains to situations where both parties have journalistic backgrounds, *i.e.* when the PR expert is a former journalist and thereby perhaps a former colleague or at least a former member of the same profession as the approached journalist. Some journalists perceive this type of situation as especially troublesome, while to others it is completely unproblematic.

Some PR agents with a journalistic background also coach corporate leaders and other organisation representatives on how to tackle the media. The interviewed journalists' opinions on this matter seem to split the professional group in two. Some dislike the phenomenon very much. They perceive it as training aimed to manipulate journalists, as a way to teach corporate leaders to "talk about hot topics and deliver half truths". The other half of the group consider it a good thing, as corporate representatives learn about the role of the media in society, so that they can master not "walking into traps or being fooled by a lie" and not being hesitant when "confronted with experienced journalists".

Bibliography

A. Kumar: *Social Change : Through NGOs*, Anmol Publication, Delhi, 2003.

A.S. Shukla: *Professional Journalism and Public Relations*, Rajat Publications, Delhi, 2010.

Abhinav Kumar Mehta: *Mass Media and Human Rights Development*, Altar Publication, Delhi, 2012.

Ajay Das: *Mass Media and Journalism*, Omega Publications, Delhi, 2010.

B. Manna: *Mass Media and Laws in India*, Naya Prokash Publication, Delhi, 1998.

Brijendra Pande: *New Heights In Modern Media and Public Relations*, Swastik Publications, Delhi, 2010.

C N Ray: *Liberalisation and Urban Social Services: Health and Education*, Rawat Publication, Delhi, 2003.

Deepak Sahay: *Mass Media and Social Change*, Pearl Books, Delhi, 2008.

Diwakar Sharma: *Public Relations : An Emerging Specialised Profession: Text and Case Studies*, Deep and Deep Publication, Delhi, 2004.

Iqbal S. Sachdeva: *Public Relations : Principles and Practices*, Oxford University Press, Delhi, 2009.

K Chandrakandan; J Venkata Pirabu; C Karthikeyan & N Anandaraja: *Mass Media and Interpersonal Communication for Social Awakening*, Authors Press, Delhi, 2001.

K. Chandrakandan, C. Karthikeyan, C. Venkatesan and C. Balaji Babu: *Public Relations*, Authors Press, Delhi, 2002.

Kapil Desai: *Media Ethics And Social Change*, Swastik Publications, Delhi, 2010.

M H Syed: *Mass Media and Journalism*, Anmol Publication, Delhi, 2006.

M. Kumar: *Social Change : Theory and Practice*, Mohit Publications, Delhi, 2010.

Manoj Dixit: *Modern Journalism and Public Relations*, Enkay Publishing House, Delhi, 2013.

Manoj Suresh Goel: *Mass Media And Social Change*, M.D. Publications, Delhi, 2009.

Manoranjan Tripathy: *Public Relations : Bridging Technologies and Monitoring Public and the Media*, Authors Press, Delhi, 2011.

Mishra, S.: *Media And Public Relations*, Alfa Publications, Delhi, 2008.

Namita Agrawal: *Mass Media and Communication : Career Opportunities*, Book Enclave, Delhi, 2012.

Narendra Ojha: *Mass Media and Communication*, ABD Publication, Delhi, 2006.

Naval Prabhakar and Narednra Basu: *Mass Media : Origin and Development*, Commonwealth Publication, Delhi, 2007.

Naval Prabhakar and Narendra Basu: *Mass Media and Contemporary Social Issues*, Commonwealth Publication, Delhi, 2007.

Naval Prabhakar and Narendra Basu: *Mass Media and Development*, Commonwealth Publication, Delhi, 2007.

Naval Prabhakar and Narendra Basu: *Public Relations : Nature and Scope*, Commonwealth Publication, Delhi, 2007.

Naval Prabhakar and Narendra Basu: *Public Relations : Principles and Functions*, Commonwealth Publication, Delhi, 2007.

Nayyar Shamsi: *Mass Media and Democracy*, Anmol Publication, Delhi, 2006.

R. Kothekar: *Economics of Welfare and Social Services*, Cyber Tech Publication, Delhi, 2012.

Ramesh H. Makwana: *Social Change Among Tribal Community Through Tribal Sub Plan Schemes*, Vista International Publishing House, Delhi, 2012.

S.B. Jogur: *Social Change Among Rural Youth*, Adhyayan Publication, Delhi, 2012.

S.R. Sharma: *Social Change Among Tribes in India*, Manak Publication, Delhi, 2000.

Sanjay Gaur: *Mass Media and Communication : A Study With Public Relations, Print and Electronic Media*, Book Enclave, Delhi, 2006.

T.V. Sekher: *Migration and Social Change*, Rawat Publication, Delhi, 1997.

Index